GAME DEVELOPMENT ESSENTIALS:

AN INTRODUCTION

Jeannie Novak

THOMSON

™

DELMAR LEARNING

Australia   Canada   Mexico   Singapore   Spain   United Kingdom   United States

Game Development Essentials: An Introduction
Jeannie Novak

Vice President, Technology and Trades SBU:	Marketing Director:	Production Manager:
Alar Elken	Dave Garza	Larry Main
	Channel Manager:	**Production Editor:**
Editorial Director:	William Lawrensen	Thomas Stover
Sandy Clark		
	Marketing Coordinator:	**Art & Design Specialist**
Senior Acquisitions Editor:	Mark Pierro	Rachel Baker
James Gish		
	Production Director:	**Cover Design:**
Development Editor:	Mary Ellen Black	Chris Navetta
Jaimie Wetzel		
		Cover Production:
		David Arsenault

Cover image from *Demon Stone* courtesy of Atari Interactive, Inc and Stormfront Studios. Special thanks to John Hight, Don Daglow, Jeff Weir, and Sarah W. Stocker. Demon Stone, Forgotten Realms and the Forgotten Realms logo, Dungeons & Dragons, D&D, and the Dungeons & Dragons logo, and Wizards of the Coast and its logo, characters, character names, and their distinctive likenesses are trademarks of Wizards of the Coast, Inc., in the U.S.A. and other countries, and are used with permission.

Library of Congress Cataloging-in-Publication Data:

ISBN 1-4018-6271-3

NOTICE TO THE READER

Publisher does not warrant or guarantee any of the products described herein or perform any independent analysis in connection with any of the product information contained herein. Publisher does not assume, and expressly disclaims, any obligation to obtain and include information other than that provided to it by the manufacturer.

The reader is expressly warned to consider and adopt all safety precautions that might be indicated by the activities herein and to avoid all potential hazards. By following the instructions contained herein, the reader willingly assumes all risks in connection with such instructions.

The publisher makes no representation or warranties of any kind, including but not limited to, the warranties of fitness for particular purpose or merchantability, nor are any such representations implied with respect to the material set forth herein, and the publisher takes no responsibility with respect to such material. The publisher shall not be liable for any special, consequential, or exemplary damages resulting, in whole or part, from the readers' use of, or reliance upon, this material.

CONTENTS

Chapter 2 Player Elements: who plays and why? 34

Chapter 3 Game Elements: what are the possibilities?.........................64

Part II: Scenarios creating compelling content 109

Chapter 4   Storytelling: creating the narrative 110

Chapter 5   Characters: creating the identity 144

Chapter 8 Interface:
creating the connection 224

Chapter 11   Production & Management: developing the process 328

Development Phases 330

Introduction

Game Development:
a new era in entertainment— and in education

When asked if he could change one aspect of the game industry, Richard "Lord British" Garriott responded, "Education—I really wish schools would catch up and support our industry, by teaching more aspects of interactive game design."

This book was written to help fulfill a wish—one that many game industry professionals and educators have had: to help students become better prepared for careers in the game industry by providing them with a thorough background in all aspects of the game industry and the game development and interactive design process.

Game industry revenues, which some have estimated exceed $30 billion per year worldwide, have now surpassed film box office and music concert revenues in the United States alone—making games the fastest-growing segment of the entertainment market, and an excellent field for career advancement. According to a recent industry impact study conducted by the International Game Developers Association (IGDA), in several countries, exports from game sales represent one of the highest exports—and well over 100,000 people are employed worldwide in the game industry.

In response to this rapid growth, hundreds of colleges and universities in the United States have launched accredited game development programs in the last few years— and textbooks providing support to these programs are in great demand. I wrote this book to satisfy the need for a comprehensive introductory text on game development for the educational and trade markets. *Game Development Essentials* also represents the launch of a new series of the same name—which is intended to help provide educators with a logical sequence of topics that might be taught in a game development curriculum.

As more schools continue to launch game programs, this book—and the companion books in this series—will become even more *essential* to game education and careers. Not limited to the education market, this series is also appropriate for the trade market, and for those who have a general interest in the game industry.

Introducing the
Game Development Essentials
Series

Game Development Essentials is just the beginning of a series that is the first of its kind: one that focuses on providing game studies, development, and design students with a complete education in all aspects of the game industry.

Upcoming books in the series will be on topics as varied as: story and character development, project management, interface design, level design, gameplay, audio, artificial intelligence, player communities, online games, mobile games, and the history of game development. All of these topics are covered in this introductory book—which is intended to be used in all introductory game development and design courses. However, this book is versatile enough that it can be used across several courses that cover the book's many topics.

About this Text

This introductory book provides an overview of the game development process—complete with a historical framework, content creation strategies, production techniques, and future predictions.

This book contains the following unique features:

- Key chapter questions that are clearly stated at the beginning of each chapter
- Coverage that surveys the topics of planning, production, prototyping, playtesting, marketing, and management of player communities
- Thought-provoking review and study questions appearing at the end of each chapter that are suitable for students and professionals alike to help promote critical thinking and problem-solving skills
- A wealth of case studies, quotations from leading professionals, and profiles of game developers that feature concise tips and problem-solving exercises to help readers focus in on issues specific to game development
- Discussions that go beyond general game development topics into emerging areas such as online and mobile game development—and non-entertainment applications for education, business, and government
- An abundance of full-color images throughout that help illustrate the concepts and techniques discussed in the book

There are several general themes associated with this book that are emphasized throughout, including:

- Differences between games and other entertainment media (such as film)
- Usability and player control as primary aspects of game development
- "Gameplay" as a new form of storytelling
- Widening game market demographics and content features
- Disappearance of the "games as violent entertainment" stigma
- Uniqueness of game development team roles

who should read this book?

This book is not limited to the education market. If you found this book on a shelf at the bookstore and picked it up out of curiosity, this book is for you, too!

The audience for this book includes students, industry professionals, and the general interest consumer market. The style is informal and accessible, with a concentration on theory and practice—geared toward both students and professionals.

Students that might benefit from this book include:

- College students in game development, interactive design, entertainment studies, communication, and emerging technologies programs
- Art, design and programming students who are taking introductory game development courses
- Professional students in college-level programs who are taking game development overview courses
- First-year game development students at universities

The audience of industry professionals for this book include:

- Graphic designers, animators, and Web developers who are interested in becoming game artists
- Programmers and Web developers who are interested in becoming game programmers
- Music composers, sound designers, and voice actors who are interested in becoming involved in this industry
- Professionals in other arts and entertainment media—including film, television, and music—who are interested in transferring their skills to the game development industry. These professionals might include writers, producers, artists, and designers.

how is this book organized?

This book consists of three parts—focusing on industry background, content creation, and production/business cycles.

Part I   Setup: Building the Foundation—Focuses on providing a historical and structural context to game development. Chapters in this section include:

- **Chapter 1   Historical Elements: How Did We Get Here?**—a history of electronic game development, from the arcade era to the online multiplayer games of today

- **Chapter 2   Player Elements: Who Plays and Why?**—explores player motivation, geographics, demographics, and psychographics
- **Chapter 3   Game Elements: What Are the Possibilities?**—reviews game goals, platforms, and genres

Part II   Scenarios: Creating Compelling Content—Focuses on how game developers create compelling content. Chapters in this section include:

- **Chapter 4   Storytelling: Creating the Narrative**—focuses on story structure, backstory, synopsis, setting, non-linear storytelling, and collaborative storytelling
- **Chapter 5   Character: Creating the Identity**—explores visual and verbal character development, point-of-view, and archetypes
- **Chapter 6   Gameplay: Creating the Experience**—introduces game theory, challenges, strategies, interactivity modes, balance, and economies
- **Chapter 7   Levels: Creating the World**—reviews structure, environmental design, perspective, style, temporal and spatial features
- **Chapter 8   Interface: Creating the Connection**—discusses player control, manual and visual interface design, and usability
- **Chapter 9   Audio: Creating the Atmosphere**—explores music, sound design, and dialogue production

Part III: Strategy (Team, Process & Community)—Focuses on project management and the development/business cycles. Chapters in this section include:

- **Chapter 10   Roles & Responsibilities: Developing the Team**—highlights the roles and responsibilities of companies and development team members, along with associated tools
- **Chapter 11   Production & Management: Developing the Process**—outlines phases in the game development cycle (including planning, production, prototyping, and playtesting), along with project management and game documentation
- **Chapter 12   Marketing & Maintenance: Developing the Community**—focuses on marketing, advertising, public relations, sales, and promotion—along with the role of player communities (including fan-produced content, modding, and fan sites)

The book concludes with **The Future: Where Are We Going?**—which presents diverse views and predictions of the future of the game industry from experts profiled in the book—followed by a **Resources** section, which includes a list of game development news sources, guides, directories, conferences, articles, and books related to topics discussed in this text.

How To Use This Text

The sections that follow describe text elements found throughout the book and how they are intended to be used.

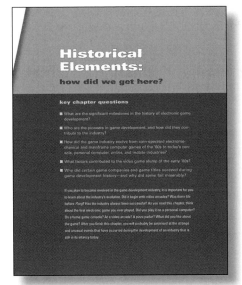

key chapter questions

Key chapter questions are learning objectives in the form of overview questions that start off each chapter. Readers should be able to answer the questions upon understanding the chapter material.

sidebars

Sidebars offer in-depth information from the author on specific topics—accompanied by associated images.

tips

Tips provide advice and inspiration from industry professionals and educators, as well as practical techniques and tips of the trade.

profiles

Profiles provide bios, photos and in-depth commentary from industry professionals and educators.

quotes

Quotes contain short, insightful thoughts from players, students, and industry observers.

case studies

Case studies contain anecdotes from industry professionals (accompanied by game screenshots) on their experiences developing specific game titles.

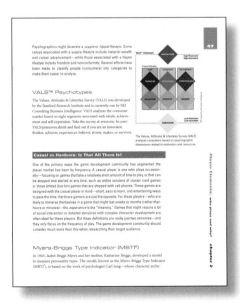

notes

Notes contain thought-provoking ideas provided by the author that are intended to help the readers think critically about the book's topics.

chapter review

A *chapter review* section at the end of each chapter contains a combination of questions and exercises, which allow readers to apply what they've learned.

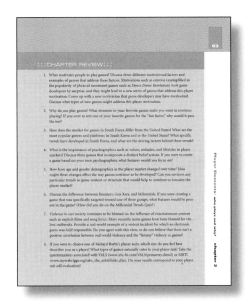

About the Companion CD

The companion CD contains the following game engine and level editing software, game documentation samples, game demos, and links to trial and full versions of key software programs, including:

- Torque game engine (GarageGames)
- Gamemaker game engine (Mark Overmars)
- Unreal Developer Network (Epic Games)
- Valve Hammer Editor (Valve Software)
- *Orbz* game demo (21-6 Productions/GarageGames)
- *Marble Blast* game demo (GarageGames)
- *Think Tanks* game demo (BraveTree Productions/GarageGames)
- *The Lord of the Rings: The Battle for Middle-earth* game demo (Electronic Arts)
- *Call of Duty* game demo (Infinity Ward/Activision)
- Maya (Alias/Wavefront) software trial
- 3D Studio Max (Discreet) software trial
- Game design document template (Chris Taylor/Gas Powered Games)
- *Sub Hunter* game design document (Michael Black/Torn Space)
- Game design document reference site (Christian Lynaes)
- Aurora Toolset Resources (Bioware)
- CryENGINE (Crytek) tech video and software demo
- The Games Factory (Clickteam) game engine

About the Instructor's Guide

The instructor's guide (available on CD format) was developed to assist instructors in planning and implementing their instructional programs. It includes sample syllabi (for using the text in either an 11 or 16 week course), test questions (with solutions), assignments and projects, lecture slides highlighting main topics and providing a framework for discussion, and other valuable instructional resources.

Order Number: 1-4018-6272-1

About the Author

Jeannie Novak is the founder of Indiespace (www.indiespace.com), one of the first companies to promote and distribute interactive entertainment online. Jeannie is also a subject matter expert and instructor for the Game Art & Design program at the Art Institute Online—and she teaches at UCLA Extension, Art Center College of Design, and the Academy of Entertainment and Technology at Santa Monica College. Jeannie has spoken extensively on game development and interactive entertainment at conferences and universities—including Macworld, Internet World, Indie Games Con (IGC), University of Southern California (USC), and University of California, Los Angeles (UCLA). Jeannie is also the co-author of three additional books on the interactive entertainment industry, including *Creating Internet Entertainment.* She is a member of the International Game Developers Association (IGDA) and has served on selection committees for the Academy of Interactive Arts & Sciences (AIAS) and the ALT+CTRL Festival of Independent & Alternative Games at the University of California, Irvine.

Courtesy of: Mark Robert Halper

Jeannie was chosen as one of the 100 most influential people in high-technology by *MicroTimes* magazine—and she has been profiled by CNN, *Billboard Magazine,* Sundance Channel, *Daily Variety,* and the *Los Angeles Times.* She received her M.A. in Communication Management from the University of Southern California (USC) and B.A. in Mass Communication from the University of California, Los Angeles (UCLA)—graduating summa cum laude and Phi Beta Kappa. When she isn't writing and teaching, Jeannie spends most of her time recording, performing and composing music. More information on the author can be found at www.jeannie.com.

Acknowledgments

I would like to thank the following people for their hard work and dedication to this project:

Jim Gish (Acquisitions Editor, Thomson/Delmar), for "getting it" right away—supporting my ideas and understanding the importance of this series.

Jaimie Wetzel (Developmental Editor, Thomson/Delmar), for her ability to maintain calm under pressure as we worked through all the details.

Tom Stover (Production Editor, Thomson/Delmar), for his positive demeanor and responsiveness during crunch time.

Marissa Maiella and Niamh Matthews (Editorial Assistants, Thomson/Delmar), for their ongoing assistance.

John Shanley (Phoenix Creative), for his focus and commitment to making this book look fantastic.

Oscar Trapp (Phoenix Creative), for his diligence and attention to detail during the layout and compositing phase.

Rachel Pearce Anderson (RPA Editorial Services), for her thorough and thoughtful copyediting.

Gail Taylor (Taylor Wordsmiths), for her excellent copyediting assistance.

Robin Sterling (RLS Images), for her help with securing permissions and high-resolution images from rights-holders.

Scott Peterson for his skill in redrawing several diagrams used throughout the book.

A big thanks also goes out to all the many people who contributed their thoughts and ideas to this book:

Jongheum Park (Nexon)

Mark Terrano (Microsoft)

Bruno Bonnell (Atari)

Pete Markiewicz (Indiespace)

James Paul Gee (University of Wisconsin–Madison)

Richard Wainess (University of Southern California)

Ed Stark (Wizards of the Coast)

Warren Spector (Ion Storm)

David Brin

Chris Klug (Brown Bear Entertainment)

Chris Swain (University of Southern California)

Mark Soderwall (Atari)

Allen Varney

Tim Langdell (University of Southern California)

Titus Levi

Edward Castronova (Indiana University)

Kevin Saunders (Obsidian Entertainment)

Aaron Marks (On Your Mark Music)

David Javelosa

Scott Snyder (Dancing Mouse Productions)

Mike Yurchak

Hope Levy

Bob Bergen

Richard Jacques

Bill Brown (Soundelux Music Group)

Alex Brandon (Midway)

Tommy Tallarico (Tommy Tallarico Studios; Game Audio Network Guild [GANG])

Rich Ragsdale

Greg O'Connor-Read (Music4Games.net)

Todd M. Fay (Todd M. Fay Media Developments)

Rob Cairns (Associated Production Music [APM])

Ron Jones (Ron Jones Productions)

Chance Thomas (HUGEsound)

Lennie Moore

Louis Castle (Westwood Studios/Electronic Arts)

Christopher Bretz (Secret Level)

Justin Mette (21-6 Productions)

Jason Kay (Society Capital)

John Hight (Atari)

Chris Avellone (Obsidian Entertainment)

Patricia Pizer

Marc Taro Holmes (Obsidian Entertainment)

Grant Collier (Infinity Ward)

KyungMin Bang (Nexon)

John Ahlquist (Electronic Arts–Los Angeles)

Jay Moore (GarageGames)

Greg Costikyan (Unplugged)

Brian Fargo (InXile Entertainment)

Brenda Laurel (Art Center College of Design)

Celia Pearce (University of California, Irvine)

Gordon Walton (Sony Online Entertainment)

Daniel James (Three Rings Design)

Rade Stojsavljevic (Electronic Arts)

Tracy Fullerton (University of Southern California)

Ed Del Castillo (Liquid Entertainment)

Don Daglow (Stormfront Studios)

David Perry (Shiny Entertainment)

Richard "Lord British" Garriott (Destination Games/NCsoft)

Graeme Bayless (Electronic Arts–Tiburon)

Starr Long (NCsoft)

Chris Taylor (Gas Powered Games)

Christian Lynæs

Michael Black (Torn Space)

Brian Reynolds (Big Huge Games)

Carly Staehlin (NCsoft)

Stephanie Spong

Mark Precious

Marianne Krawczyk

Ivo Gerscovich (Vivendi Universal Games)

Sara Borthwick (Encore Software)

Russell Burt (Art Institute of California–Los Angeles)

Jan McWilliams (Art Institute of California–Los Angeles)

Janet Wilcox

Hugh Hancock (Strange Company)

Bill Amend

David Davis

Mark Overmars

Jennifer Penton

Robert Ferguson

Aaron Nash

Melissa Adkison

Katrina Ruban

Arash John Sammander

Rebecca Voss

Kathrine Courchaine

Tracy Heilman

Carissa Reyes

Elizabeth Butler

Stephen Toth

Vincent Ramos

Mason Batchelder

William A Henderson (MPAA)

Thanks to the following people for their tremendous help with referrals and in securing permissions, images, and demos:

Holly Newman (Liquid Entertainment)

Christopher Bretz (Secret Level)

Marc Taro Holmes (Obsidian Entertainment)

Kevin Saunders (Obsidian Entertainment)

Jay Moore and Alex Swanson (GarageGames)

Janet Wilcox

Starr Long, David Swofford, and Mike Harris (NCsoft)

John Ahlquist, Craig Owens, Harvard Bonin, and Aaron Kaufman (Electronic Arts–Los Angeles)

John Hight, Nancy Bushkin, Mimi Storey, and Jon Leach (Atari)

Patrick Hudson (Ensemble Studios)

Mark Terrano (Microsoft)

ClipArt.com

DebySue Wolfcale (Origin Systems/ Electronic Arts)

Mary Suggett (Universal Press Syndicate)

Tracie Snitker (Reverb Communications)

Timothy Roberts (Infinum Labs)

Melinda Mongelluzzo (Capcom)

Mark Robert Halper (Mark Robert Halper Photography)

Alan Lewis (Acclaim)

Keith Robinson (Intellivision)

Joshua Stecker (DeLyon–Hunt & Associates)

Lee Dickholtz (Meta Motion)

Curtis Kaiser (DISCover)

Paul Mishkin (Quia)

Jamie Nye (Gunnar Games)

Sylvain Bizzoire (Old-Computers.com)

Gregory Micek (D.I.Y. Games)

Mike Doak (Socko! Entertainment)

Mike Mantarro (Activision)

Tara Reed (The Adventure Company/ Dreamcatcher)

Col. David Gardiner (U.S. Army)

Nitsa Olivadoti (Analog Devices)

Sue Runfola and Del Penny (Apple Computer)

Gail Salamanca (Atlus USA)

Redentor Quiambao

Dan Ferguson (Blockdot)

Allan Crossman (British Go Association)

Paul Gouge (Ironstone Partners Ltd/ Commodore)

Alexander Bogdanov (CSA)

Christopher Brandkamp (Cyan)

Claudia Curcio (DigiDesign)

Bruce Damer (Digital Space)

Kevin Clark (Discreet)

Margaret Adamic (Disney)

Andy Tepper (eGenesis)

Sheila Leunig (Eidos)

Mark Rein (Epic Games)

Christina Boone (Entertainment Software Ratings Board [ESRB])

Ingo Ruhnke (GMX)

Kelley Gilmore (Firaxis)

Mike Smith (Fragapalooza)

Dr. Cat (Dragon's Eye Productions)

Jean Fages (GeoWhere)

Tom Tinervin (Getty Images)

Greg Holmes (GH Services)

Helen Van Tassel (Hasbro Games)

Steve Fawkner (Infinite Interactive)

Kathryne Wahl (Interplay)

Jill Storms (Jaleco)

Tonya Huskey (Jerome Chessum Photography)

Judy Schultz (Knowledge Adventure/ Vivendi Universal Games)

Marc Franklin and Wolfgang Ebert (Konami)

Patricia Lahey (Lahey Fun Park)

Cathy Campos (Panach PR/Lionhead Studios)

Peter Morawiec (Luxoflux)

Kally Workman (Magnavox/Philips Consumer Electronics)

Zicel Maymudes (Mattel)

Richard Cahaly, Jr. (Massachusetts Institute of Technology [MIT])

Eugene Evans (Mythic Entertainment)

Mary Shinya (Namco)

Robin Zlatin (New Line Cinema)

Jerome Rankine (Newsweek)

Paul Philleo (Nexon)

Stephanie Reimann (Nintendo)

Jose Cavazos (Nokia)

Jenny Shaheen (Oddworld Inhabitants)

David Lloyd (Overclocked Remix)

Claude Vezina (PCV)

Kathy Bacon and Amy Janas (PopCap Games)

Jake Rinaldi (Prestige Casino)

Kenn Hoekstra (Ravensoft)

Erika Shaffer (Real Networks)

Nancy Glowinski (Reuters Pictures Archive)

Barbara Griffin (Riverdeep)

Jeanette Manahan and Robert Leffler (Sega)

David Berky (Simple Joe)

Julie Iverson (Sony USA)

Steve Weiss (Sony Online Entertainment)

Sonia Im and Koji Suga (Square Enix)

Kristen Thomas (SRIC)

Gregor Whiley (SSG)

Mark Cecere (Strategy First)

Peter Snell (Tascam)

Ryan Arbogast (Tecmo)

Maryann Huhs (Tetris Company)

Devon Knudsen and Danielle Conte (THQ)

Scott Miller (3D Realms)

Dan Pontes (Ubi Soft)

Doug Lombardi and Kellie Cosner (Valve Software)

Justin Ziran, Andrew Smith, Kyle Murray, and Elena Moye (Wizards of the Coast)

J. Griffin Lesher (Zenimax Media/Bethesda Softworks)

Jeff Mallett (Zillions of Games)

Delmar Learning and I would also like to thank the following reviewers for their valuable suggestions and technical expertise:

Anthony Borquez
    Director, Video Game Program
    University of Southern California
    Los Angeles, CA

Russell Burt
    Instructor, Interactive Design Department
    Art Institute of California–Los Angeles
    Santa Monica, CA

Jan McWilliams
    Department Chair, Interactive Design Department
    Art Institute of California–Los Angeles
    Santa Monica, CA

Kevin Saunders
    Senior Designer
    Obsidian Entertainment
    Santa Ana, CA

Mark Soderwall
Instructor, Media Arts and Animation
Department
Art Institute of California–Orange
County
Senior Art Director–Atari
Santa Monica, CA

Mark Terrano
Technical Game Manager
Microsoft Xbox
Redmond, WA

Richard Wainess
Senior Lecturer, Information
Technology Program
University of Southern California
Los Angeles, CA

Royal Winchester, 3D Animation
Instructor
Art Department
DigiPen Institute of Technology
Redmond, WA

Jeannie Novak
Lead Author and Series Editor, Game Development Essentials Series
—Summer 2004

Logos for the following companies are used with permission:

Activision	New Line Cinema
Nintendo	21-6 Productions
Atari	Sega
Stormfront Studios	THQ

Questions and Feedback

We welcome your questions and feedback. If you have suggestions that you think others would benefit from, please let us know and we will try to include them in the next edition.

To send us your questions and/or feedback, you can contact the publisher at:

Delmar Learning
Executive Woods
5 Maxwell Drive
Clifton Park, NY 12065
Attn: Graphic Arts Team
(800) 998-7498

Or the author at:

Jeannie Novak
Founder and CEO
INDIESPACE
P.O. Box 5458
Santa Monica, CA 90409
(310) 399-4349
jeannie@indiespace.com
jeannie@jeannie.com

DEDICATION

This book is dedicated to my family and friends for dealing with my "hibernation," to my students for their enthusiasm and creativity, and to KDS for hanging in there as long as possible—and for always being my game-playing pal.

Part I: Setup

building the foundation

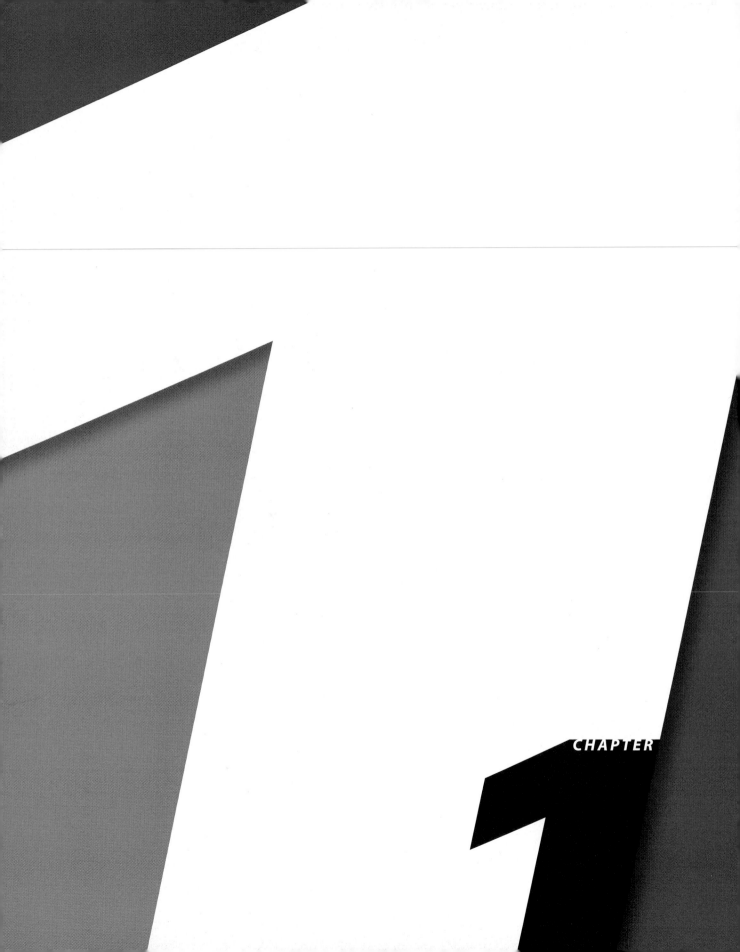

CHAPTER

Historical Elements:

how did we get here?

key chapter questions

■ What are the significant milestones in the history of electronic game development?

■ Who are the pioneers in game development, and how did they contribute to the industry?

■ How did the game industry evolve from coin-operated electromechanical and mainframe computer games of the '60s to today's console, personal computer, online, and mobile industries?

■ What factors contributed to the video game slump of the early '80s?

■ Why did certain game companies and game titles succeed during game development history—and why did some fail miserably?

If you plan to become involved in the game development industry, it is important for you to learn about the industry's evolution. Did it begin with video arcades? Was there life before *Pong*? Has the industry always been successful? As you read this chapter, think about the first electronic game you ever played. Did you play it on a personal computer? On a home game console? At a video arcade? A pizza parlor? What did you like about the game? After you finish this chapter, you will probably be surprised at the strange and unusual events that have occurred during the development of an industry that is still in its infancy today.

Before the Arcades

The first electronic games were not played at home or even at video arcades. Instead, research departments at universities, labs, military installations and defense contractors provided the backdrop for this industry. At military bases, electromechanical games were provided for the recruits to escape from the rigors of basic training. Meanwhile, a few bleary-eyed, overworked students, programmers, faculty and researchers in academic and government institutions turned their mainframe computers into game machines—relieving them of traditional duties such as performing complex mathematical calculations for research. Late at night, these pioneers spawned what would become one of the most compelling forms of entertainment in history.

The first electronic games were played at military bases (Camp Pendleton, left) and at academic institutions (Massachusetts Institute of Technology [M.I.T.], right).

Two distinct segments of the electronic game industry developed in parallel, starting in the '50s. One of these segments began in 1951 when Marty Bromley, who managed game rooms at military bases in Hawaii, bought electromechanical machines and launched SEGA (an abbreviation for SErvice GAmes). This segment of the industry grew into the coin-op video arcade industry, which experienced a boom in the 1970s. Electronic versions of arcade favorites marked the beginning of what was to become the console game industry of today.

The other segment of the electronic game industry started with mainframe computer games developed by faculty and students at universities who wanted to either hone their programming skills or entertain each other during breaks from the long hours spent working on their dissertations. Although an adaptation of one of the early mainframe games (*Spacewar!*) became the first coin-op video arcade game in the United States, it was not until the personal computer revolution that mainframe games were adapted for personal computers. It was at this time that the computer gaming industry was born.

::::: They're Not All Video Games!

Which of the above is not a video game? The term *video game* came out of the arcade business and gravitated toward the home console game business. Games played on personal computers have always been referred to as computer games—*not* video games. The term electronic game is used to refer to both.

Many companies and developers made significant contributions in the creation of game systems and content. You might recognize many companies that were formed in this era, and you might even have played some games that were developed during this time. What are the companies that made a difference in the evolution of this industry? Who were the pioneering designers, artists, programmers, and producers responsible for developing compelling games that continue to inspire developers today?

A few companies were ready to plunge in just as the electronic game industry began. Some of them maintain a significant presence in the industry today. You might be surprised at how they began—and how they continued to develop. Some of them had initially nothing to do with games, or even entertainment. Others tried, and failed, to dominate every segment of the game industry. Many came and went, and a few are still going strong. Some stepped out of the picture for a while, only to return with a vengeance during the second "golden age" of the industry. As we look at the arcade phenomenon, we'll focus on some of these companies and the popular games they developed.

The Arcade Phenomenon

The public was first introduced to electronic games not through home game consoles or personal computers, but through public arcades. Before video games were introduced, the most popular arcade games were electromechanical pinball machines. Arcades were often located in small amusement parks, attracting children and teenagers—who would challenge each other to pinball matches as part of a regular weekend social event. As video games became more popular, arcades became more accessible. Conveniently located near schools and residential neighborhoods, arcades became flooded with teens after school. At the height of the craze, kids would spend hours at the arcades—sometimes into the night, forgetting to eat, or to do their homework!

::::: Sega: Setting the 25-Cent Standard

In 1956, just a few years after Marty Bromley started SEGA, Rosen Enterprises' David Rosen began to import coin-operated electromechanical games to Japan—launching the country's coin-op business and becoming Japan's largest amusement company. In 1964, Rosen Enterprises merged with SEGA to form Sega Enterprises. Acting as a bridge between the United States and Japan, the company released the first Japanese export, *Periscope*, in the United States. Interestingly, it was due to the high shipping costs of this export that U.S. arcade owners charged 25 cents to play the game—setting a standard for future arcade games. Sega was purchased by Gulf & Western in 1969—but David Rosen and partner Isao Okawa bought it back in 1984. The price tag: $38 million.

Several games are considered milestones during this era. Although limited by the technology of the time, these games were innovative—inspiring new trends in content, genres, gameplay, and development techniques that had never been considered before. Some of these games were extremely popular—successfully capturing a broad market that went far beyond the stereotypical "male teen" demographic. They provided hope for the future of electronic games as a mass entertainment medium. Many of these games are considered so nostalgic by gamers from this era that they have been re-released in console, computer or handheld format so that they can be experienced again. You might recognize a few of them!

Computer Space

In 1961, MIT student Steve Russell developed *Spacewar!*—the first interactive computer game on the university's mainframe computer. Nolan Bushnell, who later founded Atari, saw the game and decided to bring it to a larger market by adapting it into a stand-alone arcade coin-op game. Calling his version *Computer Space*, Bushnell sold the idea to Nutting Associates in 1971. The game, which consisted

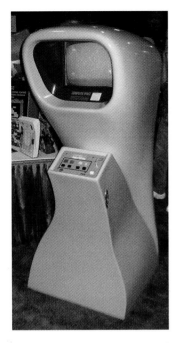

simply of trying to shoot a flying saucer, might not have been as compelling as a pinball game—and its low sales reflected this. However, Bushnell started the coin-op video arcade industry by bringing an elitist form of entertainment that had remained enclosed within the ivory tower of the university system out to the masses. In 1978, after video game arcade technology had become more sophisticated, Cinematronics released *Space Wars*—another arcade adaptation of Russell's mainframe game.

Computer Space, the first coin-op video arcade game, was an adaptation of Steve Russell's *Spacewar!*

Atari's Wild Ride

After *Computer Space*, Bushnell left Nutting Associates to start Atari with partner Ted Dabney. (The word "Atari" is from the board game *Go* and means roughly, "Look out! The move I'm about to make will be dangerous to you"—similar to "check" in chess.) After surviving a legal dispute with Magnavox over the rights to the first successful video game (*Pong*), Atari became the most prolific presence in the arcade business—churning out games like *Asteroids*, which became the first blockbuster video game and forever associated the name "Atari" with the video arcade. After Bushnell left the company to start several ventures, Atari was purchased by Warner Communications in 1976, and began to spend more energy on business affairs and marketing than design and development. Concerned about the growth of the console and personal computer industries, Atari also began to shift its focus away from its arcade business and toward console systems (such as the VCS/2600) and personal computers. In 1984, Atari was sold to Commodore founder Jack Tramiel—who in turn sold it to disk drive manufacturer JTS, who then filed for bankruptcy in 1999 and sold it to Hasbro Interactive. The Atari name was revived when Infogrames purchased it a few years later. Now Atari is back on top—publishing some of the most popular computer and console games in the industry.

Historical Elements: how did we get here? chapter 1

Pong

The beginnings of the first memorable—and controversial—electronic game appeared in 1958 when Willy Higinbotham of Brookhaven National Laboratories in New York showcased his table tennis–style game on an oscilloscope. Almost a decade later, Ralph Baer of Sanders Associates began to research ideas for an interactive "table tennis" television system. He patented his idea in 1968, and Magnavox licensed it from him in 1970. The Magnavox Odyssey interactive game console—featuring Baer's "table tennis" game—was demonstrated in 1972. The first Atari game, *Pong* (designed by Atari engineer Al Alcorn) was released that same year. The controller was a two-direction rotary dial, and the rules of the game were simply "use your paddle to avoid missing ball for high score." *Pong* soon became the first successful coin-op arcade game. Magnavox sued Atari that same year, claiming that Bushnell had stolen the idea. The case was settled out of court.

Atari, Inc.

Pong – the first successful coin-op arcade game.

> As a young child in the late 1970s, I encountered my first video game, *Pong*, prominently displayed in the children's clothing section of Macy's Department Store in San Leandro, California. I was entranced, excited to play, and mesmerized as I watched my hand control a rectangle that bounced a square to my opponent. Both of us gleefully volleyed the square back and forth, feverishly trying to get the other to miss a shot—as *Pong*'s simple "beeps" and "blips" added to our delight.
>
> — *Jennifer Penton, Experimental Animation student*

::::: Ralph Baer and *Simon*

Hasbro, Inc.

Ralph Baer, who invented the Magnavox Odyssey (the first home console system), was inspired by the Steven Spielberg film *Close Encounters of the Third Kind* when he created the successful musical memory game, *Simon*—released by Milton-Bradley during the holiday season in 1977.

::::: *Asteroids*: Goodbye, Pixels!

Atari's most successful arcade game, *Asteroids* (1979), was the first to allow players to enter their initials into a high score table. *Asteroids* (designed by Ed Logg) utilized monochrome vector graphics—which allowed the game to display fast-moving objects made up of very sharp lines instead of the crude pixel graphics common among video games of its time.

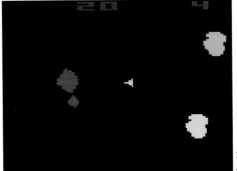

Atari, Inc.

Game Violence

In 1976, the first public controversy over video game violence occurred in response to the Exidy Games release of *Death Race*, in which players drove over "stick figures" representing pedestrians. (Compare this to today's *Grand Theft Auto* series!) The game was inspired by the 1975 cult film, *Death Race 2000* (starring David Carradine and also Sylvester Stallone in one of his first roles)—in which pedestrians are run down for points in a cross-country car race of the future. Protests were so widespread that even *60 Minutes* decided to do a story on it—bringing video games into public awareness. The publicity didn't help the game, though—as nervous arcade owners eventually refused to carry it.

My first experience with an electronic game was the original *Asteroids*. It was on the second floor of my mom's racquetball club in Cincinnati. The most memorable thing about the game was that for years I only got the chance to dream about destroying the "real detailed" silvery-looking asteroids because I was never allowed to insert 25 cents. My mom thought video games were a waste of money.

— *Rebecca Voss,*
Game Art & Design student

Pizza & Mechanical Animals:
The Family Arcade Experience

In an attempt to remove the stigma associated with the public view of arcades, Atari founder Nolan Bushnell opened up a string of pizza parlors initially known as Pizza Time Theater. Eventually becoming Chuck E. Cheese, these family restaurants offered game tokens with every meal, a video arcade for kids who would play while waiting for the pizza—and a "live" floor show featuring Chuck E. Cheese himself (along with other mechanical robot animals) for the whole family to enjoy while eating.

> I really enjoyed playing *Pac-Man*. It was exciting—and the thought of the ghosts catching me made my heart pound. It was a simple but fun game.
>
> — *Katrina Ruban, Game Art & Design student*

:::::: Bally/Midway Introduces Color with *Galaxian*

Midway Games

Bally/Midway imported some of the most popular "slide and shoot" games to the video arcades. *Space Invaders* was the first blockbuster video game, and *Galaxian* was the first video game with a full-color monitor. *Galaxian* was followed by a number of sequels—including *Galaga*, *Galplus*, *Galaga '88* and *Galaxian 3*.

:::::: "A" for "Activision"

It is not uncommon for employees in the game industry to leave and start new companies so they can retain creative leadership. Activision, one such company, was the first third-party game publisher—established in 1980 by former Atari programmers. The name was specifically chosen because it came before "Atari" alphabetically.

> *P*ac-Man was like a dream. As a child, I felt as if I became part of a cartoon world. I kept playing and playing until my parents would turn off the lights.
>
> — *William A. Henderson (Senior Analyst, Motion Picture Association of America)*

Pac-Man

In 1980, Namco released *Pac-Man*—which appealed to a much wider market, in part because it did away with the "shooting" theme that pervaded most other games. The game's controller consisted only of a multi-directional joystick. Instead of shooting spaceships, *Pac-Man* ate power pills—which allowed

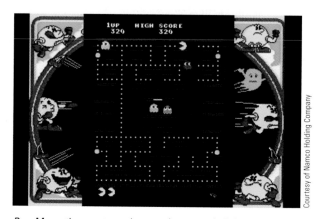

Courtesy of Namco Holding Company

Pac-Man—the most popular arcade game of all time.

him to munch on his ghostly enemies for a short while. Over 300,000 units were sold worldwide—making *Pac-Man* the most popular arcade game of all time. As players successfully completed one maze, they would move up a level—which contained the same maze, but more difficult play. *Pac-Man* spawned an even more popular, and inclusive, sequel: *Ms. Pac-Man*, the first game to star a female character. Instead of the increasingly difficult maze used in levels of play in the original game, there were four different mazes used in *Ms. Pac-Man*. The game even incorporated a rough three-act plot structure that incorporated animated sequences (a primitive form of the cinematics used in today's games) as dividers. In Act I, Pac-Man and Ms. Pac-Man meet; in Act II, Pac-Man woos Ms. Pac-Man by chasing her around the screen; and in Act III, Pac-Man, Jr. is born. The game had great crossover appeal, helping to further widen the market to incorporate girls and families. Boys played it, too—finding the game even more challenging and addictive than its predecessor.

::::: Arcade Screen Evolution

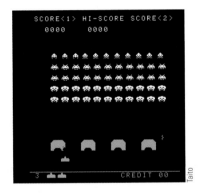 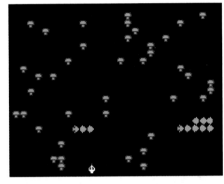 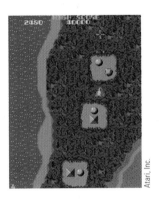

Arcade games evolved from the static screen and unlimited horizontal movement of *Space Invaders*, to the limited vertical movement of *Centipede* and, finally, to the scrolling screen of *Xevious*.

Women Enter the Arcade World

Released by Atari in 1981, *Centipede* was the first arcade game co-designed by a woman. Dona Bailey and Ed Logg teamed up to create a game with the goal of shooting quick-moving centipedes as they appeared at the top of the screen and tried to snake their way down. Each time a segment of the centipede was hit, it turned into a mushroom. The game was designed in a unique pastel color scheme.

> When I played *Space Invaders*, I really thought I was fighting aliens—and I was afraid to lose!
>
> — *Tracy Heilman, Interactive Design student*

Donkey Kong

In 1977, Shigeru Miyamoto was hired as Nintendo's first staff artist. The company initially assigned him to *Radarscope* – a submarine game that consisted of repetitive button-pushing without any real story or characters. Although this was the typical game style of the time, Miyamoto wanted to create something unique. The result was *Donkey Kong*, a game that represented a cross between *King Kong* and *Beauty and*

Donkey Kong kicked off a successful series of games that are still wildly popular today.

the Beast, where an ape steals his keeper's girlfriend and runs away. The player takes on the role of the keeper (Mario)—who becomes the hero of the story as he attempts to rescue his girl-friend (Pauline) from the clutches of the beast.

Nintendo made its phenomenal entry into the U.S. market with *Donkey Kong*. Like *Pac-Man*, the popularity of this game resulted in a series of successful, although confusing, sequels. Mario (originally called Jumpman) first appeared as the heroic carpenter whose goal was to rescue his girlfriend. The game's sequel, *Donkey Kong Junior*, switched the roles of Mario and the ape so that Mario was the enemy—an evil carpenter who had caged the now apparently innocent ape from the origi-nal game. The player took on the role of the baby ape who attempts to rescue his father (the ape from *Donkey Kong*) from Mario's evil clutches. In the third game, *Mario Bros.* (released in 1983), more confusion arose. Instead of being a carpenter, Mario was a plumber. He and his brother, Luigi, were known as the "Mario Bros." (Was Mario's full name "Mario Mario"?) The action takes place in a sewer, where two players take on the roles of Mario and Luigi to battle each other and an infinite supply of creatures (e.g., turtles, crabs, and flies) that emerge from the surrounding sewer pipes.

After *Donkey Kong*, Shigeru Miyamoto went on to develop a series of Mario titles. In fact, each time a new game system is introduced by Nintendo (starting with the original NES – discussed later in this chapter), Miyamoto designs a Mario game as its flagship title. Miyamoto's credits also include *Zelda*, *Star Fox*, *Pikmin* and *Metroid Prime*.

Why *"Donkey Kong"*?

You might wonder why a game involving a gorilla and a carpenter would be called *Donkey Kong*. Since the gorilla in the original game was "stubborn," Shigeru Miya-moto—creator of *Donkey Kong*—wanted to call the game *Stubborn Gorilla*. Wanting a more snappy English translation, Miyamoto found that "donkey" could represent "stubbornness" and "kong" could represent a gorilla (as in the film, *King Kong*)!

The U.S. arcade business reached its peak in 1981, as revenues reached $5 billion and Americans spent more than 75,000 hours playing video games. But the following year, the business experienced a decline from which it never fully recovered.

::::: Nintendo: Ancient History

What was to become one of the "big three" in today's console wars—and a major contender in the handheld market—was established in 1889 by Fusajiro Yamaguchi to manufacture and distribute Japanese playing cards known as *Hanafuda*. It wasn't until 1980 that Nintendo of America was opened by Minoru Arakawa. Nintendo jumpstarted the second "golden age" of the video game industry by releasing the Nintendo Entertainment System (NES) home console.

::::: Collecting Quarters for *Pole Position*

Namco Limited

In 1982, Namco released *Pole Position*—a first-person point-of-view game that became the first wildly successful driving game. One of these arcade games was in the break room at a now-defunct but then-successful recording studio in Los Angeles. During breaks from recording, famous bands and artists would play the game incessantly—always putting a quarter in the slot per play. Little did they know that this wasn't necessary—since the owner had deactivated the coin box control. (The staff knew about it, and they just played for free!) Every few months, the staff would use the quarters that had been collected in the machine to pay for a big company dinner—thanks to its clients' video game addiction!

> My friends and I would go to the local arcade and play games till we ran out of money or our hands developed blisters and went numb. I would get so excited when I played that I would get drenched in my own sweat and have to walk around trying to dry off so that my mom wouldn't find out that I had been at the arcade.
>
> — *Arash John Sammander, Game Art & Design student*

Tron: The First Video Game License

Released in 1982 by Bally Midway, *Tron* was the first video arcade game to be licensed from a film studio. The film itself was about characters going inside games and competing with each other, so the tie-in with an arcade game was fitting!

The Birth of Console Games

Although the Magnavox Odyssey—first home game console—was released in 1972, it wasn't until the late '70s that the home console industry began to take shape.

Pre-dating the video arcade industry boom, the Odyssey was ahead of its time. The video arcade industry was *business-to-business*—with machines sold to arcade operators rather than to consumers. The high price tag on standalone arcade machines made it prohibitive for all but the wealthiest consumers to own them. It became clear that selling directly to consumers (*business-to-consumer*) could expand the industry tremendously—so video arcades began to move into the home in the form of affordable game consoles. These systems used the television as a monitor and competed for market share much like today's Sony (PlayStation), Microsoft (Xbox), and Nintendo (GameCube).

Atari VCS/2600

Atari, Inc.

The Atari VCS/2600 successfully launched the home game console industry.

Although the first programmable home game to use cartridges (Channel F) was released in 1976 by Fairchild Camera & Instrument, the inexpensive Atari VCS (Video Computer System)/2600 took off one year later—successfully launching the home game console industry. Keeping the price of the hardware low, Atari made most of its money from the game titles it developed for the console. Popular titles included *Adventure* (where a block-shaped knight searched for keys and a magic chalice, always on the lookout for angry dragons) and *Yar's Revenge* (where a race of mutated houseflies that had taken to space seek revenge on an army setting up camp on the right side of the screen). When Atari adapted the blockbuster arcade game *Space Invaders* for the VCS format in 1980, the practice of selling home versions of arcade games began. Atari followed-up with its less-successful 5200 in 1982, and the 7800 in 1984.

It was love at first sight when I laid eyes on *Vanguard* for the Atari 2600 [cue Jekyll-Hyde transformation]. I never thought blasting those 16-color panels in *River Raid* could be so fulfilling. It was like "bending space and time." I started playing at about 8am—and suddenly it was 3pm. My friend's mom was shooing us out for being inside all day. (I believe it's some sort of singularity like a black hole; neither light nor time can escape!)

— *Aaron Nash,*
Game Art & Design student

::::: The Hidden "Easter Egg"

FoxTrot by Bill Amend
Courtesy of Universal Press Syndicate

The first video game "in joke" (known as an "Easter egg") was programmed by Warren Robinett in the VCS game *Adventure*. The hidden information was Robinett's credit—which symbolized the need for game developers to get the credit they deserved for their work. It turned out that Robinett made one pixel on a wall in a room active—linking to a hidden room containing his credit. When the Easter egg was discovered by a teenager—who wrote an excited letter to Atari about it—other developers were inspired to hide their names and other messages in games. The tradition continues today (whether or not the game companies know about it)!

Mattel Intellivision

Atari had some competition two years after the release of the VCS from an arguably superior (and more expensive) console system released by Mattel, known as Intellivision. Instead of a joystick (like the VCS), the Intellivision was equipped with an "intelligent" controller consisting of a keypad and a movement disc resembling the "track pad" on some of today's laptops. Game-specific plastic overlays were available to slide over the controllers, and the system even had rudimentary voice synthesis (with the purchase of an attachable component—the Intellivoice). In 1984, Mattel Electronics was shut down after heavy losses and sold to a Mattel vice president Terry Valeski, who renamed it Intellivision Inc.

Intellivision, Inc.

Mattel's Intellivision game console used a keypad and movement disc instead of a joystick.

::::: Mattel's Handhelds: One Sport at a Time

In 1977, the same year that Atari released the VCS/2600, Mattel launched the handheld game industry by releasing a series of LED (light emitting diode)-based portable games. Unlike today's cartridge-based handhelds, these systems would only contain one game! If you wanted to play another game, you'd have to buy another portable. Fortunately, the games were inexpensive! Some popular titles were *Auto Race*, *Basketball*, *Bowling*, *Football*, and *Sub Chase*.

Mattel Electronics

Football and *Sub Chase*—two of Mattel's popular handheld games.

> A round 1984 (I was 6 yrs old), I took a handheld football game away from my male cousin. I remember feeling a sense of excitement being a girl playing a boy's game, especially when I beat all the neighborhood boys' scores.
>
> — *Carissa Reyes, Internet Marketing & Advertising student*

ColecoVision

Coleco's entry into the console market was ColecoVision—containing mushroom-like joystick controllers and superb graphics. Blending the best of the VCS/2600 and Intellivision, ColecoVision soon became the standard to meet for reproducing the arcade experience at home. Nintendo's wildly popular arcade game, *Donkey Kong*, was included with every ColecoVision. Most of the early titles were adaptations of other memorable arcade titles such as *Venture*, *Mr. Dot*, *Lady Bug* and *Space Fury*.

River West Brands, LLC

Coleco's ColecoVision blended the best of the VCS/2600 and Intellivision console systems.

:::::: Cobbler to Cabbage Patch: Coleco's Diverse History

The Connecticut Leather Company (later shortened to Coleco) was established in 1932 by Russian immigrant Maurice

Greenberg to distribute leather products to shoemakers. The company soon began to make leather craft kits for kids based on popular icons Howdy Doody and Davy Crockett.

After competing in the first console wars of the home gaming industry with a superior system (ColecoVision) and releasing the successful Cabbage Patch Kids toys, Coleco filed for bankruptcy in 1988.

In the '70s and '80s, Coleco released some of the most memorable handheld games, including mini tabletop arcade games of popular titles such as *Zaxxon*, *Frogger*, and *Galaxian*. These mini arcade games were cleverly designed to emulate the look and feel of real stand-up arcade games, down to the joystick controller and cabinet art.

Sega Corporation

Sega's *Zaxxon* was just one of the arcade games transformed into a mini tabletop game by Coleco.

> The first electronic game I remember playing was *Smurfs* on ColecoVision. I think I was about 6 years old. I thought I was so cool—as I jumped over the fences and ducked under the bats that swooped down on me!
>
> — *Elizabeth Butler,*
> *Game Art & Design student*

Just as it seemed like the video game industry was unstoppable, it halted. The entire industry—including arcades and the home console segment—experienced a "slump" during the early '80s. The arcades never recovered from it, although the home console segment experienced an amazing recovery in the mid '80s.

What happened, and why?

The Video Game Slump & a New Golden Age

Several theories have been attributed to the video game industry slump of the early '80s. Perhaps the industry was just experiencing a temporary decline, and the platforms and titles introduced were just not revolutionary enough to reverse it. Oversupply may have also contributed to the slump—with 50 software companies producing cartridges, saturating the market with titles. There was also a lack of innovation—with low-quality and derivative games flooding the market. Market conditions forced the price of games to be lowered to $5 in order to stay competitive. Many video game developers were also concerned that home computers would take over the home gaming market altogether. Because this industry had never experienced a decline before, the general public started to question its legitimacy—wondering whether it was simply a fad, like the short-lived "hula hoop" craze!

Nintendo

Nintendo's entry into the console business in 1985 breathed new life into the home gaming industry—but it also helped push the arcade business into extinction. The system was far superior to consoles of the previous era, and the titles were graphically advanced—with compelling storylines and characters. Titles such as the *Super Mario Bros.* arcade conversion, *The Legend of Zelda*, and *Punch-Out!!* (where players had the thrill of bashing boxing legend Mike Tyson) were engrossing—with seemingly limit-

The Nintendo Entertainment System (NES) revolutionized the console industry.

less environments. Over 50 million NES systems were sold. The release of the improved Super NES in 1989 solidified Nintendo's presence in the marketplace. In 1990, Nintendo released *Super Mario Bros. 3*, the most successful non-bundled game cartridge of all time.

> The first real video game I ever played was the *Super Mario Bros.* that came with the original NES system. I played it night and day, and even taped my final victory against King Koopa. It was quite an achievement for me back then.
>
> — *Robert Ferguson,*
> *Game Art & Design student*

The NES had become so successful in the marketplace that the former industry leader Atari established Tengen, a subsidiary that exclusively focused on developing games for the NES. Soon afterward, Tengen discovered a way to bypass Nintendo's "lockout chip" and produce NES-compatible games without Nintendo's approval. Tengen then acquired the rights to sell the extremely popular puzzle game, *Tetris*. After it was discovered that Tengen bought the rights from Mirrorsoft (which did not actually own the rights), the game was removed from the marketplace—and Nintendo, which had acquired the legitimate rights to the game, released it under its own label.

::::: Alexey Pajitnov & *Tetris*

Tetris originated in Russia around 1985 and was never patented. At the time, intellectual property rights were not established in the U.S.S.R. for private individuals. The original author of *Tetris* was Alexey Pajitnov, assisted by Dmitry Pavlovsky and Vadim Gerasimov. *Tetris* has been embroiled in a strangely large number of legal battles since its inception. The IBM PC version eventually made its way to Budapest,

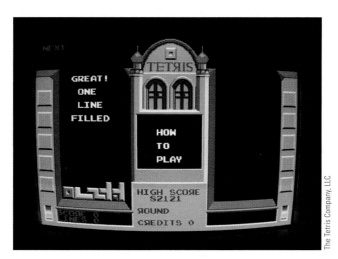

Hungary, where it was ported to various platforms and was "discovered" by a British software house named Andromeda. They attempted to contact Pajitnov to secure the rights for the PC version, but before the deal was firmly settled, they had already sold the rights to Spectrum Holobyte. After failing to settle the deal with Pajitnov, Andromeda attempted to license it from the Hungarian programmers instead. Meanwhile, before any legal rights were settled, the Spectrum Holobyte IBM PC version of *Tetris* was released in the United States in 1986. The game's popularity was tremendous, and many players were instantly hooked—it was a software blockbuster. By 1989, half a dozen different companies claimed rights to create and distribute the *Tetris* software for home computers, game consoles, and handheld systems. Nintendo released their version of *Tetris* for both the Famicom and the Game Boy and sold more than three million copies. The lawsuits between Tengen and Nintendo over the Famicom/NES version carried on until 1993. In 1996, Alexey Pajitnov and Henk Rogers formed The Tetris Company, LLC and Blue Planet Software in an effort to get royalties from the Tetris brand, with good success on game consoles but very little on the PC front. *Tetris* is now a registered trademark of The Tetris Company, LLC.

What would eventually become a great rivalry between Sony and Nintendo began in 1991, when the two companies—who had begun working together on a joint CD peripheral—ended their partnership over a legal dispute over publishing profits. Nintendo then turned to Philips to create a CD-ROM compatible with the Philips CD-i ("interactive") system. Unhappy with this move, Sony scrapped the old "PlayStation" developed for Nintendo and began working on developing a 32-bit CD-only game machine to compete aggressively with Nintendo in both Japan and the United States.

Cheating with the Genie

In 1991, Galoob Toys released the Game Genie, which lets players cheat in NES games and win more easily. Nintendo attempted to prevent Game Genie sales—citing that it reduced the long-term value of its games.

Nintendo revolutionized the industry again with the Game Boy—a portable system that launched a new era of handhelds in 1995. The ever-popular *Tetris* was the flagship title for the monochrome system. The Game Boy Advance and follow-up Game Boy Advance Color were launched in 2000. The Game Boy Advance SP (which looks like a miniature laptop and has a backlit screen) was released in 2003.

Nintendo's Game Boy (Game Boy Color, left)—followed by the Game Boy Advance (middle) and Game Boy Advance SP (right)—kicked off a new era in portable gaming.

Tiger's Multipurpose Handhelds

In 1997, Tiger released a monochrome handheld system called "game.com" to compete with the Game Boy. Unlike Nintendo's special-purpose game system, Tiger's featured a built-in solitaire game, calculator, personal contacts database, and calendar. It also included a stylus and touch-screen technology—and it could hook up to a standard modem for access to an online text-based email service.

Sega

Following Nintendo's successful launch of the NES, Sega began to release a slew of game systems in the '80s and '90s—including the Sega Master System (SMS), Genesis, Saturn, and Dreamcast. In 1991, Sega reinvented itself with *Sonic the Hedgehog*—a game that featured a fast-moving blue creature in red tennis shoes. The character of Sonic

The Sega Master System (SMS) was Sega's first entry into the console market.

chapter 1   Historical Elements: how did we get here?

was so successful that it became Sega's mascot—and a serious challenger to Mario! Although the Sega Genesis outsold SuperNES in 1992, allowing Sega to effectively take control of the U.S. console market, Sega's follow-up releases did not fare as well and were both discontinued. By 1995, Sega of America was juggling seven separate and incompatible game platforms—Saturn, Genesis, Game Gear, Pico, Sega CD, 32X, and 32X CD.

3DO & the Bit Wars

In 1992, Electronic Arts founder Trip Hawkins started 3DO—a new company that received major backing from Panasonic, Time-Warner and MCA to release a 32-bit (as opposed to the standard 16-bit) game console that would hopefully take over as the new industry leader. A year later, Panasonic marketed the console; although reviews are positive, the price (at $699) was not. Atari responded to this by jumping ahead to a 64-bit console system with the release of the Jaguar. Sega responded by releasing the 32X, a peripheral device that enabled the Genesis to run a new set of 32-bit cartridge games.

:::::: Video Game Violence:
Senate Hearings & the ESRB

Entertainment Software Ratings Board

ESRB ratings symbols include AO (Adults Only – 18+), EC (Early Childhood), E (Everyone), M (Mature - 17+), and T (Teen).

In 1993, U.S. Senators Joseph Lieberman of Connecticut and Herbert Kohl of Wisconsin held hearings on violence in computer and video games. Shortly thereafter, the industry created the Entertainment Software Rating Board (ESRB) to provide parents and consumers with detailed information on game content so that they can make appropriate purchasing decisions for their unique households. The ESRB now rates all entertainment software, providing both age ratings and content descriptions that can be found on game packages, advertisements, and marketing materials. Senator Lieberman and the Federal Trade Commission (FTC) called the ESRB "an industry model" and "the most comprehensive of all the industry rating systems," respectively. For more information, visit *www.esrb.org*.

Since Saturn had been outselling Sony's PlayStation in Japan, the assumption was made that it should be the focus in the United States. After announcing that the system would be released in the United States on "Saturnday"—September 2—Sega released the system four months earlier than expected. Overall sales were very low and few titles were released—primarily because developers had been caught off guard by the early release. Although the system continued to do well in Japan, sales remained disappointingly low in the United States. By 1996, the rumors persisted that the company would stop developing hardware and focus on game software.

In 1997, Sega announced that it would merge with Japanese toy company Bandai—which ironically was developing software for the PlayStation. After Bandai's board approved of the merger, the company reversed its decision. In 1998, Sega launched the Dreamcast—which used Microsoft's Windows CE operating system, allowing for easier game conversions to and from the PC. Even with the success of this release, President Hayao Nakayama stepped down from his position and Sega ceased distribution of the Saturn in the United States.

Sony Computer Entertainment America, Inc.

The launch of Sony's original PlayStation started a brand new era in the console wars.

Sony Launches a New Era

The entry of Sony's PlayStation into the console market in 1995 launched a new era in the console wars. Even with the release of industry leader Nintendo's N64, the PlayStation kept its top spot as the number-one worldwide next-generation game console. In 1997, Sony and Nintendo continued to compete with the PlayStation and N64.

Currently, three systems vie for the attention of the marketplace—and Sony's PlayStation 2 (PS2) appears to be winning, so far. Microsoft's Xbox is definitely a force to be reckoned with—and Nintendo's GameCube has been praised for its usability, but its titles are few and focus on a younger market. We will be exploring these systems in more detail in Chapter 3.

FoxTrot by Bill Amend
Courtesy of Universal Press Syndicate

The Personal Computer Revolution

During the mid-1970s, another segment of the electronic gaming industry would begin to enter a new era. The personal computer revolution brought technology that was once the exclusive territory of programmers and hobbyists into the home. Games that had once been developed on a whim by university students could now be adapted for personal computers—and the general consumer would get to join in the fun. Already, arcade games were being repurposed into home game systems, taking some of the business away from video game arcades. The growth of computers in the home would also contribute to the eventual decline of the arcade business—and it would also represent a threat to the game console business. Several personal computers—such as the Apple II and Commodore 64—were created with gameplay in mind. (In fact, Steve Wozniak, who designed the Apple II, was an avid gamer.) As you read this section, think about the first personal computer your or your family owned and what games you liked to play on it.

Mainframes and Text-Adventures

Colossal Cave (also known as *Adventure*—not to be confused with the Atari VCS game of the same name) was developed by assembly-language programmer William Crowther and influenced a generation of adventure game developers at colleges and defense contractors. Donald Woods expanded on it, resulting in Infocom's popular *Zork* in 1979. The two-word commands, which originally were developed by Crowther so that his young daughters would understand them—were immortalized in ZIL (Zork Interpretive Language)! Roberta Williams was so inspired by the game that she developed *Mystery House* with her husband Ken Williams—launching what would become Sierra On-Line and the Sierra Network.

Colossal Cave: Text Addiction

My father, who was a mathematician for a defense contractor, would often bring his work home with him—which sometimes included a terminal with a 300-baud modem attached to it. This is about 100 times slower than a sluggish dialup connection today! I would play *Colossal Cave*—using two-word commands such as "go west" and "get inventory" in order to move my character and see what I was carrying. As simple as this sounds, the game was highly addictive—and the lack of graphics allowed my imagination to run wild.

Other mainframe games included:

- Richard Greenblatt's *MacHack-6* (1966) – the first computerized chess program to enter a tournament (and beat a human player). The program was an expansion of Alan Kotok's BS project on the IBM 7090.
- John Horton Conway's *Life* (1970) – a cellular automata-artificial life program that allowed the "player" to set rules and watch what happened to computer-based "life-forms" as they evolved. Software Toolworks latter released *Life* for personal computers.
- Don Daglow's *Trek* (1971) – a very popular *Star Trek*-like sci fi game that began on the Pomona College mainframe. Cygnus Software later released *Star Fleet I* (a "slick" version of *Trek*) for personal computers.
- Gregory Yob's *Hunt the Wumpus* – incorporated a maze based on a dodecahedron (12-sided polygon). Players explored this "map" and attempted to kill the Wumpus (an odorous beast who hid in caves surrounded by pits and superbats). The beast would remain asleep until unwary adventurers would wake him by firing an arrow and missing. If the Wumpus ended up in the same room as the adventurer, he ate the adventurer—who would get clues during the game of how close the Wumpus was (based on the strength of the creature's odor).

::::::IBM PC: the "Business Machine"

IBM Corporation
Image courtesy of Sylvain Bizoirre at
Old-Computers.com

In 1981, IBM released the IBM PC using Intel's 8088 microprocessor. Although the system was not targeted toward the business and programming communities—and it was not designed for entertainment—it ended up capturing the market for computer programmers (including game developers) because IBM used an open system architecture and allowed itself to be cloned. Today, personal computers based on the original IBM technology are the standard hardware used by computer game developers and players.

Apple II

While at Hewlett-Packard, Steve Wozniak designed what was to be known as the Apple I and demonstrated it at the Homebrew Computer Club—a popular computer hobbyists' hangout. Steve Jobs approached him at the meeting and suggested that they start a company together. The result was the first personal computer system—and the beginning of a revolution that would threaten to compete with video arcades and home consoles alike. Computers were now out of the exclusive realm of university and research engineering students and hobbyists, and in the home.

Steve Wozniak implemented the BASIC programming language into what he called "Game BASIC" in order to develop games for the Apple II. Consumers could program the system as well, or play games such as *Zork*, *Lode Runner*, *Wizardry*, and *Ultima*.

In 1984, Apple released the Macintosh—a system with superior graphics, sound, and an accessible, user-friendly interface. A year later, Microsoft released the Windows operating system to compete with the Macintosh; although Windows eventually grabbed a majority of the market share, the initial releases of the operating system were weak.

Apple Computer, Inc.

The first home computer games were played on the Apple II.

::::: *Ultima*'s Origin

In 1979, Richard Garriott's California Pacific Computer (later Origin Systems) released *Akalabeth*—precursor to the popular *Ultima* series. A year later, a tile-based graphics version of *Ultima* was released for the Apple II. After seven sequels, the highly successful adventure/role-playing game series continues today with *Ultima Online*.

ORIGIN Systems, Inc.

Ultima III is one of eight games in the popular *Ultima* series.

Electronic Arts: Rock Stars and Sports Stars

Former Apple employee Trip Hawkins later started what was to become the largest game company in the United States: Electronic Arts. Initially treating his designers and artists like "rock stars," he referred to game packaging as "album covers" and sent his developers on in-store game signing tours. Hawkins' later decision to focus his attention on celebrity advisors in the sports industry helped make sports the top-selling game genre in the United States—with titles like *Dr. J. & Larry Bird Go One-On-One* and the ever-popular *John Madden Football*.

:::::From Console to Computer

Atari, Inc.

Atari shifted its focus to compete directly with Apple by releasing the 400 (a game machine that was also a computer), 800 (with a real keyboard and internal expansion capability), and 5200 (a pure game machine—but it did not handle 400 or 800 cartridges).

The Atari 400 was a hybrid computer-game system.

Coleco also tried to compete with Apple by releasing the unsuccessful Adam Computer. Not only did this effort detract from the ColecoVision console system, but 60 percent of all Adam Computers were returned defective.

CDTV: Commodore's Edutainment System

In 1990, when companies such as Davidson & Associates, the Learning Company and others launched the "edutainment" computer software movement, Commodore released the CDTV (Commodore Dynamic Total Vision)—a home entertainment system that was basically a Commodore 64 without a keyboard. This "interactive" system was one of many released at the time that stressed educational software as well as games. The software was sold on CDs rather than cartridges.

Commodore 64

After releasing the PET (Personal Electronic Transactor) and the VIC-20 to compete with the Apple II (and failing to do so), Commodore Computer made another attempt to enter the personal computer market in 1982. This time, the company was successful beyond belief. The affordable Commodore 64 (C-64), released in 1982,

Commodore Computers

was a formidable competitor to the more expensive Apple II. In fact, the C-64 was one of the most successful computers of all time. Its $300 price tag (equivalent to Intellivision) and programmability made personal computing affordable. Its color monitor and spacious memory made rival computer Texas Instruments' TI-99 look primitive. Software continued to be developed for the Commodore 64 into the next decade. Commodore also released the Amiga computer in 1986; designed to support high-end games, the Amiga was an exceptional platform but was marketed poorly.

The Commodore 64 made personal computing affordable.

New game companies were launched that created software for home computers only instead of arcades and consoles. Inspired by *Colossal Cave*, Roberta Williams started Sierra On-Line with her husband Ken; most of the team's game development was who done at the kitchen table! In 1984, Sierra released *King's Quest*—a graphical adventure/role-playing game targeted for IBM's PC Jr. The game became a successful and long-running series. Broderbund's focus is on educational games, such as the *Carmen Sandiego* series.

Before the personal computer revolution even began to heat up, innovations in the online world were going strong—among those who were fortunate enough to have access to the online world. It would take the emergence of networked gaming—and especially the commercialization of the Internet—to break open this world for the consumer public. Until the introduction of the World Wide Web in 1993, playing personal computer games was mainly an isolated activity. Let's look at the evolution of online games—an industry segment that began with a small, elite market decades before personal computers took over home entertainment.

Multiplayer Meets the Online Elite

You might think that online games began once the Internet became commercial, attracting a wide market of consumers. In reality, online games pre-dated this era by several decades. In the early days of online gaming, players had access to technology that was not readily available to the public. As a result, networked games evolved away from the public eye—and they really did not get public attention until the World Wide Web came into consumer use.

Here are a few milestones in the history of online gaming. You might recognize some of the services that helped fuel this segment of the industry. In fact, you might even be using them today!

PLATO

It all started with PLATO (Programmed Logic for Automatic Teaching Operations), introduced in 1961 at the University of Illinois. The system was intended to be used for research in the area of computer-based education, but Rick Blomme turned it into a multiplayer game network. Creating a two-player version of *Spacewar!*—Steve Russell's MIT mainframe game that started it all—Blomme catalyzed the growth of a new phenomenon in gaming. PLATO soon introduced a *Star-Trek*-based game for 32 players (*Empire*), a flight-simulation game (*Airfight*), and a popular precursor to today's chat rooms known as *Talk-O-Matic*—foreshadowing the importance of social interaction in online games. In the '70s, PLATO featured *Dungeons & Dragons*-inspired *Avatar* (origin of the *Wizardry* series) and *Oubliette*. This was the beginning of what would become online role-playing games—which are now played on a "massive" scale, with thousands of simultaneous players. It was also the beginning of many educational games and interactive experiments.

MUDs

Roy Trubshaw and Richard Bartle at Essex University (U.K.) created what would later be referred to as a Multi-User Dungeon (MUD) in 1979. As the Essex network became a part of ARPAnet—a worldwide computer network of academic institutions and the basis of what is now known as the Internet—students and researchers connected to the network began to create their own MUDs with the freely-available code. Like *Talk-O-Matic* and future online chat rooms, MUDs focused heavily on the social aspects of games. This, and the ability for the players to design their own environments, helped build social interaction and player design into the online game tradition.

CompuServe

The first Internet service provider (ISP), CompuServe, immediately recognized the monetary potential of allowing its customers to play games over a public network. Teaming up with developers John Taylor and Kelton Flinn of Kesmai Corporation, CompuServe released ASCII-text role-playing games such as *Islands of Kesmai* and *Megawars I*. Charging its customers a whopping $12 per hour (even more expensive primetime at $25-65) to play these games, CompuServe launched commercial online gaming.

The First Monthly Game Service

Marc Jacobs provided the first online gaming service for a monthly rate ($40) with the text-based role-playing game called *Aradath*. Jacobs' company, AUSI, was the predecessor to Mythic Entertainment—developer of *Dark Age of Camelot*.

QuantumLink

America Online (AOL) actually started as a game company. The predecessor of today's AOL was launched in 1985 to directly compete with CompuServe's online multiplayer game services. The first graphics-based online service, QuantumLink was initially available only to Commodore 64 users. The first game available on the service—developed by Randy Farmer and Chip Morningstar at LucasFilm—was

Habitat, the first graphic-based MUD online environment that focused on social interaction. Richard Garriott of Origin Systems approached QuantumLink in 1991 to develop *Ultima Online*—an online version of the successful *Ultima* series.

Why Not Play-By-Email?

Play-by-mail (PBM) games such as *Diplomacy* (which began in the 1960s) were developed as a way for geographically separated gamers to compete with each other. With the advent of online services such as GEnie and QuantumLink (AOL), pioneers Don Daglow and Jessica Mulligan launched the first commercial play-by-email (PBeM) games. Chat-based multiplayer space strategy game *Rim Worlds War* was developed by Jessica Mulligan for the GEnie online service. *Quantum Space* was designed and programmed by Don Daglow for QuantumLink (AOL).

GEnie

The GE Network for Information Exchange was an online service that competed directly with CompuServe and QuantumLink. Kesmai developed *Air Warrior* for GEnie, which was a World War II flight simulator that could be considered the first massively multiplayer online game (MMOG) that was graphically based. During the late '80s, GEnie established itself as the premier online service for multiplayer online games—licensing game environments such as AUSI's *Galaxy II* and Simutronic's *Orb Wars*. The first online 3D shooter, *A-Maze-ing* was launched in 1989.

id Software: Revolutionizing Networked Gaming

In 1993, several events took place that helped accelerate the online multiplayer game segment. The first graphical web browser, NCSA Mosaic (created by Mark Andreessen while he was a student at the University of Illinois) marked the end of text-only communication on the Internet—opening up this global network to the commercial world, as well as to the general public. The commercial online service competed for subscribers.

Then, in 1993, id Software released *DOOM*—which allowed up to four players to connect over a LAN (local area network) and play against each other in a "death-match." The company's next title, *Quake*, featured built-in Internet capabilities so that geographically-dispersed players could engage in deathmatches. Other computer game developers added modem and LAN functionality to games that allowed for simultaneous players. Yet another entirely new section of the computer game market was created, involving CD-ROM products being played over networks. Built-in Internet-based multiplayer capability also became a requirement with games—rather than an option.

:::::The LAN Party Phenomenon

The '90s saw major developments in computer graphics, processing speed, and sound—and computer games were raised to new standards. Networked multiplayer games such as *Doom*, *Quake* and *Diablo* spawned a new social trend among gamers. "LAN parties" involved friends networking their computers together in a room and playing in teams or against each other—in between bites of pizza and (root) beer.

As the information revolution, fueled by the World Wide Web, began to infuse American culture in the mid '90s, computer games became truly interactive—with the capacity for hundreds of thousands of people worldwide to play "massively multiplayer" games simultaneously. Players would immerse themselves in a simulated, persistent fantasy world—customizing their own characters, forming collaborative teams or "guilds," and engaging in adventurous quests. (Online multiplayer games will be discussed in more detail throughout the rest of this book.)

:::::The *Ultima* Saga Continues in the Online World

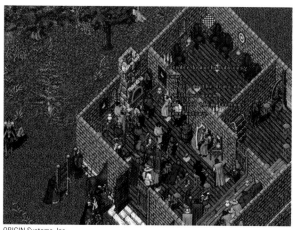

ORIGIN Systems, Inc.

The rise of massively multiplayer online games (MMOGs) in the United States began when Origin Systems launched *Ultima Online*—hitting the 50,000-subscriber mark within the first three months. Turbine Entertainment developed *Asheron's Call* and Verant Interactive (later acquired by Sony) launched *Everquest*—which was to become the largest massively multiplayer online role-playing game (MMORPG) in the United States, claiming to have over 500,000 simultaneous players. (Massively multiplayer online games are discussed in more detail in Chapter 3.)

Ultima Online was one of the first massively multiplayer online games.

Convergence: Industry Segments Come Together

Sony Computer Entertainment America, Inc.

Microsoft Corporation

Nintendo of America, Inc.

The three current dominant console systems—PlayStation 2 (PS2), Xbox, and GameCube—all offer Internet connectivity.

After decades of developing in parallel, the console and computer game segments are experiencing some technology convergence—where characteristics of once-separate industry segments are now intersecting. This has been fueled by an unexpected development involving online games. The online world has now become a popular place for communication and entertainment. Console game companies, in their desire to grab this market, now offer Internet connectivity through their systems— GameCube (Nintendo), Xbox (Microsoft), and PlayStation 2 (Sony). Convergence is the theme for most current portable and console systems —whether they connect to the Internet or incorporate cell phone technology. The PSX, released in Japan (and similar to the upcoming PS3) incorporates DVD technology.

Emulators: The Online Arcade

Even arcade and online worlds are converging in the form of online arcade emulation programs—which duplicate the function of one system with a different system, so that the second system appears to behave like the first. For example, the MAME (Multiple Arcade Machine Emulator) software emulator allows computers to run arcade games on computer hardware. One of the more creative is a *Pac-Man* emulation that was programmed through an Excel spreadsheet! A popular use of emulators is to run games written for hardware that is no longer sold or readily available—not only arcade hardware, but console and computer hardware (such as Commodore 64 and Amiga).

Nokia, Inc.

Nokia's N-Gage is a cell phone/game/MP3/ Internet system—and the N-Gage QD is a more compact, special-purpose gaming system.

Sony's EyeToy combines a camera with motion-tracking technology to give players the experience of being in the game and controlling it with their movements.

Other segments of the industry are starting to experience growth. The portable game business—first seen in the 1970s with Mattel's sports-oriented handhelds—has evolved into a full-fledged mobile game market. The release of Nokia's N-Gage (cell phone-game-Internet system) followed close on the heels of Nintendo's new and improved Game Boy Advance SP. Although the N-Gage's initial launch has not met expectations, the N-Gage QD may prove to be a success.

Developers and hardware manufacturers are jumping on the bandwagon and putting together portable gaming development initiatives (Sony's PSP), developing innovative hardware (Sony's EyeToy and Majesco's video attachment to the GBA),

Sony Computer Entertainment America, Inc.

and experimenting with techniques that address the graphics, memory, and screen size limitations (Nintendo's DS—a dual-screen handheld). See Chapter 3 for a detailed discussion of current game platforms.

Nintendo of America, Inc.

Nintendo may revolutionize the industry again with its dual-screen handheld system—the Nintendo DS.

Into the Future

You have now taken a brief look at major milestones in the history of electronic game development. Where do you think the industry will be 10 years from now? Do you see another segment of the industry bubbling under the surface? Will one particular segment of the industry experience a growth spurt? Will consumers choose portability over the cinematic experience of "home theatre"-style console gaming? If the mobile gaming industry takes off, will developers start to focus on the small screen? Will the social aspects of online multiplayer games become so compelling that players begin to spend more time in the virtual environment than in RL ("real life")?

This chapter provided you with a solid background on the history of electronic game development—including the companies, people and games that helped this industry take shape. Next, let's look at the players—who they are, where they are, and why they play. Although often overlooked by game developers, the player market must be understood in order to develop successful games.

:::CHAPTER REVIEW:::

1. What are the significant electronic game development companies that have been around since the beginning of the industry, and how did they get started?

2. Who are the individuals that have played a significant role in the evolution of the electronic game development industry, and what are their major contributions?

3. What are the key phases and milestones in the history of electronic game development? How has convergence played a role in connecting these phases today?

4. Why have some game development companies succeeded while others have failed? How can you apply this knowledge to today's industry?

5. What electronic games helped to attract a larger audience to this industry? Why did they succeed in doing so?

6. What traditions in early game development are still in existence today? How are they appealing and useful to developers and players?

7. Several theories have been used to explain the decline of the arcade industry and associated video game slump of the early '80s. Do you agree in particular with any of these theories? Do you have a theory of your own? Is there anything that could have been done to prevent this slump?

8. What was the first electronic game you ever played? Did it capture your attention? Why? What are some non-electronic games that were popular when you were a kid? Do you feel that the thrill of any of these games has been captured in digital form?

9. Choose a time in the history of electronic game development, and pretend you are a developer working in the industry. Knowing the limitations of the time, what type of game would you create?

10. You've read about the many eras and phases of the electronic game industry. Are we at the dawn of a new era? Can you predict the primary features of the next phase in game industry history?

2

Player Elements:
who plays and why?

key chapter questions

- What motivates people to play games, and how does this affect the types of games that are developed?

- What is the difference between geographics, demographics, and psychographics?

- How has the player market changed over time?

- What is the difference between the U.S. and South Korean market?

- What are the different generations of players in the United States?

Now that you have an understanding of how the game industry has evolved over the years, it's time to take a look at the people who play these games. There was a time when the profile of a "gamer" was a teenage boy—but that profile is inaccurate today. The market for players has changed dramatically since the mid-1990s, in large part due to the advent of the World Wide Web as a commercial medium. As the "multimedia" interface to the Internet, the web fueled the growth of a new communications industry. Many people have at least one personal web site (often complete with their own daily blog), if they're not already using the web as a storefront—and it's now commonplace to communicate with friends, family, and colleagues via email and instant messaging. You might even be using this textbook to supplement an online distance learning class!

If you plan to develop games, you need to understand the game *market*—the people who play games. Which portion of this market do you want to target? The answer to this question is *not* "everyone." You need to understand who *your* market is in order to create a compelling game that will suit your market's needs.

With half of all America playing electronic games, interactive entertainment is the entertainment choice of the 21st century. The Entertainment Software Association conducted a survey of over 1,000 players in August 2003. The poll found that the average player spends approximately 6.5 hours a week playing games. Almost one-third indicated that they play at least three genres of games. Contrary to popular belief, boys ages 6–17 don't spend that excessive an amount of time playing—just over an hour a day, on average.

> Even *Tetris* will take your mind off your troubles for a while.
>
> —Robert Ferguson, Game Art & Design student

Motivation

Why do people play games? Understanding this can help you develop games that will fulfill these needs. Some developers create games without considering why their audience would want to play them—and components of games that are most attractive to the players are not utilized enough by game developers to keep the players interested. Here are just a few factors that motivate players to keep on playing.

:::::: Player Suits

In 1996, Richard Bartle published "Hearts, Clubs, Diamonds, Spades: Players Who Suit MUDs" (Journal of MUD Research)—a paper

British Go Association

in which he proposed that multi-user dungeon (MUD) players fall into four categories, depending on whether they enjoy acting on (manipulating, exploiting, controlling) or interacting with (learning, communicating, examining) the game world or players. Bartle came up with four player types, corresponding to the four suits in a deck of cards:

1. **Hearts:** These players are *socializers*—those who enjoy learning about or communicating with other players.

2. **Clubs:** These players are *killers*—those who enjoy manipulating other players.

3. **Diamonds:** These players are *achievers*—those who enjoy manipulating the game world.

4. **Spades:** These players are *explorers*—those who enjoy interacting with the game world.

Bartle theorized that a healthy MUD community required a certain proportion of each type of player to sustain itself.

Social Interaction

When games are played by more than one person, players might be motivated to interact socially with their opponents or team members. This socialization could exist in simple two-person

games at an arcade or in *massively multiplayer online games* (MMOGs), with thousands of people playing simultaneously. Players in MMOGs are often allowed to communicate through the game itself—often

The *Sims Online* centers around social interaction.

discussing non game-related topics rather than "staying in character." Sometimes players who meet each other through the game arrange to meet each other in real life at game conventions. Even marriage ceremonies have taken place in games!

Physical Seclusion

The idea of *seclusion* may seem the opposite of *social interaction*. However, players who want to be secluded are still interacting socially with people—but in the privacy of their own physical environments. This challenges the definition of "being social." Some would argue that people who prefer to stay home and play an MMOG must be anti-social. Others would argue that these same people must be highly social, since they are most likely interacting with many more people than they could possibly have run into at a dinner party. Is email considered anti-social? Before it was accepted by the masses as a viable way to communicate, it most certainly was. Now it's seen as a way to broaden one's social network—which now has the capacity to transcend geographical boundaries, becoming global. Players motivated by physical seclusion would probably prefer to play games in a private place—such as their homes. Other players could easily play games in public places, such as arcades—or almost anywhere, with their handhelds in tow!

Physical seclusion and privacy are motivating factors for some players.

Competition

Some players enjoy the thrill of *competing* with other players. This concept will be discussed further in the next chapter. The competitive spirit has been associated with games throughout history—and it forms the basis of the tremendously successful sports industry. You will see in Chapter 6 that competition can also be combined with cooperation to make games more compelling and challenging.

Competition is the motivation behind playing many sports games such as *WWE Smackdown: Shut Your Mouth!*

Knowledge

Players can be motivated to gain *knowledge* of particular concepts, processes, and strategies by playing games—although this motivation can often be unconscious. If players made it clear that they truly wanted to learn while playing, game developers might market their games as educational tools—providing "fun learning" for everyone. In the next chapter, you'll learn more about how most games allow players to learn "by accident"! In Chapter 6, you'll also learn that players apply knowledge within the game and outside of the game in order to play the game successfully.

Educational games such as *Carmen Sandiego* focus on providing knowledge to players.

Score summaries, such as this one from *Bookworm*, are necessary for players who are motivated to master the game.

Mastery

Some players are motivated to *master* the game itself—demonstrating their ability to dominate the game world and figure out how to become advanced players. Mastery is most obvious during games that depend on increasing character skills in order to "win." Players motivated by mastery focus on assessing their status in the game by attaining high scores and rankings.

> Everyday stress motivates me to play games. Playing games helps me unwind and gives me a feeling of control—unlike many other parts of life.
>
> — *Katrina Ruban, Game Art & Design student*

Escapism

Lionhead Studios

Game worlds such as the vast prehistoric landscape in *BC* can provide escape for some players.

Players often indicate that they are motivated to play in order to *escape* from the ongoing stresses and challenges of real life. An imaginary game world follows its own rules, some of which are less restricted than those in real life. Although people can escape into the "worlds" of other media such as books and movies, they are not directly participating in those worlds like they are in games.

> I play games to escape the life that most of us live and live the life that most of us want.
>
> — *Arash John Sammander, Game Art & Design student*

The next chapter introduces the concept of *immersion* and how it's particularly effective in games. Players' participation in games can also involve close bonds with characters within the games—especially if a character is "inhabited" by the player. The concept of player and character identity is discussed further in Chapter 5.

Player Empowerment in *Ultima Online*

My most memorable experience working on a title was right after we shipped *Ultima Online*. We were having a terrifically hard time stabilizing and optimizing the game (i.e., it was crashing and lagging all the time). Despite our success in attracting the largest number of subscribers ever to an online game, we were a bit down on ourselves for the lack of quality in our product. About that time, we got a letter from a player who described what a wonderful time he was having in the game. In the somewhat lengthy letter, he talked about how *UO* allowed him to experience things he never had a chance to experience in real life. In *UO*, he was a strong leader with lots of friends—and he was able to explore the vastness of the land and destroy evil. At the end of the letter, he said how much he appreciated us for giving him a chance to run—which, since he was confined to a wheelchair, he could not do in his real life. That letter made all the pain and effort worth it. More importantly, it taught me that these games can be more than money-making entertainment. They can have real meaning and impact for our customers. I have never forgotten this lesson, and I still cherish that letter today.

ORIGIN Systems, Inc.

Ultima Online

— *Starr Long (Producer, NCsoft)*

Player Elements: who plays and why? **chapter 2**

Prestige Casino

Casino games such as Prestige Casino's blackjack game can be very addictive.

Addiction

Some players indicate that they are motivated by *addiction*—which is the tendency to focus on one activity at the expense of all others. A recent panel conducted by the International Game Developers Association (IGDA) indicated that one of the best compliments that can be paid to game developers is that their games are addictive. Unlike the comparatively "passive" entertainment of television and film, games do offer players the ability to take active roles in the entertainment experience—including making decisions and getting feedback. This can be highly rewarding for players, but it can also cause them to crave continuous play to the point of ignoring other more important areas of their lives. Gambling has been shown to be addictive, and some game developers are considering incorporating gambling into more sophisticated electronic games. But it can be argued that all worthwhile hobbies tend to be addictive—and that it is the player's responsibility to maintain some balance!

There are many other reasons people play. Some feel it's a form of *therapy* for them, where they can work out issues that trouble them in a "safe" environment separate from (but sometimes eerily similar to) the real world. Others, such as *Dance Dance Revolution*'s energetic fan base, play to exercise and work on some new dance moves. With Konami's follow-up to *DDR—Karaoke Revolution,* a karaoke game that allows people to sing and play—many are eagerly awaiting a game that combines the two so that everyone can become an entertainer. A game's *playability* (discussed in more detail in Chapter 10) is related to player motivation. If the game satisfies a player's particular motivation, it is more likely to be fun, engrossing, and worthwhile to that player.

Geographics

Geographics relate to the players' geographic locations—which could include various countries or even regions within those countries. The U.S. game industry alone does over $10 billion worth of business annually—and it is estimated that the industry is grossing over $35 billion worldwide. According to Loren Shuster in the technology magazine, *Compiler,* the size of the gaming industry is now approaching $40 billion, and has already surpassed the motion picture industry in terms of box office revenue.

South Korea is the most "wired" country in the world (the United States is #7)—and, despite its relatively small size, it is home to more online gamers than any other country, including the United States.

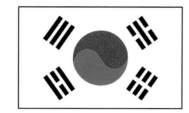

South Korea—the world leader in broadband penetration—boasts the largest subscriber base to online multiplayer games.

Jongheum Park on Developing Games for the U.S. & South Korea :::::

Jongheum Park began working as a programmer at Nexon in 1996. In addition to programming *Dark Ages*, Nexon's second massively multiplayer online role-playing game (MMORPG), he became Lead Programmer of *Tactical Commanders* (known as *Shattered Galaxy* in the United States), which won four prizes out of six in the Independent Games Festival (IGF) at the Game Developers Conference (GDC). In 2001, Jongheum became Lead Game Designer on *Crazy Arcade*, which has over 300,000 concurrent users—a record that has not been broken by any other game in South Korea (as of this writing). He is currently working as Lead Game Designer and Producer of a new, as yet undisclosed, MMORPG.

Jongheum Park
(Lead Designer,
Nexon)

Communication matters in game development—which really involves synchronizing the brains of key members of the team. (If everyone thinks the same, this is best!) When developing a game for both the U.S. and South Korean markets, we had a lot of miscommunication with our U.S. office. The only communication channel was through email. (Because of our poor English, talking on the phone was impossible.) The market is quite different, and so are the minds of the developers—so it was hard to reach agreement.

In South Korea, games are getting easier and easier. There are a lot of hit casual games. The game *Go-Stop* (Poker-style gambling) is widespread. It is phenomenal! Many companies are trying to grab the *Go-Stop* market. But these games have a short life cycle—so I think game designers will focus on the strong points of casual games and MMOGs, fusing them into one. Just as South Korean players want more simplicity, U.S. players seem to want complexity. I think it's almost impossible to focus on both markets simultaneously.

Most wired countries based on percentage of broadband penetration. (Source: eMarketer, 2001)

When NCsoft, now the largest game developer in South Korea, launched the *Lineage* massively multiplayer online game (MMOG) in September 1998, the country was experiencing an economic crisis that had resulted in a dramatic devaluation of Korean currency and an unprecedented increase in unemployment. "Refugees" from the high-tech industry, mostly middle managers, became entrepreneurs overnight—starting PC game rooms in their living rooms. A profitable industry had begun, with hourly fees of $1 (US equivalent) paid by the unemployed gamers—a low price to pay to conquer foes in "virtual worlds" and escape the real economic catastrophes in the offline world, without having to own a personal computer.

As South Korea's financial situation began to improve, and households with broadband service increased rapidly, personal accounts on home PCs began to rise. In addition to playing at PC Baangs, gamers can now download game software onto their home PCs. Baangs have also grown in popularity—making a dramatic transformation from entrepreneurs' living rooms to full-blown entertainment centers, some of which are as ritzy as Las Vegas casinos. It is commonplace to see both men and women gamers in Baangs—which often provide "his" and "hers" chairs so that couples can play online games together. Online gaming has also grown beyond being just a pastime into a competitive national sport—with many game competitions now being televised regularly. Currently, approximately 80 percent of South Korea's Internet users have played online games, and the country has the highest broadband penetration in the world. South Korea represents an online gaming market—not a console market.

Mark Terrano on the South Korean Market:::::

Mark Terrano works in the Xbox Advanced Technology Group as a Technical Game Manager. In this role, he is able to work with game developers worldwide to help them make the best possible Xbox games. Previously, he worked with Ensemble Studios on the *Age of Empires* series as a designer and programmer. He was also a network specialist involved in every area of computing from stock markets to oil pipelines. When not working, he enjoys Seattle, playing music, and—of course—all kinds of games.

Mark Terrano (Technical Game Manager, Xbox Advanced Technology Group)

When people ask where I think games are going in the near future, I always refer to South Korea. Game parlors are on every block and apartment complex, the professional gamers are on billboards and television, and everyone you meet has a favorite *Starcraft* story. Games are not just accepted in popular culture; they are integrated, and nearly everyone plays.

"Professional gamer" is a recognized career, and it is well-respected; tournament competition is fierce and followed in the media on par with any other sport. The government is a strong proponent of game developers in Korea as well—providing services, resources, information, and tools to start-ups. The students just moving into their first jobs now have grown up with games, and they understand games as an interactive medium. Even a little-known new game can easily attract 100,000 beta players—and the rate of introduction and evolution of multiplayer titles is staggering.

Courtesy of: Mark Terrano

Arcade Machines (Seoul, 2003)

Competition and tournament play are also important in popularizing gameplay. The World Cyber Games started in South Korea; this is an Olympics-style event with players competing from all over the world and converging for the world finals which lasts a week in the host country. Professional gamers work their way up through the competitive ranks and represent

Courtesy of: Mark Terrano

WCG Competiton (Seoul, 2002)

their neighborhoods, schools, and companies. Large tournaments and local heroes create media attention that follows the professionals and builds a fan base. The commercial sponsorships and endorsements follow the fans, which leads to more competition and tournament play. Full-color weekly magazines are thick with strategies, tactics, and interviews with the pro gamers and developers. Fashion, gadgets, accessories, and other media are also influenced by games.

Baang –Coex Center
(Seoul, 2003)

Korean developers are bringing new perspectives, stories, and mythologies, and even completely new social structures, to online game design. In the game *Lineage,* players gather to defend their castle from a siege which has been scheduled to take place. A group of players will actually commandeer a game room for the siege; it transforms into a base of operations, and defenders will quickly organize and change strategies as orders are shouted around the room. This is a completely new kind of game and social experience that has not been available before in any medium. While the physical and social properties of the PC game room don't always translate worldwide, the use of voice, command structure, team tactics, group balance, and shared risks and rewards are powerful gameplay devices that will shape the next generation of games.

Japan does not even appear on the list of most wired countries because it is dominated by NTT DoCoMo, a wireless service that has a telecommunications monopoly in the country. NTT's presence is so strong that it has made it financially prohibitive for Japanese citizens, who get charged by the minute for Internet use, to order broadband service. The game industry has thus revolved around video game consoles—and not online games. Most people in Japan don't have PCs, but personal digital assistants (PDAs). The wireless network (iMode) is primary, while the Internet is secondary.

Japan's game industry revolves around video consoles and wireless games.

Due to historical political rivalry between Japan and Korea, consoles (a major Japanese export) are not popular in South Korea. These same historical conflicts between Korea and Japan—especially related to the World War II occupation—also affect online gameplay. Korean players, who have more experience playing in the online arena and can easily organize into powerful teams, often seek retribution for past grievances through *player kill (PK)* targeted toward Japanese players. ("Player kill" refers to those characters getting killed in a game by other characters—where both characters are controlled by players. The term "offline PK" became used by South Korean authorities when PK would be taken out of the game and into the PC Baang—resulting in some real-world violence between players.)

Using licensed properties has become a content issue in Japan (also in France and the Scandinavian countries)—where properties such as *Star Trek* aren't anywhere near as popular as they are in the United States, Germany, and the United Kingdom.

Another content issue in market geographics includes the depiction of violence in games. *Quake II* did not have a retail launch in Germany—the second largest computer game market in the world—due to the game's level of violence. In order to sell *Command & Conquer Generals: Zero Hour* in the German market, the game's graphics had to be modified so that all military units were robots—not people—ensuring that no humans were killed in the game. In Germany, games must avoid showing blood, shooting humans, and anything that glorifies Hitler, the Nazis, or the Third Reich. Other countries, including Australia and Korea, have also banned titles that are identified as being too violent.

Germany is the second largest market for computer–based games.

Bruno Bonnell on Playing Global vs Local Culture :::::

Bruno Bonnell, Chairman and Chief Executive Officer of Atari, Inc. (formerly Infogrames, Inc.), is one of the foremost visionaries in the interactive entertainment industry. In June 1983, Bruno co-founded Infogrames with Thomas Schmider to bring interactive entertainment to consumers around the world across every available distribution platform. Since then, Bruno has propelled the company to a leadership position within the multi-billion dollar video game industry. In December 2000, Infogrames acquired Hasbro Interactive and that company's line of well-known brands—including Atari, Monopoly, Scrabble, and Jeopardy. In May 2003, Infogrames formally adopted Atari as its corporate name for its worldwide operations. Today, Atari is one of the top interactive entertainment publishers in the world. Bruno has also continued to look beyond traditional gaming platforms and has been a pioneer in extending the reach of entertainment software. In conjunction with TV Canal + (Europe's pay-per-view cable giant), he founded Game One—the first European TV channel dedicated to video games. Prior to founding Infogrames, Bruno was involved with the launch of the Thomson TO7, one of the first computers designed for domestic use. Outside of Atari, Bruno is a shareholder in Lyon's UEFA soccer team, the Olympique Lyonnais—and he is the creator of SELL, an association for

Bruno Bonnell
(Chairman & CEO, Atari)

French software publishers. A graduate of the University of Paris Dauphne, Bruno received degrees in Economics and Chemical Engineering. Bruno says his real job is "Dreambuilder—a simplified version of Santa Claus—who, after all, is a simple toy manufacturer…"

The U.S. market is by far the largest coherent interactive market and has a deeper penetration level into the player population than the overseas market does. In Europe, languages, cultural differences, and taxes don't help the development of a unified interactive market—but at the end of the day, we see the major worldwide hits being the same, and some local successes finding an economy at a country level. We are definitely moving towards a global interactive market.

I do hope that the installed base in particular areas will grow enough to allow the emergence of a generation of specific titles supporting a local culture—because interactive entertainment is about diversity, and we shouldn't be limiting our investments to only global production. Local is beautiful, too—especially when you play your own culture.

Markets can differ widely—even on a national level. In the United States, certain pastimes such as hunting and fishing are popular in certain regions—such as the Midwest. This might affect the sales of a game such as *Bass Fishing* or the *Deer Hunter* series. Similarly, games associated with sports that are particularly popular on the East Coast (such as squash, lacrosse, and fencing) might have a much larger market there than on the West Coast.

Psychographics

Psychographics consist of people's values, attitudes, and lifestyles. How do they like to spend their time? How do they see the world? Are they social people? Are they ambitious? How do they feel about money, religion, culture—themselves? Are they cynical or optimistic? Do they participate in social and environmental causes?

A Bobo Could be Playing *Your* Game

In his book *Bobos in Paradise: The New Upper-Class and How They Got There,* David Brooks defines an interesting psychographic: the "bourgeois bohemians ("Bobos" for short). The combination of "bohemian" (concern with the environment and nature) with the "bourgeois" (material wealth and elitism) could result in irony—such as driving around in an SUV sporting a "save the environment" bumper sticker.

Psychographics might illustrate a *yuppie* or *hippie* lifestyle. Some values associated with a yuppie lifestyle include material wealth and career advancement—while those associated with a hippie lifestyle include freedom and nonconformity. Several efforts have been made to classify people (consumers) into categories to make them easier to analyze.

VALS™ Psychotypes

The Values, Attitudes & Lifestyles Survey (VALS) was developed by the Stanford Research Institute and is currently run by SRI Consulting Business Intelligence. VALS analyzes the consumer market based on eight segments associated with ideals, achievement and self-expression. Take the survey at www.sric-bi.com/VALS/presurvey.shtml and find out if you are an innovator, thinker, achiever, experiencer, believer, striver, maker, or survivor.

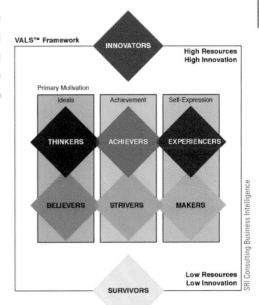

The Values, Attitudes & Lifestyles Survey (VALS) analyzes consumers based on psychographic dimensions related to motivation and resources.

Casual vs Hardcore: Is That All There Is?

One of the primary ways the game development community has segmented the player market has been by frequency. A casual player is one who plays occasionally—focusing on games that take a relatively short amount of time to play, or that can be stopped and started at any time, such as online versions of classic card games or those limited (but fun) games that are shipped with cell phones. These games are designed with the casual player in mind—short, easy to learn, and entertaining ways to pass the time. Hardcore gamers are just the opposite. For these players—who are likely to immerse themselves in a game that might last weeks or months (rather than hours or minutes)—the *experience* is the "meaning." Games that might require a lot of social interaction or detailed storylines with complex character development are often ideal for these players. But these definitions are really just two extremes—and they only focus on the frequency of play. The game development community should consider much more than this when researching their target audience.

Myers-Briggs Type Indicator (MBTI®)

In 1943, Isabel Briggs Myers and her mother, Katharine Briggs, developed a model to measure personality types. The model, known as the Myers-Briggs Type Indicator (MBTI®), is based on the work of psychologist Carl Jung—whose character arche-

Myers- Briggs Type Indicator (MBTI)

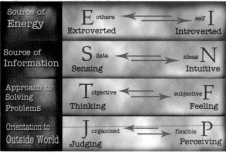

Preferences on each scale of the MBTI instrument combine to yield a 4-letter psychological type [e.g., ISFJ, ENTP]. (Source: Myers & Briggs Foundation, Inc.)

types will be discussed further in Chapters 4 and 5. The Myers-Briggs personality types contain four letters, each corresponding to one of two opposing personality characteristics:

- **Extrovert (E) vs. Introvert (I):** Energy is more outer- or inner-directed
- **Sensing (S) vs. Intuitive (N):** Perception is more present or future-oriented
- **Thinking (T) vs. Feeling (F):** Judgment-formation is more objective or subjective
- **Judging (J) vs. Perceiving (P):** Approach to world is more structured or spontaneous

Linking Players to the Experience

During the early years of the computer game industry, developers paid little attention to who its customers were. Most game concepts were based upon the personal preferences and opinions of the developers. In more recent years, some gaming companies have employed demographics to consider our target populations. Most game industry efforts to profile customers and potential customers are limited to the demographics of age, gender, and gaming preference (hardcore versus casual). These parameters are of limited usefulness because they do not directly tell us how to best entertain these players. The more directly any demographic information can be linked to how the game is played, the more readily we can apply it to our design. Studying player personalities and motivations brings us one step closer to the real question: What makes a game fun for a certain type of person?

— *Kevin Saunders (Senior Designer, Obsidian Entertainment)*

The game industry is beginning to take notice of psychographics such as MBTI®. International Hobo—a company founded by game developer and author Ernest Adams—is currently developing a research study that applies the Myers-Briggs personality test to the player population.

Behavior patterns can also be seen as part of psychographics. As U.S. citizens continue to play more games, they are clearly spending less time on other activities. According to the Entertainment Software Association (ESA), 52 percent of players who are spending more time playing games report watching less television as a result. In addition, 47 percent of gamers are going to the movies less—and 41 percent watch movies at home less often. The decline of television viewing is becoming such an issue that advertisers are now considering in-game advertising as a more viable way of reaching much of their market. The ESA also reports that over half (54%) of U.S. households have purchased or plan to purchase one or more games in 2004—which may further contribute to the decline of other traditional entertainment pastimes in the United States.

Demographics

The *demographics* of players include statistical information such as gender, age, income level, education level, marital status, ethnicity, and religion. Let's take a close look at a few of these demographics with regard to online game playing to see how they have changed over the years.

Early arcades were populated more by boys than girls.

Gender

As discussed in Chapter 1, public arcades reached a market of kids who played after school and on weekends. The atmosphere and marketing strategies did not attract the adult population—so this player demographic was ignored. Although these arcades could have easily reached young girls as much as boys, that didn't happen. Even with games such as *Pac-Man*—which were specifically designed to reach a wider market—the arcades continued to be dominated by teenage boys.

Gender Role Representation in Toy Commercials

Toy commercials aimed towards girls focus on toys that encourage nurturing play (e.g., domestic items such as baby dolls and toy ovens), while those targeted towards boys focus on toys that encourage aggressive play (e.g., military items such as guns and tanks). I theorize that this is the result of childhood socialization by parents and the media—which has been perpetuated by many game developers. My theory comes from a content analysis study I conducted in 1992 at UCLA on gender role representation in toy commercials. I analyzed over 300 toy commercials for type of toy, gender of children depicted in the ad, cooperative versus competitive behavior—and features such as camera movement, music tempo, cuts and pans. Among other results, I found that girls in the ads cooperatively played with dolls and other domestic toys, while boys played competitively with vehicles or war-themed action figures (e.g., GI Joe).

Very rarely did both genders appear together in these ads. Toys depicted in ads with both genders were board games—and all but one ad showed boys teaming up against girls and winning the games. I concluded that children are socialized at a young age by the media to play with certain toys (in certain ways) based on their gender. This socialization is most likely perpetuated by parents, who often begin their children's lives decorating and clothing their children in pink or blue. If girls are truly being taught to play nicely and cooperatively with baby dolls and Barbies, wouldn't they feel "out of place" walking into a noisy, dark arcade—where most games involve shooting or destroying creatures and spaceships?

Jumping ahead to the dawn of the home console era, arcade gamers encouraged their parents to buy these games so that they could play at home with their friends, using their television sets as monitors. Although there were plenty of female siblings around, their more experienced arcade-going brothers (and their friends) may have initially dominated these games.

Early home console systems were often played by boys.

In Chapter 1, you learned about the computer segment of the game industry—including home personal computers and mainframes. This industry was also male-dominated. It was not until the advent of the commercial Internet—fueled by its multimedia interface, the World Wide Web—that electronic games became more gender-balanced.

The 2003 ESA poll found that adult women make up a larger percentage of players than boys ages 6–17—dispelling the age-old stereotype that games are for boys. Females of all ages now make up almost 40% of the game-playing population.

Early personal computer gaming was dominated by boys.

Adult women gamers currently outnumber male gamers ages 6–17.

:::::Games Are Not Just For Kids Anymore!

The 2003 ESA survey also showed that men and women over 18 make up 64 percent of the gaming population—and that the average age of players is now 29 years old. A full 17 percent of players are over age 50, which is up from 13 percent in 2000. Although most of the women are playing online no-fee puzzle games, this is still a major change in player demographics.

The game industry has clearly seen a dramatic change in the consumer marketplace in the past few decades. Some developers haven't addressed these changes—preferring to focus on an outdated profile of their audience. Others have begun to take steps to build a more intricate model of their customers—focusing not only on demographics such as age and gender, but on the deeper values, attitudes, and beliefs shared by certain groups of players. There is another age-related demographic that borders on a psychographic. Its importance cannot be overlooked in any industry.

Generation

Generations are considered part of both demographics and psychographics. Although associated with a discrete age range, members of each generation as a group have experienced particular historical events and climates—including economic, cultural, social, and political shifts—during their lifetimes. Therefore, they are likely to have developed a particular set of beliefs, attitudes, and values. This assumption is based on what is known as *cohort analysis*—which suggests that people of a certain group do not necessarily change over time (e.g., if people were "liberal" when they were younger, they would continue to be liberal as they grow older). *Life stage analysis,* on the other hand, assumes that people's beliefs change over time (e.g., that people get more conservative as they get older). Generational analysis is based on the idea of cohort analysis. If you assume that people as a group retain generally the same values over time, those people may continue to like the same types of entertainment over time.

Generation birth years in the United States since 1900 (based on information from William Strauss & Neil Howe).

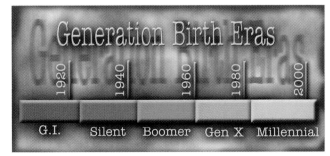

There are four *generations* of players currently in the United States:

1. Silent Generation (~60-80 years of age)
2. Boomer Generation (~40–60 years of age)
3. Generation X (~20–40 years of age)
4. Millennial Generation (under 20 years of age)

A *generation* is composed of people whose common location in history lends them a collective persona. The span of one generation is roughly the length of a phase of life. William Strauss and Neil Howe—authors of *Millennials Rising, The Fourth Turning,* and *Generations*—have provided an extensive analysis of generations throughout U.S. history. Their theories form the basis of my discussion on generational player demographics.

Silent Generation (born 1924-1943)

The Silent Generation grew up staying at home under the secure wing of over-protective parents, while older siblings (GI generation) fought in World War II and joined the Civilian Conservation Corps. Once entering the workforce, this generation donned nondescript "gray flannel suits" and opted for the job security offered by large, faceless corporations. Sandwiched in between two active generations—the civic-minded group of GIs who fought in World War II and rebuilt America after the Great Depression, and the inner-focused group of Boomers that questioned authority and ushered in a major cultural shift in music and politics—the Silent Generation was like a "middle child," taking cues from others. Preferring to reap the benefits of America's unprecedented post-war prosperity, this passive generation consumed more than it created. As the first mass consumer audience, they used credit cards, cooked in space-age designer kitchens, and managed to escape the isolation of suburban life through the medium of television—which offered a superficial connection to the outside world. Not until adulthood did this generation finally break its silence—initiating a "midlife crisis" that resulted in the splintering of the very nuclear family system they had helped strengthen during the 1950s.

If you were to create a game that focuses on the Silent Generation, what type of content would you include? Perhaps a game that made order out of chaos would work for this generation. Other than games based on traditional Silent heroes—such as James Bond—no current games come to mind that might truly target this group. Games with heroes who are clean and cold—but who are not motivated by cynicism or revenge—might connect with this generation. An ideal example might be a combination of the slick sophistication of James Bond and the intricate, romantic, yet uptight nature of Thomas Crown. (According to exit interviews conducted by Cinema Score, even the 1999 remake of *The Thomas Crown Affair* appealed to an older demographic but did not prove sufficiently engaging to a younger audience.)

Boom Generation (born 1943-1961)

The Boom Generation (also known as the "Baby Boomers") grew up sheltered in the suburbs during post–World War II economic prosperity—with their parents following the permissive child-rearing philosophies of Dr. Spock and working to keep the nuclear family intact. Death rates, drunk driving, suicide, illegitimate births, unemployment, and crime doubled or tripled as this generation came of age. The Boomers rebelled strongly against their parents, creating what is now known as the "generation gap." They also participated in an "awakening" that their families couldn't understand—establishing an unprecedented counter-culture involving music, drugs, and sexual promiscuity. As this generation grew into adulthood, they became "yuppies" with mainstream careers, immersed themselves in New Age enlightenment, and took up yoga—realizing that their "sexual revolution" and once-dominant liberal lifestyle had come to an end because of the realities of AIDS and conservative Reaganomics.

In *Ultima IV: Quest of the Avatar*, players must master eight moral virtues (honesty, honor, humility, spirituality, sacrifice, compassion, justice, and valor)—which are comprised of the three principles (truth, love, and courage).

If you were to create a game that focused on the Boomer generation, what type of content would you include? Perhaps a game with a social, spiritual, or political message would be ideal. Famed game designer Richard "Lord British" Garriott continues to tap into the worldview of this generation—most recently with *Tabula Rasa*, a sci-fi game of epic salvation that distinguishes itself from other games of its kind with its spiritual focus. Characters in *Tabula Rasa* are built around three attributes: mind, body and spirit.

ORIGIN Systems, Inc.

Generation X (born 1962–1981)

Members of Generation X grew up in an era when America experienced its lowest birthrate ever, and where it was commonplace for families to be torn apart by divorce—only to be stitched back together, patchwork-style, by remarriage, step-siblings, and half-siblings. As teens, Xers became independent "latchkey kids" who worked odd jobs or at fast food restaurants instead of receiving an allowance. These kids came home to *After School Specials, Sesame Street, Electric Company,* and *Mister Roger's Neighborhood* on television, which became a de facto babysitter (instead of having after-school activities monitored by teachers or parents). During this era suicide, murder, and incarceration rates skyrocketed. Growing into young adults, members of this generation have continued to assert their independence. They have expressed their cynicism and angst creatively through their art, while using their entrepreneurial tendencies to innovate do-it-yourself small businesses. Known as "Generation X," they were not given a descriptive name—although "X" has now come to mean "Xtreme" (a term that captures this generation's risk-taking, cutting-edge spirit).

Tomb Raider's Lara Croft and *Half-Life*'s Gordon Freeman are both depicted as lone heroes.

Eidos/Core Design, Ltd.

Valve Software

If you were to create a game that focused on Generation X, what type of content would you include? Perhaps a game that focuses on an independent, nomadic character who's "on the edge" and takes risks would be ideal. Sound familiar? Since the Generation X age group makes up most of the game developers these days, games like this are pretty easy to find!

Millennial Generation (born 1982–2002)

Before reading ahead, take the Millennial Generation Quiz on page 55 and discover some surprising statistics from the U.S. Census Bureau, Gallup Poll, and other national surveys that reveal a drastically different upbringing and social climate experienced by the Millennials. No cheating!

A New Generation

During the last 10 years, most of the miserable trends in crime, divorce, illegitimacy, drug use, and the like that we saw in the decades after 1965 either turned around or stalled. Today Americans are consciously, deliberately embracing ideas about sex, marriage, children, and the American dream that are coalescing into a viable… normality. What is emerging is a vital, optimistic, family-centered, …and yes, morally thoughtful, citizenry…. [M]arketers who plumb people's attitudes to predict trends are noticing something interesting about "Millennials," the term that generation researchers Neil Howe and William Strauss invented for the cohort of kids born between 1981 and 1999: they're looking more like Jimmy Stewart than James Dean. They adore their parents, they want to succeed, they're optimistic, trusting, cooperative, dutiful, and civic-minded. "They're going to 'rebel' by being, not worse, but better," write Howe and Strauss.

— *Kay S. Hymowitz, "It's Morning After in America" (City Journal; Spring 2004)*

::::: Millennial Generation Trends Quiz

Do you think that the following trends have gone UP or DOWN since 1992 for teenagers ages 12–17?

	Up	Down
1. School shootings	☐	☐
2. Crime	☐	☐
3. Sexual activity among boys	☐	☐
4. Abortion rate	☐	☐
5. Out of wedlock pregnancies	☐	☐
6. Non-alcohol drug use	☐	☐
7. Academic performance	☐	☐
8. Closeness to parents	☐	☐
9. Time spent with fathers	☐	☐
10. Divorce rate of parents	☐	☐
11. Time spent studying	☐	☐
12. Time spent watching TV	☐	☐
13. Time spent playing organized sports	☐	☐
14. Hours spent in community service	☐	☐
15. Suicide rate	☐	☐
16. Importance of religion	☐	☐
17. Trust of the police, government, and teachers	☐	☐
18. Respect for celebrities and athletes	☐	☐

Answers on next page :::::

Millennials were born in an era of parents who proudly displayed "baby on board" placards on their minivans. As these kids grew older, their soccer moms helped organize their team sports and other activities, while their dads spent more time with them than any other living generation had previously experienced. Movies popular during this generation's childhood included *ET: The Extra Terrestrial, Parenthood,* and *Spy Kids.*

::::: Millennial Generation Trends Quiz (Answers)

Most people get almost every one of these answers wrong. How did you do? Are you surprised by the correct answers? If you are, there's a good chance that you are making the assumption that kids today are exactly the way kids were 20 years ago. You also might be influenced by the media, which currently focuses a lot more energy on reporting news related to teenagers. The media didn't focus on teens 20 years ago. Why?

1. DOWN by 20%

2. DOWN—comparable to 1960s levels

3. DOWN by 30%

4. DOWN—now the lowest ever recorded

5. DOWN—now the lowest ever recorded

6. DOWN—all types of drugs

7. UP—particularly in math and science

8. UP by over 80%—highest ever recorded

9. UP—5 hours per week more than in the 1980s

10. DOWN 20%

11. UP—3 times more homework since the 1980s

12. DOWN—has been dropping steadily since 1997

13. UP—coincides with the "soccer mom" trend

14. UP since the 1980s

15. DOWN for the first time since World War II

16. UP—teens are now the most religious group in the United States

17. UP—even before September 11

18. DOWN—is this the end of the "cult of celebrity"?

Sources:
U.S. Census (1990–2002); Gallup Polls (1990–2002); UCLA Annual poll of Incoming College Freshmen (1967–2002); University of Michigan, Institute of Social Research (1999); ZOOM and Applied Research & Consulting LLC; 2001 survey of nearly 10,000 kids ages 9–13 for PBS; Horatio Alger Association (1999); U.S. Department of Justice Statistics/Juvenile Statistics (2001); National School Safety Center (2001); ChildTrends DataBank (2002); Alan Guttmacher Institute (2001); CDC Youth Behavior Surveillance Survey (2002); U.S. Substance Abuse and Mental Health Services Administration (1999); SAMSHA–Substance Abuse and Mental Health Services Administration (U.S. Department of Health and Human Services); University of Michigan MTF (Monitoring the Future); SAT College Board; University of California Berkeley Survey Research Center, as part of the center's Public Agendas and Citizen Engagement Survey (PACES) project, 2002

Thanks to Pete Markiewicz, PhD. for providing the statistics for this quiz.

From a combination of parenting patterns, interviews, and cultural depictions, here are what appear to be the main characteristics of Millennials:

- **Networked peer-to-peer communication:** This phenomenon isn't surprising, considering that the Millennial Generation is the first to grow up using Internet technology for communication in their daily lives. Some Millennial teens have several hundred friends on their IM buddy lists!

- **Collectivist team-players:** Think of how Millennials might make music, film, literature, and art more collaborative. Many of these forms of popular culture are already happening, often by using the Web as a communication medium. Could this mean that Millennials also like to be more active audience members—rather than engaging in more passive activities, such as watching television?

- **Special:** Millennials are considered to be "golden children" and are depicted in film as "power kids" (e.g., the *Spy Kids* film series, in which children help out and save their spy parents).

- **Sheltered:** As opposed to the "latchkey" Gen Xers, this generation has grown up with over-protective parents. With the emphasis on national security, this theme will probably continue in their lifetime. Although teens feel "pressure" from their parents, they get along with them.

- **Confident:** This generation displays a confidence that exceeds that of the Boomers in the '60s.

- **Open:** Millennial confidence seems to transcend into privacy issues. Millennials are so used to sharing everything with their parents that the notion of privacy doesn't seem to concern them. Since the first crisis faced by the Millennials was as children during the September 11th terrorist attacks, it has been speculated that Millennials have grown up in a national (as well as familial) atmosphere of concern over security at the expense of privacy.

- **Female-dominated:** "Girls rule" in the Millennial generation. More girls than boys are enrolled in college, and girls are getting better grades in both elementary and secondary school.

- **Structured:** Millennials believe that rules have value. When you took the Millennial Trends Quiz, you discovered that Millennials generally trust the government but do not necessarily respect celebrities. This generation appears to follow the rules of society, rather than rebel against it. Will entertainment lose its "edge" when the Millennials begin to contribute to the culture?

Pete Markiewicz received his doctorate from the University of Chicago in Theoretical Biology. After a decade of research in molecular biology (where he helped developed a powerful method for protein engineering), he entered the brave new world of the Internet in 1993. He is co-author of three nationally-distributed books on the Internet revolution and co-founded Indiespace in 1994. Recently, Pete has developed futurist theories based on an analysis of rising U.S. generations and their impact on technology—in particular, robotics. He currently teaches interactive design at the Art Institute of California–Los Angeles.

Courtesy of: Daniel Hayes Uppendahl

Pete Markiewicz, PhD
(Indiespace)

Understanding generational personality characteristics requires familiarity with the events, trends, and changes in culture during a generation's childhood and young adult years. It is also necessary to remember that a generational personality is an averaged aggregrate; it describes traits of large populations of similar ages and does not predict the behavior of individuals in the generation:

Silents—"90% of life is just showing up" (Woody Allen): Members of this generation experienced the Great Depression and World War II as small children—and came of age during the 1950s as the U.S. postwar economy boomed. As children, they were sheltered and protected—and as young adults they displayed a conformist, adaptive mentality. Their media entertainment featured subtle images of rebellion, "lonely crowd" attitudes (seen in movies like Hitchcock's *Vertigo*), irony, and emotional sensitivity—as opposed to the stoic hero of G.I. culture. Silents tend to compromise rather than divide, and see more shades of gray than Boomers in terms of cultural behavior. Their media shows two sides to every issue, and tends toward the personal rather than ideological. In the 1960s and 1970s they experienced a "midlife crisis" and turned away from their earlier "gray flannel" conformity, leading feminism and the sexual revolution in particular. Gender differences are great within this generation (relative to younger ones). Their archetypal hero is seen in James Bond—the ultra-cool, behind-the-scenes agent striving to maintain the balance of power. Relations with their children (mostly Generation X) are relatively distant compared to younger generations. As they have aged, they have redefined the image of the old from being sadly immobile in nursing homes to the current "grandma drives a sports car" mentality. Throughout their lives, they have reaped society's benefits; the economic boom of the

1950s appeared when they started work, and numerous senior entitlements support their lifestyle today.

Boomers—"The times, they are a-changing" (Bob Dylan): Members of this generation were small children during the postwar boom. While young, they experienced a relatively safe but confined social climate based on material well-being. In reaction to this, they started a society-wide, values-oriented "spiritual" revolution in their famous coming-of-age during the 1960s and 1970s. As young adults, they sought to recast the moral underpinnings of society and have done their greatest work in the "culture and values" arena. More divisive and confrontational than Silents, they tend toward a more black/white ideology (ignoring shades of gray) and are responsible for the "culture wars" of the 1990s. Their politics focus on grand, sweeping solutions rather than adjustment and compromise. Their media heroes tend to be a lone voice rising up against a faceless system, denouncing it prophet-style, and changing it to a new "spiritual" utopia. Instead of compromise, their heroes convert the masses. Boomers led the rise in "bad" behavior in teens and young adults—and teen crime, drug use, and other negative social indicators peaked in their generation during the 1970s. Boomers were responsible for the huge shift in attitudes toward children during the 1980s and 1990s. Increasingly successful outside the home, Boomer women have managed to "have it all"—while Boomer fathers play a greater role in the lives of their kids than in earlier generations. Rejecting their own parents during their youth, they have surprisingly close relationships with their mostly Millennial children. As their children leave home, they are currently entering a new stage in their lives—one in which some expect their old radicalism to intensify as they gain political and cultural power over society.

Generation X (born 1961–1981)—"There can be only one" (*Highlander*): Members of this generation were children during the social turmoil of the 1960s and 1970s—and were the targets of an anti-child cultural bias difficult for younger generations to understand. In their youth, they experienced the divorce epidemic, hands-off parenting, "latchkey" self-reliance, falling fertility, and declining investment in children. Many Xer media workers today mock the crude, low-budget animation and slasher/devil child programming that they experienced as kids. As young adults during the 1980s, they were often seen as a "disappointing" generation and were characterized as the "New Lost"—alienated, poorly-educated slackers. Despite this, Generation X has actually began reversing many negative social trends (e.g. drug use), has started more businesses than any in history, and was the first generation to be generally comfortable with technology. Instead of rejecting the system, they have made it on their own without any help from anyone. Compared to older

> **P**laying ... games is as normal to the younger generation as hanging out at the malt shop was to their grandparents.
>
> — *Arizona Republic* editorial (July 9, 2003)

groups, gender relationships are more equal within this generation. Their media "heroes" emphasize survival rather rebellion; they aren't out to change the world—just to keep their place within it. Politics and ideology hold far less interest for them than older generations, and they are more conservative on social issues than Boomers or Silents. Possibly due to their latchkey upbringing, they are drawn to media depicting edgy, "gladiator-style" death matches—everything from the lone girl left alive at the end of slasher movies to the ruthless voting of television's *Survivor*. Where Boomers might endlessly discuss the value of a conflict, Xers just make sure they win the conflict. Xers push the boundaries; being "X-treme" is primary. As they enter middle age, older Xers are showing surprisingly strong parent/family orientation, continuing the pro-child trend started by Boomers.

Millennials (born 1982–2001)—"No one left behind" (originally from the U.S. military; popularized in the films *Black Hawk Down* and *Lilo & Stitch*): Members of this generation are growing up during the 1982–2000 economic boom—the greatest in history and one fueled by high-technology. A "wanted" generation, they have enjoyed parents who deliberately sought to conceive and raise them. Compared to Xers, they have benefited by increased spending by their parents and rising standards in education. However, these benefits include a close, controlled, ultra-organized, "soccer Mom" parenting style and ideologically-driven teaching. GenX experienced a "hands off" childhood, while Millennials have had a very "hands on" one—ranging from standards-based and "no tolerance" classrooms to school uniforms. This has resulted in a generation which has successfully reversed many of the negative social trends long associated with youth; compared to Boomers and Xers, Millennials commit fewer crimes, use fewer drugs, get pregnant less often, and score higher on their SATs. Compared to earlier generations, they are female-dominant; girls lead the way in leadership and education. Despite this gap, gender relations are good. With ideologically-driven parents, Millennials may ultimately become a "hero" generation—achieving great things in the exterior world and thereby supporting the expectations of their parents.

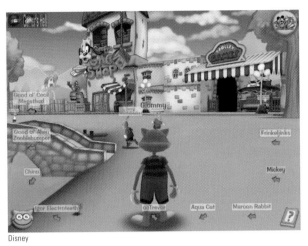

Disney

Mythic Entertainment, Inc.

In *Toontown Online*, players team up to rid Toontown of evil robots (the Cogs). *Dark Age of Camelot* is touted for its "realm vs. realm" combat, where players cooperate in teams to compete with other groups.

If you were to create a game that focused on the Millennial generation, what type of content would you include? Perhaps an online game involving a lot of communication and cooperation between players would be ideal. You learned in Chapter 1 that massively multiplayer online games (MMOGs) involve a lot of collective, teamwork behavior. This sounds like a great form of entertainment for the Millennial Generation, doesn't it?

eGenesis

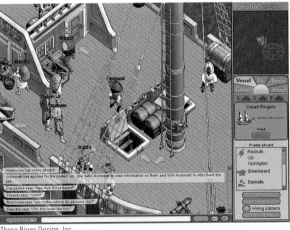

Three Rings Design, Inc.

Games that incorporate cooperation—such as *A Tale in the Desert* and *Puzzle Pirates*—might be ideal games for the Millennial Generation.

If Millennials are so focused on collective, team-based behavior, why is the United States dominated by consoles and not online multiplayer games? As you learned earlier in this chapter, the player market no longer consists of one (youngest) generation, but at least three generations. That's a market spanning a 60-year age range. Generation Xers and Baby Boomers gravitate toward a certain type of entertainment—and they also have a great influence on their Millennial children, many of whom are still living at home and have a close relationship with their parents. Since the Millennials are still too young to have an impact on the creation of popular culture, they are consuming the culture of the generation just above them. Could the fact that Generation X makes up the bulk of game developers today have something to do with the lone hero, single-player console focus of the U.S. game industry?

You might wonder why the Millennial Generation is significant when over half of the game-playing population is over 18. At 85 million people, the Millennial Generation is even larger than the Boomer Generation (60 million)—and it dwarfs Generation X (35 million). As the Millennials come of age, *they* will begin to make up most of the playing population—and they will certainly be creating most of our entertainment.

Now that you've learned about the much-overlooked areas of the player market—including motivation, location (geographics), values (psychographics), and statistics (demographics)—let's look at some of the basic game features developers need to consider in order create great games targeted toward their preferred market segments.

Applying Player Markets to Genres, Platforms & Applications

In the following chapter, we will look at game elements—including platforms, genres, and applications—that developers consider when putting together game projects. How would you apply player characteristics—including motivation, generation, and other demographics and psychographics—to these elements? Use the knowledge you have gained from this chapter to help you decide which game elements are right for your player market.

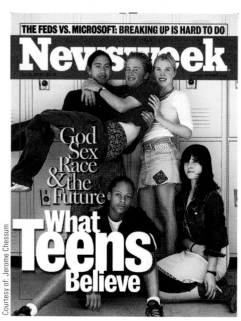

Generation X and the Millennials have been depicted very differently by the media.

:::CHAPTER REVIEW:::

1. What motivates people to play games? Discuss three different motivational factors and examples of games that address these factors. Motivations such as exercise (exemplified in the popularity of physical movement games such as *Dance Dance Revolution*) took game developers by surprise, and they might lead to a new series of games that address this player motivation. Come up with a new motivation that game developers may have overlooked. Discuss what types of new games might address this player motivation.

2. Why do *you* play games? What elements in your favorite games make you want to continue playing? If you were to test one of your favorite games for the "fun factor," why would it pass the test?

3. How does the market for games in South Korea differ from the United States? What are the most popular genres and platforms in South Korea and in the United States? What specific trends have developed in South Korea, and what are the driving factors behind these trends?

4. What is the importance of psychographics such as values, attitudes, and lifestyles in player markets? Discuss three games that incorporate a distinct belief system. If you were to create a game based on your own psychographics, what features would you focus on?

5. How have age and gender demographics in the player market changed over time? How might these changes affect the way games continue to be developed? Can you envision any particular trends in game content or structure that would help to continue to broaden the player market?

6. Discuss the difference between Boomers, Gen Xers, and Millennials. If you were creating a game that was specifically targeted toward one of these groups, what features would be present in the game? (How did you do on the Millennial Trends Quiz?)

7. Violence in our society continues to be blamed on the influence of entertainment content such as explicit films and song lyrics. More recently, some games have been blamed for violent outbreaks. Provide a real-world example of a violent incident for which an electronic game was held responsible. Do you agree with this view, or do you believe that there isn't a positive correlation between real-world violence and the "fantasy" violence in games?

8. If you were to choose one of Richard Bartle's player suits, which one do you feel best describes you as a player? What types of games naturally cater to your player suit? Take the questionnaires associated with VALS (www.sric-bi.com/VALS/presurvey.shtml) or MBTI (www.myersbriggs.org/take_the_mbti/links.cfm). Do your results correspond to your player suit self-evaluation?

CHAPTER 3

Game Elements:

what are the possibilities?

key chapter questions

■ What are some non-entertainment goals associated with game development?

■ What platforms are available for games, and what are the specific elements associated with each?

■ What are the characteristics of popular game genres?

■ How do modes based on number of players affect the way games are created?

■ What are time interval options, and how do they change how a game is played?

In Chapter 1, you were introduced to some games that succeeded (or failed) during the brief history of electronic game development. In Chapter 2, you learned about the players: who they are, and what motivates them to play. Now let's take a look at the basic options that are available as you consider developing your own game. The elements introduced in this chapter are applied to all other areas of game development. As you continue to read through this book, you will notice that these elements will come up repeatedly in other contexts.

Goal

Why do you want to create a game? Do you want to entertain, educate, support, market, build a social community—or get players to work up a sweat? In Chapter 2, you learned that people play for many different reasons. Games can also be developed for a variety of purposes—and pure entertainment is just one of them!

Entertainment

It is a common assumption that games should be developed purely to entertain the players. You learned in Chapter 2 that many people play to escape from the stresses of daily life—or to relieve boredom. There are also those who play for the same reason they might watch a movie or read a book. It's a diversion that immerses them in an alternate world, engaging them emotionally. Some games specifically allow players to become someone new—to role-play as characters, some of their own creation. Others keep them occupied by having to react quickly to physical reflex and mental problem-solving challenges. Notice that players are not just passively sitting down and letting the entertainment unfold in front of them. Instead, they are involved in actions such as role-play, physical movement, and problem-solving. This medium is uniquely interactive—allowing the player to manipulate, modify, and sometimes even take part in creating the entertainment experience.

Oddworld Inhabitants

Most games, such as *Munch's Oddysee*, are created for entertainment purposes.

Dragon's Eye Productions

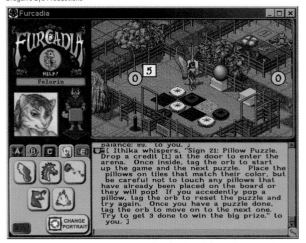

Some games, such as *Furcadia*, focus on community-building.

Community-Building

In Chapter 2, one of the motivating factors for playing games was noted as social interaction. Some multiplayer online games, discussed later in this chapter, are developed for this purpose. In these cases, entertainment in the traditional sense takes a back seat to community-building.

A non-game example of community-building would be an online dating site such as match. com—where people spend a lot of time browsing profiles of each other and communicating through secure email, IM, and chat sessions. (Some of the profiles read like game character descriptions!) There are other types of multiplayer games (such as LAN-based and "local") that also result in a great deal of social interaction. These are discussed in the "Player Mode" section below.

Community-building as a focus can happen by accident. The original purpose of *The Sims Online* was to entertain players through scenarios that involved role-play and character maintenance. The ability to communicate through the game attracted players who preferred to discuss non-game topics to actually playing the game itself. (Player communities within and outside of online games are so significant that I have devoted an entire section of Chapter 12 to this phenomenon.)

Games developed for the specific purpose of creating communities need not be limited to online games with a large customer base. These games would be appropriate for support groups, membership associations, religious organizations—or even "family and friends" networks.

Education

Educational games are those created to teach while they entertain. In Chapter 1, you learned about the *edutainment* era in CD-ROM game development. These games were specifically developed for educational purposes, and they were all aimed at children. Examples include *Oregon Trail, Reader Rabbit,* and *Math Blaster* (from Sierra On-Line, The Learning Company, and Davidson & Associates, respectively). These games feature in-game knowledge acquisition—where knowledge of certain topics (such as geography, math, and reading) is taught or accessed within the game itself. In most edutainment games, the topics are taught overtly. All types of simulation games discussed later in this chapter allow players to acquire in-game knowl-

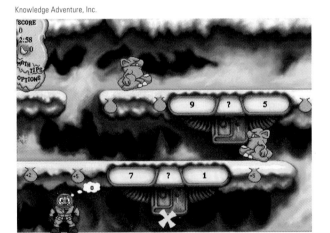

Knowledge Adventure, Inc.

Math Blaster was one of the first children's edutainment games from the early 1990s.

edge about real-world objects (such as the controls in the cockpit of a jet) and to apply knowledge they have learned outside of the game (such as how an economic system works).

Why were *edutainment* games designed mainly for children? There is a large market of adults in colleges, universities, research institutions, vocational schools—even in

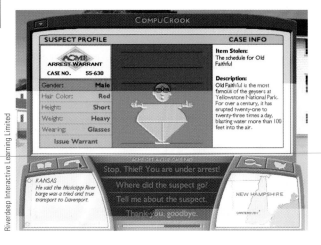

In Where in the USA is Carmen Sandiego? players chase Carmen and her gangster sidekicks through all 50 states as they learn about regional U.S. history, culture, and music.

corporations—who would benefit from games that serve an educational purpose. As we saw in Chapter 2, players are not just kids! An interesting educational application might be online distance learning. Most online classrooms consist of discussion threads—which enhances social interaction (as it does in online multiplayer games). Instead of only posting discussion threads—which greatly enhances lateral learning but does not involve constructivism (learning by doing)—students could be playing online multiplayer games that incorporate real-world simulations, such as economics, archaeology, auto mechanics, music, marketing… even surgery!

Economic Missteps During the "Edutainment" Era

Ten years ago the best educational games had similar budgets and quality to what you found on the game shelf. Then some of the educational game marketers set out on a campaign to "increase market share by cutting prices." Rival publishers struck back by combining what had been three to six different titles in one box for the same price.

In the short term, consumers saved lots of money for software for their children. Then the chain reaction started. You could no longer charge full price for educational software, so budgets for innovative new titles shrank, often to 10% of their prior levels. The warring software publishers, drained by the loss of profitability on these titles, were often acquired or parted out through bankruptcy. Broderbund, one of the highest quality publishers, was acquired three times, then subdivided and sold again to different buyers. Parents and kids have joined the publishing company shareholders as the losers in this MBA-driven scheme. Only a broken publishing model separates us from a new generation of inspiring and impressive educational games.

— *Don Daglow (President and CEO, Stormfront Studios)*

MMOGs as Online Distance Learning Applications

My research at the University of Southern California showed that massively multiplayer online games (MMOGs) incorporate many elements associated with *constructivist* theory that provide a perfect framework for learning—including *active learning* (character-customization game-world modification); *social interaction* (communication and interaction with other players); and *problem-solving* (observing processes and applying real-world knowledge to simulations in the artificial game world). This led me to theorize that MMOGs would be perfect online distance learning applications. Instead of joining an online class, students would join a game! (For more information, see my research at www.jeannie.com and www.indiespace.com.)

Even though education can be a specific goal when designing a game, many electronic games are educational "by accident" (just like community-building). Several motivating factors discussed in Chapter 2 have a lot to do with learning. In addition to gaining and applying knowledge about real-world events (the traditional definition of an educational game), there are other forms of learning going on in most (if not all) games.

James Paul Gee on Games as *Real* Learning :::::

James Paul Gee is a theoretical linguist by training, but he has worked on issues in education for the last two decades. He has served as Professor of Linguistics at the University of Southern California and as the Jacob Hiatt Professor of Urban Education at Clark University. He is now the Tashia Morgridge Professor of Reading in the School of Education at the University of Wisconsin–Madison. He is a founding member of the New London Group, an international group of scholars that has stressed the importance of design and design thinking for students in the modern world. He has been published widely on issues dealing with cross-cultural communication, literacy learning, and learning inside and outside schools and workplaces. A few years ago, inspired by his then-six-year-old son, he began playing and eventually doing research on computer and video games, and has written short pieces for *Wired* and *Game Developer,* as well as a number of more academic papers. His books include *The Social Mind, The New Work Order,* and most recently, *What Video Games Have to Teach Us About Learning and Literacy.*

James Paul Gee, PhD (Tashia Morgridge Professor of Reading, School of Education - University of Wisconsin–Madison)

Real learning is not about "facts"—but about having such deep experiences of the world… that the facts become part of what it takes to "play the game" or take on the identity. Real learning means learners cannot just talk about what they have learned, but actually do things with it. Real learning should be assessed by asking how the current experience has prepared learners for future learning. If the experience makes them do better on a later—perhaps even more important—learning task, who cares how many "facts" they get right or wrong today?

For example, *mastering* the game is tied into a learning process. Players are not usually satisfied with investing time into playing a game, only to lose. Most people play to win. The game accommodates this by allowing the player to save the game at different intervals (discussed in more detail in Chapter 8), so that players can go back to a point in the game *before* they made decisions that may have resulted in losing the game. Winning is also accommodated by providing the player with feedback—which sometimes appears in the form of a "score" or even a letter grade! For example, Nintendo's *Advance Wars* involves a series of missions that a player must complete in order to eventually finish the game. At the end of each mission, the player receives a numerical score and letter grade ("S" for "Superior," followed by A, B, C, etc.). If the player has made a few mistakes while playing the mission and wants to start over, the player can exit out of the mission and start again at any time before completing it. The letter grades assigned to the missions provide a form of "assessment" for the player, who now has an idea of how well he or she is playing. It's like getting feedback from an instructor every time a student finishes a homework assignment! *Advance Wars* also offers a "field training" section—a tutorial that helps teach new players how to play the game, which can be a more entertaining alternative to reading the instruction manual for some players.

Active Learning

Students tend to take more "ownership" of knowledge when they acquire it through a dynamic interactive experience. In a game setting, students receive immediate feedback on their performance in a problem-solving activity. This is an environment that inherently encourages active learning.

— *Jan McWilliams (Artist & Director of Interactive Design, Art Institute of California, Los Angeles)*

Recruitment & Training

In *America's Army* (www.americasarmy.com), military recruits prepare to face a 250-foot jump tower.

Games have also been used by the military and government for recruitment and training purposes. Simulation games (discussed later in this chapter), which replicate processes, environments, and objects that exist in the real world, have been used by government and military institutions such as NASA and the Air Force to train astronauts and pilots to adjust to changes in atmosphere and navigate vehicles. *America's Army* (www.americasarmy.com)—the first online simulation game used as a military recruitment tool—was so popular when it was launched that the web site was jammed with requests. Corporations also use games to help build their employees' leadership and management skills.

Turning Games into Learning Machines

When adapting games for learning, developers should create:

- Strong identities that learners can create or inhabit (e.g., being a scientist of a certain sort).

- Immersive experiences that naturally cause people to learn important things by living through and actively thinking about the experience. Make the meanings of words, concepts, and symbols concrete through experiences and actions.

- Well-ordered problem spaces, which give meaningful practice that eventually makes skills routine, and then challenges that routinization with a new higher-level problem. Give learners plenty of opportunity to interact both within and outside the game. Encourage learners to talk and think about their experiences outside the game (e.g., debrief them about their strategies).

— James Paul Gee (Tashia Morgridge Professor of Reading, School of Education - University of Wisconsin–Madison)

Playing games can also improve physical and mental skills—providing unexpected "training" for certain professions. A recent study by found that surgeons who played games for three hours or more a week made 37 percent fewer mistakes than doctors who did not play games. Conducted by Boston's Beth Israel Medical Center and Iowa State University's National Institute on Media and the Family, the study also found that the surgeons who played games were also 27 percent faster than their counterparts. The study sampled 33 doctors and medical-school residents from May 2003 to August 2003. The next step? Surgery simulations!

Marketing & Advertising

Some games are created for the purpose of marketing a product or service to consumers. *Advergames* are games that are specifically designed as advertisement tools. Many of these games exist online and are created in Flash or Java—tools that are efficient for developers and players due to quick downloads and short development cycles; these tools will be discussed further in Chapter 10. These games are used as an alternative to other web-based advertising, such as banners. Advertisers pay sites to host these games, which usually feature the advertiser's brand. Another online form of game-related marketing is *advertainment*—in which sites developed for the purpose of showcasing a brand contain games and discussion forums,

Blockdot, Inc.

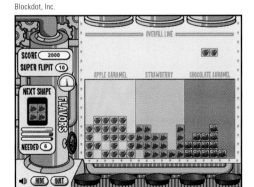

FlipIt Frenzy—created for Mrs. Smith's to promote a new cake product—is one of several advergames created by Blockdot (www.blockdot.com).

becoming a fun hangout for customers. An early example of advertisement is the *Joe Boxer* site (www.joeboxer.com), which invited customers to download a virtual pair of underwear before entering a circus-themed site—complete with carnival games and a chat room. Movie sites containing games, screensavers, and trailers focus on creating a fun experience for site visitors while marketing the film series. Game areas on movie sites include the interactive spy center at *Spy Kids* (www.spykids.com); episodic games at *Scooby Doo* (www.scooby-doo.com); and *Bloodline*—a *Half-Life* game modification (or *mod,* which will be discussed in Chapter 12) of Sony's *Underworld* (www.sonypictures.com/homevideo/underworld).

Many film and television shows have been used as vehicles for advertising products. For example, *Seinfeld* was notorious for its blatant advertising of Diet Coke—a supply of which was always available in Jerry Seinfeld's refrigerator. This form of advertising is known as *product placement*—and advertisers pay large sums of money for this. In-game product placement could soon be just as common. As you learned in Chapter 2, falling television ratings in the U.S. are causing advertisers to turn to games to promote their products. Activision and research organization Nielsen Entertainment reported that television viewing among men aged 18-34 in the U.S. fell by nearly 10% in 2003. In a recent study of 1,000 males, Nielsen found that 75% of the subjects owned a game console and watched less television. Over 25% recalled advertising from the last game they had played—and 33% said in-game ads helped them decide which products to buy. Interestingly, more than 50% actually liked the inclusion of real products in games. Major corporations are now considering product placement in games as a significant form of advertising. Sports games such as *NBA Street* and *Tony Hawk* feature popular clothing labels and sports accessories. McDonald's and Intel have spent more than $2 million on being part of *The Sims* community. Players have used Intel-branded computers in their virtual homes and offices; they can not only buy virtual Big Macs, but they can even become McDonald's franchisees.

Platform

You are familiar with the evolution of arcade, console, computer, handheld, and online games from Chapter 1. All of these formats are known as game systems or *platforms.* Since each game platform has distinct characteristics, games developed for each platform differ in several important respects. Let's review the platforms, discuss their distinctions, and look at how this might affect game content.

Mach 3 arcade game being played during the Classic Gaming Expo at the Electronic Entertainment Expo [E3], 2004.

Arcade

Arcade games are standalone game systems that are found in public venues—such as video arcades, bowling alleys, amusement parks, and pizza parlors (a trend begun by Atari founder Nolan Bushnell). Most games are played standing up—with player controls consisting of buttons, joysticks, or a combination.

Two-person "cocktail table" arcade games were introduced in the mid-'80s and became popular items in diners and hotel lobbies. Some games use other types of controllers—such as pedals and steering wheels (sit-down driving simulators), "guns" (shooters), and foot pads (dancing, as in *Dance Dance Revolution*). These games evolved from black-and-white/grayscale to full-color displays. Since these games are usually coin-operated, it is important from a business perspective to get players to deposit as many coins as possible into the game—so arcade developers focus on creating fast-moving, time-limited games that do not involve detailed story or character development. During the height of the arcade craze, there were also many technical issues such as memory limitations that made it difficult to provide this complexity. Since time is limited in arcade games, "action" is one of the main elements of this platform. Arcade games gave birth to the *action* genre—which still focuses primarily on "speed" and certain types of skills (eye-hand coordination, aim, and navigation—as in shooting and racing games). Other elements, such as story and character, have been emphasized more in the action genre on other platforms.

Crystal Castles is one example of a cocktail table arcade game—often seen in diners and hotel lobbies in the mid-1980s.

Atari, Inc.

There are three main entities associated with arcade game development:

1. *Hardware manufacturer*—owns the rights to the hardware and has control over what content is played on it
2. *Game (or content) developer*—often develops the game for the manufacturer, but is sometimes the same company as the manufacturer
3. *Venue operator*—licenses or purchases the game from the manufacturer and collects revenue from the players.

Since the hardware manufacturer owns and controls the content, it is involved in the planning, development, and testing process. In cases where the developer and manufacturer are separate entities, the developer has to answer to the manufacturer—who has final approval over whether the game will be developed.

Console

Console systems are usually played in the home, hooked up to a television set. The systems support four controllers. There are three proprietary console systems currently on the market that are vying for audience attention: Sony's PlayStation 2 (PS2), Microsoft's Xbox, and Nintendo's GameCube (GC).

Microsoft Corporation

Sony Computer Entertainment, Inc.

Nintendo of America, Inc.

The Xbox, PS2, and GameCube are the dominant console systems currently on the market.

Like the arcade platform, the console platform is proprietary—which means that hardware manufacturers such as Sony, Microsoft, and Nintendo have control over what software is developed for their respective platforms. An advantage of developing for a proprietary console system is that the hardware will not vary from player to player. (As you will see in the next section, this is a problem for the computer platform.) When a game is developed for the PS2, there's no doubt in the developer's mind that the game will work on *all* PS2s (assuming the hardware is working correctly). Another feature of game consoles is that (like arcade systems) they have traditionally been "special-purpose" devices that have been created specifically for playing games. The hardware controllers, for example, are designed to provide an optimum game-playing experience. This is in contrast to computer platforms, which were not originally intended as game-specific machines. Console systems are also moving away from their special-purpose roots—not only used for playing games, but also for DVDs, MP3s, and IM sessions. This is a dramatic move toward multi-purpose convergence. All the major systems have the ability to link to the Internet for online play. This introduces the idea of technology convergence, discussed at the end of Chapter 1. Will console systems eventually support *all* features associated with computers?

::::: The Phantom: A New Challenger in the Console Wars?

Infinium Labs Inc.

Phantom receiver and lapboard—part of a new console system with an online game subscription service

Infinium Labs is launching its sleek console system and on-demand online game subscription service. The Phantom Online Gaming Service will be delivered online over any broadband network and will offer a large library of games designed to appeal to both the avid gamer as well as the casual player. Could the Phantom be a possible rival to the "Big 3" console manufacturers? At the very least, its online game subscription service could help provide new opportunities for online game developers who depend on subscription fees for their revenue.

Computer

Like console systems, computers are usually played in the home. Unlike the console and arcade platforms, the computer (or PC) platform is not proprietary. This frees the developer from having to answer to the manufacturer. However, there is so much variation in hardware setups between players that it is next to impossible to predict the average speed, hardware space, and memory allotment players will be using. In the planning stages of creating a game, the development team will need to create prospective technical specifications for the game and try to develop the game around these requirements. Both *minimum* and *recommended* tech specs should also be available to the player. Minimum specs are those that are necessary in order to load and play the game from beginning to end (e.g., processing speed, memory, disk space). Recommended specs expand further on the minimum specs—also allowing for an enhanced game-playing experience (e.g., high-end sound and video cards). Many games have a variety of advanced graphics and sound options that a player can disable if the system is incapable of handling them. A computer has sharper graphics than a console system because it has a higher resolution; even a computer's lowest resolution (640 x 480) has twice the resolution of any console designed for standard television.

Online

Online games are played on a computer platform (and, more recently, through a console system connected to the Internet), but the technology behind them differs so greatly from games on any other platform that they deserve their own section. Players need an Internet connection to play, and game information might be stored on a *server*. The largest online games actually involve thousands of simultaneous players, which sometimes requires that the information for the game be stored on several servers. For example, millions of people are playing *Half-Life: Counterstrike* online at any given time—making the game one of the most popular in the online world—but only a few people are playing a particular instance of the game simultaneously. If you join a game, you won't run into millions of people! *Massively multiplayer online games (MMOGs)* can entertain thousands of players simultaneously. Due to their subscription-based payment model and the 24/7 nature of the Internet, MMOGs are also ongoing *persistent worlds*—posing some unique develop-

Client-Server Network

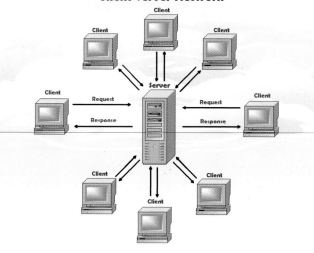

Peer-to-Peer Network

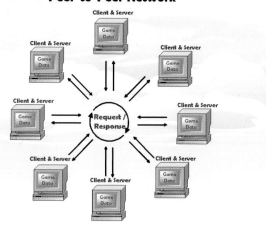

ment and maintenance problems. Most online games (and all MMOGs) utilize a subscription revenue model, where players pay a monthly fee in order to continue playing the game. This is often combined with an initial fee to purchase the game software (either hard copy or download).

There are two main communication models associated with online games. In the *client/server* model, each player runs a client program (in the form of game software) on their computer that communicates with a server that stores the game. The client presents the game to the players.

In the *peer-to-peer (P2P)* model, utilized by many strategy and action games, all player computers communicate directly with each other. If you haven't yet played a P2P game, you might have seen first-hand how a P2P model works if you've ever downloaded music from a file-sharing system such as Gnutella or Kazaa. Since each machine (all player computers) are on equal footing (hence the term "peer"), it's a completely decentralized system. Some services, such as Gamespy Arcade, allow players to find one another and connect in P2P networks.

Another technical issue related to online games includes connection speed. Players with slower connections are at a disadvantage. Although this problem has been addressed by player services that match opponents up on the basis of connection speed, players still can lose their connections while playing. In some games, any "slow" player (due to the computer or connection speed) can cause the game to slow down for everyone.

Also, live 24-hour customer service is essential for subscription-based MMOGs—since players expect to get help immediately on a diverse set of issues. Customer service reps must be trained to solve online-specific problems, including connectivity issues and player misbehavior. Content issues related to online games are discussed in the "Persistent State Worlds" genre section in this chapter. Customer service such as this is of primary importance for any game that involves a subscription fee. Some of these reps are referred to as *Game Masters (GMs)* (see "Role-Playing Games" in this chapter for the history of this term)—who provide technical support, create new content (e.g., quests, events) for the players, and participate in online game-related discussions with players.

Handheld

The small size of handheld devices makes it convenient for them to be taken with the player almost anywhere. Nintendo's Game Boy series initially focused on kids—but, with the release of the Game Boy Advance SP (GBA SP), this format is becoming much more popular with adults. The GBA SP is a significant improvement over the original GBA—with a back-lit screen and fully-rechargeable (and long-lasting) battery. Add-ons such as Majesco's GBA video player software with a DVD-style interface allow players to experience the GBA as a multipurpose device—watching movies as well as playing games. The Nintendo DS (a dual-screen portable) presents another innovative expansion of the handheld experience—as players experience simultaneous perspectives and points-of-view during a game.

Nintendo's Game Boy Advance SP (GBA SP) and Nokia's N-Gage QD are examples of handheld game systems.

> ### The Mobile Market
>
> The mobile market is closer, in some ways, to the market for light online games (puzzle games, classic board and card games) than it is to the conventional PC/console market. People use mobile games to have fun and kill a little time, rather than for an intense game experience.
>
> — *Greg Costikyan (Chief Creative Officer, Unplugged, Inc.)*

In addition to handhelds such as the Game Boy series and Sony's PSP, which have been created specifically for playing games, other portable devices such as mobile phones and PDAs have also been used as platforms for games. These devices are more popular outside of the United States and often contain puzzle or trivia games that don't require a lot of time investment to play. Nokia made the first effort to combine a cell phone with a handheld platform with the release of its N–Gage in 2003. Although the N-Gage's initial launch did not meet expectations, the QD (its follow-up release) is a vast improvement—and Nokia's effort has inspired other manufacturers to consider the possibilities of the mobile gaming market.

Tabletop

A "tabletop" game refers to the traditional analog (rather than digital) game platform—including games that might be played on a tabletop. Examples of tabletop games include board, card, dice, tile, block… and even pen-and-paper games such as *Dungeons & Dragons,* where the game pieces literally consist of pens (or pencils) and paper! It's extremely important to study tabletop games in order to understand the underlying gameplay challenges and strategies behind games in general. (See Chapter 6 for a discussion of gameplay.) Another important use of tabletop games is as prototypes for future electronic games (discussed in Chapter 11). Many game development companies create preliminary versions of their games in tabletop form in order to ensure that the gameplay is functioning properly.

Time Interval

Time intervals are time-dependent elements that affect the pacing of the game. This pacing affects whether the game is played *reflexively* or *reflectively.* Would you develop a game that allowed the players to spend an unlimited amount of time responding to challenges—or one that encouraged them to react quickly to them? What about something in-between the two extremes: allowing each player a limited amount of time to make decisions? There are three basic time intervals used in games. (See Chapter 7 for a more detailed discussion of how time is used in games.)

Turn-based

In traditional board and card games, each player takes a turn moving a token along the board or playing a card. Usually, the time allotted for each turn is unlimited (unless the player's opponents begin impatiently drumming their fingers on the table). In this case, players have as much time as they need to plan their moves and decide how to play their hands—allowing for reflective, deliberate thought. These games are *turn-based*— meaning that each "player" (whether artificially-generated or human) may take a "turn."

Pool—also known as billiards—is a classic turn-based game.

Real-time

The opposite of a turn-based game is known as a *real-time* game. In this case, there is no time interval between turns. In fact, there are no "turns" at all. Winning a real-time game requires having quick physical reflexes, as opposed to the reflective thought required for turn-based games. Real-time games are difficult to play online due to performance-related technology issues—including the speed of the player's connection, server load, and regional Internet traffic bottlenecks. However, real-time games are extremely popular online—partially due to the ability to communicate in real-time with other players.

Cross-country marathon racing is a real-time sport.

Time-limited

Boxing is a time-limited real-time game.

Timed chess is a time-limited turn-based game.

A *time-limited* game is a compromise between turn-based and real-time games. Time-limited games limit the time each player has to take a turn. In the case of some single-player puzzle games (discussed later in this chapter), a time limit is placed on the game itself. In timed games containing more than one player, each player could take their turns separately (as in chess) or at the same time (as in some online games). In the latter case, each player has the experience of taking a turn—but the game itself is actually happening in "real time," since neither player is actually waiting while the other player is taking a complete turn.

Deciding on an interval for your game is the first step in considering how the game will be played. How does the interval affect a player's involvement in the game? Do real-time games feel more "real"? If turn-based games encourage reflective thought, does this mean the game always appears to be slow-paced? These are some questions to consider when considering time intervals.

Player Mode

There are several possible *player modes,* which directly correlate to the number of people playing a game. These modes range from single-player to "massively multi-player"—involving thousands of players. Your choice of player mode—as well as the content—will have a significant impact on how your game is played. What platforms might work better in certain modes? Can you combine a real-time interval with a single-player mode? Think of ways you could combine intervals and modes together to create a unique game.

Single-player

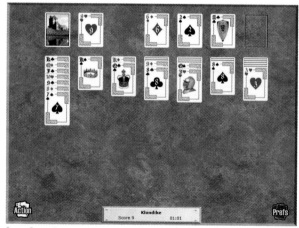

Gunnar Games, Inc.

Only one person can play a *single-player* game. Any additional "players" (usually opponents) in the game are known as *artificial intelligence (AI)* characters or *non-player characters (NPCs).* (Player characters and NPCs are discussed in Chapter 5.) The limited amount of screen space (known as *screen real estate,* discussed further in Chapter 8) on handheld platforms such as Nintendo's Game Boy Advance SP and Sony's PSP makes these systems ideal for single-player games. If you were to create a single-player game, what platform might you avoid?

Solitaire is a classic
single-player card game.

Two-player

Two-player (also known as *head-to-head*) games initially evolved from single-player arcade games. The first two-player arcade consoles contained two start buttons—one for single-player mode, and one for two-player mode. Players would take turns playing against the game itself. Each player's experience of playing the game was identical to what it would have been in single-player mode. The only difference was that the game kept track of both players' scores and compared the two in order to determine the winner. Players did not compete against each other on-screen, but they both knew that the game would declare only one of them the "winner." This idea of player-to-player competition was akin to trying to beat a high score on the arcade console—but instead of a faceless set of initials on a screen, your opponent was standing right next to you.

These early games were turn-based. It wasn't until *Double Dragon* that a two-player arcade game had a real-time interval. In this game, two players were able to share the console and play side-by-side at the same time—using buttons and joysticks to control the movements of their characters as they fought each other.

Local 2-Player & Local Multiplayer (3-4 Players)

In *local* player mode, all players sit in the same space and play the game on the same machine—sharing the same screen using separate *input devices* (controllers). This is a common mode of play on console systems, which allow for local play of up to four players. Since all players are sharing the same screen, each player can see what the other players are doing. Players cannot hide information from each other; this poses a problem with creating games that require players to make "secret" moves and decisions. Since consoles have introduced network capability, this pattern of local play might change or disappear. Players with Game Boy Advance systems can plug them into the GameCube console as controllers. This allows the players to hide information from each other.

The *Bubbles* arcade game had a two-player option. Count the fingers to choose (but don't count the thumbs)!

Dance Dance Revolution (played at the Electronic Entertainment Expo [E3], 2004) is a two-player, real-time arcade game where players dance side by side and control the game with footpads.

Local console games allow 2–4 players to share the same screen and use separate input devices.

Players can also engage in local play on a personal computer—which involves not only sharing a screen, but input devices (in this case, a keyboard and mouse) as well. Needless to say, a real-time interval would be next to impossible in this case. (Some early computer games, such as *Rampage,* were developed for local play—requiring each player to use a different area of the keyboard.) Interestingly, local play has been increasing in recent years as parents play games with their children—who sit on their laps!

"Co-op" Play

Some two-player and multiplayer games are known as co-op two and co-op multiplayer. In these cooperative games, players team up to play against the game itself. An early co-op two game was *MicroSurgeon* for the Intellivision console—where one player would move a robot inside a human body and find viruses, while the other player would shoot antibodies at the viruses to heal the person. *Gauntlet* was an early co-op multiplayer local arcade game with four joysticks that involved up to four simultaneous players. Each player was either a wizard, warrior, valkyrie, or elf; all players cooperated with each other to kill monsters, ghosts, grunts, and demons.

Gauntlet's four joysticks enabled four players to cooperate simultaneously to fight a common enemy.

Fragapalooza

LAN-based games allow several players to plug their machines into a Local Area Network (LAN). Fragapalooza is the biggest LAN party in Canada.

LAN-based Multiplayer

LAN-based games allow players to share the game on a *local area network (LAN)* without sharing the screen or input device. In Chapter 1, you learned about how LAN-based games represent an intersection between the personal computer and online multiplayer phases of electronic game history. With LAN-based games, it was possible to combine the networking capabilities of online mainframe games with personal computers that could be placed in one local area. A simple LAN can be created by linking 2–4 Game Boy Advance handheld systems together through "gamelink" cables. Unlike home console-based local play, the players *can* hide information from each other because they are not sharing the same screen—only the game itself. At a LAN party, players might bring their personal computers to one location (anywhere from a modest living room to a large convention hall), plug them into the LAN, and play games together as one large group. (Workplaces are also often on LANs, making LAN play popular as a lunch-time or after work activity.)

Online Multiplayer

Like LAN-based games, *online* games represent a form of *networked* play—where players connect their computers to a network and share the game. In the case of online games, the network is the global *Internet.* You've already seen that *online multiplayer* games can be played by thousands of players simultaneously. Although single-player and two-player games can be played online (and on a LAN, for that matter), it is the multiplayer mode that has become closely associated with online play.

:::::: *Crazy Arcade*: Online Local Play?

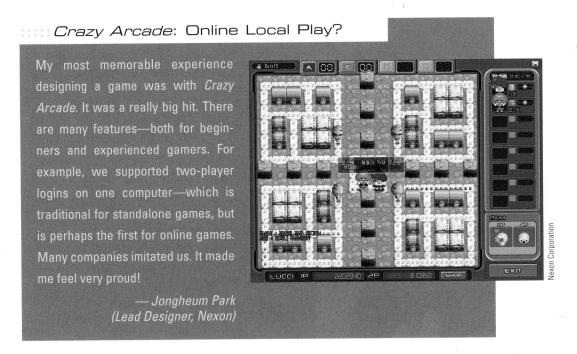

My most memorable experience designing a game was with *Crazy Arcade*. It was a really big hit. There are many features—both for beginners and experienced gamers. For example, we supported two-player logins on one computer—which is traditional for standalone games, but is perhaps the first for online games. Many companies imitated us. It made me feel very proud!

— *Jongheum Park*
(Lead Designer, Nexon)

Nexon Corporation

When do online games become "massively multiplayer"? This mode is associated with games that persist 24 hours per day and maintain a subscription-based revenue model in which players pay a monthly fee to continue playing the game. The sheer number of players (who may or may not be playing at certain times of the day) can greatly affect the way this sort of game is developed and maintained.

These games often encourage team-based play, where players form groups and cooperatively defeat opponents or solve problems together. Since the game involves a large number of players who could easily be playing from locations throughout the world, it's fairly easy for players to find other players at any time of the day or night.

MMOGs: "Splashing in the Shallow End of the Communication Pool"

What hasn't been done yet in MMOGs? Enabling people to communicate and connect on a deeper level. Why? Because life is about connecting with others, sharing ideas, and coming away richer for the experience. So far, we've been splashing in the shallow end of the communication pool. There's so much lost through a simple text chat. Right now, I find this to be the single most compelling challenge in game design: How do you capture and convey the energy of a group playing together in a room when the people are spread out all over the globe?

— *Patricia A. Pizer, Game Designer*

MMOG developers have learned that the society of the game (friends made while playing) is a primary incentive for many people to keep playing the game. By offering team-based play, the developers are encouraging friendships to form, thereby strengthening the game's society and increasing its player retention rate. It is next to impossible to expect large numbers of people to play the game the way it was originally meant to be played. Instead, players drop in and out of the game and socialize with other players about topics unrelated to the game. Are "massively multiplayer" games really social communities? Isn't the *player control* and a sense of "freedom of choice" important in almost every type of game? These ideas will be discussed in more detail in Chapter 4.

:::::Player vs. Player (PvP)

Valve Software

Player-vs-player combat scene from *Half-Life: Counterstrike*

The player vs. player (PvP) mode specifically refers to instances in MMOGs in which players compete against each other. The usual MMOG mode involves players forming cooperative teams to defeat non-player characters [NPCs] (discussed in more detail in Chapter 5). Many players prefer PvP, since combat is more interesting if it occurs against another player. Some players in an MMORPG (massively multiplayer online role-playing game—an MMOG subgenre discussed later in this chapter) would rather kill a member of a competing guild than kill a computer-generated monster.

As you learn more about game genres in this chapter, apply what you know about platforms, intervals, and player modes. What genres work best in single-player mode? Would it be better to develop a real-time game for a particular platform or genre? If you were developing a game for a handheld device, which genres might you choose?

Genres

Game *genres* are categories based on a combination of subject matter, setting, screen presentation/format, player perspective, and game-playing strategies. In looking at your target market, consider what genre these people play. From Chapter 2, you learned that some people focus on playing one particular genre. Certain genres are more playable on particular platforms. If you were to choose a mobile phone as your primary development platform, do you think a puzzle game or a role-playing game would be most appropriate? Which of these genres would be more appropriate for a massively multiplayer online game (MMOG) using a high-end, multiple server platform? Think of putting these components together—market, platform, and genre—as you read through this section.

Genre: Setting or Style?

Unlike genres in books and movies, current game-industry genres are not necessarily related to story, plot, and setting. Instead, they focus on how the game is played—its *style.* The traditional definition of genre relates more to what is known as the *setting* of a game. Some examples of setting include fantasy, sci-fi, horror, and crime. Setting will be discussed in more detail in Chapter 4.

Action

The *action* genre has been around since the arcade craze. In fact, almost every arcade game (such as *Pac-Man, Asteroids,* and even the comparatively slow-moving *Pong*) is an action game. The goal of most action games involves quickly destroying your enemies, while avoiding being destroyed yourself. These games tend to be simpler because they focus on player reaction time. Simplicity is necessary in action games because the average brain cannot process much additional information in a fast-paced environment. Eye-hand-coordination is necessary to excel in action games— also known as "twitch" games (a term that comes from the quick hand movements associated with using joysticks and pressing buttons repeatedly).

::::: Bemani: A New Genre?

Japan's Konami has launched a series of games where players perform in some way (by either dancing or singing) to create music. The goal of play involves either completing a song, dance, drum pattern, guitar solo, or hand wave. Examples of Bemani games include *Dance Dance Revolution*, *Beatmania*, *Drummania*, *Guitar Freaks*, *Dance Maniax*, and *Karaoke Revolution*. These games are becoming so popular that they are quickly defining a new genre.

Dance Dance Revolution in action at the Electronic Entertainment Expo (E3), 2004

The relentless fast-paced nature of these games means that they are always played in a *real-time* interval. People are motivated to play action games for the adrenaline rush involving quick reflexes and snap judgments—focusing on *reflexive* actions rather than *reflective* thought—while sometimes a much-needed reflective break can appear in the form of *mini* games (games within the larger *meta* game) that involve puzzle-solving or turn-based strategy. Once the player solves the puzzle or finishes the game, it's back to the action of the larger game experience!

Donkey Kong is a classic platformer arcade game.

Nintendo of America, Inc.

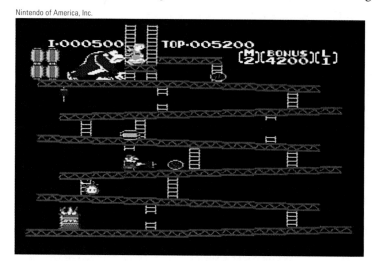

There are a few sub-genres in the action category that have taken on styles of their own:

Platformers

The *platformer* action sub-genre focuses on players moving quickly through an environment—often jumping and dodging to avoid obstacles, and sometimes collecting items along the way.

Examples of platformers include early arcade games such as *Donkey Kong* and *Sonic the Hedgehog,* and newer 3D console games such as *Ratchet & Clank* and *Jak & Daxter.* These games have clearly identifiable and memorable characters (such as Mario and Sonic) that often act as mascots for the companies that develop these games.

Shooters

The *shooter* action sub-genre focuses on combat between a player and the other characters in the game world—usually in the form of "shooting" with guns and other weapons controlled by the character's hands.

The shooter sub-genre is dominated by a style-based genre known as a *first-person shooter (FPS).* In these games, the player has a first-person perspective and cannot see his or her character on-screen. The player can see the character's weapons, as well as the other characters in the game (usually a mix of team members and opponents). The action in an FPS is sometimes thought to seem more immediate because the perspective can provide the feeling of being thrown into the game world. Perspective is discussed in more detail in Chapter 7.

Third-person shooters allow the player to see his or her character, along with the rest of the game world. If you develop a third-person shooter, it's important to ensure that the player's character can be easily differentiated from the others on-screen. An advantage of third-person shooters is that the player has a much wider perspective than in an FPS—which is limited to straight-ahead vision (without even the normal peripheral vision experienced in a real-life first-person perspective).

Eidos Inc.

Deus Ex is an example of a first-person shooter.

Eidos Inc.

Tomb Raider is an example of a third-person shooter.

Racing

Games in the *racing* sub-genre also use first-person or third-person perspective. The standard scenario involves the player's vehicle (usually a racecar) racing one or more opponents on a variety of roads or terrains. The player attempts to make the vehicle move as quickly as possible without losing control of it.

GravRally is an example of a racing action game.

Fighting

Many *fighting* games are two-person games in which each player controls a figure on a screen and uses a combination of moves to attack the opponent and to defend against the opponent's attacks. These games are often viewed from a side perspective, and each session only lasts a few minutes. The combination moves that have been a focus of the fighting sub-genre have been incorporated into larger action games.

Tekken is a classic fighting arcade game.

Genre: A Double-Edged Sword

I tend to de-emphasize genre in my designing and thinking. I feel that genre is a bit of a double-edged sword for designers. On one hand, genres give designers and publishers a common language for describing styles of play. They form a shorthand for understanding what market a game is intended for, what platform the game will be best suited to, and who should be developing a particular title.

On the other hand, genres tend to restrict the creative process and lead designers toward tried and true gameplay solutions. I encourage students to consider genre when thinking about their games from a business perspective, but not to allow it to stifle their imagination during the design process.

— *Tracy Fullerton,*
Assistant Professor
(Electronic Arts Interactive Entertainment Program,
USC School of Cinema–Television)

Adventure

In Chapter 1, you learned about the first text-adventure game known as *Adventure* (or *Colossal Cave*). In this game, the player was an explorer, wandering around in an enormous cave filled with treasures and dangers. The goal of the game was to gather the treasures and bring them out of the cave. In order to find all the treasures, the player had to use objects to unlock areas that allowed deeper access to the cave. This game may have been the first to give the player an illusion of freedom of choice, which is still an important quality of adventure games today. The game also gave feedback to the player in the form of "human-like" sentences, such as "I don't know how to do that" (instead of the "value too high" error messages exhibited by other mainframe games). The *adventure* genre was named after this game.

Myst is the most popular adventure game of all time.

Replayability in Adventure Games

The idea of being able to replay a game is very appealing to most players. Not only does this often more than double the hours of play, but it also provides a different perspective of the game's story (e.g., whether it involves playing the game from a different character's perspective, a different location, or a different time period). Unfortunately, most adventure games are intrinsically not replayable because they often consist of puzzles with a single solution. Once the game is over, the player has solved the game's mystery—and there isn't an opportunity to "re-solve" the game in a different way. How can adventure games be modified so that they can be replayable?

This game spawned a series of text-adventures that went beyond puzzle-solving and exploration—adding strong story elements. As graphics capabilities on game platforms increased, text-adventures gave way to graphic-adventures —leading to titles such as *Myst*, a point-and-click graphic adventure that became the best-selling computer game of all time (until *The Sims* came along).

Currently, only a handful of adventure games are released each year—but there is still a niche group of adventure fans out there. Characteristics of adventure games include exploration, collecting, puzzle-solving, navigating through mazes, and decoding messages. Unlike action games, adventure games are usually *turn-*

I'm attracted to adventure games because they challenge my intellect. I feel as I become a part of the intricate puzzle that my survival depends on my intellectual ability. Not too far from my own reality.

— *William A. Henderson*
(Senior Analyst,
Motion Picture Association
of America)

based—allowing the player time for reflective thought. This key difference in the way the game is played is most likely the primary reason adventure gamers are not into action-adventures.

::::: Survival-Horror: A New Trend in Story Genres?

A group of games with a dark, menacing theme—such as *Resident Evil, Silent Hill, Clock Tower, Fatal Frame* and *Alone in the Dark*—are being referred to as survival-horror games. This might mark the beginning of a new trend in game classification that could incorporate story and content genres.

Silent Hill is an example of a game in the "survival-horror" genre. Some of the most seasoned players find this game disturbing—and even terrifying!

Konami Digital Entertainment

Action-Adventure

The *action-adventure* genre is the only hybrid genre that has truly distinguished itself as an accepted genre in its own right. The "action" component allows for quick, reflexive movements as the character dodges and hunts down enemies—while the

"adventure" component adds conceptual puzzles and story elements to the game. Pure adventure gamers aren't usually interested in action-adventures because they are used to the slower pace of adventure games. The action-adventure hybrid has attracted a new audience as well as some pure action players.

Beyond Good & Evil is an action-adventure game in which the player takes on the role of an action reporter who must fight a sinister conspiracy using "stealth, force, and wits.".

Ubisoft Entertainment

Casino

In Chapter 2, you learned that addiction can be a motivation to play games. This is particularly apparent in *casino* games, which are often electronic versions of popular games—such as roulette, craps, poker, blackjack, and slot machines—found in on-ground casinos. The addiction motivation is closely tied to gambling, and many online versions of this genre are run by online gambling sites. Related to this genre are classic card games such as bridge that are available for the "casual" player market.

Prestige Gaming

Prestige Casino duplicates the gambling experience—right down to the slot machine visuals.

Puzzle

Although puzzle elements appear in many game genres, a pure *puzzle* game focuses on the player solving a puzzle or series of puzzles without controlling a character. There is little or no story surrounding puzzle games, which can be either real-time or turn-based. The pattern-based puzzle game *Tetris*—one of the most popular puzzle games of all time—is in real-time, involving a fast-paced game-playing experience. Many puzzle games (such as *Rocket Mania*) are timed—falling in-between real-time and turn-based intervals. Others, such as the *Scrabble*-esque *Bookworm*, are turn-based—giving the player all the time needed to form words out of adjacent scrambled letters. Handheld platforms—which can be played while standing in line or waiting in doctor's offices—are ideal for these games.

The Tetris Company, LLC

Tetris is the most popular electronic puzzle game of all time.

Rarely, puzzle games involve more than one player or a non-player opponent. One example of a multiplayer puzzle game is *Puzzle Fighter,* in which players simultaneously solve puzzles. This game goes beyond just solving a puzzle and brings in elements characteristic of the *strategy* genre (see next section), since each player must also pay attention to what the other is doing.

::::: Puzzles Everywhere

  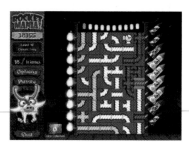

PopCap Games, Inc.

Rocket Mania, *Tip Top*, and *Bejeweled* are just a few of the many puzzle games that can be played at PopCap Games.

A great site for online puzzle games is PopCap Games (www.popcap.com), a Java-based game collection that includes all types of puzzle games—from the maze-like *Rocket Mania* to word-scrambling *Bookworm*, to the color/pattern-matching *Alchemy*. Some games, such as *Insane Aquarium*, are fast-paced and incorporate reflex skills specific to action games.

Role-Playing Games (RPGs)

Role-playing games (RPGs) originate from the tradition of the *Dungeons & Dragons®* paper-and-pencil fantasy role-playing games that originated in the 1970s. In these

Sir-tech Canada Ltd.

games, players take on roles such as fighters, wizards, priests, elves, or thieves. Players also explore dungeons, kill monsters (such as dragons and ogres), and gather treasure. One player, the Dungeon Master (later known as a Game Master), sets up the game world and takes on the roles of the other (non-player) characters in the game.

Wizardry 8 is part of one of the very first RPG series.

The term *Game Master (GM),* which originated from paper-and-pencil role-playing games, is currently used in online multiplayer games to refer to those who play an important role in supporting players online. GMs are discussed in more detail in the online multiplayer section of this chapter.

Like adventure games, RPGs are characterized by containing strong storylines—but RPGs also contain player-characters that improve throughout the course of the game. Due to the strong emotional character development—and because winning is tied in with this character advancement—RPG players usually experience close emotional involvement with their characters. The genre's presentation is diverse, ranging from simpler arcade-style games such as *Dungeon Siege* to the graphically-rich environments in *Final Fantasy.* Themes in RPGs are usually variations on "save the world"—such as finding the person responsible for a murder, rescuing someone who's been kidnapped, destroying a dangerous object, or killing monsters.

Immersion (discussed in more detail in Chapter 4) is an important element of RPGs. In playing a character role in these games, players often become highly involved in the game environment. We will see later on in this chapter that this element can be difficult to preserve in MMOG versions of these games.

Is An RPG Always Fantasy?

Why do most RPGs take place in fantasy worlds—and involve killing monsters, embarking on quests, and "saving" someone or something (usually "the world")? It is only within the past few years that RPGs such as *Star Wars Galaxies* allow for other goals (fame, wealth, and power)—and roles (musician, smuggler, doctor, bounty hunter, storm trooper). What about creating a modern-day RPG? If you were to create an RPG, where would it take place—and what roles would exist? *Anarchy Online,* with its strong political backstory, is a good example of an RPG that has steered away from the traditional fantasy structure.

The characters in RPGs are often termed "heroes" since they engage in heroic quests—usually in a team, known as a guild in online multiplayer versions of this genre. Combat is one way in which the heroes advance—gaining strength, experience, and money to buy new equipment. Chapter 5 goes into more depth on character development in all genres.

Ed Stark on Tabletop and Digital RPGs:::::

Ed Stark (Special Projects Manager— RPG Research & Design Group, Wizards of the Coast)

Ed Stark is currently the Special Projects Manager for the RPG Research & Design Group at Wizards of the Coast. He has been a game designer, author, creative director, and all-around game professional since 1991 when he started at West End Games. He came to TSR in 1995 and then moved out to Seattle with the Wizards of the Coast acquisition in 1997. He became the Creative Director for *Dungeons & Dragons*® shortly before the launch of the Third Edition of the game and stayed in that position for about four years. Ed now spends much of his time working with licensing and scheduling for the RPG R&D group and doing anything else deemed a "special project" by the boss!

Playing pen-and-paper "tabletop" RPGs such as *Dungeons & Dragons* continue to attract audiences all over the world. Paper-and-pencil RPGs promote socialization, group cooperation, and a level of commitment to group enjoyment that few other games demand. You have to play RPGs with other people—that's the whole point of a role-playing game—and you have to be willing to make sure everyone has a good time.

I predict that the tabletop industry will continue to flourish as people look for more excuses to actually get together. I believe that our industry will look at ways to utilize existing technologies to promote socialization. Playing an RPG *sans* pen-and-paper is still a fun activity. But technology should give us more ways to get together—not more excuses for being apart.

Socialization, imagination, and cooperation remain at the heart of every RPG—and, even after 30 years, *D&D* still has the same focus. However, we've learned a lot about game design, story development, and other aspects of RPG play in those 30 years! We've grown up into an industry where our educated, vocal players have a critical eye for balanced rules and interesting stories. We've learned to adapt our design philosophies to reflect what people want— not just to mimic what has gone before.

I think computer-based RPGs have helped us do this. When we see what's popular in the virtual universe of RPGs, we on the pen & paper side learn from that and try to build upon it. If you look at the current version of the *D&D* rules system, you'll see a much more streamlined and intuitive approach to game resolution than the earlier versions of the game ever had. We may have started the whole RPG trend, but it was the computer games' dependence on math and consistent system design that spurred us to solve a lot of the independent resolution systems inherent to prior versions of the *D&D* rules. Now, instead of resolving every separate action in a *D&D* game differently, you learn one metarule—the d20 rule—and you're good to go.

Simulations

Simulations (sometimes referred to as *sims*) attempt to replicate systems, machines, and experiences using real-world rules. Earlier in this chapter, you learned that some simulations are used in military and government institutions for training and recruiting. There are also many simulations that have been created for sheer entertainment purposes. Types of simulation games include vehicle, process, and participatory sims. Rules associated with all simulation games are based on real-world situations and objects. Players familiar with the subject matter associated with a simulation game often enjoy applying these real-world rules to the game-playing experience.

Vehicle Simulations

In *vehicle simulations,* the player usually operates complicated machinery (often vehicles such as jet fighters, ships, or tanks). Microsoft's *Flight Simulator* (discussed in Chapter 1) was the first widely popular vehicle simulator. Most of these games are highly accurate, right down to the equipment controls and user manual—which is often thick with text describing the intricate details of the machine. In addition to being developed for entertainment purposes, adaptations of these simulators have been used widely by the military for training and recruiting purposes. (Non-entertainment applications such as education, training, and recruitment are discussed below.) Flight and racing simulators (both military and civilian) are popular applications of machine simulators.

Microsoft Corporation

Microsoft Flight Simulator 2004—a descendent of the first widely popular vehicle sim.

Process Simulations (Construction & Management)

Process simulations involve real-world systems or processes. These games are also known as *construction and management sims (CMSs), god* or *toy* games. Examples of these games include *Rollercoaster Tycoon, Sim City,* and *Black & White.* Instead of focusing on operating machinery and understanding how to use controls, this type of sim focuses on the ongoing maintenance of a system, which could include anything from social to economic constructs, involving people, creatures, objects, or whole worlds. Although some of these games are set in fantasy worlds complete with unusual creatures and rituals, all of these duplicate the rules of real-world socioeconomic systems. The goal in process sims is not to defeat an enemy or opponent, but to build something within a process. These games are considered *constructive*—involving building and creating—rather than destructive. In order to win these games, players need to understand and control these processes. The success of *Sim City* proved that games don't need high-speed action or violence to be popular. The game also appealed to a broad audience.

Electronic Arts Inc.

Disaster strikes in
Sim City 4.

Games Without Goals?

Many process sims have often been referred to as "toy" or "god" games in which there is no goal involved and players can "do no wrong." However, the process of building and maintaining systems incorporates the ongoing goals of system balance—whether it's ensuring that your roller coaster does not malfunction, that your city does not go into deficit, or that your creature does not (or *does*) "misbehave."

Richard Wainess on Education through Simulation :::::

Richard Wainess came to the game arena from a circuitous route—as a musician, graphic designer, programmer, 3D animator, interactive multimedia developer, video writer, producer, and director. Richard has also taught a wide range of media-related courses, including multimedia authoring, 3D modeling, character animation, digital media design, and media management. Along the way, he has created board games and programmed arcade-style games. Currently he teaches game design and level design at the University of Southern California (USC), and he's involved in the development of two of the university's cross-disciplinary video game minors. His PhD research focuses on cognitive issues related to video game use, and he is partnering with other researchers to develop a video game–based science curriculum. When he's not working, he's an obsessed FPS player.

Richard Wainess, M.S.Ed. (Senior Lecturer, University of Southern California)

Simulations provide players with the opportunity to experience inaccessible environments—those that are dangerous (inside an active volcano), microscopic (inside a molecule), or remote (such as visiting Mars). By combining a gaming environment (goals, rewards, and realistic 3D visualization) with a simulation (i.e., scientifically-based experimentation), students are given the opportunity to *virtually* visit unique locations to experience scientific concepts and conduct experiments *first-hand*—and to feel as if they are really there, all within the comfort of the classroom.

Sports & Participatory Simulations

Participatory simulations engage the player to experience the simulation as a participant within it. The *sports* genre is a type of participatory sim because—like other sims—sports games often accurately reproduce real-world rules and strategies associated with the sport. Players vicariously participate in their favorite sport—as a player *and* often a coach. Why is the U.S. game-buying public so fascinated with this genre? Perhaps because it allows players to experience "wish fulfillment"—to

Acclaim Entertainment, Inc.

become extraordinary athletes, and to accomplish things they may not be able to in real life. Wish fulfillment can apply to many other real-world experiences. What about the ability to play a musical instrument, become a master chef, or create a work of fine art? In *Project Rockstar*—where the player manages a rock band—"it's a rock band instead of a football team." Perhaps other participatory simulations will begin to surface as the game industry continues to mature.

All-Star Baseball 2005 includes online head-to-head play, downloadable rosters, authentic Major League Baseball™ parks, legendary players—and a realistic "between the lines" experience.

Sports: Going Beyond Simulation

Electronic Arts devotes two company divisions to sports—EA Sports (which focuses on creating simulation sports games with real-world rules), and EA Sports BIG (which goes beyond simulation and delivers "larger-than-life" sports experiences). The creation of the EA Sports BIG division may mark the beginning of a new trend in the sports genre—one that steers away from playing by the rules and alters sporting conventions.

Microsoft Corporation

Age of Mythology is a strategy game in which players control figures from ancient mythology—assembling troops, building societies, and conquering enemies.

Strategy

Strategy games have their origin in classic board games such as chess, where players are required to manage a limited set of resources to achieve a particular goal. Most strategy games take place in a military setting. Unlike RPGs, the player's character is relatively unimportant. (In fact, sometimes the player has no character.) Instead, the player's resources (e.g., troops, weapons) become central to the game experience. Resource management typically includes constructing a variety of buildings or units, and deciding how and when to put them into action. The strategy in these games is based on comparative resources and decisions between opponents.

What's Wrong with a Detective Strategy Game?

Most strategy games take place in a military setting and involve traditional warfare. Of course, the elements of building units and expending resources can be applied to a variety of situations that don't involve warfare. How about criminal investigations? *Emergency Fire Response* is an example of a unique strategy game where players are firefighters who must defeat a natural enemy and put out fires. See if you can think of some other innovative ideas!

Turn-Based Strategy (TBS)

Until the early 1990s almost all strategy games were turn-based. This interval lends itself nicely to strategy games because it encourages players to take time to think "strategically" before making decisions. In turn-based strategy games, resource management involves discrete decisions such as what types of resources to create, when to deploy them, and how to use them to the best advantage. The player's ability to take the time to make these decisions is part of the game's appeal.

Firaxis Games / Atari, Inc.

Civilization III is an electronic turn-based strategy game.

Real-Time Strategy (RTS)

Real-time strategy (RTS) games incorporate a real-time interval. Although strategic thinking doesn't really lend itself well to real-time action, RTS games have become surprisingly popular. RTS players are under such constant time pressure that they don't have the opportunity to truly ponder a move. Multiplayer RTS games have to be played in one sitting.

Electronic Arts Inc.

Command & Conquer is a classic electronic RTS.

RTS Challenges

RTS games need a lot of time for game balance of two types—for the single-player campaign, and for the multiplayer experience. This isn't easy—and it occupies a lot of effort throughout the middle and end of development. RTS titles have been borrowing bits and pieces of other game genres recently. This is a useful experiment… but some don't fit well.

— Frank Gilson (Producer, Atari)

Another issue in RTS games is referred to as "micromanagement"—the process of balancing sets of resources (e.g., troops). Since the game is moving quickly in real-time, one set of resources might flourish while others fail, since the player can't feasibly focus on all sets at once. A player might decide to concentrate on managing one set of troops, who might be engaging in combat to defend the player's territory. In the meantime, another set of the player's troops—left "helpless" without the player to control them—is defeated. These games involve such a great deal of action and reaction time that the genre should really be referred to as an Action-Strategy hybrid!

Mix It Up!

One of the more interesting trends today is the plethora of "mixed-genre" games. It seems that one way to mitigate risk, while still trying to innovate, is to take several popular genres (e.g., action, adventure, and role-playing) and mix them to create a new style of game. *Deus Ex* is a great example of this hybrid.

— Tracy Fullerton, Assistant Professor
(Electronic Arts Interactive Entertainment Program,
USC School of Cinema–Television)

This computer and Internet technology "challenge board" trivia game was built using *Quia's* mini-game system for instructors and students.

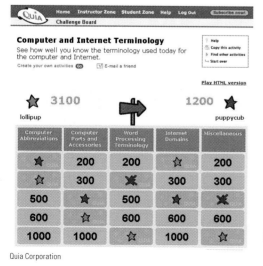

Quia Corporation

Trivia

The *trivia* genre focuses on games that "test" real-world knowledge. In *Trivial Pursuit,* for example, players must answer questions in several categories (including entertainment, history, art and literature, science and nature, and sports and leisure) in order to progress through the game. There is some crossover between a trivia game and a "quiz" that might be given to a student on a particular topic. In fact, part of the original "edutainment" educational software began with a trivia-style Q&A (question and answer) format. Sites such as *Quia* (www.quia.com) allow instructors to create trivia games based on their own course information using templates in the style of *Concentration,*

Hangman, Battleship, and others. Quiz shows such as *Jeopardy* have been immortalized with "home game" versions that are now available online. Many trivia games have movie tie-ins that are developed for marketing purposes (discussed earlier in this chapter). Much like casino games discussed earlier in this section, trivia games appeal to a "casual" player market.

Massively Multiplayer Online Games (MMOGs) & Persistent-State Worlds (PSWs)

Earlier in this chapter, you learned about technology issues related to massively multiplayer online games (MMOGs). Now let's look at the content and genre characteristics of these games. Under the MMOG umbrella, there are several variations on some genres you've already seen—known as massively multiplayer online role-playing games (MMORPGs), massively multiplayer first-person shooters (MMOFPSs), and massively multiplayer real-time strategy games (MMORTSs).

Planetside is an example of an MMOFPS.

One of the biggest issues in MMOG development is balancing social interaction with *immersion.* This poses a problem for MMORPGs in particular. Traditional RPG players want to escape into a fantasy world and become involved in rich storylines and character development. If MMORPG players discuss real-world topics during the game or don't stay in character, other more traditional players might not enjoy the experience of playing. Does a developer try to enforce role-play, or do the players have to accept that the game cannot be fully immersive? Issues related to story and immersion are discussed further in Chapter 4.

::::: Chatting in Digital Space

One of the benefits of MMOGs is the ability to "meet" new friends in a virtual world. In some ways, this is equivalent to what one of the first graphics-based chat rooms, *The Palace,* tried in the mid-'90s. *The Palace* became a very popular hangout for those who were using the Web at the time.

The Palace was one of the first graphics-based Internet chat rooms.

Sony Online Entertainment Inc.

EverQuest: The Planes of Power—part of the first popular MMORPG series in the United States.

Another related issue involves player misbehavior. Some players are simply rude—while others harass, cheat, or even commit fraud… providing a more serious threat to others' enjoyment of the game. The anonymity provided by the Internet is a primary reason this type of behavior is as prevalent as it is. This could pose a threat to the current trend in which parents and children are playing online games together (discussed in Chapter 2). Fortunately for young children, there are now some interesting MMORPGs created just for them—such as Disney's *Toontown Online*.

:::::: *Yohoho! Puzzle Pirates:*
The First MMOPG?

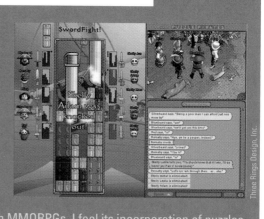

I created *Puzzle Pirates* because of my love of pirates—both as a concept and pretending to be a pirate—combined with the realization that puzzle games made the ideal gameplay backbone to an MMOG. My girlfriend at the time becoming pathologically addicted to *Bejeweled* was a tip-off. [Author's Note: Although *Puzzle Pirates* has elements associated with MMORPGs, I feel its incorporation of puzzles into the game makes it the first of its kind—an MMOPG (puzzle game)!]

— *Daniel James (CEO, Three Rings Design)*

Three Rings Design, Inc.

MMOGs are also referred to as *Persistent-State Worlds (PSWs)* because they are available 24-hours per day and do not end when a player logs out of the game—allowing the player's character to "persist" in time. This persistence can pose some interesting challenges. Since an MMOG is never completely over, content for the game is produced on an ongoing basis, and it is expected to change periodically to keep players interested in the game.

Shattered Galaxy: A Rewarding MMORTS

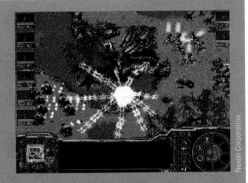

Unlike most other MMOGs, *Shattered Galaxy* is based completely upon player versus player combat. Every player belongs to a team, or faction, that competes with other factions for game resources. Since we wanted players to actively support their team, we made several changes to traditional RTS gameplay. For example, penalties for death are negligible, and we reward players for participating in battles whether they win or lose. When you're not afraid of dying, you're able to sacrifice yourself for teammates without hesitation.

— *Kevin Saunders (Senior Game Designer, Obsidian Entertainment)*

The Pros & Cons of MMOG Development

For MMOGs, the list of cons is huge. MMOGs are risky, very technically challenging—and they also have to be incredibly robust and secure. The technical challenges alone usually occupy so much of the developers' time that they have difficulty creating the content, and tuning and balancing it in time for any kind of reasonable launch. On the "pro" side, an MMOG can be the most immersive experience that a gamer can imagine. It's still early for the genre. Right now, the genre is still very derivative and too dependent on consumable content, instead of replayable and fun experiences in a social setting.... I'm pleased to see some independent MMOG developers focusing on non-combat activity. Games such as *A Tale in the Desert* and *Puzzle Pirates* utilize cooperation, collaboration, and gameplay that didn't descend from *Dungeons & Dragons*.

— *Mark Terrano (Technical Game Manager, Xbox Advanced Technology Group)*

Now that you've learned the basic elements of game applications, platforms, and genres, try applying this to what you learned in the previous chapter about player markets.

Market

In Chapter 2, you learned that there are many different types of people who enjoy playing games. Who do you want to reach? This set of players is your *target market.* Are you interested in developing a game that attracts a wider market of teens (without being gender-specific) or an even wider market consisting of teens and young adults?

Now tie the market into applications, genres, styles, and platforms. How about focusing only on women who enjoy playing MMORPGs? Or perhaps creating an educational game for adult students attending a nationwide culinary school? In this case, you'd probably be marketing to the school itself instead of (or in addition to) the students. You could also concentrate on developing games for a particular platform—such as the handheld. Since the popularity of the Game Boy Advance SP has already shown that the market for handheld devices is growing beyond children into adult gamers, why not develop adult-themed games for this particular device?

Generational Games

Generation X is the first generation that grew up with arcade and, later, console-style games. Xers have a great interest in both online and console games. Game content for Xers often skews toward "man against computer," rapid-fire action, shoot-'em-up games. Xers tend to favor personal, individual competition—so gladiator death-matches win over team play and multi-user game content. Growing up in the arcades, older Xers are comfortable with simple, abstract game visuals. There is significant potential for re-creating classic arcade games online and in consoles as Xers become old enough for nostalgia. Older Xers show significant interest in online games, but younger generations are likely to overtake them in this area due to its communication and multiplayer gaming style. Younger Xers (sometimes referred to as Generation Y) have less interest in classic-style "arcade" games and demand great realism, motion, graphics, and so on. In content, they continue the "gladiator" trend of individual combat—although there is significant interest in "team-play" gaming in the LAN rather than in muliplayer online gaming style.

The Millennial generation is the first to treat the Internet and games as "normal" and not as something new. Popular Millennial games emphasize communication over competition. This generation has many more female gamers, and this trend is likely to continue. The girls (and many boys) display interest in "social engineering" games such as *The Sims*. Millennials expect high-quality game graphics as a given. They show interest in using game environments as a way to communicate rather than simply compete—though competition is also okay. Many Boomer and Xer parents have close relationships with their kids, and the decision to buy a game often involves a parent-child co-purchase. Therefore, games aimed at Millennials must pass the test of parental acceptability. Although many Millennials play console games, this is most likely due to influence from their parents. As Millennials begin attending college and moving away from their parents, their tendency to use the Internet to communicate may translate into the continued growth of Millennial online gaming.

— *Pete Markiewicz, PhD (Indiespace)*

Generation

From our discussion of the Millennial Generation in Chapter 2, you might have a particular idea of what games this age group might be interested in playing. If you wanted to create a game that provided the opportunity for this group to engage in teamwork behavior, you would most likely choose a multiplayer mode. Age might also correspond to the genre. Gen Xers might prefer horror-themed games or single-player games that concentrate on a lone "hero" who overcomes incredible odds to vanquish a series of foes.

What types of game platforms and genres would be ideal for the Millennial generation?

Rating

Entertainment Software Ratings Board (ESRB)

In Chapter 1, you learned about the establishment of the Entertainment Software Ratings Board (ESRB)—the industry's reaction to the Senate hearings on game violence. Like the film ratings established by the Motion Picture Association of America (MPAA), the ESRB ratings are tied into the age group of the target market. Ratings include:

- EC (Early Childhood)
- E (Everyone)
- T (Teen)
- M (Mature – 17+)
- AO (Adults Only)
- RP (Rating Pending)

What rating would you propose for a game you'd like to create? Many EC-rated games are educational, since certain developmental skills (such as learning to read) are stressed at that age. Interestingly, almost all massively multiplayer online games (MMOG) are rated T. This rating is based on the game itself *before* it is played by multiple players. With open communication between people within the game world—where "anything goes" with regard to language—it appears that deciding members of the ESRB may not have much experience actually playing an MMOG! (Ratings for some now note: "Game experience may change during online play.")

Concept Development & Documentation

All of the elements described in this chapter help form the beginning of your game concept. It's important to understand how these elements work together to give your game a strong foundation. A complete concept also includes the areas covered in Part II, which focuses on creating compelling content—including storytelling, character, gameplay, levels, interface, and audio. As you read through Part II, try to apply the basic historical, player, and game elements to content development. In Chapter 10, you will also learn to incorporate some of the basic elements in this chapter into game documentation such as the concept document (which will include your target market, genre, and platform[s]).

:::CHAPTER REVIEW:::

1. What are some unique game applications? In this chapter, you learned about several applications that are distinct from pure entertainment. Can you think of a new game application not mentioned in this chapter that you might want to create?

2. The ESRB has used a "T" rating on all MMOGs. This rating is not necessarily accurate. Why is this? What do you feel motivates people to play MMOGs? How does the structure of an MMOG differ from LAN-based multiplayer and single-player games?

3. What are the benefits and disadvantages of developing *turn-based* and *real-time* games? How do genre, platform, and player mode (single-player, two-player, networked, massively multi-player) affect the game-playing experience for both of these styles?

4. Create a brand new game genre that is distinct from those discussed in this chapter. Tie this genre into what you learned in Chapter 2 about player markets. What type of player might be interested in playing a game in your genre, and why?

5. Combine two genres discussed in this chapter to create a new hybrid (mixed) genre. What type of game would you create for this new genre? List five unique features of the game and discuss what would motivate players to try your game.

6. Your company has recently acquired the rights to port a computer game to all other existing platforms (arcade, console, handheld, online, and tabletop). Choose two of these other platforms and discuss how you would modify the game so that it was optimal for your chosen platforms.

7. Local play is common on console systems, but it can be awkward on computer systems. Can you think of a situation in which it would be fairly comfortable for two players to share a keyboard and mouse? Your company has been asked to develop a local play game for the computer platform. What type of game would you develop for this player mode—and why?

8. Adventure games have declined in popularity in the last 10 years. Why do you think this has happened? What would you change about the content or structure in adventure games to incite new interest in this genre?

9. Strategy games don't always need to have a military backdrop. Discuss three settings or scenarios *not* related to the military that could be incorporated successfully into a strategy game.

10. Do you feel that all games are educational "by accident"? Why or why not? The 'edutainment' movement of the 1980s and early 1990s focused on the early childhood market and players in the K–12 grades. What about games created specifically to educate beyond K–12 (post-secondary)? Create an idea for an educational game geared toward adults who are taking a college course.

Part II:
Scenarios

creating compelling content

4

Storytelling:
creating the narrative

key chapter questions

- How do stories in games differ from those in films and other entertainment media?

- What are some traditional story structures and how do they relate to plot?

- What is *interactivity* and how can it be applied to storytelling?

- What are some dramatic storytelling devices used in games?

- How does story affect *immersion* in a game?

Although a great deal of this chapter focuses on some traditional aspects of storytelling and how narrative can be incorporated into games, the most powerful storytelling device involves what the player experiences while playing the game. This is the *gameplay* itself, discussed in detail in Chapter 6.

Where do game ideas come from? Why do these ideas seem compelling enough to get produced? Why do they succeed or fail? This chapter focuses on the mechanics of putting story ideas into practice—from learning about story structure and formats, to ensuring that these stories work with all the other game elements, including platform, genre, and gameplay. We'll focus on the specifics of character development in Chapter 5.

Storytelling Traditions

Cave paintings were flat, 2D images that told simple stories without words or sound. This was the beginning of the visual storytelling tradition, which has evolved into the visual media of today—including film, television, art, and interactive entertainment. Games form a significant proportion of the highly visual medium of interactive entertainment; this medium incorporates the visual storytelling tradition,

Cave paintings are considered the first examples of visual storytelling.

but it has also revolutionized the way stories are told. Other storytelling traditions (including oral, audio, and text) have also been folded into the game medium—as music, sound effects, voice-over narration and dialogue, player-to-player chat, and on-screen text dialogue.

Why do we tell stories? Noted psychologist Carl Jung explains this in terms of the *collective unconscious*—a knowledge that we are all born with and yet can never be directly conscious of. Within this collective unconscious are universal themes and *archetypes* (discussed in more detail in Chapter 5), which appear in our culture in the form of stories and character types in art, literature, music, film—and games.

Electronic Arts Inc.

American McGee's Alice is an "evil" parody of Lewis Carroll's *Alice in Wonderland*.

Generating Ideas

Without reading further into this chapter and delving into story structure and unique features of the game storytelling process, consider how story ideas are generated. You've heard the phrase "write what you know." That's a start. But if we all wrote what we knew, there wouldn't be anything but stories based on real-world events—and there certainly wouldn't be fantasy, science fiction, or horror stories! How would we ever experience the fantastic or the surreal: aliens taking over the earth, superheroes that can fly "faster than a speeding bullet," time machines, parallel universes?

Writers often get ideas from thoughts that just come to them throughout the day. These ideas could be anything from observations of the people and the environment around them to portions of dreams they remember from the night before. Direct personal experience is another common idea generator. Have you ever been in a difficult situation and had to do some clever problem-solving in order to "escape" from it? Do you know anyone who's unusual or eccentric (and you caught yourself thinking, 'This person would make a great character in a story!')? What was it like for you growing up?

You can also be inspired from stories that already exist. What are your favorite movies, television programs, plays, and books? What was it about these stories that involved you emotionally? Have you come upon some interesting news stories? You might be inspired by a television situation comedy, such as *Seinfeld,* to create a game that involves ordinary characters in ordinary situations. Or you might be inspired by a musical (such as *Moulin Rouge*) to create a game in which the characters sing!

My favorite game storyline is from *Final Fantasy 2.* It forced the entire spectrum of emotions in the player to emerge. I felt anger, love, envy, and jealousy over the various players, and also cried at several points in the game where characters sacrificed themselves to further the game. This game was released in the United States in the 1990s. It is very difficult for me to find a game from our next-generation systems that is able to bring back the type of feelings I felt from this game.

— *Arash John Sammander,*
Game Art & Design student

:::::: Adaptations

Existing movies, books, plays, and television shows can inspire you to create original games. But if you decide to do a direct adaptation of a pre-existing work, you need to clear the subsidiary rights with the copyright owner and make a licensing deal. This can be rather expensive—and these rights are often already taken. For example, Electronic Arts and Vivendi Universal have made deals with New Line Cinema and the estate of J. R. R. Tolkien, respectively, to create games based on the *Lord of the Rings* trilogy.

Electronic Arts Inc.

Fell beast attacks Gondor soldiers in *Lord of the Rings: The Battle for Middle-Earth*—an adaptation of a story from another medium.

Start carrying a notebook with you at all times so that you can jot down any ideas that come to your mind throughout the day. Make sure you use the notebook only for this purpose—not for writing down "to do" lists or contact information. If you get into the habit of doing this, you'll start to notice that you have many creative ideas. The tough part will be transforming them into good game storylines.

Marianne
Krawczyk
(Writer)

After writing professionally for the last few years, Marianne Krawczyk got her break when her first feature, *Popular Myth,* was optioned. Moving on to the hit children's show, *Sweet Valley High,* Marianne learned the ins and outs of the writers' room. She was then hired to write and develop the animated project, *Swamp & Tad,* for Wild Brain Studios—and she also wrote *Caffeine,* a pilot for Studios USA/Universal Television. Transferring her skills to the game industry, Marianne wrote the story and script for the Sony PlayStation 2 AAA title, *God or War*—and she recently was hired to write for unannounced game projects with Sony and Midway. Marianne also has projects under consideration at National Geographic Film and Television and United Artists Pictures.

Good writing is always challenging. You need interesting twists, truthful characters that drive stories, and compelling worlds. If writing were easy, every film would be a blockbuster, every TV show a hit, every game a 500,000-unit seller. Obviously, this isn't the case.

Introducing game design into how stories are told is a whole new challenge. To further complicate matters, good stories are linear while games are not. A common mistake is to start out with something too complicated that will only get more so throughout the ever-changing organism that is a game. Negotiating a simple, direct story in a world that is designed to drift sideways is difficult—but, ironically, it's probably a better metaphor for life itself than the medium of film.

Traditional Story Structure

Story structure has been the topic of Hollywood screenwriting classes for decades. It is seen as a "formula" that, when applied correctly, can ensure an audience's emotional involvement in a film. The most common structure is known as the three-act plot structure. Other story structure formulas are considered to be more universal and philosophical, such as Joseph Campbell's *Hero's Journey,* and, in turn, Christopher Vogler's *Writer's Journey.* Let's take a look at these approaches.

Hollywood 3-Act

The *three-act* structure touted in the Hollywood screenwriting community emphasizes the simple idea that a good story has a beginning, a middle, and an end. The beginning introduces the main character's *problem;* the middle focuses on *obstacles* that prevent the problem from being solved; and the end illustrates a *resolution* of the problem, following the ordeal of having to remove or defeat the obstacles:

1. **Beginning (Act I):** The most interesting stories begin by placing the audience into the action or drama of the story. The backstory and any background events leading up to this moment can be introduced later. The goal is to capture the audience's attention. Act I focuses on the character's problem. The story should introduce this problem immediately.

2. **Middle (Act II):** The middle of the story focuses on the obstacles that stand in the way of the character's ability to solve the problem introduced in Act I. There are usually a series of obstacles in Act II that the character must overcome. This act comprises the bulk of the dramatic tension in the story.

3. **End (Act III):** The story ends when the problem introduced in Act I has been solved. The character often has to systematically face and remove each obstacle in Act II in order to reach this resolution.

Screenwriters are encouraged to begin their stories in the middle of the action (e.g., the main character is chased by the police), which allows the immediate introduction of a problem. In a game, it has been argued that players need to learn how to use the game and bond with the character before the problem is introduced. This is especially important in games that allow the player to take on the role of the character.

Most Hollywood films employ a simple three-act story structure.

In film, all scenes in the middle of the story should advance the plot or reveal an important aspect of a character's personality. This is related to the closed nature of linear media. In addition to being limited by time (usually no more than 2½ hours), movies are not meant to be vast worlds for the audience to explore. In a game, there's all the time in the world for an unrelated storyline, twists and turns, and other tricks—which help create the illusion of freedom for the player as well as a more realistic game world with endless experiences. Players are also given the option of taking any number of paths in the game, which can further allow for a rich game-playing experience.

Linear stories include tragic endings (and sometimes even non-endings) that leave the audience guessing what will happen to the character. One or more main characters could even meet with disaster (such as the *Romeo & Juliet*-inspired *Moulin Rouge* and *Westside Story*) as the story ends. However, games can have numerous endings that are specifically related to the many paths available for the players to take in the game. Each of these endings should make sense to the player and correspond to the actions chosen. These endings should range from total success to complete failure.

Monomyth & Hero's Journey

In *The Hero With a Thousand Faces,* Joseph Campbell introduced the concept of the *monomyth*—a specific story pattern that legends and myths of all world cultures share. Campbell calls this monomyth "hero's journey," where a fictional hero must leave his community and go on a dangerous journey—usually to recover something (or someone) of value. Campbell attributed George Lucas' success with the original *Star Wars* trilogy to a story structure that made use of this monomyth. The path taken by the hero is marked by various characters, which often represent Carl Jung's *archetypes* (discussed further in Chapter 5). Some examples from *Star Wars* include the hero (Luke Skywalker), the nomad (Han Solo), the mentor (Obi Wan Kenobi—and, later, Yoda), and the shadow (Darth Vader).

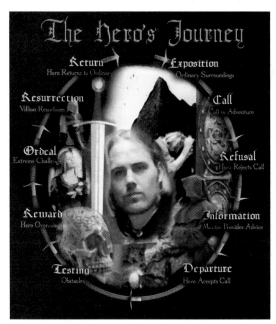

Joseph Campbell's "hero's journey," is a monomyth that can be found in all legends and myths.

In *The Writer's Journey,* Christopher Vogler applied Joseph Campbell's "hero's journey" to screenwriting. I've used Vogler's steps as a framework below. Some of the titles and explanations differ from his original material:

1. **Exposition:** This section introduces the main character in his or her "ordinary" surroundings. In *Final Fantasy,* the ordinary world is alluded to with the introductory slogan, "It was a day like any other."

2. **Call:** The main character gets a "call to adventure." In this section, the alternate (or "special") world is introduced to the main character. Usually, elements in the alternate world somehow intersect with those in the ordinary world—and the main character is asked to enter this alternate reality and embark on a quest or journey.

3. **Refusal:** The hero initially rejects the call, not wanting to leave the relative comfort of the ordinary world—but also hesitating and experiencing self-doubt, which sets the stage for future conflict.

4. **Information:** On the surface, the hero has rejected the call—but he continues to question his decision. A mentor figure (often a "wise old man") provides the hero with some information and advice relevant to the refused call.

5. **Departure:** From the knowledge the hero gained in the "information" stage, the hero makes a final decision—usually changing his mind and deciding to embark on the journey. The hero prepares to leave the ordinary world.

6. **Testing:** During the journey, the hero faces a series of challenges. This section usually makes up the main action in a story. This is where the hero must solve problems, face fears, rescue others, defeat foes—often accompanied by a transformation of some sort.

7. **Reward:** After completing this series of challenges, the hero will receive a reward. This section could mark the end of the story… but not always!

8. **Ordeal:** Just when the hero appears to be beginning a safe return to the ordinary world, the hero must face another ordeal. This is the big conflict—the one the storyteller saved for last—which often plays on the hero's deepest fears. In this section, the hero displays vulnerability (like Superman and kryptonite)—and it isn't clear whether the hero will succeed or fail.

9. **Resurrection:** "Just when you thought it was over" and the hero overcame the final ordeal, the enemy (usually a major villain) resurfaces briefly. (This is the moment in a horror film when the audience is shouting at the main character, "Turn around! He's not dead yet!") This is also the place where the storyteller might include a "trick ending"—something completely unexpected. Perhaps the villain isn't really a villain at all. Maybe the mentor was an imposter. (Could Yoda have been evil? Hmmm.)

10. **Return:** This marks the end of the story. The hero returns to the ordinary world and resumes life as usual. The structure is circular, with the hero returning back to the beginning. This makes it easy for the audience to draw "before and after" comparisons and notice how the hero has been transformed. The circular structure also leaves room for open-endedness. Could the hero be called upon again in the future? Has the enemy really been defeated? Is another threat on the horizon? Will the hero ever really be at rest? Leaving questions like these open—instead of opting for a neatly tied-up ending—not only intrigues the audience but makes way for sequels. The ending could actually answer these questions. What if the hero is unexpectedly transported back into the artificial world right at the end of the story? The main character in *Back to the Future* finds out right at the end of the film that his journey into the past has caused some major changes in the future. He must answer another call and travel into the future in order to save his family from disaster. In *Half-Life*'s last-minute plot twist, main character Gordon Freeman is just about to escape when he is approached by the "man in black" and is offered a difficult choice.

Although it's important to have a framework for traditional storytelling, using these structures could result in tired, overused stories. Instead, try to see these as guidelines and expand upon them. These structures also don't account for scenarios involving multiple main characters who all share equal importance in the story. As discussed in Chapter 3, there are several player modes (ranging from one to thousands of simultaneous players) that allow for groups of characters to go on journeys together. How would you incorporate some of this structure into MMOGs where players needed to cooperate with each other?

::::: Generational Storytelling

Generation X is thought of as a more independently-minded generation, and the Millennial generation is thought of as a more team-oriented generation.

You learned about generations of gamers in recent U.S. history in Chapter 2. What types of stories do you think would work well for games that were created for the Millennial generation? Knowing that the Millennials are more team-oriented and collective, perhaps games involving cooperation, communication, and heroic teamwork will appeal to them.

Valve Software

Half-Life and *City of Heroes*—examples of generational storytelling?

Cryptic Studios, Inc. / NCsoft Corporation

What types of games work for Generation X? Knowing that this generation is more independent, cutting edge, and entrepreneurial, is it any wonder that *Half-Life, Metal Gear Solid* and other games involving the "lone" nomadic hero are so appealing? If you are a member of this generation, do you find yourself wanting to develop a storyline like this?

How about games that can only be played in teams made up of heroes? Going further, each hero could have a unique power that is potent only when combined with the powers of the rest of the team. Can you think of some comic book series and Saturday morning cartoons that fit this description? *City of Heroes* takes this tradition and brings it into a massively multiplayer environment. Players take on the roles of heroes to defend Paragon City from "super-powered villains, alien invaders, and underground monsters." Superhero statistics, skills, powers, and costumes can be customized by the players.

Story Elements

In traditional entertainment media such as film, literature, television, and radio, it is conventional for writers to produce stories—complete with compelling characters and specific settings—that form the basis of the content. Although storylines also exist in many games, they are not necessary for a satisfying game-playing experience. In Chapter 3, you learned that puzzle games often do not incorporate stories. Consider *Tetris*, an extremely popular puzzle game without a storyline that has captivated players since the mid-'80s. On the other side of the spectrum, some role-playing games (RPGs) rely heavily on story. In fact, an RPG is most like a movie for some players—where the game can become merely a "delivery vehicle" for the story.

Chris Klug on the Importance of Dramatic Form :::::

Chris Klug has been designing games for over 23 years—shipping approximately four dozen games, supplements, adventures, and add-ons. Before joining the game industry, Chris was trained as a theatrical lighting designer—working on Broadway, in regional theater and opera, and touring with various rock 'n' roll bands in the 1970s. Starting his game industry career in 1981 with Simulations Publications, Inc., he assisted with the design of *Universe*, the second edition of *DragonQuest* (winner of a Game of the Year Award), *Horror Hotel*, and *Damocles Mission*. When TSR bought SPI in 1982, Chris and the rest of the SPI staff moved on to form Victory Games—where Chris headed up the role-playing games group, designed the *James Bond 007* role-playing game (also a winner of a Game of the Year award), and oversaw the

Chris Klug (Owner, Brown Bear Entertainment)

entire Bond product line. Most recently, Chris Klug worked as Creative Director for Electronic Arts' MMORPG *Earth & Beyond*. A leading proponent of making the game industry realize its full potential, Chris was a keynote speaker at the Second International Conference on Entertainment Computing hosted by Carnegie Mellon University in May 2003. He also serves on the advisory board of Indiana University of Pennsylvania's Applied Media and Simulation Games Center, as well as a Program Advisory Committee Member for Game Art & Design for the Art Institute of Pittsburgh.

The best writers I've worked with are not novelists, but playwrights—who understand dramatic form: that scenes have to turn; that dialogue must be written with subtext, allowing room for the actor; and that the theme has to be delivered and visible in every scene and beat... like the best movies and plays.

The following story elements—premise, backstory, synopsis, theme, and setting—will help you begin to take your rough ideas and structure them into a preliminary form.

Premise (High Concept)

The *premise* (sometimes referred to as the *high concept*) is a one- to two-sentence summary of the game's purpose and overall theme, and it often appears on packaging associated with the game. It is intended to intrigue customers, enticing them to purchase the game. A premise can be written from any point of view, but I suggest focusing on a second-person perspective so that you are addressing the player directly. Here are just a few examples:

- *Devastation:* "As the leader of a group of Resistance fighters in a future devastated earth, you must assemble your army and travel the globe, restoring peace and sanity in a very dangerous world."
- *Wolverine's Revenge:* "You have just 48 hours to find the antidote for the virus that was implanted in Wolverine. Along the way, you'll face some of the greatest X-Men villains, including Sabretooth, Juggernaut, and Magneto."
- *Driver:* "Drive a getaway car for the mob in this action-packed street-racing game."
- *Metal Gear Solid 2 – Sons of Liberty:* "Assume the role of Solid Snake, a one-man army determined to stop a deadly high-tech weapon from falling into the hands of the wrong people. Snake must utilize his skills in stealth, weaponry, and counter-terrorism to fight off the competing powers and destroy the gigantic killing machine, Metal Gear Ray."
- *Half-Life:* "Take on the role of Gordon Freeman, an ordinary technician who is forced to battle trans-dimensional monsters after an accident at a secret research facility."

This summary should focus on what is unique about your game. In addressing the player directly, you also might want to indicate the game's genre. For example, if one of the unique features of the game is that it's played in a massively multiplayer context, try to incorporate this into the summary. As you come up with your high concept, you need to think like a "marketer"—understanding that this is one element used to sell the game to the public and potential investors.

Backstory

A *backstory* provides information that leads up to where the game begins. It usually consists of a short paragraph in the game instruction manual, or it appears as text (usually accompanied by a voice-over) at the beginning of the game. This helps orient the player to the purpose and action involved in the game, as well as allowing the player to sometimes establish initial bonds for certain characters.

Cyan Worlds, Inc.

Myst has a strong backstory that is referred to throughout the game as the character solves mysteries related to events that happened in the past.

Synopsis

The story can also exist throughout the game itself. In this case, the player might be involved in the setting and actions that take place in the game. A *running storyline* can also help a player escape from reality and become immersed in the "artificial" game world, during which the player can become emotionally involved with the game's characters (discussed in more detail in Chapter 5).

Theme

The theme represents what the story is *really* about. Themes usually relate to a primary obstacle in the story faced by the main character(s). Is the obstacle an enemy (villain), nature, society, fate—or the characters themselves? What is the philosophical idea behind the story? The theme could be a defining question—such as "Is murder justified?" or "Can love triumph?" What theme do you want to explore in a story?

Setting

The *setting* or *backdrop* represents the world that is being explored by the audience, characters, or player. In creating a game story, think of the world in which your characters will live and interact. Think beyond the stereotypes. Will it be a

Firaxis Games / Atari, Inc.

Lionhead Studios

Alpha Centauri takes place on a distant planet orbiting the star, and *BC* takes place in prehistoric times.

real-world location (e.g., Sahara Desert, Alaskan tundra), or a specific time period (e.g., Victorian era, Roaring '20s)? Will it take place in the world of organized crime, behind the scenes of network news, or among the "uncomplicated" lifestyle of the Amish people? What is the history and geography of the world? (Elements of the game environment are discussed in Chapter 7.) How about settings associated with traditional media genres such as science fiction (space), horror (haunted house), or mystery (crime scene)? The setting is often tied-in with the game's genre. Many puzzle games do not have a real setting (or story)—but exist in an *abstract* world—and most RPGs take place in a fantasy world.

Card & Board Games: Building a Story from a Premise

Let's say you have decided to explore the world of archeology in a game. Within this world, you have the opportunity to go on an archaeological dig in five different locations (volcano, underwater, desert, jungle, and polar). You could build an interesting story to go with each of these settings. However, this card game (*Lost Cities*) focuses on the mechanics of playing the game (gameplay—discussed further in Chapter 6) rather than a storyline. Although there's a "premise" (you and your opponent are archaeologists competing to for the most funding and return for your respective digs), there is no focus on story synopsis. The goal is to build cards that represent a particular dig in a certain sequence. It's all about chance, ordering, numbers; you could play the game without knowing anything about the setting. When playing games such as these, players either keep the game abstract or imagine a story going along with the gameplay. While playing *Bohnanza*—a highly-addictive card game that focuses on bean farming—my friends and I find ourselves discussing our bean fields and the process of planting, nurturing, and harvesting our beans. After a while, it's easy to imagine taking a game like this and integrating it with more story. The next time you play a card or board game, imagine creating a digital version of the game and expanding the game's premise into a meaningful storyline.

Plot

Plot is more about *how* the story unfolds rather than *what* the story is about. Earlier in this chapter, you learned about story structure. Each of the structures contained plot elements that guided the story along. In Vogler's *Writer's Journey,* the hero's initial refusal to heed the call to adventure and the appearance of the mentor (who supplies important information to the hero) are both plot elements. Game plotting can be part of the game's story structure—but it can also be dictated by how the game is played. In Chapter 6, you'll learn about *gameplay*—which involves how a player might

DEAD OR ALIVE 3
© TECMO,LTD. Team NINJA 2001

Tecmo Ltd.

Combat scene from *Dead or Alive 3.*

react to challenges faced in the game. Doesn't this sound similar to the classic "hero," who must make decisions related to tests and obstacles along a journey? In this way, plot and gameplay are interconnected. The key to making these challenges and obstacles interesting to a player is to relate them to the story with the use of various plot devices that optimize dramatic tension.

Balancing Conflict

Dramatic tension in a story is maximized when the player seems to often be on the brink of disaster but is able to escape repeatedly from this situation by just the narrowest of margins. In a multiplayer game, this same balance needs to be maintained between the players as well. (More on game balance is discussed in Chapter 6.)

Shifting Focus

Even though players make choices and have apparent freedom while playing the game, players can be drawn back to the main storyline. This effective storytelling technique can be accomplished by shifting the player's focus while capturing the player's interest—such as widening the scope of the game by providing more sub-quests or by introducing new characters or objects that lead the player into other unexplored areas.

Foreshadowing Events

Foreshadowing is a device that ominously alerts the audience about an important event or change that will happen in the future. In *Half-Life,* main character Gordon Freeman catches glimpses of strange alien landscapes that feature heavily in later parts of the game. Neither the character nor the player is aware of this as they are introduced to these powerful images.

Oddworld Inhabitants

Oddworld: Munch's Oddysee provides suspension of disbelief through unusual characters and situations.

Suspension of Disbelief

Suspension of disbelief means that the story you create must somehow make the players forget real life and accept the artificial reality you've created. This is related to immersion, but it more specifically refers to the players' acceptance of rules and experiences that may not make sense in the real world. Any film or book set in the future—or a story involving monsters or aliens—has to convince the players to believe that what is happening in the story is important… and "real." What if people in a game could fly without the aid of air transport? What if the game world included a rule indicating that all characters that resembled humans were evil, while the horrific-looking demons were good? If you're caught up in the story behind the game, you will disregard the real world while you're playing it and adopt the artificial world as yours for a while.

Activision, Inc.

Realism

Realism, in contrast to the *suspension of disbelief* device, can be used in games to mimic the real world as closely as possible. In the discussion of simulation games in Chapter 3, you learned that the application of real-world rules to these games is often the most significant element for the players. In this case, play-

True Crime: Streets of LA uses visual realism by replicating the environment of Los Angeles.

ers want reality and "authenticity." Such stories might include the visual realism of a contemporary real-world setting—such as Luxoflux/Activision's *True Crime: Streets of LA*, in which LA streets were replicated in the environment, right down to signs on the surrounding buildings. Related to realism is *harmony*. In order to ensure that a game is harmonious, nothing should seem "out of place" or inconsistent. For example, characters in a story set in Medieval times should not be wearing watches. These types of temporal inconsistencies are known as *anachronisms*.

:::::: *Call of Duty:* Realism & Ratings

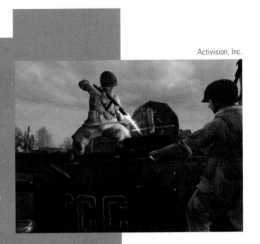

Activision, Inc.

When game characters end up looking like real people, others might want to stop people from seeing graphic things happen to them. We experienced this a bit during the ratings process for *Call of Duty*. Because of the level of immersion provided by the experience, it was almost rated a mature game.

— *Grant Collier (President, Infinity Ward)*

Many military games employ realism to appeal to their fan base. *Call of Duty*—which takes place during World War II—contains authentic weapons used during that time—along with realistic depictions of wartime violence.

David Brin on What Drives Storytelling :::::

David Brin's 15 novels—including *New York Times* bestsellers and winners of the Hugo and Nebula awards—have been translated into more than 20 languages. His 1989 ecological thriller, *Earth*, foreshadowed global warming, cyberwarfare, and the World Wide Web. *Kiln People* explored a near future when people may be able to be in two places at once. *The Life Eaters* rocked the world of graphic novels with a stunning and heroic portrayal of an alternate World War II. A 1998 movie directed by Kevin Costner was loosely based on *The Postman*. David wrote the scenario and introduction for the highly-touted video game *ECCO the Dolphin*. His "Uplift Universe" was adapted by Steve Jackson Games as GURPS Uplift and features a unique system for creating new alien life forms. Simulation game *Tribes* allows players to strive for survival and reproductive success in the Neolithic Age. David is also a scientist and commentator on public policy. His non-fiction book *The Transparent Society: Will Technology Make Us*

David Brin (Author, Scientist & Public Speaker)

Choose Between Freedom and Privacy?—which deals with issues of openness and liberty in the new wired age—won the Freedom of Speech Award of the American Library Association.

Story is driven by two things—game-playing procedure and depiction technology. You might expect a storyteller like me to resent this, but I don't. As a science fiction author, I have always felt that the constraints of a fictional world—its science and technology background—should play a role in constraining the plot. So when Sega asked me to write the story for *ECCO,* I studied their gameplay and images first before putting down a single word. Games tell stories in much the same way that movies do—with far more attention to gloss and surface than background or character. In a book, the point-of-view character thinks—and shares those thoughts with the reader. In a movie or a game, the hero or heroine is supposed to snarl "Oh yeah?" at the villain and then blow up 100 henchmen. That may change as multi-user dungeons (MUDs) start lacing their worlds with greater layerings of texture and meaning....

Many people think that sci-fi is driven by science—but the real driver is *history:* the long, horrible saga of nasty existence under brutal chieftains and kings and mystics. I look around at a new civilization that is at last based on a principle of personal choice by educated and fiercely independent people. I am awed that we live in an era when, at last, we can all choose to find some way to be creative... or at least to have fun.

Chris Swain on Games as the New Storytellers :::::

Chris Swain (Professor, USC School of Cinema–Television)

Chris Swain is a game designer, writer, and educator. He has worked on games for Microsoft, Sony, Disney, Activision, Acclaim, and many others. He currently consults as a designer for several game developers including Bandalong Entertainment and PopNYC. Chris recently co-authored *Game Design Workshop*—a hands-on design book for aspiring game designers. Chris has had a long-time interest in games for mass audiences. He was leader of the team that created *NetWits* (for the Microsoft Network)—the world's first massively multiplayer online game show. Other notable projects include *Multiplayer Wheel of Fortune* and *Multiplayer Jeopardy!* for Sony Online Entertainment, and *webRIOT*—a mass audience interactive television show—for MTV. He was a founding member of the New York interactive design firm, R/GA Interactive, which grew from 4 to 80 employees during his tenure. He was also a founding member of the convergence technology start-up, Spiderdance, Inc. He serves on the Board of Directors for the Academy of Television Arts and Sciences (the Emmys).

When thinking about story, I like to draw an analogy between games today and films from the early 20th century. Back in the 1910s, films were silent and black-and-white—and the stories were told almost exclusively using techniques borrowed from theater. Those films really didn't make much of an emotional connection with people. If you could have told someone back then that film would become the literature of the 20th century, they would have laughed you out of the room. However, film evolved and became transformed through technical (sound, color) and creative breakthroughs (close-ups, flashbacks, camera movement) to become the most influential storytelling medium that we've ever known. I think of games today like films from 1910—crude from a storytelling perspective, not able to make real emotional connections with people—and I see them becoming transformed through technical and creative breakthroughs into an incredibly powerful storytelling medium.

It's an exciting time to be a game designer because there are many technical and creative avenues for breakthroughs, innovation, and original thought. I may get laughed out of the room today, but I'll go on the record to say that games will become the literature of the 21st century.

Game Story Devices

There are several game-specific story devices—many of which differ from traditional story devices.

Interactivity

Games have a higher level of interactivity than other media. If a consumer only wants a story, they would watch a movie or read a book. In Chapter 6, you'll learn that games depend even more on *gameplay* than story for player satisfaction. Stories by nature are not interactive. They come out of the storyteller's mind and are meant only to be received by the audience passively (and not actively manipulated by the audience in any way). In games, players don't only have to play

Electronic Arts Inc.

In *The Sims 2,* the player takes on the role of storyteller.

the role of the traditional "audience." They can also be co-storytellers—and sometimes, they can even be the *only* storytellers.

Traditional Storyteller Backlash

After the Web became commercial in the mid-1990s, several well-known authors attacked the medium publicly. "I don't want feedback from my readers!" one exclaimed in an interview—appalled at the online forums, in which his fans were discussing details of one of his recent novels. Some traditional storytellers such as authors and filmmakers still have a problem with this. How would they react if their stories were made into games that allowed players to take part in the storytelling process?

Bantam Books

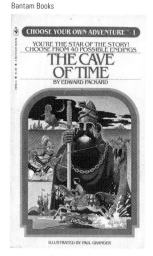

The *Choose Your Own Adventure* book series allowed readers to choose different paths within one story. The first book in the series, *The Cave of Time* (written by Edward Packard), was made into a computer game for the Apple II and Commodore 64 in the mid-1980s.

Non-Linearity

Linear stories follow a physical and temporal straight line—beginning with the most distant events and ending with the most recent. Games do not have to follow a linear storyline. This is tied to the apparent freedom of choice attributed to the players, who might take any number of paths through the game.

For a simple example of a non-linear story, consider the *Choose Your Own Adventure* book series—which provided the reader with several choices (represented by page numbers) in the book at certain moments in the story. The reader could take any combination of paths and experience the story differently each time. This idea most closely resembles an interactive game experience.

Non-Linearity in Film

Filmmakers and authors have played with non-linearity. The structure of Quentin Tarantino's *Pulp Fiction*—in which several interconnecting storylines (each related to a specific set of characters) are presented out of sequence—gives the impression that time is not running in a "straight line." Tom Tykwer's *Run Lola Run* provides three different possible paths the main character could take in the story—one right after another; the film also pauses on characters and shows images of how their lives differed depending on the particular path taken by the main character. The screen in Mike Figgis' *Timecode* is divided into four quadrants, each of which follow parallel storylines. All four storylines can be followed by the audience visually, but only one audio track can be emphasized at a time. Director Figgis has physically "performed" live remixes of the audio tracks during some screenings to give audiences a completely different storytelling experience. Christopher Nolan's *Memento* is composed of a series of scenes that run in reverse order—so that the film begins with the final chronological scene and ends with the first one.

Even though some filmmakers have provided the audience with unique non-linear experiences, there is no way for individuals in the audience to choose which paths to take within the film itself. Therefore, the audience is still engaging in a passive experience. This is due to the linear medium of film—which must run from beginning to end on celluloid film or video tape. The DVD format allows for interactivity—but this has so far been utilized for the bonus features associated with the film, and not the film itself.

Player Control

Players have the ability to manipulate the game in some way—in sharp contrast to an audience watching a movie or a television show. The game's story can change based on who's playing the game. In this way, players can be storytellers in games—something they cannot do in books and movies.

A common form of player control involves *character customization* (discussed in Chapter 5), where players create their own characters with personalized features. Players are also given the ability to choose *paths* to take in the story. Although there are a finite number of possible story paths within a game, the mere fact that the player can make choices in the game means that the player is involved in the creation of a custom plot. Players can also often build their own versions of a game with the use of *world-building* tools—which allows them to take on the role of game developer as well as storyteller. Finally, multiplayer games often allow players to *communicate* within the game itself—which adds unpredictable behavior patterns and dialogue to the game. (See Chapter 5 for a more detailed discussion of character dialogue.)

ORIGIN Systems, Inc.

MMOGs such as *Ultima Online* allow for player control—including the ability to customize player characters.

Persistence

Persistent-state worlds and *MMOGs* were discussed in Chapter 3. How does story relate to these worlds? Traditional narrative doesn't apply. You cannot guide the player through the story. Instead, you create the environment (see Chapter 7) and provide options for the players—but *they* create the real story. A persistent-state world is really a playground!

Story in the traditional sense can be seen as the backdrop or framework associated with the game, while all the details are supplied by the players. This idea becomes more obvious when the game is replayed. Games often have *replayability*—which means that they can be played to the end, replayed (usually many times), and still provide an enjoyable (and unique) experience each time around. The adventure genre, discussed in Chapter 3, has little replay value—in part because it is heavily focused on traditional storylines and puzzle-solving (where there can only be one solution). But most games are developed with replay value in mind. Players get more play time for their money, and they get to experience different story angles every time they play.

In games, the storyteller role isn't always filled by those who create the game. The players themselves play an important role in the storytelling process. Knowing this, it's important for game developers to avoiding overwriting the story. For example, players don't need extraneous dialogue or narrative that holds up the game and takes players away from truly participating in the story themselves.

Warren Spector on the Player as Storyteller:::::

Warren Spector received a B.S. in Speech from Northwestern University and an M.A. in Radio-TV-Film from the University of Texas. In 1983, just shy of his PhD in Communication, Warren worked on a variety of boardgames, RPGs, choose-your-own-adventure books, and novels, with Steve Jackson Games (where he rose to Editor-in-Chief) and at TSR, which he joined in 1987. Warren entered the world of electronic games with Origin Systems in 1989, co-producing *Ultima VI* and *Wing Commander* and producing *Ultima Underworld 1* and *2*, *Ultima VII: Serpent Isle*, *System Shock*, *Wings of Glory*, *Bad Blood*, *Martian Dreams*, and others. In 1997, after a year as General Manager of LookingGlass Austin and producer on *Thief: The Dark Project*, Warren started Ion Storm Austin. He was project director on Ion's award-winning action/RPG, *Deus Ex*—published in June 2000 and reissued in a 2001 Game-of-the-Year edition and, in 2002, as *Deus Ex: The Conspiracy on PS2*. As Studio Director, he oversaw development of *Deus Ex: Invisible War*, released in December 2003, and *Thief: Deadly Shadows*, released in June 2004.

Warren Spector
(Studio Director,
Ion Storm)

The biggest stumbling block for people thinking about story and games is failing to recognize the centrality of the player. Most narrative forms are vehicles of expression for authors. Games, at their best, are different, allowing a level of collaboration between creator and consumer that's completely unprecedented. Everything in a game story is driven by player choice, by player action. If what you want to do is impose a narrative on your players, you might as well write a novel or make a movie. What that means is that you have to focus on the consequences of player decisions. You have to think in terms of active verbs, rather than passive ones (i.e., the player *does* things; the game doesn't do things *to* players). You should focus on story as it contributes to player experience rather than on story as a vehicle for communicating ideas to players. It's easy to lose sight of this kind of thing when you're working out a game story with your team; paradoxically, players often get lost in the shuffle of creativity.

Collaboration

The multiplayer game mode introduced in Chapter 3 makes it possible for players to engage in *collaborative* storytelling. This is most pronounced in massively multiplayer games in which thousands of players could conceivably personalize their character roles, introduce new plot points, and modify the environment itself, all while playing the game. Collaboration is similar to interactive theatre—where the players are performers improvising with each other and with the audience itself. As character and game-world customization become more sophisticated, developers may play an even more "hands-off" role in these games—and the players may take over as the primary storytellers. A collaborative storyline could be initiated by the game development team, and the paths of the story might be added by the players. As players become more involved in this storyteller role, the line could blur between developers and players. This phenomenon is much like a *prosumer* effect (a term coined by futurist Alvin Toffler), where consumers (players) and producers (developers) become one and the same.

A story tree is used in collaborative storytelling to map out different possible paths in a scene.

A simple model for collaborative fiction is a *story tree*. You can experiment with this model easily. Let's say Author A writes a few paragraphs of a story. Authors B and C pick up where Author A left off and write the continuation of the story (with or without knowing what the other is writing). Authors D and E write the continuation of B, and so on. Multiple paths are created, and the authors have engaged in a collaborative writing experience. In a more sophisticated and organized model, a theme and set of characters are created before the writing process starts. The online world is a great place to find countless examples of collaborative storytelling—including art (virtual graffiti walls), music (jams, remixes), and stories (hypertext trees, blog entries).

Why not create collaborative games? In a possible collaborative game scenario, players could develop plots that make up possible paths in the game—much like a story tree. A very basic example would involve starting off with a story (just like Author A does with the tree). Authors B and C (and more) consider all possible decisions a player character could make in the game—and so on. This could be done for all possible player characters in the game—who may be introduced at the very beginning. Taking an adventure-style opening and a "hero" player character as an example: A soldier has been left for dead on a battlefield in the middle of a vast desert wasteland. The soldier awakens, unable to remember anything that has happened. There are several objects lying nearby (weapon, rope, canteen, satchel) and some sounds in the distance. At this point, Authors B and C (and maybe others) decide for each object what will happen if the soldier either picks it up, uses it (fires weapon, drinks from canteen, etc.), throws it, combines it with another object, and so forth. Other authors might decide to focus on other aspects of the environment (sounds in the distance, surroundings) in order to anticipate what a player might want to do. Notice that the idea of collaborative storytelling is connected to the characters in the story. Most game storytelling is *character-driven,* in which the stories revolve around the characters' actions. This is because players often inhabit the role of the game characters, and the decisions they make through these characters enable them to play the game.

Storytelling Consistency

The most challenging aspect of the storytelling process is *consistency:* tying myriad threads together so that they all make sense—and tying them together at the right moment in the plot.

— David Brin
(Author, Scientist & Public Speaker)

Immersion

Game storylines play a significant role in what is known as game *immersion*—in which the story, characters, and gameplay are so powerful and engaging that the players find themselves deeply caught up in the game world. Valve's *Half-Life* and Square Enix's *Final Fantasy* both have strong, emotional storylines. Infocom's text-adventure *Zork* (inspired by *Colossal Cave*) and the graphically-rich *Myst* are also extremely immersive games because they create an atmosphere and a mood that is rich and consistent. The experience of roaming through the graphically-rich yet uninhabited environment in *Myst*—while putting together the missing details of a mysterious story—can elicit feelings of dread and anticipation. Developing effective game environments is discussed further in Chapter 7.

The concept of immersion was originally introduced in Chapter 3 with regard to MMOGs. In massively multiplayer mode, the social interaction between players (which sometimes can involve discussions of non game-related topics such as the news headlines of the day or new movies that have just been released) can take the players "out of character" and out of the game world itself. In this case, player *immersion* is compromised. If indeed players often feel that the storylines in RPGs are of highest importance, than this can be a big problem in MMORPGs (which are the most popular type of MMOG).

In *Puzzle Pirates,* players continue to stay in-character by maintaining "pirate-speak" during in-game chats.

Three Rings Design, Inc.

Cinematics

Another way immersion can be compromised in a game might be surprising to the film industry, since it's a device that's borrowed from linear media. In Chapter 1, you learned that cinematics were introduced in the arcade era as mini-movies that were created to "reward" the player for completing difficulty levels in *Ms. Pac-Man. Cinematics* are sequences that run like movies, usually at the beginning or end of a game. *Cut-scenes* are mini-movies that run within the game. The goal of a cut-scene is to either develop characters, introduce new environments, advance the plot, or set out goals for a new section in the game. The assumption in the film business is that these "cinematic" scenes allow players to become immersed in the game, just like an audience might get emotionally involved in a film. However, this is not necessarily the case. If players have been actively playing the game—making decisions, solving problems, communicating with characters, or engaging in some game-related action—a cut-scene introduced at the wrong time (e.g., right in the middle of real-time combat) could be a disaster for the player's enjoyment of the game. Instead of providing the total emotional involvement this same scene might provide during a film, it could ironically have the opposite effect.

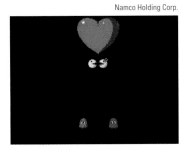

Namco Holding Corp.

Ms. Pac-Man may have been the first arcade game to use cinematics as "rewards" for completing difficulty levels.

Cinematic Inconsistency

Imagine the contrast of being able to make decisions—only to have those decisions taken away from you as you watch your own character act in a specific way. The contrast could actually result in unintended laughter. When playing *Grand Theft Auto: Vice City* for the first time, I was having difficulty controlling the motorcycle driven by Tommy Vercetti (the main character), and the poor guy was bumping into poles and flying off the cycle half the time, only to bravely get back up and try again. But when he walked into various buildings and met with the seedy drug dealers, the cut-scenes took over—and he became "cool" and composed (not the bumbling character I had created)! Not only was I eager to get back to playing the game instead of watching a "movie," I was laughing uncontrollably during the cut-scenes because of the apparent split-personality disorder of my character! The key to the "cut-scene" problem is that it's a non-interactive sequence. If a game is a form of interactive entertainment, the introduction of elements that do not allow for interaction (as defined earlier in this chapter) might no longer feel like a game at all to the player.

:::::Story Layers in *Earth & Beyond*

Electronic Arts Inc.

To understand how we increase tension in *Earth and Beyond*, we need to look at the plot in a different way. The following outline tells the story of the shard: who has it, who stole it, who wants it back, and so on. Control of the shard is simply what organizes this level of the story. This is the plot. Sometimes writers call this the A-story. If *Earth and Beyond* were a fairy tale, we could leave the story like this and call it successful:

Act I The Search for the Shard [excerpt]

Story Step 01   The shard is missing

Story Step 02   The loss of the shard brings Kahn back to Vega

Story Step 03   The search for the shard forces Merjan to admit Antares

Kahn blockades Gallina

New factions are proposed by Ariad, Cassel, and Loric

Story Step 04   Herrera steals the shard for deWinter

Story Step 05   Kahn attacks Cygni; Herrera informs on Infiniti

The trouble is we've been telling stories for a long time now and fairy tales are too simple for most people. The technology of writing has gotten more sophisticated.

So how did writers make stories more sophisticated and satisfying? There are a hundred ways to analyze this, but here's a simple one: To keep up, writers didn't mess around with the plot. Fairy tales have worked for centuries. Why try to fix what isn't broken? No, writers left the plot alone, but they added another layer to the story. A lot of times this is the personal side of a plot, the hero's perspective or problem, relative to the plot. In Act 1, we added MacGregor's story (see below) to make the plot more personal. Specifically, we added MacGregor's personal struggle: Should I do what's right or should I just get rich? Does the shard mean anything to me? That's the second layer in our plot.

You can call this layer a lot of different things—sometimes it's the theme, sometimes it's the hero's journey, sometimes it's the B-story. It makes the story richer by giving it another dimension. And if something changes in the B-story, the A-story notices that and acknowledges the change. MacGregor's attack of conscience on the B-level brings about SolSec, the handoff, and the transfer of 61 Cygni on the A-level. The two levels of the story are separate, but they talk to each other:

Act I The Search for the Shard [excerpt]

Story Step 01   The shard is missing

MacGregor looks for Amah

Story Step 02   The loss of the shard brings Kahn back to Vega

MacGregor agrees to arm Kahn's warriors and dismisses the value of the shard

Story Step 03   The search for the shard forces Merjan to admits Antares

Kahn blockades Gallina

New factions are proposed by Ariad, Cassel, and Loric

MacGregor is shocked by Kahn's blockade

Story Step 04   Herrera steals the shard for deWinter

MacGregor sees the shard is a serious issues; he begins to recruit warriors of his own

Story Step 05   Kahn attacks Cygni; Herrera informs on Infiniti

MacGregor bans the sale of arms to the Centuriata, but tries to avoid an all-out war

So, this is nice, and if *Earth and Beyond* were a novel or a movie, we could just stop here and call the story successful. But the technology of writing is becoming interactive, and this much storytelling just isn't good enough anymore. All it does is tell a story. It doesn't give the players anything to do. We need more now.

So what do writers do about that? One thing you can do is fool around with the A-story, or the B-story, or both. You can write a branching plot, multiple endings, all kinds of complicated story wizardry to let the players determine plot events. These devices give players a role in the plot and a big stake in events, but there's a problem—interactive plotting doesn't usually improve stories. In some cases, an interactive plot actually makes a story too big to manage and can even confuse the main story idea. In other cases, interactive plotting is too demanding technically, requiring a lot of code and art assets that won't be used extensively enough to justify their cost in money, time, and imagination.

On *Earth and Beyond,* we went back to the idea that inspired the creation of the B-story. Rather than mess around with what works, whether the fairy tale or the hero's journey, we leave those two layers alone. In fact, we put them beyond the reach of interaction and beyond the reach of the players and let them go on above game play. But… we add another layer—a third layer of story that the players can affect. This is the faction layer of the story and it's completely controlled by player actions.

At launch there are six player factions at work in the galaxy. These factions give the players choices, choices that are argued by the NPCs. Your class leader offers you a story step mission, presented along with his or her views on the situation. But other NPCs will offer opposing missions that reflect conflicting points of view. The players will choose to follow one NPC over another, to stay within their faction, or to shift to an opposing action. By the time we reach this layer of the story, the search for the shard is a pretext that forces players to make decisions and by extension gives them control over their level, the type of missions they take on, who their friends are, and who their enemies will be. The plot stays the same, but the effects of the plot on the players and the number of player pathways through the story reaches into the hundreds of thousands—all because the story is interactive at the third level:

Act I The Search for the Shard

Story Step 01 The shard is missing

MacGregor looks for Amah

Shinwa: Do I look for the shard or investigate the explorers?

Sha'ha'dem: Do I look for the shard or explore Antares?

Centuriata: Do I fight the Sabine or protect them?

Sabine: Do I look for the shard or help the warriors?

InfinitiCorp: Do I look for Amah or sell guns to the Progen?

EarthCorp: Do I support Infiniti or help the Psionics?

Story Step 02 The loss of the shard brings Kahn back to Vega

MacGregor agrees to arm Kahn's warriors and dismisses the value of the shard

Shinwa: Do I protect the Sha'ha'dem or abandon them?

Sha'ha'dem: Do I lie to the warriors or tell of Antares?

Centuriata: Do I support Kahn or aid the Sabine?

Sabine: Do I help Vinda or spy for Cassel?

InfinitiCorp: Do we arm the Progen or support EarthCorp?

EarthCorp: Do we protect Infiniti or stop Infiniti?

Story Step 03 The search for the shard forces Merjan to admit Antares

Kahn blockades Gallina

New factions are proposed by Ariad, Cassel, and Loric

MacGregor is shocked by Kahn's blockade

Shinwa: Do I attack the Antares or defend the Sha'ha'dem?

Sha'ha'dem: Do I accept the warriors or reject them?

Centuriata: Do I enforce the blockade or help the Sabine?

Sabine: Do I aid the Sabura or aid the Centuriata?

InfinitiCorp: Do I support GetCo or oppose it?

EarthCorp: Do we allow the blockade or oppose it?

Story Step 04 Herrera steals the shard for deWinter

MacGregor sees the shard is a serious issues, he begins to recruit warriors of his own

Shinwa: Do I stay Shinwa or join the Pirates?

Sha'ha'dem: Do I stay with the Sha'ha'dem or join the Mordana?

Centuriata: Do I stay with the Centuriata or join the Sabine?

Sabine: Do I remain with Vinda or align with Cassel?

InfinitiCorp: Do I stay with Infiniti or join EarthCorp?

EarthCorp: Do we support Infiniti or oppose Infiniti?

Story Step 05   Kahn attacks Cygni, Herrera informs on Infiniti

MacGregor bans the sale of arms to the Centuriata, but tries to avoid an all-out war

Shinwa: Do I help the Progen or help the Terran?

Sha'ha'dem: Do I go to Aragoth or go to Antares?

Centuriata: Do I attack Cygni or join the Sabine?

Sabine: Do I help the Sabura or turn them in?

InfinitiCorp: Do I defend Cygni or sell guns to the Progen?

EarthCorp: Do I fight the Red Dragons or join them?

Now there are a lot of choices in the game and there's a lot for players to decide—all because of this third story layer. And that's why the factions [e.g., InfinitiCorp, EarthCorp—controlled by players] are important. They give players choices. In fact, the factions carry virtually all of the story interactivity we have here.

So we have an A-story, a B-story, and a player's story. Terrific. Now, how do we control it? How do we increase and decrease drama with all these layers of story? Well… the same way we increase and decrease drama in any other story. Drama increases as the characters involved face tougher and tougher decisions with more and more at stake. If we wanted to increase the drama of the A-story, we would raise the stakes in the A-story. If we wanted to increase the drama in the B-story, we would give MacGregor a few more high-risk decisions. But what we're concerned with is that third layer of story, the factional layer, because that's the layer the players will experience and control first-hand. What we would like is a tense A-story and a tense B-story, and a very, very wonderful tense third layer—because that's what the players will feel. By asking the players to make tough choices, we raise the stakes on their story layer, and that's how this game gets more dramatic.

—*Chris Klug (Owner, Brown Bear Entertainment)*

Machinima: Storytelling Convergence?

Machinima is a blend of "machine" and "cinema." The machine in this case is a game engine (discussed further in Chapter 10) that is used by filmmakers to create an animated movie instead of a game. From the film industry side, machinima can be seen as an example of technology convergence—adopting a tool originally created for game development to make movies. From a game-industry perspective, machinima takes cinematics and cut-scenes even further away from the game experience itself and toward linear storytelling.

Strange Company

Machinima pioneer Strange Company's *Steelwight* is a tale of "swashbuckling heroes and Victorian streets where monsters lurk in places of power... "

The low development costs associated with using game engines to make animated movies adds machinima to DV technology as another revolution in independent film-making. Compared to a computer-generated animated film such as *Toy Story* or *Final Fantasy*, it costs next to nothing to produce a full-length machinima feature. Strange Company founder and artistic director Hugh Hancock was inspired to blend game engines with cinema after being involved in player communities that modified the original *Quake* game by developing in-game mini-movies. (Player communities and game mods [modifications] are discussed in Chapter 12.) According to Hancock, "Machinima is important because it opens up a third way of creating films. Steering a course between digital video (quick to produce but restricted) and animation (unlimited but extremely slow), Machinima opens up entire genres of filmmaking to hobbyists and low-budget filmmakers. Now, rather than just making *Clerks*, upcoming Kevin Smiths can cut their teeth on making films with the scope of *Star Wars* or *The Matrix*."

Scripted Event

Another storytelling device is a *scripted event*—a brief sequence that is either time-based or triggered by a player's actions. These contain either small portions of dialogue (discussed in Chapter 5) or action, and their purpose is to either build character, convey backstory, or redirect the player toward a new goal.

What movies remind the audience that it's "just a movie"? If you've ever seen unintentional bad acting before, you were probably reminded of this. However, some movies specifically reference the real world—often through popular culture and expressions of the time. The *Scream* series references other horror movies and contains "inside jokes" for those who are familiar with these films. There are other examples of entertainment that purposely remove the "fourth wall." This is when characters in a story talk directly to the audience (also called an *aside*).

Games Need More Than Story

Like a film, a game is a powerfully dramatic medium—one that requires ideas and vision in order to move the audience, whether they are players or viewers, emotionally and intellectually. Growing up, we are not really taught how to communicate ideas using dynamic systems in the same way that we are taught to write essays or tell stories. But there is a lot we understand about the world that can't be told using linear media. Game systems offer us a new way of making stories and communicating this type of knowledge.

One thing that I find over and over with the games I play, and with the games I've worked on—including student games—is how difficult it is, and yet how important it is, that the *mechanics* (associated with gameplay) drive the storytelling. The mechanics provide structure—objectives, procedures, and rules; these create the action and the play. But there needs to be dramatic elements that give context and meaning to that play, overlaying and integrating these structural elements.

A gratuitous story, not supported by the mechanics, won't add to the experience; that's pretty clear. But when dramatic elements are completely integrated into the mechanics, the player's connection to the game can be extreme. I'm thinking of my own obsession with a particular *Sims* family. I could tell you their story, but it would take too long. Suffice it to say that it was epic and tragic, and other than some custom skins and my own imagination, they emerged completely from the dynamics of the system in play.

— Tracy Fullerton,
Assistant Professor
(Electronic Arts Interactive Entertainment Program,
USC School of Cinema–Television)

Game Storytelling & Documentation

Once you have come up with a game story, you will need to incorporate components of the story into several game documents (discussed in more detail in Chapter 10). These documents help to organize your ideas and to clearly convey them to others. The *concept* document is intended to express the basic vision of the game, and it includes the game's premise. Sometimes, this document is expanded into a proposal—which provides more detail on the game's story and characters. The *story treatment* is usually a one- to two-page summary of the game's overall storyline. It should not be a detailed discussion of all the possible paths that characters can take in the game. Instead, it should incorporate the story's theme, structure, and a few significant plot elements. A standard script containing dialogue might be created for cinematics and cut-scene producers/dialogue sessions, while a story tree or flowchart might be created to map out the story's structure. Finally, the *game design document* provides a reference for the development team and includes plot elements related to gameplay.

Gameplay: The Real Storytelling Device?

You've learned how to tell stories in the traditional sense, and you've learned how stories can be very different when applied to games. This difference is tied-in directly with gameplay. I would argue that gameplay is the essential storytelling component in games—a non-traditional device that allows the player to take on the role of storyteller. This is why writers are often not hired to write game stories. Instead, game designers often get this privilege—usually because it's more important for a game to incorporate compelling challenges than a well-crafted plot. Writers interested in getting involved in this industry should make sure they have a clear understanding of gameplay. The assumption in the game industry is, "What does a writer know about gameplay?" If a Hollywood screenwriter were hired to write a game, do you think "gameplay" would be on this person's mind? Instead, the screenwriter might submit a traditional script containing one linear storyline. As more writers with game knowledge get involved in the game industry, there will most likely be more opportunities for them. Before we get to Chapter 6, which focuses on gameplay, Chapter 5 will look at specific elements of creating game characters.

chapter 4

:::CHAPTER REVIEW:::

1. Members of the film industry are beginning to migrate to the game industry, in part due to revenue reports depicting the game industry as fast-growing, Several game studios are also attempting to recruit members of the "Hollywood" community. Discuss the differences between these two forms of entertainment (film and games), and provide three examples of how the intersection of these two forms of entertainment could change game content, structure, and delivery.

2. There has been great debate in the game industry on which is more important—story or interactivity. Do you feel one is more important than the other? If so, which one—and why? What might you do to balance story and interactivity in a game?

3. Why are game developers utilizing classic story structures such as Hollywood's three-act structure and Campbell's "hero's journey" scenario? These classic structures provide a good base for game story development, but their somewhat predictable formulas don't necessarily lend themselves to innovative game content. What elements of these story structures do you think work best? How would *you* choose to tell a story through a game environment?

4. Create a premise, backstory, and synopsis for an original game idea that targets either Boomers, Xers, or Millennials. Describe your target market in detail, and outline why you chose to create this sort of content for this group.

5. Expand on your original story idea in the previous question by creating an outline of your story's "acts"—using the *Earth and Beyond* example provided in this chapter. Try to incorporate story layers in your outline by identifying A, B, and C levels.

6. What are some dramatic storytelling devices used in games? Choose one of these devices and discuss how you would make it work within your original game storyline.

7. What role do *cut-scenes* play in a game, and how can they sometimes compromise *immersion*? Choose a cut-scene from a pre-existing game, and identify three reasons why you feel the cut-scene is being used in the game. Is the cut-scene necessary? Does it compromise immersion? If you were on the game-development team and were told that the scene had to be removed, what would have to be done in order to ensure that the "reasons" for the cut-scene were still being fulfilled? Create a synopsis for an original cut-scene and discuss why the cut-scene is essential to the game experience.

8. How is *machinima* an example of industry convergence? What are the two industries involved, and how do they intersect? How does this new way of creating games affect game storytelling? Can you think of another way to intersect two industries so that storytelling is affected?

9. How have some filmmakers experimented with non-linear storytelling (in a linear medium)? Choosing one of the films mentioned in this chapter (or another film that you feel experiments with non-linear story structure), discuss how you would create a game adaptation of that film. How might the game medium expand the filmmaker's vision?

10. Choose a "tabletop" (especially card or board) game with a distinct setting or premise. (If you want to see some cleverly-designed "tabletop" games, go to Funagain Games at www.funagain.com.) After familiarizing yourself with the game, discuss how you would adapt the game to electronic form. What story elements would you expand upon in order to create a more enriching, immersive experience for the player?

CHAPTER

5

Characters:
creating the identity

key chapter questions

- How are game characters different from characters in other media?

- What are *avatars* and how do they relate to player identity?

- How does visual character development differ from other forms of character development in games?

- What are some character types and *archetypes,* and how do they relate to story structure?

- What are several purposes of dialogue in games?

In Chapter 4, you learned how storytelling devices can be used in games to enhance players' enjoyment and emotional involvement. What about the characters within the story? What sort of impact can game characters have on the player? The importance of characters in a game environment can add a personal dimension to a player's experience. Unlike characters in other entertainment media, game characters can interact directly with the player—who might also play a character role. This chapter introduces all aspects of game character development—including how they look, act, move, feel, and communicate.

Game Characters

Game characters are either player characters or non-player characters (also known as NPCs). Sometimes, one player can control several player characters (often in a group, such as sports teams or military troops). Of course, some games do not contain any characters at all. This is the case with most puzzle games—in which the player only interacts with the puzzle and does not take on the role of any character. As discussed in Chapter 4, these games also often do not have stories. Many games, however, contain characters that are controlled by the players or the game itself.

Tomb Raider's Lara Croft is a player character.

Player Characters & Avatars

Player characters are characters or other entities in a game world that are controlled by the players. When a player controls only one character, that character is called an *avatar*. The direct connection between the player and the avatar can sometimes result in a player assigning personal identity to the avatar. This can be more pronounced if the avatar displays realistic features and actions. When you play games, do you feel that you have actually taken on the role of the character in the game? Do you sometimes see some of yourself in the character?

A player can control several characters. This is common in strategy games and process simulations, in which players often manage sets of resources that include several characters. Most of the time, these characters are all fairly distant from the player—and no emotional bonding occurs. Some of the time, one particular character stands out as a main character—becoming the player's avatar. There are also a few games in which the player bonds with all of their characters. This happens most often in role-playing games (RPGs) involving guilds, in which every member of the group might connect with the player emotionally. Intelligent Systems' *Fire Emblem* is a strategy RPG in which all units have a distinct history and personality. Death is permanent, so a player is emotionally encouraged to take care in combat to prevent fatalities.

Parasocial Interaction

An interesting effect known as *parasocial interaction* can occur when an audience becomes so attached to characters that they actually believe the characters are real people. This effect has occurred with audience members who bond strongly with characters and the make-believe world they observe week after week on television series. "Evil" characters are hated by these audience members, who often send threatening letters addressed to the characters (not the actors). Parasocial interaction is extremely powerful—even though these audience members are not taking on the roles of any of the show's characters and are only "passive" viewers. Couldn't this type of character bonding be even stronger in games?

Cocktail Party Character Quotations

I was at a cocktail party shortly after *The Space Bar* shipped. The woman I was chatting with started telling me about a game she'd been playing and how much she was enjoying it. Then she began to quote characters in the game—my game! Hearing my writing being repeated was astounding. All those hours of sitting at a computer, writing, rewriting, wondering if it worked, all melted away. I had reached her, given her a meaningful experience, and she wanted to share that with someone else. It's magic.

— *Patricia A. Pizer, Game Designer*

Non-Player Characters (NPCs)

Non-player characters (NPCs) are characters in a game world that are not controlled by players. Instead, these characters are created and controlled by the game's artificial intelligence (AI) engine. An NPC can range from a merchant who sells you food to a monster you must defeat.

Lionhead Studios

NPC creature from *Black & White: Creature Isle.*

Character Types

There are five common character types used in games: animal, fantasy, historical, licensed, and mythic:

- **Animal:** Sonic the Hedgehog is an example of an *animal* character. Common in games that are marketed toward families or children, animal characters are often given human characteristics (e.g., Sonic's sneakers) in order to allow for more identification between player and character. Animal protagonists were popularized in animated cartoons that catered to children—with characters such as Bugs Bunny and Mickey Mouse. Not all games featuring animal protagonists are family-oriented. (See the adult-oriented *Conker's Bad Furr Day,* discussed later in this chapter.)

- **Fantasy:** Characters that do not have counterparts in the real world fit into the *fantasy* category. Examples include Mario, Luigi, Wario (Mario's nemesis), Lara Croft, Duke Nukem, and Pac-Man. This category covers any character that was specifically created for a game—and not licensed from a pre-existing source.

- **Historical:** Characters that are *historical* have distinct counterparts in the real world—but often from past history. Political and military games focusing on real-world events contain historical characters—including Benjamin Franklin, General Lee, Cleopatra, William the Conqueror, and William Wallace in games such as *Ally's Adventure* and *Medieval: Total War*.

- **Licensed:** A *licensed* character also already exists in the real world—but in a pre-existing medium. These characters are usually fantasy-based, but already have established recognition in literature, comic books, films, and television. James Bond, Frodo (*Lord of the Rings*), Neo (*The Matrix*), Harry Potter, and Bart Simpson would be examples of licensed characters. When licensing pre-existing characters, game developers do not have to start from scratch on character development—whether visual, personality, or verbal.

- **Mythic:** Characters in the *mythic* category have counterparts in mythology from all over the world. Many role-playing games such as *Neverwinter Nights* and *EverQuest* make use of standard mythic characters—including orcs and trolls. *Age of Mythology*—a mythology-specific strategy game—contains the Cyclops, Medusa, and other characters from Greek, Egyptian, and Norse mythology.

These character types can be either player characters or NPCs. Have you noticed that you gravitate toward games that focus on a certain character type? In addition to these broad character types, there are classic, specific character types that are often used in games and other media. Let's take a look at these types of characters in detail.

Classic Character Archetypes

Chapter 4 introduced the idea of psychologist Carl Jung's *collective unconscious*—which forms the basis for our connection to certain universal character types. These archetypes are used in all entertainment media to heighten the audience's connection to the story.

Namco Holding Corp.

Xenosaga

Shion Uzuki is the hero in *Xenosaga Episode I: Der Wille zur Macht*.

Hero

In Chapter 4, you learned that the *hero* archetype is the central character in a single-player game. When you create a hero character, keep in mind that the hero will be the player's avatar—and the player needs to identify and bond with this character. Chapter 4 also discussed Campbell's "hero's journey" *monomyth* and the process by which the hero transforms during this classical story form. The hero is always presented with a problem toward the beginning of the story, and he embarks on a physical or emotional journey to eventually solve this problem. The hero performs most of the action in a story and assumes the majority of risk and responsibility. Luke Skywalker is a classic example of a hero character.

Shadow

The *shadow* is an extremely important character—representing the hero's opposite, often the ultimate evil character in a story. The shadow could be the adversary who is responsible for the hero's problem. Sometimes this character remains hidden until the story's climax, which can add to the story's dramatic tension. Sometimes the shadow represents the "dark side" of the hero. This was explored symbolically in Robert Louis Stevenson's classic, *Dr. Jekyll & Mr. Hyde.* Darth Vader is another example of a shadow character—someone who has gone completely over to the "dark side."

Electronic Arts Inc.

Command & Conquer's Kane is a shadow character.

Mentor

The *mentor* is a character who often guides the hero toward some action. In Chapter 4, you learned that the mentor character provides the hero with the information needed to embark on the "hero's journey." The mentor is often an older "advisor" character—someone who might have been in the hero's shoes at one time, who can provide the hero with wisdom learned from that experience of making a similar journey. Obi-Wan Kenobi and Yoda are examples of mentor characters. In the *Civilization* series, the advisors (military, domestic, culture, science) provide warnings and hints to the player. Sometimes a mentor character can give bad advice to the hero—deliberately leading the hero down the wrong path. In the tutorial for *Black & White*, a devilish advisor only gives evil advice to the player.

Eidos Interactive/Core Design Limited

Werner Von Croy

Lara Croft's former mentor, Werner Von Croy.

Square Enix Co. Ltd.

The Chocobo are ally characters from *Final Fantasy Tactics*.

Turbine Entertainment/Vivendi Universal Games

Skeleton guardians block the entrance to a barrow in *Middle-Earth Online*.

Eidos Interactive

The Trickster from *Thief*.

Allies

Allies are characters that help the hero progress on the journey and also assist the hero with tasks that might be difficult or impossible to accomplish alone. Han Solo and Chewbacca are examples of allies.

Guardian

The *guardian* blocks the progress of the hero by whatever means necessary—until the hero has proven his or her worth. A classic guardian character is the sphinx who guards the gates of Thebes in the Greek play *Oedipus*. In order for the hero (Oedipus) to gain access to Thebes, he must answer the famous riddle posed by the sphinx. The guardian character tests the hero. By answering the riddle correctly, the hero has proven to be worthy of continuing on the journey. Sometimes the guardian character is the shadow's henchman. The guardian could also be a "block" that exists within the hero's mind—such as self-doubt, fear, discomfort—that makes the character hesitate to continue on the journey.

Trickster

The trickster is a neutral character who enjoys making mischief. Trickster characters can either cause severe damage through their pranks—which can stop the hero from progressing along the journey—but they are more often simply "jesters" who provide comic relief for the story. Examples of these characters include C3PO and R2D2. These characters can be the hero's sidekicks or even a shadow character.

Herald

The *herald* facilitates change in the story and provides the hero with direction. An example of a herald character is Princess Leia, whose call for help motivates Luke Skywalker to take action toward a specific goal.

In addition to Jungian archetypes, there are other classic character types that are associated with every story—including the *protagonist, antagonist,* and *supporting characters.*

Protagonist

The *protagonist* is the main character. A single-player game centers around this character, and the game's story is told from this character's point-of-view—even if the game is not played in the first-person. The protagonist in *Half-Life*—Gordon Freeman—is central to the action that takes place in the story.

The protagonist must always drive the story forward—*acting* instead of reacting, *making things happen* instead of waiting for them to happen. Any *reaction* on the part of the protagonist is out of the character's control—and the immediate goal in the story then becomes regaining control. For example, a character could be goaded by bullies and lose control—reacting to their taunts by taking physical action (such as throwing a punch at one of the bullies).

The protagonist is unusually strong physically or morally—but not always "good." In fact, the protagonist often has a fatal (or "tragic") flaw. A protagonist's tragic flaw is universal and reflects vulnerability. This makes the character likable and human—allowing the audience to identify and empathize with this otherwise larger-than-life character. The flaw could be in physical form (e.g., paralysis, scarring, stuttering) or appear as a personality characteristic (e.g., greed, stubbornness, envy). Consider any classic Greek or Shakespearian tragedy. In Sophocles' *Oedipus Rex,* the protagonist loses his temper and kills a man (who turns out to be his father). In *Othello,* the flaw is jealousy—as the protagonist is led to believe that his wife has been unfaithful to him, Othello's jealousy is so powerful that it drives him to murder. Even Superman (as discussed in Chapter 4) is greatly weakened when exposed to kryptonite. Your goal is to develop a protagonist that is believable, likable, and flawed—with the ability to grow and transform throughout the story.

Dark Age of Camelot's Herald.

Mythic Entertainment

The Adventure Company

Sherlock Holmes is the protagonist in *The Mystery of the Mummy.*

The Adventure Company

Kate Walker is the protagonist in *Syberia.*

Antagonist

A story's *antagonist* is the opposite of the protagonist. The Jungian archetype conforming to the antagonist is known as the *shadow* (or "opposite"). This does not mean that the antagonist is "bad." The protagonist and antagonist could simply have opposing views—political (liberal vs. conservative), ethical (privacy vs. security), or lifestyle preferences (business vs. family). As you learned in Chapter 4, stories derive dramatic tension from conflict—and this opposition between the protagonist and antagonist is one form of conflict.

When the protagonist and antagonist want the exact same things (e.g., love interest, precious stone, or leadership of a clan), they become linked together in the story. This device is known as the *unity of opposites,* and it makes any conflict or competition more relevant.

Players can become attracted to an evil force in a game. Here are some types of evil antagonists that often appear in stories:

Sephiroth represents the antagonist in *Final Fantasy VII.*

Square Enix Co. Ltd.

Transformational

A *transformational* antagonist is an *antihero* character who could have been a protagonist. This antagonist receives punishment at the end of the story to satisfy the audience's need for justice. Stephen King's *Carrie* is a great example of this: As a reaction to being victimized by her classmates, the protagonist uses her telekinetic power to destroy. Although the anger and humiliation faced by this character might stir up feelings of empathy in the audience, her power causes the deaths of innocent people. In the process of destroying others, she is killed—and the audience feels some sense of relief. (The ending, however, suggests she may come back from the grave… Stay tuned!)

Nintendo of America, Inc.

Mario's antagonist is the greedy Wario—with an upside-down "M"!

Mistaken

Mistaken antagonists are characters who the audience initially thinks are villains—but they turn out to be innocent. These characters are very popular in murder mysteries and crime dramas. Sometimes a mistaken antagonist could turn out to be the protagonist!

Exaggerated

Exaggerated antagonists are those who are larger-than-life, bizarre, and sometimes even comedic villains who might even dominate the story because they are often more interesting than the protagonist. Examples of these exaggerated antagonists include Dr. Evil in *Austin Powers*—and most of the villains in *Batman* (e.g., Joker, Riddler, Cat-Woman).

Realistic

Realistic antagonists are the opposite of exaggerated—and the toughest to create. They are mild-mannered, fairly "normal" characters (which can sometimes make them seem a bit creepy—especially if it is revealed that he or she is the "killer next door"). Stories containing realistic antagonists usually also have more colorful protagonists.

Nintendo of America, Inc.

Co-Protagonists

Co-protagonists join forces with the protagonist in a story. These characters often appear in games such as massively multiplayer online games (MMOGs) that require teams. Sometimes these characters do not start out as co-protagonists, but as antagonists. For example, some characters compete with each other for resources. If a natural disaster strikes or a major villain shows up which threatens to deplete everyone's resources, co-protagonists often band together to defeat the larger "evil" (a common enemy). In Chapter 6, you will learn that competitors can sometimes cooperate as well as compete in order to win the game. This can be applied to the roles of protagonist, antagonist, and co-protagonist.

Brothers Mario & Luigi and pals Jak & Daxter are examples of co-protagonists.

Naughty Dog/Sony Computer Entertainment, Inc.

Sony Online Entertainment, Inc.

Supporting Characters

In Chapter 4, you learned about how Act I in a three-act structure introduced a problem to the main character. *Supporting* characters—also known as *pivotal* characters—exist primarily to prevent the protagonist from walking away from this problem. An example of a supporting character is the mentor in Joseph Campbell's "hero's journey" monomyth. The supporting characters often jump-start the action in the story—sometimes even through carrying out the bidding of the antagonist. Think of supporting characters as sets of troops under both your (the protagonist) command *and* your enemy's (the antagonist) command during a military strategy game. These characters bring a variety of viewpoints to the story. They can be your sidekicks or the antagonist's henchmen.

The orc is a supporting character on the side of evil in *EverQuest 2*.

Character Development Elements

Basic character development in a story involves the relationships between characters and the changes they might undergo throughout a story. The elements of the *character triangle* and *character arc* play a significant role in development of character relationships and character change.

Love Triangle

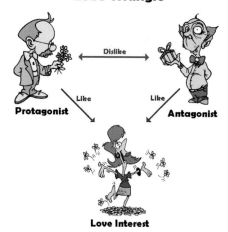

The character love triangle is the most common type of character triangle.

Character Triangle

A *character triangle* forms a powerful three-way relationship between characters in a story. In this relationship, contrasting characters (usually the protagonist, antagonist, and supporting) are connected in threes. The most common example of this is a "love triangle," in which the protagonist and antagonist are both vying for the attention of the same love interest (supporting character). There can be many triangles in a story, and the character's role can change based on each of these triangles. For example, the same protagonist that's involved in a love triangle might also be involved in a career triangle—where the protagonist and antagonist are vying for the same position at a company. Each of these triangles represents subplots in a story and must be connected in some way.

Character Arc

A protagonist rarely changes during the course of a story—but the character always *grows*. Even a passive protagonist learns how to turn the tables on an antagonist and become strong enough to reach a specified goal—growing as a result of the events in the story. The process of character growth and development is called the *character arc.* This arc consists of several levels and is illustrated through a character's behavior rather than monologue or dialogue. Understanding a character's value system is the core of character development. The following character development levels are based on sociologist Abraham Maslow's *hierarchy of needs* model. The levels begin with the smallest unit, the self, and expand to the largest (and most abstract) unit, humanity.

Character Development Levels

Maslow's Hierarchy of Needs.

Level 1: Intrapersonal

In the *intrapersonal* level, the protagonist is only concerned with his or her own needs and thoughts.

Level 2: Interpersonal

In the *interpersonal* level, the protagonist bonds with another character in a one-on-one relationship. This other character could be a lover, friend, colleague, or family member. The protagonist is no longer just looking out for himself or herself, but another character as well.

Level 3: Team

In the *team* level, the protagonist bonds with a small group of characters who have common interests. These characters could be members of the protagonist's circle of friends, family, sports team or activity club. The need to *belong* is fulfilled at this level. An example of this level occurs in many MMOGs that involve the formation of guilds with other players.

Level 4: Community

In the *community* level, the smaller team becomes part of a larger organized network, which could include a neighborhood, city, school, or company.

Level 5: Humanity

In the *humanity* level, the protagonist often goes through what Maslow calls *self-actualization*—spiritual growth that can occur now that the protagonist has achieved comfort, love, and acceptance among a larger community.

Sometimes protagonists can start at a higher level and move down the ladder. Michael Corleone in *The Godfather* is one example. These characters are really anti-heroes or transformational antagonists. The character arc illustrates that the protagonist is either better or worse off from experiences in the story.

Point-of-View

Games usually have specific player *points-of-view (POV)*. Some POVs are seen through the eyes of the player's avatar in first-person perspective, and some allow the player to observe the avatar in third-person perspective.

First-Person POV

In a *first-person point-of-view (POV)*, the player sees through the eyes of the avatar. In a *first-person shooter (FPS)*, the player also sees the avatar's hand holding a weapon in the lower portion of the screen. This POV can sometimes enable the player to bond with the character, because the player steps into the character role physically and cannot observe the avatar separately. However, this POV makes it more difficult for

Crytek/Ubisoft Entertainment

First-person POV in *Far Cry.*

the player to form a mental image of the avatar because the character cannot be seen on-screen. Some developers use cut-scenes and in-game scripted sequences to address this—shifting the perspective of the game so that the avatar can be seen in third-person POV. As discussed in Chapter 4, these sequences can sometimes feel like an interruption and take the player out of the game world. This can be avoided by creating a cinematic sequence as an introduction to the game, and by including images of the avatar in the game interface menu system (discussed further in Chapter 8). Packaging and poster art associated with the game (and usually handled by the marketing department) can also depict images of the avatar. First-person games can also use reflective surfaces (e.g., mirrors) to show the character to the player.

In RPGs that feature a single character, the protagonist is often left deliberately undefined because the character is the player's alter-ego in the game world. The character creation process in RPGs gives the player the freedom to personalize the avatar. In this case, the character becomes the player. In first-person games with a story, the player must become the character—taking on the role of a character such

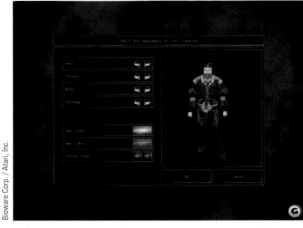

Character creation and customization screens from *Neverwinter Nights* and *Earth & Beyond*.

as *No One Lives Forever's* Cate Archer, in a process similar to acting. Unlike many strategy games and process simulations, first-person games allow you to become the protagonist and get right in the middle of the action.

First-Person Identity in Film

Assuming that a first-person POV could help the audience identify with the protagonist, several filmmakers in the '50s tried this technique. The first and only film shot in first-person POV was *The Lady in the Lake*. Although innovative at the time, audiences didn't relate to the character—partially because they were never able to form a mental image of him. In *Dark Passage*, starring Humphrey Bogart, the film begins with first-person POV (as Bogart, hiding in a garbage can, is dumped out of a truck and rolls down an embankment). The transition is made to third-person POV as we see Bogart's character—but we don't see his face because it is wrapped in bandages. As the bandages are removed, the POV shifts again to first-person—and then permanently shifts back to third-person after the bandages have been completely removed, revealing a new identity. We never see the character's "original" face.

Eidos Interactive/Core Design Limited

Tomb Raider's third-person POV.

Third-Person POV

In *third-person POV*, the player can see the avatar on-screen. This allows the player to retain a mental image of the avatar, but it does not provide the feeling of truly inhabiting the body of a character and seeing the world through the character's eyes. The ability to see the avatar at all times could put the player in the role of *observer* rather than *player character*. However, players often allow themselves to eventually bond with the character on-screen as the game continues. When you create an avatar that will be seen on-screen, it's especially important to ensure that the avatar's look (including color scheme) can be easily differentiated from the rest of the characters on-screen. In third-person action-adventure games, players can often see the game by looking over the character's shoulder.

Since movies are rarely shot in first-person POV, a third-person game often has more of a cinematic feel—and the main characters of a third-person game are often marketed as "movie stars." The character of Lara Croft represents the first attempt at creating a game icon. Cinematic suspense is created by allowing the protagonist to be seen on-screen, especially when players can see a threat—such as an enemy approaching—before the character does. There is also more emotional response when we feel for the hero (rather than becoming the hero).

What's in a Name?

Each of your characters (especially your protagonist) should have a strong, distinctive, and memorable name, which might even reflect the character's personality traits. Here are some examples:

Gordon Freeman (*Half-Life*): The last name indicates a "hero" character—someone who wants or fights for freedom. This has universal appeal.

Max Payne: The possible translation of this name into "maximum pain" suggests someone who is in pain—and might give a great deal of pain to others. Since this character is motivated by revenge over the death of his wife, this name is particularly fitting.

Duke Nuke'Em: This name suggests that the character is the "duke" of "nuking" or "killing" people.

Cate Archer (*No One Lives Forever*): The last name suggests the character is precise and "on target," just like an archer.

Leisure Suit Larry: This name suggest a bachelor character who might have a "Vegas" lounge-lizard style.

Kate Walker (*Syberia*): This is an appropriate name for an adventure character who spends much of the game walking into various buildings, exploring strange rooms, and uncovering hidden secrets.

Fox McCloud (*Star Fox*): This name suggests that this character is clever (as a fox), and spends most of his time in the air rather than on ground.

Master Hand (*Super Smash Bros.*): It's no accident that this character consists of a white glove that is larger than any of the other fighters in the game. Master Hand's moves range from flicking, poking, slamming, swatting, punching, and throwing.

Protoman (*Megaman III*): This name suggests the "first" of its kind—and it is! Protoman was the first robot created by Drs. Light and Wiley together: the prototype of what was to become the Megaman cyborg.

Sam Fisher (*Splinter Cell*): This undercover cop is good at "fishing"—baiting enemies and performing stealthy operations.

Sonic the Hedgehog: The "sonic" moniker is related to the speed of the character, who's faster than the speed of sound!

Viewtiful Joe: Normally an "ordinary Joe," this character can transform into the larger-than-life "Viewtiful Joe"—a virtual superhero who can slow down or speed up time.

Visual Character Development

The physical characteristics of game characters are art-driven, but they also need to correlate with the character's role in the story. For this reason, you need to develop a character's personality before you create the character's appearance. If you were creating a *hero* character, how would you indicate strength while hinting at vulnerability? You might make the character tall and muscular, but you might make the character appear sad. If your character is a *trickster* that starts off as an *ally* but becomes a *shadow,* how would you provide a subtle visual hint that this character is not quite what they seem to be? You could have the character's hands clench into fists periodically, or make their eyes dart around occasionally.

Aspects of a character's physical appearance include gender, age, facial features (including hair and eye color), body type (tall, short, large, small, muscular, flabby, angular, round), skin color, health, and abnormalities or distinctive physical characteristics (moles, acne, nervous ticks). Your character should also have an identifiable pose that differentiates the character from the others. Would players be able to pick your characters out if they were all in shadow?

You should also consider each character's costume—including clothing, armor, and accessories such as shoes,

Sony Online Entertainment, Inc.

"The long and the short of it": Characters from *Everquest 2.*

Sega Corporation

Sonic the Hedgehog has a distinctive color scheme, profile, and pose.

glasses, hats, gloves, and watches. What is the color scheme of the character's costume? If the character is a protagonist and the game is viewed in a third-person perspective, make sure that the character's colors stand out against the environment and are differentiated from the colors worn by other characters in the game.

Are there any props associated with this character? Consider weapons, bags, briefcases, and any other items the character might be carrying. Make sure your character's prop can be identified with the character. A great example of a character prop is the hat belonging to Odd Job in *James Bond;* the hat is only worn by the character and is also used as a weapon.

::::: *Magic: The Gathering—Battlegrounds*: From 2D to 3D

Wizards of the Coast, Inc., Hasbro, Inc., Secret Level, Inc., Atari, Inc.

Magic: The Gathering— Battlegrounds character sheet

Our team worked on *Magic: The Gathering—Battlegrounds* by Atari for Wizards of the Coast. There were many challenges in turning a 2D, turn-based card game into a 3D, real-time, spell-casting/fighting console game. Graphically, the original character cards are created by numerous artists, each with his or her own visual style—and there are thousands of cards, often representing the same creature in three to four different incarnations! It took time to find a graphical interpretation in 3D that satisfied our technical restrictions—as well as the visual expectation the licensor had of the Xbox. And no matter how good the reference materials we received, there was always some nugget of information which was only obtained by talking with the licensor directly and getting at all of the "unwritten" personal histories of the characters and places of *Magic: The Gathering*—things that seem insignificant on the surface, but help tie the world together and remain faithful to the source.

— *Christopher Bretz
(Art Director, Secret Level)*

Techniques

There are several art techniques used in games that help to convey the physical characteristics of game characters. Software associated with these techniques and phases of game art production are discussed in Chapter 10.

Character concept drawings from *Tabula Rasa*.

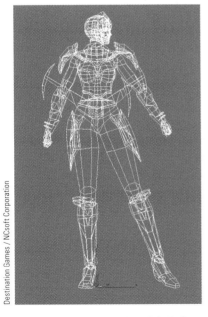

Character wire meshes from *Tabula Rasa*.

Destination Games / NCsoft Corporation

Concept art involves creating several views of a character (front, sides, back) using pencil sketches or 2D digital renderings. A strong profile or silhouette is essential for your character to be instantly recognizable. The color scheme of your character's costume should not be too busy and contain no more than three to four colors. A character should also have distinctive features, which could include particular facial characteristics (Mario's moustache), accessories (Harry Potter's spectacles), or even a hairstyle (Lara Croft's braids).

Modeling involves creating a character's size and stature in 3D (from 2D assets). The modeling process begins with the creation of a 3D wire mesh, to which 2D textures related to the character's skin and costumes are applied.

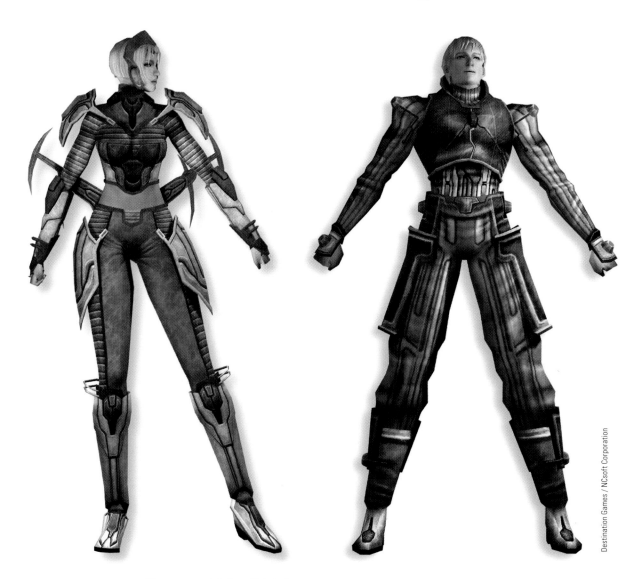

Character models from *Tabula Rasa*.

Destination Games / NCsoft Corporation

The majority of 3D programs use polygons as building blocks because these shapes provide the illusion of 3D on the 2D surface of a screen. The artist starts with a 3D space of infinite size within the computer, defined by its center (or origin). From this point, distance is measured along three axes: X (side to side, or horizontal), Y (up and down, or vertical), and Z (toward and away). A point in space can be defined by providing figures for X, Y, and Z. Once three points are defined, the computer software joins them together and fills in the space—creating a polygon. Models are constructed by joining several polygons to the initial polygon.

Unlike film and television animation, 3D models in games must work in real time. Although computer graphics systems are getting more powerful, they still have limits to the number of polygons they can move around. Modelers attempt to build efficient, low-polygon models. As the hardware becomes faster, artists will be able to work with more polygons, allowing characters to have less angular curves and more detail.

Texturing involves creating 2D surface textures (e.g., skin, costumes) known as *texture maps* that modelers apply to 3D wire meshes. Texture maps are used to give depth to the character's physical appearance. Applying texture maps involves cutting apart, peeling, and spreading a model's parts out flat for painting. Some programs contain an integrated painting program that allows the artist to paint directly onto the model in 3D. In addition to texture maps, other maps can be applied to models—isolating areas of the model that contain the map's property, such as reflection, transparency, glow… and even bumps!

Character movement is conveyed through *animation*. Initially, *rotoscoped animation* allowed an actor's movements to be photographed and traced to add realism to character movement. In most 2D games, animation is restricted to small areas of the screen that are controlled by the player or in response to commands given by the player. These small areas are often referred to as *sprites,* and might contain a character or object that moves over a static or scrolling background. These sprites are animated in short sequences, which isolate an individual action made by a character. The process of 3D animation is similar to stop-frame animation. Using the *keyframing* technique, an animator creates each pose of a movement and sets sequential keyframes to generate animation files. *Motion-capture*—where an animator captures the motions of real people, placing markers on joints of the person in order to track movement and create motion data—is becoming more popular. All of these techniques will be discussed further in Chapter 10.

Mark Soderwall on Game Character Development :::::

Mark Soderwall has worked in the game industry for 14 years. In that time, he has directed and created 3D/2D art content and animation for over 21 published titles. His career began by chance—after winning a Fiction & Fantasy Art competition in California in the late 1980s, right after graduating from high school. One of the judges on the panel owned a game studio that created content exclusively for the Nintendo Entertainment System (NES). Mark became hooked, and gained even more experience and creative understanding of innovative CG tools, techniques, and technologies with every title he completed. This momentum only fueled his resolve to push the limits of CG art and animation in every company he has worked for over the next decade. Mark has held exciting positions in numerous interactive development and publishing studios throughout the industry. These include, Art Director at Virgin Interactive Entertainment, Senior Lead Artist for Electronic Arts, Canada, and his most recent position as Senior Art Director with Atari Inc., Los Angeles. Mark also gives back what he has learned by moonlighting as a professional instructor of advanced 3D character animation and compositing at the Art Institute of California, Orange County.

Mark Soderwall
(Senior Art
Director, Atari)

There are many unique features that set game characters apart (from characters in other media)… One concerns characters in a game setting and how well they stand out from their environment, while still maintaining a visual compliment to the overall visual look and style of the game.

Since most game characters need to interact with their environments (e.g., pick up items, non-player characters), there is always the fear that they may blend or become lost in the scene—making it difficult for the player to readily distinguish the avatar from everything else.

Movies have the ability to place cameras wherever and whenever they need in order to bring focus back to a character. Unfortunately, game environments are usually not afforded such luxuries.

Techniques like distinct lighting, contrasting colors, particle effects, and unique animations can be applied to a game character—helping to create enough distinction to prevent them from becoming too obscure or lost within lush environments or crowded scenes.

:::::Character Development in
Tabula Rasa

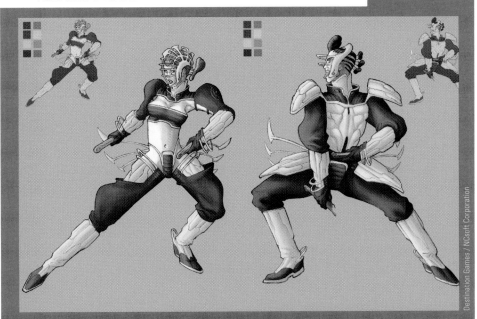

Destination Games / NCsoft Corporation

Character concept art from *Tabula Rasa.*

A meticulous attention to detail marked the development process for the avatar models and creature concepts for *Tabula Rasa.* With a design maxim that required a strong fictional basis for every aspect of the fictional environment, the concept art team found themselves exploring character creation at a fundamental level. In a universe where a mere thought could manifest physical matter, what would that matter look like?

The result of this exploration provides an insight into ergonomic fashion, alien physiology, and the aesthetics of an alternate reality. The clothes worn by the human inhabitants of Sanctuary (shown above) reflect their vocational path of being a warrior of mind, body, or spirit. Where the body-oriented warriors tended to heavy, serviceable garments, the mind-oriented warriors expressed themselves in lighter, softer styles.

This intuitive evolution of physical manifestation can also be found in the creatures known as the "Thrax" (shown in Chapter 10). Their forms are a corruption of what was once a beautiful and angelic race. They evoke an almost demonic presence that is tied to a descent into chaos and destruction. Even the animations of the final models reflect a menacing, disjointed feel. This is consistent with the idea of what would happen to a creature if it gave up its individuality and succumbed to the taint of evil and covetous self-interest.

Additional thought was given to how players would interact with the characters they were role-playing. Unlike many games, the men and women of Sanctuary aren't overly muscular or buxom. This was a conscious decision, in order to increase the sense of connection between player and avatar. It was important that the avatars have proportions more in tune with reality. This small detail may never be widely publicized, but it is certain to be appreciated in some capacity.

Overall, the driving force behind character development was to find a harmonious balance between fantasy and reality—an original conceptual iteration that honored the unique vision of the game's creators. To this end, a variety of artistic and intellectual influences can be seen in not only the sentient beings of the *Tabula Rasa* universe, but also in its environments, architecture, and weapons.

— Starr Long
(Producer, NCsoft)

Electronic Arts Inc.

American McGee's Alice: Not an exact retelling of the classic Lewis Carroll story!

Style

The characters in the game world are often created in a style that fits with the look and feel of the game environment. (More detail on the environment is discussed in Chapter 7.) A consistent character style helps to maintain the game's harmony. In many children's games, for example, the character style might be referred to as "cute." In *Conker's Bad Fur Day*, cute characters were transplanted into an adult-oriented game—complete with vulgar dialogue. The irony worked for the adult audience. If this had been reversed—and a villain in a children's game appeared as an HR Giger-esque alien, this might terrify a young audience! Many artists feel that they have to copy popular styles in order to get noticed. This myth occurs in all areas of entertainment—music, screenwriting, filmmaking—and it couldn't be further from the truth. Exposing yourself to game-art styles is a valid way to learn your craft, but the important thing about style is to make it your own. Art styles used in game worlds are discussed in more detail in Chapter 7.

Verbal Character Development

Narration, monologue, and *dialogue* refer to verbal commentary, discussions, or interactions among any number of characters in a game. The use of verbal communication in a game can occur through voiceover audio (discussed further in Chapter 9) or on-screen text.

Narration

Narration specifically refers to verbal commentary made by the narrator in a game. The narrator could be one of the NPCs in the game, or a special "narrator" character whose role is only to inform the player about the game's backstory or provide unbiased comments on events that are happening in the game. The narrator may or may not appear visually on-screen.

Monologue

A *monologue* is usually a lengthy "speech" given by one of the characters in a game for the purposes of illustrating the character's emotions or personality characteristics—or to reveal that character's inner thoughts. Shakespeare's soliloquies—including Hamlet's angst-ridden "to be, or not to be" speech—are examples of monologue.

Dialogue

Dialogue technically refers to two-person verbal interaction. However, it is used in games to refer to verbal interactions between any number of characters. Keep in mind that characters are a part of the story and should not talk about the story. The events that occur in your story are much more important than what the characters say. The purpose of dialogue is not just conversation. Go to a public place and eavesdrop on a conversation. It will most likely take at least a few moments for you to understand what is being discussed. This is because conversation is *context-specific*—depending almost entirely on the relationship, backgrounds, personalities, and motivations of the speakers. In multiplayer games that allow the players to interact through their characters, the dialogue is often more context-specific (and realistic) because the characters are real people. However, this sort of dialogue often does not move the game forward. In fact, as discussed in Chapters 3 and 4, in-game conversations sometimes do not have anything to do with the game at all. Dialogue created for non-player characters (NPCs), on the other hand, should fulfill the following purposes:

Reveal Character

The dialogue should reveal the character's background—including personality, physical, and social characteristics. (See the end of this chapter for a discussion of incorporating these characteristics into a character synopsis.) Text dialogue will need to reflect any specific vocabulary and choice of words. Each of your characters will have a certain way of talking, so any voice-over dialogue will also need to reflect certain audio speech patterns—such as tone, volume, pace, accent, and any speech abnormalities (like stuttering or lisping). If one of your NPCs is an impatient person, you might want the voice-over artist to speak at a hurried pace and an irritated tone.

Reveal Emotion

Dialogue can reflect any emotion—anger, sadness, happiness, disappointment, excitement. Understand how each character might express any of these emotions. If the impatient character above was always impatient, how would you change the character's tone if they were to become angry or *extremely* impatient?

Advance the Plot

The game story's plot can be advanced through conversations between characters, but this method often sounds forced. Narration is the preferred method of advancing the plot. Some games get a bit tiresome when players have to scroll through endless dialogue between the characters explaining what's going on in the story. Perhaps this could be handled better by having a text-based or voiceover narrator filling players in on the plot. Some well-written character dialogue can advance the plot brilliantly, but this takes a great deal of subtlety and a lot of practice.

Reveal Conflict

A dialogue exchange can reveal that there's conflict happening between the characters in a game. However, a much better way to handle conflict is through the actions of the characters. This will be discussed in more detail in Chapter 6.

Establish Relationships

Dialogue can help establish relationships between the characters. If not written well, this can also be very awkward. You've probably noticed forced dialogue in games where characters say things like, "Remember—you're my brother!" or "Brother John,...", to make it clear to the player that the characters are siblings.

Comment on Action

Some dialogue exists so that characters can comment on or react to the action in the game. Again, this needs to be written subtly to avoid throw-away dialogue such as "Ouch—that hurt!" (unless this is a comedic moment) or "Why do you think Mary hit Bill?"

Dialogue in *Earth & Beyond*

This sample dialogue from Loric (an NPC) shows specifically how game dialogue differs from screenwriting. Game designers need to anticipate all possible dialogue choices that could be made by a player. Note that the following excerpt reads more like a "map" of these possible choices (similar to the story tree discussed in Chapter 4). Loric's dialogue is much more extensive, revealing the character's personality and mood, while advancing the story. The player dialogue, on the other hand, is terse—representing choices rather than revealing the player's personality (which cannot be assumed by the designer). The script reads like a flowchart—with "if/then" statements involving the player dialogue. "If" the player chooses response A, "then" Loric says this set of dialogue:

Electronic Arts Inc.

```
          LORIC                        005T
     Never mind. Why imitate the Ancients and
     their celestial example when you can hang
     around Earth Station, have a Coke, and bore
     yourself into a daze? Why dream when you can
     phase out? You know? You think deWinter is
     doing something to the air here?

[If the Player responds:]

          PLAYER
     I don't know.

          LORIC                        006T
     Breathe in. Go on. It's like there's
     something in it. It's like she's desperate
     to have us think it's wonderful. She owns
     the air, you know.

[Continue after 005]
```

[If the Player responds:]

> PLAYER
>
> Yes.

> LORIC   007T
>
> I think so too. I think she's changing things. Things most people take for granted—like the air. Know how long it's been since I had a breath of independent air? Know how long?

> LORIC   008T
>
> Aw, never mind. I need some money to get to Deneb. Ten credits is all I ask. Will you help me or not?

[If the Player responds:]

> PLAYER
>
> Forget it.

> LORIC   009T
>
> I just want to stand where everything in sight hasn't been bought and sold and already owned by somebody else. What's ten credits to you?

[Continue after 008]

[If the Player responds:]

> PLAYER
>
> I guess I can spare ten credits…

> LORIC   010T
>
> You made the right choice. Be generous to the adventurers. You never know when you might be one yourself.

> LORIC   011T
>
> When I get there, I'll remember you. You and the ordinary people just like you. It'll be different there. Better. I'm sure of it.

[Continue after 009]

Movement

There are several forms of movement that should be considered for all characters:

Signature

A *signature* movement is an action move (usually a gesture) that showcases a character's personality and character type. If an antagonist character (such as a sharp-clawed monster) is supposed to instill fear in the player, you might want to include a signature move that appears foreboding—such as having the monster slice through all objects in its path with its claws.

Nintendo of America, Inc.

In a signature movement, Link gestures with his sword in *The Legend of Zelda.*

Idle

An *idle* movement takes place when the character is "waiting" for something to happen—usually for the player to make a decision that involves that character. Sometimes these idle movements can be humorous. Leisure Suit Larry, for example, holds his breath and changes colors accordingly while waiting for the player to resume control over him.

Walking Cycle

The *walking cycle* is the most basic of character actions, and it reveals much about a character's personality. For example, Mario's comfortable yet energetic walking cycle illustrates his easygoing nature. The importance of reflecting character attributes through movement cannot be overlooked. As discussed earlier, motion capture is one way of accomplishing this.

Background, History & Advancement

Aspects of a character's social background include race, religion, class, home life, education, occupation, skills, relationships with other characters, political views, and hobbies. The concept of character advancement is integral to a game's story, a character's history, and the concept of player control discussed in Chapter 4.

Nintendo of America, Inc.

Mario's walking cycle reflects his personality.

Many MMOGs allow players to create customized character profiles. This is a set of attributes associated with the character, such as name, gender, age, clothing, and skin/eye/hair color. Gender swapping has become a common practice in these games, enabling players to assume identities that they do not get the opportunity to play in the real world.

Race selection screen from *Icewind Dale II.*

Class & Race

In many games, character attributes such as *class* and *race* can be chosen by the player. The MMOG *EverQuest,* for example, allows players to choose from over 14 different attributes—each of which is tied to a unique skill level. Here are some examples of online games and their associated classes or races:

- *World of Warcraft:* human, orc, or tauren (minotaur)
- *Allegiance:* Iron Coalition, Gigacorp, Bios, Belters, or Rixian Unity
- *Starcraft:* Terran, Zerg, or Protoss
- *Return to Castle Wolfenstein:* soldier, medic, engineer, or lieutenant

Skill

Character advancement is usually accomplished through an increase in statistics—such as strength, experience, and skill. Characters in particular classes or races are often further divided into various skill levels. One fighter might be skilled with a sword and another with a bow. Most game characters have at least one special skill or power that is identified with them. If your character fulfills the "hero" archetype, create a skill that fulfills a fantasy. Look at some classic superheroes for examples: Superman has x-ray vision and can fly "faster than a speeding bullet." Spiderman can climb walls and has unusually strong intuition ("spider sense").

When characters advance in *Neverwinter Nights,* they allocate points among dozens of possible skills.

Character Description

In order to get started with character development, you will need to write a *character description* (also known as a *character synopsis*) for each major character. A character description represents a brief summary of a character's life. The purpose of putting together a character description is to explore each of your characters in depth—to understand where they come from and who they are. Think of your characters as real people. (Even if they're fantasy creatures or monsters, try to give them some human characteristics.) How will they react or respond to situations that might have absolutely nothing to do with your story? How will they relate to others in the real world? Elements of a good character synopsis include all the elements discussed in this chapter, such as:

- Name
- Type (class, race, archetype, fantasy/mythic/historical)
- Gender/age
- Physical appearance (body type, height, hair color/style, eye color, skin tone, costume, color scheme, signature pose, profile, gestures, facial expressions, distinguishing marks)
- Background and history
- Personality characteristics (reflect these back onto the character's physical appearance; mood, motivation, nervous ticks, idle moves)
- Vocal characteristics (vocal tone and pace)
- Relevance to story synopsis

The following is a character description of Ariad from *Earth & Beyond*:

> Ariad: Leader of the Jenquai Traders. Young and appears a bit flighty at times—but this is a cover for a shrewd negotiator. Ariad may be described physically as light, airy, flowing, almost elfin. In typical Jenquai fashion, she has spent her life in low-G, and she is unnaturally tall and thin, with long, precise fingers and fragile limbs. She possesses an unearthly grace. Less a trader than an artisan, she sees trade as a vehicle leading to truth, order, and beauty. Typically dresses simply but elegantly, adorning herself with one or two exotic baubles of unsurpassed beauty. She is in her late 20s.

After you complete your character synopsis, summarize each character's physical appearance, personality traits, and relationship to the story in just a few sentences. Use one paragraph per character and identify each character by name. Character synopses and summaries can be incorporated into documentation as part of the planning process. This will be discussed in detail in Chapter 11.

Now that you have learned the basics of game story and character development, it's time to look at what might be the most distinguishing feature of games—the *gameplay* itself. The next chapter focuses on what players actually *do* while playing a game.

1. In what ways can players identify with avatars during a game? What is the significance of being able to customize a player character? If you were to create a character based on yourself, what traits would it possess?

2. In what ways do characters "develop" in games? Discuss all aspects of character development and tie them in with story structure.

3. Choose a character archetype and discuss its significance. Why are archetypes such as these used in games, film, and other media?

4. Name three of your favorite game characters. Why do you like these characters? What are their character types and archetypes?

5. If you were to create a customized character based on yourself, what would it be like? Describe yourself in terms of a game character. What are your physical and personality characteristics, goals, strengths and weaknesses, likes and dislikes, general mood? Discuss other characters that might also appear in the game. (Note: These characters may not necessarily be helpful, but could represent obstacles that prevent you from reaching your goals.)

6. Create a name for an original character. Tie the name into the character's physical and personality characteristics. How does the character name relate to the game's genre and style of play?

7. Write descriptions for three characters associated with an original game idea. At least one character should be a player character. What elements will you include in your character descriptions, and how will the player and non-player characters differ?

8. How do you distinguish the main player character from the game environment? Choose one of your original characters and discuss three specific ways that you could ensure that players can always easily detect where the player character was and what the character was doing.

9. How do the visual features of a game character reflect the character's personality? Discuss how you would utilize profile, facial expressions, gestures, poses, costume, character movement, color scheme, and even associated objects to reflect the personality of one of the original characters you created.

10. Using the original game story you created in Chapter 4, construct a five-page scene involving at least two of the characters you described in the previous exercise. Make sure one of your characters is a player character and one is a non-player character. How will you distinguish between the dialogue written for the player characters and NPCs? (Note: You are not writing a linear cut-scene, but one in which the player still has control of the avatar.)

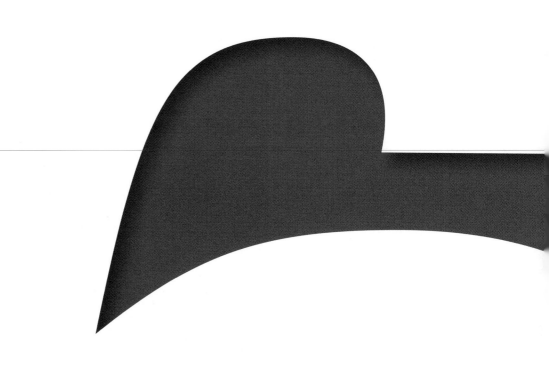

CHAPTER

6

Gameplay:
creating the experience

key chapter questions

- How are a game's *challenges* and *strategies* associated with gameplay?
- What are *interactivity modes* and how do they relate to gameplay?
- What is the relationship between gameplay and story?
- What is the difference between *static* and *dynamic* balance?
- How can the *Prisoner's Dilemma* and the *tragedy of the commons* be applied to cooperative gameplay?

What makes games different from other forms of media? It can be argued that games allow for more interactivity than other media. In Chapter 2, you learned about what motivates people to play games. Did you notice that most (if not all) of the reasons had something to do with the process of actually *playing* the game? Players seem to tie in their motivations with *doing*, or engaging, in some activity. In Chapter 4, you learned that *gameplay* is actually a storytelling device that is unique to game development. The *experience* of playing the game is really what allows the story to unfold.

Gameplay *is* Story

Gameplay and story are the same. The best game systems tell a story through the system itself. We really hit home runs when gameplay goals and story emotional goals intersect.

— *Chris Klug*
(Owner, Brown Bear Entertainment)

Gameplay can be defined as choices, challenges, or consequences that players face while navigating through a virtual environment. Now that you understand some of the basic elements of story structure and character development, apply these to gameplay. Think about how challenges in a game are often linked together—almost as if they represent plot points in a story. For each challenge (or plot point), consider the many strategies that can be used by a player (or character in a story) to overcome it. It can be argued that the gameplay is what truly makes a game compelling.

Rules

All games contain rules. Even the first popular arcade game, *Pong,* was equipped with the simple instructions, "use your paddle to avoid missing ball for high score." Many games contain rules that are much more complicated. These rules are documented in an instruction manual (and also often on-screen) to aid play. Components of the instruction manual are discussed in Chapter 10. (For more complicated games, players can even purchase strategy guides that provide tips on how to best play them.) The rules of a game define the actions or moves that the players may make in the game (and also those that they cannot make). In order to formulate rules for a game, it's important to first understand the *conditions* or terms of the game. The rules of the game should be communicated to the players. Although this can be accomplished through in-game tutorials and hints, an instruction manual often accompanies the game.

The Dynamic Language of Games

Only the active contribution of the players can determine the actual outcome of the game, the specificity of the experience. I have noticed that it is very hard for students to get past this aspect of game design; the fact that the player input will intrinsically change the nature of what they've created. But once they do understand this, and start thinking about games as a dynamic language, rather than trying to force a particular experience on the players, they realize just how exciting this type of entertainment can be—both for players and designers.

—*Tracy Fullerton, Assistant Professor*
(Electronic Arts Interactive Entertainment Program,
USC School of Cinema–Television)

Victory Conditions

A game's *victory conditions* correspond to how players win the game. Is there only one winner, or can there be several? What does a player have to do in order to win? Does the player have to rescue a kidnapped family member, slay a dragon, save the community from a disease outbreak, defeat an alien race, or solve the mystery of a friend's death? At what point in the game can it be said that this victory condition has been met? In the classic two-person game, *Battleship,* you know you've won when your opponent says, "You've sunk my battleship!"

Allen Varney on the Importance of Gameplay :::::

Allen Varney has worked at the Austin office of Looking Glass Technologies (under Warren Spector), at Sony Online Entertainment, and he has freelanced for Origin, Interplay, SimTex, and others. In the paper-game field, he has published board games, role-playing games, 7 books, and over 200 articles, columns, and reviews. Most recently he was principal designer of the 2004 revision of the classic 1980s paper role-playing game *PARANOIA*. With Enspire Learning, he is currently designing the computer version of the *UT Executive Challenge*, a 3-day, 100+-player business ethics simulation he created in 2003 for the University of Texas McCombs Business School, sponsored by Dell Corporation.

Allen Varney
(Designer
& Writer)

A good game design defines and explores an unstable boundary between decision spaces. But today, whole categories of computer games—seduced by 3D graphics—minimize interesting gameplay decisions in favor of environmental exploration or minimally interactive narrative. These are fine recreations, but not really games. Although many players in online role-playing games enjoy the standard level grind in the same recreational way outdoorsy folks enjoy whittling (as Raph Koster observed), that "gameplay" doesn't contribute much to the game design discipline.

Many puzzle games have no victory condition. In *Tetris*, the game just gets increasingly difficult until the player decides to stop. Any notion of victory stems from comparing your game score to others. (This is like the "high score" technique used in arcade games.) Process sims usually don't have any explicit victory conditions, but the ability to help your resources improve through the game is most certainly a type of ongoing victory. In *The Sims*, you maintain a victory condition as long as your Sim doesn't die. Multiple victory conditions can be incorporated into a game for replayability and to appeal to different playing styles. For example, in *Civilization III*, two of the victory conditions are conquering the world (which appeals to players who prefer strategic warfare) and achieving a dominant culture (which appeals to players who prefer construction and management activities).

Namco Holding Corp.

"You win!" indicator from *Tekken*.

Redentor Quimbao

"You have been defeated" screen from *Battle of the Generals*.

Loss Conditions

A game's *loss conditions* specify how players lose the game. Two types of loss conditions are *implicit* and *explicit*. Losing because you're not the first to achieve victory is an *implicit* loss condition—common in games that require competition between the player and other players or non-player characters (NPCs). Losing because your character dies or runs out of vital resources is an *explicit* loss condition—common in construction and management games such as process sims.

Tim Langdell on Adaptive Gaming :::::

Tim Langdell, PhD (CEO, EDGE Games; Lecturer and Chair, Game Curriculum Committee, Information Technology Program, University of Southern California)

In 1979 Tim Langdell started one of the first British computer and video game companies, EDGE Games, which he still runs to this day. Over the years he has been responsible for bringing over 180 games to market, combining many roles as developer, designer, producer, and company CEO. In addition to founding EDGE, Tim has authored a number of books on computer games. He also launched the *UK EDGE* magazine, which remains one of the leading game magazines to this day. Prior to forming EDGE, he was in academia as a research cognitive psychologist, and in the early 1990s he returned to academic life to combine running EDGE with forming a curriculum on interactive entertainment at the USC Film School. In 2003 he spent some time as a Director of the Game Art & Design Program at the Art Institute of California, San Francisco, where he taught and developed curriculum, and then joined the Information Technology Program (ITP) at USC in the fall of 2003. At ITP he has been heading up the game curriculum committee.

I have a number of academic research projects underway that all pertain to how game developers can create better games. These projects draw on my background as a research psychologist with expertise in cognitive psychology, looking at ways to make games better by determining what factors impact playability and whether a game is fun or not for any given individual. I am also researching the idea of adaptive games, which change their gameplay according to the individual differences of players. I am also working on next-generation artificial intelligence (AI) for games, which is related in part to my work on adaptive gaming.

In the mid-1980s, we faced a dilemma with a game we were doing based on the *Snoopy/Peanuts* license, which we realized had a fan base with young kids as well as with adults. We thus devised a game that had many levels of play in it—from play that would suit a 5- to 10-year-old, to very complex puzzles that would challenge the most hardened adult gamer. What we then did is build in a relatively low-level AI that tried to determine who the game was being played by and to present gameplay to that player accordingly. This led to some amusing results when some magazine reviewers (not realizing what we had done) proudly and unwittingly announced they had beaten the level intended for the 5-year-olds (that is, the game thought it was playing with a young child)! Since that work I have continued to evolve ideas for how games can become real-time adaptive to the skills of the player as well as the individual differences of players. Is the player more visual in their thinking? Responds better to tactile or visual cues? Are they a left-hemisphere or right-hemisphere thinker? How does a game adapt itself in real time to provide better (more challenging, more fun) gameplay by balancing and tuning the play and the interface to that actual player? A lofty goal perhaps, but we are making some significant strides in this already, and we have only just begun with the hard research at the academic level, where we finally have the time and facilities to do it.

Interactivity Modes

The concept of *interactivity* was introduced in Chapter 4 as an element of game storytelling. There are several types of interactivity that affect the gameplay. In each of these modes, the interactive element originates with the player—which illustrates how important the player's decisions are in the gameplaying process.

Player-to-game

In Chapter 3, you learned about player modes associated with the number of people playing the game. In single-player mode, the player is interacting only with the game itself and the platform. Even though the non-player characters (NPCs) might exhibit many human characteristics (and the player might sometimes think they *are* human!), they are still generated by an artificial intelligence (AI) system. *Player-to-game* interactivity is a very common form of interactivity, especially when it involves single-player mode. Player-to-game interactivity involves

Cyan Worlds, Inc.

Player-to-game interactivity includes how the player interacts with a game environment (such as *Myst*).

issues such as the game's spatial representation, mapping, environment, atmosphere, and content. Multiplayer games utilizing the player-to-game interactivity mode are really expanded single-player games, since the players do not interact with each other (e.g., *Bingo*).

Player-to-player interactivity often occurs in chat windows during an online game, such as in *Puzzle Pirates*.

Player-to-player

In multiplayer mode, players are not only interacting with the game, but with each other. *Player-to-player* interactivity is the connection between players: how they communicate with each other and ways in which they play the game together (which could include cooperative and/or competitive behavior). As you've learned with MMOGs, developers can only create the *potential* of player-to-player interactivity, but cannot easily predict how players will actually interact during the game. Competition between players can be structured in several ways. One-on-one player competition is common in fighting games and classic "tabletop" games such as chess. *Unilateral* competition involves two or more players competing against one player (e.g., tag, dodgeball). In the board game, *Scotland Yard,* one player is the criminal, while the other players are detectives. The game maintains a balance between the criminal and the group of detectives; the criminal has all the information associated with the game, while the detectives cooperate with each other as a group in order to catch the criminal. *Multilateral* competition involves three or more players directly competing with each other (e.g., *Monopoly*). This pattern reflects most multiplayer games. However, there are many MMOGs—such as *EverQuest*—that allow players to *cooperate* with each other by forming teams or guilds while competing against non-player characters (NPCs). (The tension between cooperation and competition will be explored later in this chapter.) Traditional team sports such as soccer, football, and baseball involve *team* competition, with equal groups of players competing against each other.

Player-to-developer

It is also possible for players to interact with those who have actually developed the game. *Player-to-developer* interactivity is most commonly illustrated in chat rooms and discussion forums available on the game's web site. Many developers take great care to read comments and concerns from the players, and they will often participate in the conversations directly.

Player-to-platform

The *player-to-platform* interactivity mode is the connection between a player and the game platform's hardware and software. Issues involved in player-to-platform interactivity include the system's graphics or sound capabilities, input devices, memory, battery, and storage.

Sony Computer Entertainment, Inc.

Player-to-platform interactivity involves how players interact with game input devices such as the PlayStation 2 controller.

Game Theory

Much of gameplay applies elements of classical *game theory*—which focuses on the types of conflicts that exist in games, and how players might respond to these conflicts. Game theory applies to games that contain two or more opponents. (One of the opponents could be an NPC that is not controlled by a player, but by the game itself.) Understanding some of the basic elements of game theory can help you ensure that the player is challenged when playing the game. These challenges are closely tied to the story's plot, and both heighten the dramatic tension in the game.

Chess is an example of a zero sum game.

Zero Sum

Zero sum games involve situations where players have completely opposing interests. In chess, for example, each player's goal is to win the game. Since there can only be one winner, it is impossible for both players to ultimately get what they want. Therefore, zero sum games can only involve *competitive* behavior.

Non Zero Sum

Non zero sum games involve situations in which players do *not* have completely opposing interests. These types of games are common in MMOGs where players form teams or guilds in order to compete against NPCs. In this case, the players are

Bioware Corp./Atari, Inc.

Neverwinter Nights: Hordes of the Underdark is a non zero sum game.

cooperating with each other (while *competing* against common enemies). This scenario gets more complicated when players are considered enemies, but they must cooperate with each other in order to ultimately win.

Although this might at first sound highly unusual, this situation is quite common in real life. For example, competing businesses often cooperate with each other to achieve their respective goals. Why do malls contain more than one department store? A combination of cooperation and competition (known as *coopetition*) describes this type of behavior.

In designer Reiner Knizia's *Lord of the Rings* board game, players (as Hobbits) compete and cooperate with each other simultaneously. Although only one Hobbit can win the game, no player wins if Sauron (represented by a black token with a menacing red "eye") gets close enough to any of the Hobbits to steal the ring. The structure of this game allows for a tension between cooperation and competition.

Prisoner's Dilemma

The classic game theory example known as the *Prisoner's Dilemma* illustrates what happens when all players try to compete with each other in a non zero sum situation. As you will see, the result can be disastrous for all:

In the *Prisoner's Dilemma*, there are two "players" involved. You and your partner in crime are arrested on suspicion of theft, but the authorities have no proof. You are each placed in a cell and questioned. You are each offered a deal: squeal on your partner, and you will be released. If you don't squeal, the authorities threaten to put you in prison for 5 years. Since you are separated from your partner, you have no idea what deal has been offered to him—if any. You have two choices: cooperate with your partner and keep your mouth shut, or "compete" with your partner and squeal. Not given any additional information, which option would you choose?

What happens if you both decide to squeal on each other? Would you both go free? That doesn't make much sense to the authorities. What if you both decide to cooperate by keeping silent? Does this mean that both of you will be put in prison for 5 years? But neither of you really confessed to the crime, so how could this be?

There are four possible outcomes to this dilemma, based on how you and your partner decide to respond:

The *Prisoner's Dilemma* payoff matrix shows four possible outcomes.

Reward: You are both rewarded for cooperating with each other. (Neither of you have confessed to the theft, and the authorities can't prove that either of you were involved in the crime.) You are hounded by the authorities for a year until they finally give up (or you are kept in jail as long as possible before your lawyers come to get you!). You both earn 3 points.

Punishment: You are both punished for squealing on each other. (The authorities now know that both of you were involved.) You don't have to stay in jail for 5 years, but 3 is bad enough! You both earn only 1 point.

Temptation: You decide to squeal, but your partner keeps quiet. (The authorities have what they need on your partner.) This is the best possible outcome for you personally, but your partner suffers. You are free to go. You earn 5 points.

Defeat: You decide to keep quiet, but your partner squeals on you. (The authorities have what they need on you.) This is the worst possible outcome for you, but your partner is home free. You must stay in jail for 5 years. You gain nothing—earning 0 points.

Each player has two choices [cooperate/keep quite (C) or defect/squeal (D)], but each must make the choice without knowing what the other will decide. If a player chooses D, that player will either earn 1 or 5 points. If a player chooses C, that player will either earn 0 or 3 points. If both players choose D, they will both do worse than if they both had chosen C.

The above scenario illustrates one "turn" in a game that could have many possible turns. A game like this could also be played in real-time, where both players lodge their decisions simultaneously. What do you think would happen initially? What if one player gets "suckered" by the other on the first turn? Perhaps the player who just lost 5 years might think, "I'm certainly not going to cooperate next time!" When a player decides to make the same decision the other player did on the previous turn, that player is engaging in a strategy known as *tit for tat*. This strategy could continue endlessly until both players are consistently competing with each other (losing 3 points per turn). The reverse could also happen: A player could "risk" cooperating with the other player, who might follow suit and cooperate.

A variation on the *tit for tat* strategy is known as *tit for two tats*. In this variation, a player would only copy the other player's strategy if that player used it two times in a row. Let's say Player A cooperated the first time, but B defected. Player A might initially think, 'I'm not going to get suckered again!' However, Player A might reconsider—giving Player B one more chance to cooperate. If Player B defects again (twice in a row—or "two tats"), Player A will subsequently copy Player B's strategy—and defect the third time. If Player B cooperated, however, then Player A would continue to cooperate.

Tragedy of the Commons

David Davis

A real-world *tragedy of the commons* would occur if no one chose to vote in an election—or if people slow down to look at a traffic accident clean-up, and cause a traffic jam in the process.

A related problem in game theory is known as the *tragedy of the commons*. This is a social "trap" in which a rational decision based on resources leads to an irrational result. As a real-world example, you might see an accident cleanup at the side of the freeway and slow down to take a closer look. This decision is rational in that it satisfies your curiosity and doesn't hurt anybody. However, in order to catch a glimpse of the accident, you have to slow down and drive under the speed limit. By doing this, you are alerting other cars behind you to do the same—changing the flow of traffic. If *everyone* behind you followed your lead and did the same thing, this could cause a collective "disaster" (a major traffic jam).

Similarly, the rational decision to not vote during an election won't hurt anybody. What could one vote possibly do to change things? However, if *everyone* made this same rational decision, there would be no election. In games involving closed systems with limited resources, players could hoard all the resources for themselves—which could result in inflation and an imbalanced economy.

Types of Challenges

Gameplay involves a series of *challenges* that are linked together. The types of challenges that occur in a game are often related to the game's genre. In fact, players who focus on playing particular genres have come to expect certain challenges to occur in these games, and they might deem a game inappropriate if the challenges don't match the genre.

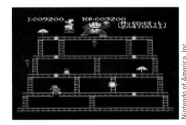

In the arcade action game *Donkey Kong,* Mario must engage in the explicit challenge of jumping over rolling barrels.

Implicit & Explicit

An *explicit* challenge is intentional, immediate—and often intense. In an action game, an explicit challenge might involve the exact timing required to jump over rolling barrels or on to a moving platform. In an adventure game, the appearance of a locked door always suggests the challenge of unlocking it.

An *implicit* challenge is not specifically added to the game, but an emergent feature of the game itself. Examples include determining how to divide up resources or deciding which units to deploy first in a strategy game.

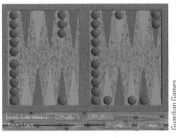

In the RTS *Command & Conquer Generals,* players face the implicit challenge of deciding which units to deploy.

Perfect & Imperfect Information

When *perfect* information is provided, the complete state of play is known to the players at all times. Perfect information yields *logical* challenges, where players assimilate the information and use it to decide upon the best course of action. In chess, both players are always aware of the state of the board and the position of all the pieces. This allows players to come up with strategies that will yield the maximum benefit.

With *imperfect* information, players are only provided with a fraction of the information needed to make the best decision. In contrast to the logical challenges in games with perfect information, the challenges in these games also require *inference* (or the ability to make a guess about the nature of the missing information). In "closed-hand" card games, all players are provided with incomplete information—since no player can see any other player's hand. *Mastermind* centers around this idea. Player A hides information (order of four pegs with six possible colors) from Player B, who spends each turn making inferences about the hidden information as Player A provides feedback after each of B's turns. Sometimes, the game platform can affect the amount of information supplied. In Chapter 3, you learned that console games involving *local* play cannot display complete information due to the limitations of sharing one screen.

The game of *backgammon* contains perfect information.

Games such as *Magic: The Gathering Online* provide imperfect information to the players.

Firaxis Games / Atari, Inc.

Fog of war is a common way of graphically representing incomplete information in a strategy game such as *Civilization III*.

A standard way to graphically represent incomplete information in a strategy game is through a *fog of war*—in which each player cannot see enemy units that are beyond the sight range of their own units. Inference is used by the player to estimate where the enemy units are located. The tension in the *Prisoner's Dilemma* game theory example results from imperfect information given to the two players about each of their decisions.

Imperfect information is commonly used in games because it challenges players to interact with and participate more in the game world. It also ties in with story components to create an element of mystery in the game. With perfect information, there wouldn't be any detective stories, spy thrillers, soap operas—or any stories with unexpected plot twists (think *The Sixth Sense* or *The Usual Suspects*). Imperfect information draws players into the game through human nature—appealing to our curiosity!

Intrinsic & Extrinsic Knowledge

Hasbro Inc.

Intrinsic knowledge is gained from within the game world. For example, a player could discover the purpose of a magical machine after getting some information from an alchemist NPC in the game. The memory of spells, combination moves, maze layouts, and character personalities throughout the game is also a form of intrinsic knowledge. Games that completely rely on memory include the *Simon* musical imitation game discussed in Chapter 1.

In a memory game such as *Simon 2*, players apply knowledge acquired within the game.

Extrinsic knowledge is gained outside of the game world and applied to the game. This type of knowledge can add an element of reality to the game and often involves facts such as "wood floats," "ice melts," "paper burns," "diamonds cut glass" and "a magnifying glass focuses light." These common sense facts can be used to solve various puzzles or meet challenges in the game. If your character possesses a magnifying glass or lens and some paper, you could direct sunlight onto the paper with the lens and start a fire. Similarly, if you are trapped in a glass room, you might use a diamond amulet to cut through the glass. Players must rely on this type of knowledge completely in order to play trivia games. Another form of extrinsic knowledge involves a player's understanding of legends referred to in the game. For example, a mirror could be used in a game to detect a vampire.

Pattern Recognition & Matching

Pattern recognition and matching challenges are common in puzzle games such as *Tetris,* where the blocks fall too fast for players to make conscious decisions about where to put them. The process by which we subconsciously match or recognize patterns is related to learning theory. This behavior is common in a lot of action games, where players simply don't have time for reflective thought and must rely on *automatic thinking* in order to master the game. It's no wonder that players fall into trances while playing these games!

Spatial Awareness

In *spatial* challenges, players usually have to navigate through an environment. These challenges are very common in puzzle games and vehicle sims—where the entire gameplay experience depends on the ability to understand spatial relationships in order to reach a destination.

Micromanagement

Many games allow players to manage settings and actions associated with their resources or characters. This *micromanagement* is one way of allowing the player to have many options in the game. For example, let's say a player's character is being threatened by several opponents. The player will need to decide how the character will respond to this threat. If the character has a series of powers and types of weapons, and can only target one opponent at a time, the player must choose which power to use, which weapon to use, and which opponent to target.

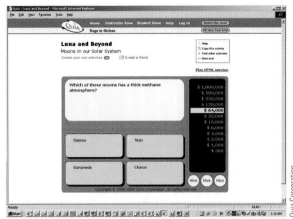

In a trivia game such as *Quia's "Rags to Riches"* challenge board, players apply extrinsic knowledge gained outside of the game.

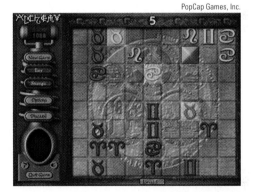

In a puzzle game such as *Alchemy,* players match patterns such as shapes and colors.

Players must navigate through air space in *Microsoft Flight Simulator 2004.*

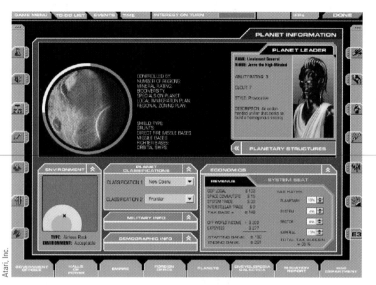

Atari, Inc.

In *Master of Orion 3,* players use multitasking to micromanage resources.

Micromanagement can get particularly exhausting when it's combined with *multitasking,* in which players must make these choices simultaneously. This is often found in real-time games, such as real-time strategy (RTS) games and first-person shooters (FPS), which involve reaction challenges. In *Warcraft 3,* "hero" units have many abilities, requiring a player to micromanage them in battle if they want to maximize their effectiveness. However, only one hero can be controlled directly at a time—forcing the player to multitask. In an FPS, multitasking might involve players having to steer vehicles while shooting at targets that are moving quickly around the game environment. In *Halo,* this multitasking is removed—since the driver can only drive, while another player rides "shotgun" and shoots. This way, neither player is driving and shooting simultaneously.

THQ Inc.

In *Red Faction 2,* players must react quickly in response to challenges.

Reaction Time

Action games challenge a player's *reaction time.* This is especially significant when the speed at which a player responds to a challenge is directly related to the speed at which the player's character reacts in the game. This could mean life or death for the character if slow reaction time results in a missed opportunity to defeat the enemy or take the treasure before it vanishes.

In a game, tension builds in a place where I am alone—with little or no resources—and I am required to accomplish a task that has a direct impact on the direction of the game. Tension also builds when I am trying to clear a point that has caused me repeated failure.

— *Arash John Sammander*
(Game Art & Design student)

All the challenges discussed can be applied to specific goals within the game itself:

1. **Advancement:** Reaching a higher "level" in the game. Each successive level might increase in difficulty (as in most arcade and puzzle games—often termed "leveling up") or allow your character to be more powerful (as in many RPGs).

2. **Race:** Accomplishing something before another player does. This is a reaction-time challenge associated with some action games.

3. **Puzzle-solving:** Applying mental processes to solving riddles and cryptic codes. This is a mental challenge that involves almost every type of challenge discussed in the previous section—and it's used most widely in puzzle and adventure games.

4. **Exploration:** Moving into new areas and seeing new things. This goal satisfies the curiosity of the player, and it's popular in adventure games and RPGs.

5. **Conflict:** Conflict, discussed in Chapter 4, usually refers to disagreements or combat between characters, and it's used in almost all game genres to provide dramatic tension.

6. **Capture:** Taking or destroying something of an opponent's without being captured or killed in return. This remains one of the most over-arching game goals across all genres (including action and RTS games).

7. **Chase:** Catching or eluding an opponent—often by utilizing either quick reflexes or stealth strategies.

8. **Organization:** Arranging items in a game in a particular order—often by utilizing spatial and pattern-matching strategies (common in puzzle games such as *Bejeweled* and *Tetris*).

9. **Escape:** Rescuing items or players and taking them to safety—often involving analytical reasoning and resource management.

10. **Taboo:** Getting the competition to "break the rules"—often involving physical or emotional stamina (e.g., *Twister*, *Don't Break the Ice*).

11. **Construction:** Building and maintaining objects—common in process simulations, and involving resource management and trade.

12. **Solution:** Solving a problem or puzzle before or more accurately than the competition does—involving analytical reasoning and knowledge application. This goal is common in adventure games, which incorporate a lot of detective work.

13. **Outwit:** Applying intrinsic or extrinsic knowledge in order to defeat the competition.

Balance

A game is *balanced* if players perceive that it is consistent, fair, and fun! The ease of winning the game also increases as the players' skills increase. Random events (e.g., a meteor hitting the area, destroying a player's resources) can still occur in the game that might cause a skilled player's chance of winning to decrease. However, a "better" player should be more successful in general at the game than a less-skilled player—unless the game is based purely on *luck* instead of *skill*. In order to implement this balance, a game often has to be "tweaked" during the *testing* process (discussed in Chapter 11). To set up a balanced system for players, the gameplay needs to provide:

1. **Consistent challenges:** Players should experience gradually more difficult challenges.
2. **Perceivably fair playing experiences:** Players shouldn't be doomed from the start through their "mistakes."
3. **Lack of stagnation:** Players should never get stuck with no way to go on.
4. **Lack of trivial decisions:** Players should only be *required* to make important decisions in the game, even in games that incorporate micromanagement.
5. **Difficulty levels:** Players should have a choice of difficulty or the level should adjust to the player's ability throughout the game.

There are two forms of game balance: static and dynamic.

Static Balance

Static balance is associated with the rules of the game and how they interact with each other. This type of balance does not depend on time and exists before the game is actually played. For example, the rules might indicate the relative strengths of units in a war-strategy game. Players might use this information as a reference when making decisions of what units to deploy during the game. The following are some ways to ensure static balance in a game:

Obvious Strategies

A game should contain one or more *obvious strategies,* which are superior to

Nintendo of America, Inc.

In *Advance Wars 2,* the character of Max has the power to give his tanks more firepower.

Nintendo of America, Inc.

other possibilities under many circumstances. In *Advance Wars,* each character has specific strengths and weaknesses. When a player is controlling a certain character, part of that player's strategy is to make decisions that correspond to that character's strengths. One of the game characters, Max, has powers that give his tanks more firepower—while his indirect-damage artillery vehicles are comparatively weak. When given the option to deploy tanks, those who are playing "Max" will attempt to do so—unless other circumstances arise that make this an unwelcome decision.

Symmetry

Symmetry, the simplest way to balance a game, involves providing each player (including NPCs) with the same starting conditions and abilities. This ensures that the outcome of the game will depend only on the relative skill levels of the players. This often works well in abstract puzzle games, but it would be difficult to achieve successfully in a real combat simulation. It's not very natural or realistic for opposing armies to have the same exact troops and abilities—and it can make the game much less exciting. However, symmetry is used often in RTSs such as *Age of Empires*—and it could work quite well in a participatory sim such as a team sports game. In the real world, teams do start with more or less the same resources (although the skill level of each team member differs).

Symmetry is associated with the relationships between resources. There are two types of symmetric relationships: transitive and intransitive.

A *transitive relationship* is a one-way relationship between two or more resources. For example, you could construct a set of characters (A, B, and C) in which A is more powerful than B, who is more powerful than C, who is not more powerful than anyone. Since this relationship is hierarchical, you can easily apply this relationship to a world with a caste system in which the royalty (A), merchants (B), and peasants (C) interact.

One way to utilize this relationship is to have all characters begin as "C"s (or to initially give the players access to "C" level units or abilities). As a player's skill level increases during play, the player graduates to a "B," and so on. In this case, all players start with the same conditions (symmetry)—but

Microsoft Corporation

In *Age of Empires,* players begin the game with the same resources.

Transitive Relationship

Royalty ⟶ Merchant ⟶ Peasant

A hierarchical caste system is a type of linear, transitive relationship.

chapter 6

Intransitive Relationship
(Rock-Paper-Scissors)

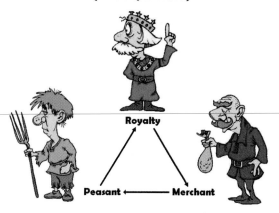

A "rock-paper-scissors" system is a type of circular, intransitive relationship.

some variation occurs in the game if players advance up the food chain at varying speeds. This is a form of character *advancement* discussed in Chapter 5.

Game theorists often refer to an *intransitive relationship* as "rock paper scissors" (RPS)—from the game of the same name. In RPS, rock beats scissors, which beats paper—which, in turn, beats rock. This relationship differs from the transitive in that it is circular rather than linear—with each resource having the ability to defeat and be defeated by another. This relationship can't be hierarchical in the classic sense, since the "weakest" characters are able to beat the strongest.

However, story elements can work with gameplay in this case. For example, the transitive caste system we set up could be turned into an RPS (intransitive) relationship if the peasants (C) were given special powers, abilities, or knowledge that would enable them to defeat the royalty (A). For example, they could storm the castle unnoticed! In this example, A beats B, which beats C—which beats A. This gameplay device works better if the relationships between the resources varies throughout the game. For example, what if the peasants (C) were no longer able to defeat royalty (A)—but they somehow developed the ability to defeat the merchants (B)? In order to keep the intransitive relationship, the abilities of the other characters would have to change as well—so that A beats C, which beats B, which beats A. (But be careful—this could provide some serious story continuity problems!) Intransitive relationships can also be defined by the actual abilities of the resources. For example, archers (A) defeat infantry (B) because they are quicker; infantry (B) defeat cavalry (C) because they have heavy armor; and cavalry (C) defeat archers (A) because they can get to them before they have a chance to fire their bows enough times.

Electronic Arts Inc.

Trade-offs

Not all relationships involve transitions between inferior and superior characters or resources. In fact, it's more common for some to be better than others in some ways. For example, in *The Sims,* expensive furniture is more "aesthetic"—but cheap furniture is more comfortable. In order to make a decision on which furniture your character

In *The Sims 2,* players weigh *trade-offs* in order to make decisions with regard to domestic issues.

Creating Meaningful Choices

The most important task for any game designer is to create meaningful and interesting choices for players. The nature of what makes a choice meaningful is something that varies widely from game to game. Is it a meaningful choice when I decide how to dress my character in a role-playing game? When I choose how many units to create for production and how many for combat in a real-time strategy game? When I determine how to use my roll in backgammon?

All of these examples present good, interesting choices for players. Yet they don't offer us easy solutions for designing such choices in our own games. Studying how other games create choice is one way to learn; another way is to design by setting *player-experience* goals, rather then *feature-driven* goals (e.g., "the game will encourage shifting alliances between groups of trading partners," rather than "players will be able to trade resources"). With this goal in mind, the game can be tested to see when the player experience works as described (e.g., when players are making interesting choices about who to trade with and when to break an alliance with a partner).

Learning how to create choices like this means getting inside the head of the player—not focusing on the game as you designed it. When you're just beginning to design games, one of the hardest things to do is to see beyond the game you envisioned to the actual game the players are playing. What are they thinking as they make choices in your game? How are they feeling? Are the choices you've offered as rich and interesting as they can be? Asking these types of questions means opening up your design process to player feedback—and this is a difficult, emotional process for most designers.

— Tracy Fullerton,
Assistant Professor (Electronic Arts Interactive Entertainment Program,
USC School of Cinema–Television)

will purchase, you have to weigh *trade-offs*. When players are provided with options that aren't entirely positive or negative, they face a decision-making puzzle.

Combination

Players can sometimes *combine* resources or characters in order to meet a challenge. For example, in *Advance Wars* players can join two sets of troops that might have been weakened by combat. Combining these troops adds the power of both together so that the new entity is stronger.

Feedback

As a game progresses, it can get out of balance and fall back into balance. The tension between players can be increased with the aid of *feedback*.

If one player is ahead in the game, for example, the game could get more difficult for that player—which would be *negative feedback*. This player could be advanced enough to be able to get resources from the other player—but there could be a high price for these resources.

On the other hand, if a player is behind in the game, challenges could get easier for that player—which would be *positive feedback*.

An application of positive feedback involves ending the game once it's clear that the game has been won. In some games, players can get to the point when they know they're going to win—but they still have to play until the "victory conditions" are met. (For example, if a player has defeated all but one of the 1,001 monsters, that player will clearly win the game. However, if that one remaining monster is hiding somewhere, the player could spend hours trying to find and defeat the creature.)

Completely random events should also occur in the game to keep it unpredictable, but these could throw a game off-balance. For example, a volcano could erupt just near one of the "underdog" player's characters—which could severely affect this player's ability to catch up.

In *Sim City,* random events such as natural disasters can affect the game's balance.

Dynamic

Games begin with *static* balance—but once they're set in motion by the players, a *dynamic* balance emerges. It is this *dynamic* balance that allows players to truly interact with the game. Players can interact with dynamic balance in several ways:

1. **Destroy:** The game is initially balanced. However, instead of maintaining this balance, the player(s) act as the opposing forces and attempt to throw the game off balance.

In *Black & White: Creature Isle,* players can sometimes destroy order.

2. **Maintain:** In this case, the game is initially balanced. Once the player(s) interact with the game, opposing forces emerge that threaten to throw the game out of balance. The object of the game is to prevent these forces from overrunning the system.

3. **Restore:** In this case, the game is initially unbalanced and perhaps even chaotic. The object of the game is for the player(s) to move the system back into equilibrium—cleaning it up and making it "orderly."

Economies

Game *economies* are systems in which resources move around—either physically (from place to place) or conceptually (from owner to owner). Resources can be money, troops, characters, weapons, property, skills—anything that players can "own" in the game (information, too!). In an FPS, a primary resource is often ammunition that can be found or obtained by "stealing" it from dead opponents. This resource is consumed by firing weapons. Health points are other resources that are consumed by being hit—and are restored with medical kits. Since resources interact with each other, players can't produce too much or too little of them—or the economy will be thrown out of balance. In process sims such as *Black & White* and *The Sims Online,* the game economy is balanced by nurturing and caretaking resources (characters); the focus in these games is on the characters and their needs.

Edward Castronova on MMOG Game Economies :::::

Edward Castronova obtained a BS in International Affairs from Georgetown University in 1985 and a PhD in Economics from the University of Wisconsin–Madison in 1991. In between, he spent 18 months studying German postwar reconstruction and social policy at universities and research institutes in Mannheim, Frankfurt, and Berlin. After graduating, he held professorships in political science, public policy, and economics at the University of Rochester and at California State University, Fullerton. Since the fall of 2003, Castronova has been an Associate Professor of Telecommunications at Indiana University. Author of numerous articles in scholarly journals, he is currently preparing a book on synthetic worlds for the University of Chicago Press. His paper, "Virtual Worlds," is the most-downloaded economics paper at the Social Science Research Network.

Edward Castronova, PhD (Associate Professor of Telecommunications, Indiana University)

In the multiplayer context, *all* economic theories can be effectively applied to games. Economics is about the interactions of human beings—so if human beings meet up in a game world, economics takes place. Economies are critical elements of immersion. Designed well, they sit in the background unnoticed and give a constant sense of value—and hence, reality—to every object in the game. Designed poorly, they are obvious at every turn—and make worthless items seem valuable (and make valuable items seem worthless).

The laws of game economics are the same as in the real world—just under rather unusual circumstances. There are thousands of real-world economic situations that could be adapted well into game environments: different monetary institutions; auctions under different rules; population response to shortages; production teams; income redistribution effects; tax effects; location decisions and urban development—and on and on!

The *EverQuest* Economy

In *EverQuest* and many other MMOGs, characters gain skills and objects they can trade with other players using the game's currency. In 2001, some *EverQuest* players decided to take the economy outside of the game and began selling their assets for real money through auction and trading sites such as eBay. Economist Edward Castronova studied thousands of *EverQuest* transactions initiated through eBay to determine the real-world economic value generated by the inhabitants of Norrath—the fantasy world of *EverQuest*. The verdict? Norrath's gross national product per-capita was $2,266. (If Norrath were a real country, it would be the 77th most wealthy in the world—just behind Russia!)

In persistent-state world (PSW) economies, players can collect and trade items of value. Since thousands of people can react in ways the developer can't possibly anticipate, it's very difficult to design and adjust (fine-tune) a PSW. *Ultima Online* was originally designed to have a completely self-contained, closed economy with a fixed number of resources. Players, acting in a way that had not been anticipated by the developers, hoarded objects without using them. Resources were depleted, which caused an "inflation" in the game economy (in which the "hoarders" could charge ridiculously high fees for these objects). Developers eventually had to do away with the closed system and had to adopt an open economy in which new resources were spawned.

Titus Levi on the Flexibility of Multiplayer Economies :::::

Titus Levi is an economist working as a consultant for individuals and organizations working in the arts and media industries. His clients include Interep, Susquehanna, and the Durfee Foundation. Titus has been a faculty member at the University of Southern California's Annenberg School for Communication—where he taught classes in business strategies and conducted research on the economics of the radio industry. His work in radio has spanned more than a decade, including serving as program host and producer for KUSC-FM and KPFK-FM. Titus also worked as a freelance journalist, most significantly writing for *Keyboard Magazine's* new talent column, "Discoveries." He has also been an arts administrator, organizing and producing concerts for the California Outside Music Association and the Los Angeles Festival.

Courtesy of Kathleen Pittman

Titus Levi
(Economist; Media
& Arts Consultant)

Game economies add *flexibility* to the game experience. By adding in side bargains and incentives to create new systems, players, and so on, the game continues to change and adapt. Economies also give players more reasons or *incentives* to continue playing the game—due to their *dynamic* nature, providing novelty and discovery. This means that you don't get bored!

Gameplay & Level Design

The gameplay elements discussed in this chapter exist in the game world—the environment of the game which contains the structures, terrain, objects, textures, and style of the game itself. *Level design,* discussed in the next chapter, focuses on creating the game world and incorporating gameplay into it.

:::CHAPTER REVIEW:::

1. What is the difference between gameplay and story? Choose one game and discuss its story and gameplay elements separately. How do these two elements intersect during a game?

2. How do players make a static game dynamic—and what does this have to do with game balance? Contrast the static and dynamic elements of an existing game. How do players modify the game to make it dynamic?

3. What are the players' goals in a *non-zero-sum* game? How can the *prisoner's dilemma* and the *tragedy of the commons* be applied to gameplay? Create a scenario around one of these theories and discuss how a game involving both cooperation and competition could be compelling and interesting.

4. Play a card or board game (such as one that can be found at Funagain Games [funagain.com]). Analyze the rules—including victory conditions, loss conditions, gameplay process, and game goals. What steps would you take to create a digital version of this game? (Consider expanding upon the game's story as one strategy.)

5. How do game goals relate to challenges in a game—and what strategies can be utilized in order to overcome these challenges? Choose one game goal and write a high concept (premise) that incorporates that goal. List three plot points that incorporate challenges associated with the game goal you chose. Discuss several strategies that a player might utilize in order to overcome each challenge. By doing this, how are you integrating gameplay with story?

6. You decide to create an original game in which you and other players must escape from a deserted island. There are three objects that could be built that may help players leave the island: boat, raft, and lifesaver. The boat is the most difficult to build, but it is the most stable escape object, whereas the lifesaver is easier to build, and the less-stable raft is in-between. The relationship between these three objects is linear, or *transitive*. How would you revise this relationship (or alter the objects) so that it becomes *intransitive*?

7. A game's premise indicates "You are given immunity from a deadly disease that causes humans to age rapidly. It is up to you alone to find the cure. Use your powers of deduction to uncover the mysterious origins of this disease and find an antidote—before it's too late!" Discuss the specific victory and loss conditions for this game. Using a genre of your choice, make up a possible set of rules for this game.

8. In a game's setup, players divide a deck of 10 cards between them and then begin to play them by placing them on the table in a certain order, according to the rules of the game. The players hide their cards from each other as part of the game's strategy. However, Player A realizes that she knows the contents of Player B's hand, which takes all the guesswork out of the game. What is the problem with the game—and what is your proposed solution? Would the same problem occur if this game was played on a console system? What if it were played with networked computers?

9. There are plenty of games that focus on the application of either *intrinsic* or *extrinsic* knowledge, but it's not as common to combine both in one game. Create an original *game idea that makes use* of both forms of knowledge as strategy elements.

10. *Unilateral* player-to-player interactivity is not common in electronic games. Create an original idea for an electronic game that involves this form of interactivity. How would you incorporate the idea of cooperation and competition into the game?

Levels:

creating the world

key chapter questions

- What is *level design* and how is it related to gameplay?

- What is the importance of the structural features of game worlds—such as duration, availability, relationship, and progression?

- What is the importance of the temporal features of game worlds—such as authentic, variable, player-adjusted, and altered?

- What is the importance of the spatial features of game worlds—such as perspective, scale, and boundaries?

- How are reality and style achieved in a game environment?

The process of creating game worlds is often focused on *level design*—an area of game design that is wrought with confusion. Some are under the impression that level designers are members of art teams and primarily focus on 3D modeling. Others believe that level designers are programmers and focus heavily on scripting gameplay events. In this chapter, I will take a physics or "space-time" approach in my discussion of level design—focusing on how designers construct the architecture and visuals of the physical game environment, and how they divide up the basic structure of the world into different sections (levels). (Gameplay—which involves events that might occur in each level—is closely associated with level design, but this topic is discussed separately in Chapter 6.)

Level design is defined as the creation of environments, scenarios, or missions in an electronic game. A level designer usually utilizes level design tools (or "level editors"), such as Valve Hammer Editor (Valve Software), Unreal Editor (Epic Games), CryENGINE (Crytek), or the Aurora Toolset (Bioware)—and/or 3D graphics editing software, such as 3D Studio MAX, Maya, or Lightwave. Traditionally, *level design* involved the creation of game worlds for real-time strategy (RTS) or first-person shooter (FPS) genres. However, this form of design is now necessary in all but the simplest of games.

Consider what function the level fulfills in the game. The level could introduce a new character or object, focus on a plot point (such as discovering a secret or preventing an attack), or create a mood through visuals or storyline. The level's function should center around an idea that becomes a unifying theme.

Structure

Levels can be used to structure a game into effective subdivisions, organize progression, and enhance gameplay. When designing levels, consider their goal, flow, duration, availability, relationships, and difficulty.

Goal

Each level should have a set of objectives that the player understands. Otherwise, the players are simply moving, shooting, puzzle-solving, and collecting until a signal appears indicating that the level is complete or that a new level is loading.

Microsoft Corporation

Open-air level in *Microsoft Flight Simulator 2004*.

Sometimes developers ensure that players understand the objectives for each level by creating a "briefing" in the form of a cut-scene or interactive tutorial at the beginning of each level, and by providing access to a status screen during the course of the game. The players might also be immediately thrown into the game's action, engaging in tasks that are fairly easy to solve and situations that immediately illustrate the rules of the game in the context of the game's environment. You should let the players know where they stand in relation to their goals by giving them progress reports—preventing a surprise defeat. This applies to a single-player mode. In multiplayer mode, the focus is on balance and strategic/tactical options presented to the player in FPS or RTS games.

Flow

There are two main issues with game flow that you should address while designing a level. You first want to make sure that a player stays in a particular area of a level until he or she has accomplished necessary objectives. For example, in "open-air" levels, there aren't any natural barriers to the player's movements. A player can then run past opponents rather than engaging them in battle (which is sometimes a strategy in itself). This problem can be solved by creating natural barriers that are destroyed as a by-product of the player's progress in the level. You also might want to prevent the player from returning to a particular area once the objectives associated with that area have been met. A method for doing this is to close off the area after the player has completed it (creating a one-way barrier, such as a door that locks after the player walks through it), which lets the player know that he or she is making progress.

Children's levels in *Toontown Online* and *Spongebob Squarepants*.

Duration

How much time should be spent on each level? One universal rule seems to be that a player must complete at least one level of any game in a single session. For computer games, these sessions should be fairly short, 15-minute spurts for children, to approximately 2 hours of continuous concentration for hardcore gamers. Console game levels usually run about 45 minutes. If you'd prefer to develop a game with much longer sessions (e.g., strategy games such as *Age of Mythology* or *Civilization III*), make sure you provide milestones of achievement, such as advancement or task completion, on a regular basis.

Availability

How many levels will you include in the game? You will need to consider the various gameplay goals in the game and ensure that each level covers one primary goal. A greater issue is how many levels should be available to a player at once. If you were to allow only one level to be available at a time, this would work for games that require first-person immersion. If you were to allow only a small number of open levels at a time, this could alleviate frustration for many role-playing game (RPG) players, who might have several quests to fulfill and need to shift their focus. If you were to allow many open levels at a time, many players might become confused—but these levels would work well in process sims and real-time strategy (RTS) games.

Ubisoft Entertainment

Players can choose from several open levels at a time in *Warlords Battlecry 2.*

Electronic Arts Inc.

Mission level within a campaign in *Command & Conquer Generals.*

Relationship

What are the relationships between levels in the game? Think of each level as a scene or even an episode within a larger story. From Chapters 4 and 6, you learned that story and gameplay are intertwined—and that story structure often consists of several acts or plot points. Levels in puzzle games are often only related through some increase in difficulty. Some levels are related through storylines—similar to traditional media such as television. In this episodic relationship, each level is self-contained, with its own internal plot line and conclusion. For example, many strategy games use the term *campaign* to describe a series of levels (known as *missions*) that need to be completed in order to finish the game. Some games contain several campaigns that are all separate from each other. Each time players complete a mission, they are closer to completing a campaign.

Progression

How do you pace the game's progression through level design? As discussed in Chapter 6, you want to make sure that a game's difficulty slowly increases as it continues. Just like story and character development structures discussed in Chapters 4 and 5, you need to make sure that each level builds conflict in a series of arcs. Vary the pace of your levels—allowing the player to alternately struggle to stay alive, systematically explore the environment, and reflectively solve challenging puzzles. Always keep the player occupied with things to do. Don't make your level a ghost town! Challenge is a good thing, but don't make your levels so difficult that only experts can survive, while other players die again and again.

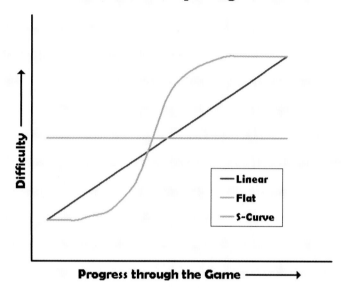

Game Difficulty Progression

Comparison of linear, flat, and s-curve progressions.

A game does not have to be *linear*—consisting of challenges that steadily increase in difficulty as the game continues. It could also be *flat*—where difficulty does not vary from one level to the next. There is also the *s-curve* model, a combination of the linear and flat models that begins with a flat section consisting of a tutorial during which the player learns the game. After this training period, the difficulty level rises steadily throughout the game, and then flattens again a few hours before the game ends so that the players who get through most of the game will eventually be able to finish it.

Depending on the goals of the level, you may want to warn players of impending danger, such as a monster behind a door or a sniper on a rooftop. One way of doing this is through audio (which will be discussed further in Chapter 9). It's also debatable whether developers should pit players against powerful enemies with only one weakness that the player must discover while trying to defeat the enemy. Although sometimes frustrating for the player, this is done in most platform-style console games. In order to challenge expert players, you can either build more difficult versions of your levels that can be accessed separately by the expert players—or you can build different levels of challenges within the level. There should also be several ways in which a player can meet each challenge and complete a level. Ideally, the different methods of success would appeal to different playing styles.

Kevin Saunders on Level Design :::::

Kevin Saunders programmed his first game, a 'port' of Intellivision's *Astrosmash*, on a ZX81 at the age of six. His official career as a game designer evolved from his graduate research in environmental engineering. This research included lab experiments that required 24-hour monitoring over 2-3 day periods. These lengthy experiments gave Kevin the time to explore the world of online games and led to an opportunity to work on Nexon's *Nexus: The Kingdom of the Winds*, which launched in 1998 to become one of the world's earliest MMOGs. Kevin subsequently designed and produced *Shattered Galaxy*, the world's first MMO real-time strategy game. More recently, Kevin has worked at Electronic Arts (*Command & Conquer Generals: Zero Hour* and *The Lord of the Rings: The Battle for Middle-earth*) and Obsidian Entertainment (*Knights of the Old Republic II: The Sith Lords*). Kevin earned his Master of Engineering degree from Cornell University.

Kevin Saunders
(Senior Game
Designer,
Obsidian
Entertainment)

The first step in designing a level is usually outlining its design on paper. This process generally takes only an hour or two and includes answering questions such as:

- What is the player's primary goal?

- How long should the level take to complete?

- What emotions is the level attempting to invoke in the player?

- What is the setting of the level?

- What additional art assets will be required?

- What resources (e.g., characters, troops, items) will be available to the player?

- Who will the player encounter?

- What side quests will help lead the player through the level?

After fleshing out the design, it is generally best to create a rough layout for the level, and then incorporate all scripting before making the level beautiful. By completing the scripting early in the level design process, you can test the game play before investing time in its aesthetics. If a level plays well, you'll find a way to make it pretty, but the reverse isn't necessarily true.

Complete creation and testing of a level generally takes from two to six weeks, depending upon the tools available and the type of game.

Time

The concept of time was introduced in Chapter 3 in the discussion of time intervals (turn-based, time-limited, and real-time). Time can also be thought of with respect to "real-world" time. "Game time" can move slower, faster, or not any differently than "real-world" time. In many turn-based and action games, there is no concept of time passing at all. Everything idles or runs in a continuous loop until the player interacts with it in some way.

Authentic

Some games try to portray time authentically and use the passage of time as a game-play characteristic. The cartridge for *Boktai*, developed for the Game Boy Advance, contains a sensor that detects the amount of light where the game is being played. The object of the game is to drag vampires out of the darkness into the sunlight. The game must be played outside during the day, and weak sunlight will negatively affect your character's energy level. You must enter the correct time of day in order to configure the game before playing. Lionhead Studios' *Dimitri* provides a variant of authentic time through its characters, who progressively age as the game continues. In Wide Games' *Prisoner of War*, the player character must participate in both morning and evening roll calls. If the player is absent during any call, the POW camp officers will conduct a search. In the game *Shrek*, the player can control time of day to accomplish different tasks. *Animal Crossing* also uses the date to trigger special events.

Konami Digital Entertainment

Konami Digital Entertainment

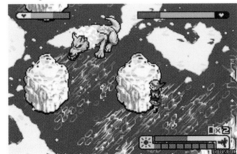

Boktai utilizes a sensor to detect the presence of daylight.

Limited

Time is sometimes implemented as a part of the setting of the game but not of the gameplay itself. Time creates an atmosphere and provides some variety, but it doesn't alter gameplay. Game time can feel artificial because players can do the same things at night that they can do in the daytime. However, there are a few games in which time is meaningful. Sometimes a player is put under pressure by being given

Black Isle Studios/Interplay

Baldur's Gate: Dark Alliance II allows players a limited amount of real-world time to accomplish tasks within the game.

Electronic Arts Inc.

The Sims depicts both day and night – but time speeds up when the characters go to sleep.

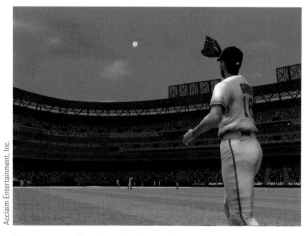

Acclaim Entertainment, Inc.

Players can adjust the time interval in sports games such as *All-Star Baseball 2005*.

a limited amount of real-world time to accomplish something. In *Baldur's Gate,* the shops are closed at night and characters run an increased risk of being attacked by monsters (because it's darker, and the monsters are harder to see).

Variable

If time is significant, the virtual time in a game usually runs out much faster than in reality, and it jumps around—skipping over periods when nothing interesting is happening. War games generally don't bother to implement a night-time or require that soldiers sleep. Since players often want to play continuously without having to pause and wait for "morning," the night-time portions of the game are not missed. *The Sims* depicts days and nights because the game is a process simulation and the characters require rest and sleep for health. However, time speeds up when the characters go to sleep.

Player-Adjusted

In many sports games, players have the opportunity to modify the time associated with game levels. For example, players can sometimes play shorter (5–10 minute) quarters instead of the standard 15-minute quarters in a football game. When creating a game, you need to provide time options to players when it makes sense. Many players do not want to devote a whole hour to playing a simulated football game. In some flight simulators, there can be long periods where nothing interesting is happening during the flight. In these cases, players might have the option of speeding up the time.

Altered

Several games incorporate altered time as an effect. *Max Payne* pioneered the use of *bullet time*—the technique of going into slow motion while retaining the ability to move the camera's viewpoint at normal speed. Since the game models bullets as real objects, it is possible to see a bullet in flight while this feature is activated. This same effect is seen in action movies such as *The Matrix* and *Crouching Tiger, Hidden Dragon*. In *Blinx,* the player can rewind time—and in *Prince of Persia: The Sands of Time,* the main character has the power to stop time during the game so that he can avoid getting defeated by opponents.

Players can stop time in *Prince of Persia: The Sands of Time.*

Elements of Level Design

Level design is the process of taking the world envisioned by the lead designer (discussed further in Chapter 10) and the design document and creating a world filled with goals, sub-goals, and lots of obstacles between the player and those goals. The level designer is responsible for designing the level's world; determining which enemies, weapons, and power-ups appear in the level; how and when the enemies appear or spawn; and the overall balance of the level (so the level is neither too easy nor too hard). More recently, the level designer may also be expected to build the 3D environment or at least some of its elements, using 3D programs such as Maya or 3D Studio Max, and even program some of the triggers or other interactions, using scripting languages. While the level designer is constrained by the rules and mechanics envisioned by the lead designer, the level designer is also in the position to offer changes to those rules, if those changes (a) will result in a more engaging game and (b) do not alter the world or the game to the point that it doesn't match the overall vision intended for the game.

— *Richard Wainess,*
M.S.Ed. (Senior Lecturer,
University of Southern California)

Space

Space incorporates the physical environment of the game—including its perspective, scale, boundaries, structures, terrain, objects, and style (color, texture, look, and feel). In Chapter 5, you were introduced to some visual character creation techniques—including concept drawing, modeling, texturing, and animation.

Tabula Rasa: Crafting the Setting & Story

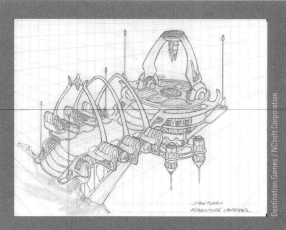
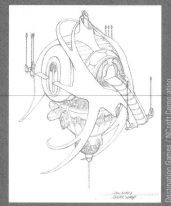

Structures, objects, and characters in the science fiction MMOG *Tabula Rasa* were first created as concept sketches. The mission-launching device (left) warps space to send squads to battle in distant worlds instantly—and the weapon shop (right) is a structure that is visited by warriors interested in purchasing and upgrading weapons.

Tabula Rasa is the latest massively multiplayer entertainment experience to come from the mind of Richard Garriott and Destination Games. Developed from the ground up to be stable, fast, and fun, *Tabula Rasa* represents a refreshing new approach to the design of multiplayer online games. In crafting the history and setting for *Tabula Rasa,* the team drew from many wells: ancient history, science, philosophy, and more. It was no accident that a strong correlation can be drawn between the benevolent Benefactors and angelic beings or the malevolent Thrax and creatures linked to demonology. The very essence of *Tabula Rasa* is the age-old tale of Good versus Evil, a familiar theme that invites a participant to reach within himself to become the hero that saves the day.

Taking this premise to a new level, the Destination Games team abandoned the traditional "sword and sorcery" models to explore new paths. Musical instruments, such as harps and drumsticks, have been fashioned into weapons that vanquish foes with energy extracted from the warrior's mind, body, and spirit. Characters live in a virtual world built by a society so advanced that a single trained thought may produce something as wondrous as a complicated construct or as simple as clothing. *Tabula Rasa* also has innovative features such as simplified character creation, squad-based missions, reduced downtime, and stylized martial arts-type combat techniques.

— Starr Long (Producer, NCsoft)

Environmental art is created in the same way—although it often is not animated specifically but utilizes some special environmental effects. Concept artists often sketch out a scene related to a game, which can reflect a particular level's style. After a sketch has been completed, you might use a level editor in order to build a 3D version of the level. Software for level design is discussed in more detail in Chapter 11. The editor should allow you to view the world in multiple perspectives (including the player view); modify geometry while you place characters in the world; and navigate through a level as you are building it.

Instantiated Spaces

More and more massively multiplayer games are incorporating instantiated spaces into their design in order to help solve some of the problems with a wholly persistent world. Persistent spaces offer an open play space in which players can interact spontaneously with the entire player base of that game, but fail to provide the much needed guidance that helps players understand how to succeed and grow within that game. On the other hand, instantiated spaces can offer a more directed/guided experience for players, but require much more work to create, and can potentially isolate players from opportunities to discover new friends within the player base. Over the next few years, I expect that we'll better understand the pros and cons of the instantiated space model, and hopefully developers will work to further refine them.

— Carly Staehlin (Lead Designer, NCsoft)

Perspective & Camera

In Chapter 5, you learned about the importance of both first-person and third-person *point-of-view (POV)* with regard to characters in a game. POV is related to the *perspective* of the game world—or how the player views the game environment.

Omnipresent

Lionhead Studios

In the *omnipresent* perspective, the player has the ability to view different parts of the game world and can take actions in many different locations of the world (even if parts are hidden at times). The omnipresent perspective allows players to look down at the game world from above. In Chapter 3, you learned about process simulations and god (or toy) games. *Populous* and *Black & White* were coined "god games" by the

Black & White: Creature Isle uses an omnipresent perspective.

press because they not only utilized the omnipresent POV, but also allowed other characters to view the player as if he or she was above the game world—akin to a god looking down upon the other characters.

Ingo Ruhnke

Aerial (Top-Down)

The *aerial* (or *top-down*) perspective shows the player the game as seen from above, from a bird's-eye view. This view is popular for games such as the original *Legend of Zelda* and *Pac-Man*.

Feuerkraft uses an aerial (top-down) perspective.

Nexon Corporation

Isometric

In the *isometric* perspective, the player can look slightly across the landscape at a 30- to 45-degree angle. In an isometric world, you can create many different angles of objects, and then place those objects on the screen. This allows you to create reusable objects rather than having to render them in real time. This perspective also makes the player feel closer and more involved with events than a top-down or aerial view. However, the fact that artists must create several (usually four) different versions of all objects from each angle can cause the process to get a bit tedious if the camera rotates. (Many RTS and strategy games were created in 3D isometric view without camera rotation.) Early versions of *Sim City* and *Civilization* were almost entirely aerial views—mainly because the hardware at the time didn't support enough detail for any other view. Eventually, these games adopted an isometric view using 2D technology to create a pseudo-3D world—creating the effect of playing with scale models, appropriate for process simulations!

Dark Ages uses an isometric perspective.

Nintendo DS: Shifting Perspective

The launch of Nintendo's dual screen handheld (DS) could dramatically change the way games are designed. Players now have the ability to play the game simultaneously with two perspectives—which could remain constant or shift to other perspectives, depending on the design. Not only do players have the ability to view the game environment in different ways, they are able to experience a game character in both first- and third-person perspective simultaneously—which might challenge and expand a players' identification with their avatars. The ability to have both a *macro,* "big picture" view of the game's events and underlying story, coupled with a *micro,* "personal" view of a character's thoughts and feelings, could revolutionize the way games are experienced and created.

Side-Scrolling (or Flat/Side-View)

In 2D space, characters can only run from left to right or jump up and down. They cannot run toward the player or away from the player. Working around these limitations, classic 2D arcade games used *side-scrolling* navigation to create the illusion of space. The player character would travel from left to right horizontally across the screen as the background moved from right to left. If the character changed direction and moved from right to left, the background would often stand still. This technique is also known as *parallax scrolling.*

Goliath uses side-scrolling navigation.

Designing Levels for RPGs

There's really not a lot of specific design issues—as long as you: stick to the RPG formula (explore – kill – loot – sell/power up – level-up – repeat); make sure you space out your carrots along the level (here's a unique item, here's an area where the player can gain a bonus feat, here's a part of the level where a new part of a story mystery is solved, here's a nice vista in the level for the player to look at, etc.); and then, if you can, try to give the player options to pursue their goals depending on how they made their character (like being able to sneak into a situation if you have a rogue, talk their way out of a situation if they're a diplomat, or just slaughter their way to the end if they're a gunman, etc.). A game should stroke the players' egos, and there's no better way to do this than to present them with levels and situations that allow them to flex the skills and abilities they spent the most points in.

— *Chris Avellone (Lead Designer, Obsidian Entertainment)*

Height Maps

A popular technique for generating landscapes, a *height map* is a contour picture depicting the elevations of intersecting points on a 3D grid. Height maps translate quite well to 3D landscapes and are created by using grayscale to represent height.

Terrain & Materials

21-6 Productions, Inc.

Valve Software

Interiors made of concrete, brick, metal, and wood textures in *Half-Life 2* contrasts with exteriors made of grass, dirt, and water textures in *GravRally*.

Environmental *materials*—such as metal, glass, sand, gravel, sky, and clouds—directly influence the look and feel of the game. A shading model defines how materials behave when they are lit. It combines the attributes of each material—such as texture, color, shininess, and translucency—with the attributes of light sources, including color and direction. Materials can then be shaded differently depending on their physical attributes. Terrain refers to textures that appear on ground surfaces—such as dirt, grass, tile, and pavement.

Radiosity & Effects

Radiosity (lighting) is just one effect that is used on game environments. Without the proper application of radiosity, players will not be able to navigate through the game environment—nor will they be able to notice details that might be necessary to see and interact with in order to progress through the game. Radiosity can also be used

A scene before and after radiosity is applied.

Many styles have been overused in games. Don't borrow a style or setting from another game, but try something new. Forget the same old villains and environments. Think about the emotion you would like the world to bring out in the player: awe, fear, excitement, amusement? This will help you formulate your style.

Oddworld: Munch's Oddysee is filled with surreal characters and environments.

Oddworld Inhabitants

:::::: Cel-Shading

Cel-shading is the art of rendering objects to look like hand-drawn cartoons—in contrast to photorealistic renderings. The most simplistic algorithms simply fill the object with a solid color and then overlay lines on the edges of the objects. More complex algorithms engage in shading; take into account light sources and shadows; or attempt to mimic a more stylistic cartoon style—such as charcoal, watercolors, or etching.

Viewtiful Joe uses cel-shading to bring a 2D look into a 3D world.

Capcom USA, Inc.

In this chapter, you learned the importance of the structural, temporal, and spatial environment within the game world. Now let's move from the game world and look at the direct connection between the player and the game.

1. What is level design and how does it relate to gameplay, story, and character development?

2. What are some unique ways games have utilized time—both real-world and game-world—to make a game more compelling? Create an original game concept around one of these methods. Can you think of another method that hasn't been used?

3. What are some spatial perspective "tricks" used in level design that sometimes overcome the limitations of the game environment? Which of these tricks might you incorporate into your original game?

4. How can a game retain authenticity through environmental design? Discuss some features you might use in developing a game centered around real-world rules.

5. The 3D game development tradition has been criticized for being too imitative—creating worlds that aren't distinct enough from one another. If you were to develop a 3D game, how would you ensure that the game reflected your unique style?

6. Play a game in any genre and analyze how the game handles structure. Is the game split up into levels? Does each subsequent level increase in difficulty? Does the game follow a linear, flat, or s-curve progression?

7. Design a game environment for your original game idea. What materials or terrain will you use? What sorts of objects or structures will you add to the environment?

8. How does a game's style relate to its mood? Describe the mood of your original game. Then describe a particular scene in terms of setting and environmental atmosphere—incorporating that mood in your description.

9. Go "location scouting" and take pictures of some unusual objects, textures, and scenes. Incorporate these textures into concept sketches of an original environment.

10. How does a game's cultural context affect its environment? Create a culture around your original game idea, and discuss how this culture might determine the look of interiors, exteriors, objects, vehicles, structures, and rules of the game world.

CHAPTER

8

Interface:
creating the connection

key chapter questions

- How do game interfaces relate to player-centered design?
- What are the components of game interfaces?
- What is the difference between a manual and visual interface?
- What is the difference between a passive and an active interface?
- Why is *usability* important in game interface design?

A game-specific interface is the connection between the player and the game itself. The primary function of this interface is to help the player make choices in order to achieve certain goals within the game. The interface is the closest connection players can have to the game without being able to jump right into the game itself, like characters in the movie *Tron*! Game interfaces differ from other interfaces because their purpose is tied to a more immersive experience than surfing the web or even talking on the phone. Even games that only involve one player must allow for an intensely high level of interactivity between the player and the game itself. The player must be able to focus solely on the game experience without external (environmental) or internal (mental) distractions. In addition to providing this connection and immersion, a game interface still needs to fulfill its general function: to help the player actually *play* the game. In order to ensure this, interface designers need to understand the many tasks, actions, needs, and challenges the player has to deal with throughout the game.

Player-Centered Design

The importance of interface design—the connection between the player and the game—is often overlooked. In order for player activity to exist, there has to be a connection between the player and the game itself. In this way, interface design is closely linked to the idea of player control.

> I like any interface I can't remember. I appreciate an interface that does its job well and stays out of my way.
>
> — Robert Ferguson (Game Art & Design student)

Interface design is traditionally known as *user* interface design. A user is someone who makes use of a certain technology—such as a web site, computer, or cell phone—in order to achieve a certain result. The term was coined during the advent of the home computer revolution, and it traditionally characterizes the user as an expert who fully understands the technology that they are utilizing. In web design, the term *user* is now commonly changed to *customer* because this better represents the role of the person who is utilizing the interface. In the same way, a *user* can be referred to as a *player* in game design.

Let's look at the concept of *player-centered design*. Who are you designing a game for? Is it for yourself, your company, or the players? Who will actually interact with the game? In all aspects of game design, constant focus needs to be on the player's needs, tasks, and choices. If you lose sight of the player, the game will be unplayable. The most important and obvious feature of a game that allows for player-centered design is the interface itself. When you catch yourself thinking of how to design an interface so that it's cool, complex, cutting-edge, and flashy, pretend that you're the player for a moment and see if your great idea will help the player play the game without getting frustrated! The interface should always be helpful and functional.

::::: **What's Wrong with this Picture?**

This ad (for American Cybercast, circa 1995) is missing a connection between the "audience" and the "content"—causing the content to resemble a television-style broadcast model rather than interactive entertainment. Can you describe the missing connection?

The interface allows the player to take control of game characters, navigate through the game environment, and make decisions throughout the game. Without an interface, a game would be no more than a presentation, animation sequence or a static environment—an "unplayable" game!

Interface & Game Features

You've already learned that the primary purpose of a player interface is to allow players to actually *play* the game, and that there are many player tasks, choices, and needs that must be addressed by the interface design. Let's split these tasks, choices, and needs into two categories: *actions* and *information*. During a game, each player will need to access information that might not be available from game characters or the environment. This information might include player status—such as lives remaining, power depleted, and skills attained. This information often changes based on where the player is in the game, or what the player decides to do during the course of the game. All of this information needs to be available through the player interface. The player also takes various actions during the course of a game. These actions might involve navigating through the game world, picking up an object, or firing a weapon. Each of these actions will need to be accounted for in the player interface. You've already learned about some basic game features—such as gameplay, story, character, and the game world (which is often structured in levels). How do these features interact with the game interface?

- **Gameplay:** The connection between the player interface and *gameplay* is what truly allows for the game's interactivity. As you learned in Chapter 6, gameplay is the core of the game experience. It involves all actions the player takes during the game. If a player chooses to take a certain path down a fork in the road or attempt to crack a code in a safe, the player will need to carry out those actions through the game interface. Designing an interface for a particular game involves understanding and allowing for all possible player actions in that game.
- **Story:** The game interface must reflect the game's *story*. The visual style of the interface should incorporate the setting, mood, time period, environment, and culture of the game. If the interface is created separately without knowledge of the game world, its presence will take the player out of the game instead of allowing the player to become even more immersed in the experience.
- **Character:** Just as a game interface needs to incorporate the story, it also needs to incorporate aspects of the story's *characters*. A player who takes on the role of a *player character* will have specific needs and goals, all of which should be addressed by the interface. It may be essential that a character have

access to certain weapons, clothing, powers, vehicles, and even personality traits. Access to these items, characteristics, and abilities can often be found through the game interface, or a specialized character interface. When choosing or creating a character, players could utilize a character selection or customization screen, which is a specialized type of interface. Even *non-player characters (NPCs)* have information associated with them that often needs to be accessed by the player. For example, a player might want to look at what types of skills and abilities are associated with his or her NPC opponent in order to choose a character with matching (or complementary) skills and abilities.

- **Audio:** Some game developers consider audio part of the player interface itself. Audio works with the visual or manual interface to bring a feeling of reality or tactile "feeling" to the experience. Types of audio include music, sound effects, and spoken dialogue/narration. In addition to providing a soundtrack to the game, music can also provide information—for example, cluing the player into trouble by becoming more dramatic right before an enemy appears on-screen. In this case, audio could be seen as being part of the "information" component of an interface. Sound effects and music can be triggered when a player accesses areas of a game interface. When a player decides to fire a weapon, the sound of that weapon firing will often occur in response to the player's action. When a player opens a jewelry box, music from within the box could be triggered by the action. A spoken word option could be available within the interface itself for the visually impaired. If a player wants to find out what items are in his or her character's inventory, these items could be "read" to the player by the voiceover in addition to being seen. Audio will be discussed in more detail in Chapter 9.

- **World:** In Chapter 7, you learned about how the game world might be structured in many ways. In addition to specific environments (interiors and exteriors) that reflect the condition and focus of the world, a game could contain parallel worlds or a series of worlds that become more or less complex depending on where they appear in a sequence. Sometimes a player interface is modified based on which portion or type of world is being accessed—and more or less components may appear in the interface. One of the most common ways of dealing with level design structure is through the use of maps that can be accessed through the game interface. These maps might appear on the periphery of the game "playing field" or be accessed separately through a menu system.

As you can see, interface design is related to all other aspects of game development—and it helps bridge the gap between the game and the player.

Interface Types

In Chapter 1, we discussed the history of game development in the context of the dominant hardware platforms associated with particular eras. Each of these platforms had distinct *manual* (hardware-based input devices) and *visual* (software-based on-screen displays) interfaces.

Arcade games did not achieve a standard interface style for either manual or visual interfaces. Before a player deposited coins into these games, the screen would display the title along with instructions or a set of screens that also included a list of players' high scores and (later) a demo sequence from the game itself. The manual interface usually consisted of a start button and direction buttons or a joystick. *Centipede* was one of the few arcade games to use a trackball—which became a fairly popular manual interface (possibly because it was more durable than a joystick). Other interfaces, often associated with arcade "simulation" games such as driving and shooting, mimicked real-life objects (such as a rifle, periscope, or steering wheel/gas pedal). Visual interfaces in arcade games were fairly straightforward—consisting of score, level, and "lives remaining" displays. Due to the relative simplicity of the technology at the time and the coin-op business model, the interfaces had to focus on functionality rather than aesthetics. Arcade-goers would not take time out to read complicated user interface instruction manuals; they had to be able to understand how to play the game almost immediately, with a minimum of text instruction (which usually needed to fit on one screen).

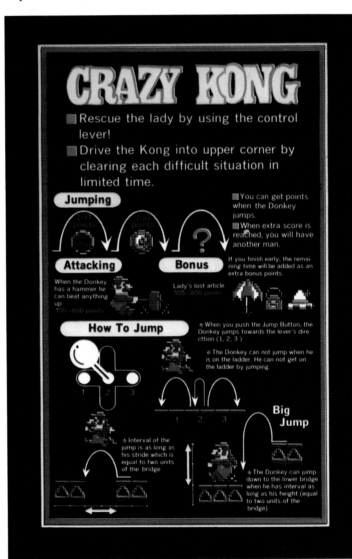

Nintendo of America, Inc.

Crazy Kong instruction screen and *Donkey Kong* visual interface.

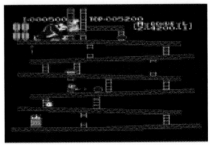

Sega Corporation

Sega Corporation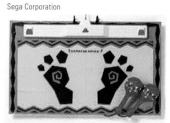

Konami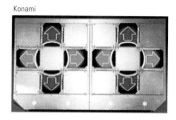

Manual interfaces for *Bass Fishing* (fishing pole), *Samba de Amigo* (maracas and foot pads), and *Dance Dance Revolution* (dance platform).

In Chapter 1, you also learned about the evolution of *computer* games, beginning with text adventures, which relied on two-word commands from the player in order to navigate through the game. In these games, the manual interface consisted of the computer's keyboard (pre-mouse), and there was no visual interface. Players simply had to look up the various commands to know how to move through the game.

When computer games evolved to contain graphics, the visual interface was still virtually non-existent. Much of the time, the visuals depicted what was going on in the game world—but did not illustrate how the player could interface with that world. The introduction of the graphical *point-and-click* interface allowed games to be much more accessible to players—attracting a much larger consumer base.

Elements of a Game Interface

The interface is one of the least understood yet most critical elements in the game. The interface is the connection between the player and the game world. The invisible interface elements [referred to in this book as *manual*] include the control triggers, keys, and mouse, which are used to select and use weapons, move around the world, and communicate with both NPCs and other players. The visible elements are the on-screen features that can let the player know his or her health, available weapons and their status, locations of enemies, distance to targets, position within the world, and any other information that is considered critical to game play, both in terms of what the player can do and what the player may not want to do (such as not attacking a powerful enemy when health is low). While much or most of what makes a good game (i.e., level design) is intuitive, what makes a good interface is largely dependent upon a vast number of cognitive issues that are generally unknown to interface designers, yet are slowly beginning to make their way into the video game industry. Understanding these issues can greatly advance the quality and usability of video game interfaces, and, ultimately, of game play.

— *Richard Wainess,*
M.S.Ed. (Senior Lecturer, University of Southern California)

Visual Interfaces

Visual interfaces are either displayed on-screen at all times, or can be easily accessed by the player through the manual interface. There are two types of visual game interfaces: passive and active.

Active

Players can interact with an *active* interface—usually by clicking on items displayed in the interface. This is because these items are meant to be manipulated in some way by the player as part of the gameplay process. One type of active interface includes a *menu system*. This often contains items that allow the player to make general decisions related to the game, including:

- start a new game and reset
- save the game
- play a saved game
- access a tutorial
- configure the game
- navigate through the game
- customize their character
- choose a player mode (such as single or multiplayer)
- get help/customer support

Syberia (upper right), *Conquest: Frontiers* (bottom right), and *I Was an Atomic Mutant* (below).

I enjoy games that integrate the interface into the game and have little or no menus. Therefore I don't enjoy an onscreen menu. I believe that menus take away from some of the immersion from the game because it reminds the individual that they are 'playing' a game and not 'living' one. How often do you interact with people and suddenly have numbers and menus pop up around you? Another option is being able to adjust the amount of information on the screen as needed. In this way it gives more options for various types of players.

— *Arash John Sammander*
(Game Art & Design student)

The Adventure Company

Canopy Games

Ubi Soft Entertainment / Game Holdings, LLC

Menu systems are usually easily accessible throughout the game, even if they aren't always visible.

Another common active interface is the *action* (also known as communication or interaction) system, which contains player choices related to gameplay. The *action* interface accepts player input (or "commands") and is related to the extent of player control available in the game. Choices available in this interface all contain action words (such as attack, talk, or retrieve), which allow the player to engage in combat, exploration, communication, and other gameplay elements (discussed in Chapter 6).

Electronic Arts Inc.

Wizards of the Coast, Inc. / Hasbro, Inc. / Bioware Corp / Atari, Inc.

Three Rings Design, Inc.

Radial and pie menus in *The Sims Online, Neverwinter Nights,* and *Puzzle Pirates.*

Some action interfaces, such as in *The Sims Online,* are *radial*—appearing around the character or target object. Since many of these actions are related to movement, some of them are handled by the manual interface.

Passive

Players cannot interact with the items displayed in a *passive* interface. This is because the items are unchangeable and cannot be directly manipulated by the player without compromising gameplay. This interface displays the player's (or character's) *status*—such as score, lives, energy, time remaining, or strength. This information could be displayed in one area of the screen, or the items could be spread out across the screen. For example, arcade games often display status items such as the score, lives, and time remaining in different areas of the screen (usually in separate corners).

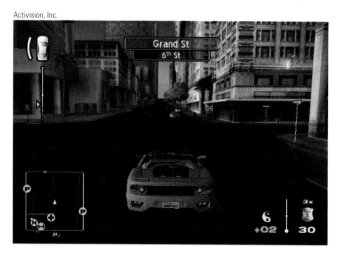
Activision, Inc.

True Crime: Streets of LA utilizes a heads-up display (HUD).

On-screen interfaces include *heads-up displays (HUDs),* which overlay the interface onto the entire game action screen, ad *wrappers,* which display the interface in a smaller area of the screen—usually in the corner. *Return to Castle Wolfenstein* utilizes a HUD that provides information on the player's power, ammunition, compass, and health at all times. When the voice command menu is accessed, it appears as a wrapper in a small box at the corner of the screen.

Sometimes the status menu is not displayed on the main screen, often due to space considerations. Instead, the information is accessed through a menu or submenu.

Visual Interface Styles

There are several interface styles used in games that can appear as passive or active interfaces.

Split-Screen

In the *split-screen* interface style, the player selects actions in a selection area of the screen and observes the results on a portion of the screen. *Maniac Mansion* and *The Adventures of Fat Man* are adventure games that contain this interface style.

Socko Entertainment

The Adventures of Fat Man uses a split-screen interface style.

Whole Screen

In the *whole screen* interface style, the player moves the cursor around the screen and clicks on objects or characters of interest. The story progresses visually by player interaction. Although it loses some flexibility, it makes up for that with gains in atmosphere and immersion. *Myst III: Exile* is an example of an adventure game that uses this interface style.

Testing Gameplay through Interface Design

Interface design is an excellent proving ground for gameplay features. After you have an idea for a new feature (or an improvement upon an existing one), consider how the interface will work. If you can't come up with a seamless interface, you should seriously consider abandoning or redesigning the feature.

— Kevin Saunders
(Senior Game Designer, Obsidian Entertainment)

Cyan Worlds

Myst III: Exile contains a whole screen interface style.

Lionhead Studios

Black & White: Creature Isle contains an invisible interface style.

Invisible

Black & White: Creature Isle attempts to immerse the player in the game with only the thinnest layer of interface separating the two. In *Black & White's invisible* interface, the player's avatar is a disembodied hand that responds directly to the movements of the mouse. There is virtually no other status information displayed on-screen, and no icons or buttons for the player to click on. Everything is performed by moving the mouse. To cast a spell, the player traces a certain shape (such as a spiral) with the mouse. *Black & White* and *Sacrifice* both also use gesture input.

Manual Interfaces

Manual interfaces are the hardware-based controllers, keyboard-mouse combinations, and other input devices that players interact with physically in order to play the game. These interfaces are closely associated with the game's hardware platform.

Arcade

Manual arcade interfaces are usually integrated into an arcade game's cabinet and consist of items such as buttons, joysticks, and sliders. Driving games often use steering wheel/pedal combinations. Specialized manual interfaces have been developed for particular games--including *Silent Scope* (gun), *Karaoke Revolution* (microphone), and *Periscope* (periscope – surprise!).

Larry Downing / Courtesy of Reuters

Silent Scope uses a gun as a manual interface.

::::: Creating a Game for the EyeToy

In Chapter 1, you learned about the motion-sensing EyeToy manual interface—which allows players to control actions in the game through physical movement. What type of game might be ideal for this kind of interface?

Sony Computer Entertainment, Inc.

In Groove is just one game for the EyeToy that incorporates the system's motion-sensing features.

Computer

Manual interfaces for computer games almost always consist of a keyboard-mouse combination. Players often navigate through the game environment on computers using the keyboard (sometimes "w,a,s,d" or arrow keys), the mouse, or both. Keyboard combinations can sometimes be used to open onscreen menus or take

Gyration

Computer manual interfaces usually consist solely of a keyboard-mouse combination.

quick action in a game. Peripheral devices used in arcade games are seldom packaged with computer games. Even though there are many other input devices for computers (e.g., joysticks, steering wheel/pedal kits, flight yoke systems), developers can *only* assume a player will use a mouse/keyboard combination.

Console

Console controllers often consist of navigation and action controls—handling action games much better than the keyboard-mouse combination, since they were specifically designed to enable simple, quick reflexes. Like arcade games (and unlike most computer games), console games also incorporate peripheral manual devices – such as foot pads (*Dance Dance Revolution*), fishing rods (*Bass Fishing*), maracas (*Samba di Amigo*) and microphones (*Karaoke Revolution*).

Digital Interactive Systems Corporation (DISC)

The *DISCover* game console uses a USB Logitech racing wheel as a manual iªnterface for its arcade-style driving game.

Each of the current primary console systems has a unique controller – with several variations manufactured by third-party companies. Features of each standard controller include the following:

- *PS2*: Dual analog mini-sticks, 8 analog action buttons, 1 D-pad (8-way directional pad), start and select buttons
- *Xbox*: One D-pad, left and right analog sticks, left and right shoulder triggers, 6 pressure-sensitive multicolored analog buttons
- *GameCube*: 7 buttons, 2 analog sticks, and 1 D-pad

Compare these specs to the old Atari 2600 joystick! All controllers now also have rumble and vibrational feedback—providing a more tactile game experience.

More complex input is required in other genres (such as role-playing games [RPGs], real-time strategy games [RTSs], and adventure games). The *point-and-click* interface style came out of computer plat-

Nintendo of America, Inc.

The GameCube and other console controllers are designed to enable quick reflexes.

form necessity. RTS games are well-suited to a keyboard-mouse interface and have not yet been well-adapted to a console control scheme. In a computer RTS, a player drags a selection box over several units in order to select them. Until recently, this was awkward on a console system. However, a selection convention has been developed (initially popularized in Shigero Miyamoto's *Pikmin*) that allows players to press or hold a button to make a selection box larger. *Goblin Commander* is an RTS game that has been specifically developed for console systems.

Jaleco Entertainment

Goblin Commander is a console-based RTS.

Handheld

Many handheld systems are like miniature console systems that contain their own screens. In this way, a handheld can be thought of as a cross between a console and a computer system. Handhelds also have their own built-in specialized controllers.

Handhelds include single-purpose portable systems such as Nintendo's Game Boy Advance (GBA) and Sony's PlayStation Portable (PSP)—and multipurpose wireless and mobile devices, such Nokia's N-Gage and QD. While designing a player interface for a multi-purpose device such as Nokia's N-Gage QD—which combines the utility of a cell phone with a game system—the designer must ensure that all features of the system remain fully functional. As a "player" becomes a "caller," there is a shift in the needs of the person using the device—making design flexibility essential. How would you design an interface so that it incorporates multiple uses?

The Game Boy Advance SP handheld contains a T-pad (4-way directional "+" pad), A/B buttons, select/start buttons, and left/right buttons on the back ("shoulder") of the system.

Interface Design for Consoles vs. Computer Games

The controller is one factor (without a mouse and keyboard, you have to be careful about the options and navigation through options in a console game), and screen resolution is another (you have to be careful about color usage and resolution—what looks great on a PC isn't going to hold true for what you see on a TV). Otherwise, the general interface rules apply: try to make it unobtrusive, keep the steps to select similar options logical and consistent throughout, try to provide the player with customizable controller options, and try to make sure it doesn't take more than a little d-pad [directional pad] switching or one or two button presses to get to what you need.

— *Chris Avellone*
(Lead Designer,
Obsidian Entertainment)

Platform-Specific Visual Interfaces

Visual as well as manual interfaces are tied to a game's platform. Here are just a few guidelines for incorporating platform-specific features into a visual interface:

- **Arcade:** Visual interfaces for arcade games are generally simple—partially because these games are designed for quick play (maximizing the amount of quarters that are deposited into the game). Usually an arcade game contains an instruction screen—followed by a series of in-game screens that often contain passive interface displays. Therefore, it isn't surprising that early arcade games such as *Pac-Man* and *Donkey Kong* never contained active interfaces—but only passive displays showing lives remaining, score, and occasionally time remaining in the game.

- **Computer:** Visual interfaces for computers range from heads-up displays (HUDs) to a series of menu systems that can be accessed by clicking on buttons using a mouse or accessing menus using the keyboard. Some games employ a "point-and-click" style, where players click on various objects in order to access them.

- **Console:** Visual interfaces associated with current console systems are tied to the way these games are played. Initially similar to the computer platform, many console games provided a combination of visual displays and active menu systems. However, as discussed in Chapter 3, local console play involves 2–4 players sharing the same screen. This means that no "hidden" information can be displayed to particular players. In contrast, a multiplayer computer game interface could reveal information to a player that might be unavailable to an opponent. This concept is readily seen in traditional card games—where players don't share what's in each other's hands. Another feature of visual console interfaces is that many players like to hook up their systems to very large television screens. It's not as common for consumers to purchase large computer screens (such as cinematic displays)—partially because of the focus on computers as multi-purpose (business as well as entertainment) devices, rather than the special-purpose (games only) emphasis of console systems. The possibility of a very large screen often affects the design of console games in terms of scale and detail—although the resolution of a computer screen is higher than that of a television monitor!

- **Online:** When games are played online—whether the hardware consists of a computer or a console system—player interfaces are affected by how many people are playing a game simultaneously. Interfaces for single-player online games are often identical to those created for the associated hardware platforms. In massively multiplayer online games (MMOGs), in which player characters often interact with each other by forming teams (or guilds), it becomes necessary for the interfaces to allow players to access information associated with each member of the team. These interfaces should also enable communication between players (often involving chat windows or discussion boards—whether private or public).

- ■ **Handheld:** The key feature of handheld systems is that the screen size is much, much smaller than that of consoles or even computers. This size drastically affects the way player interfaces are designed for these platforms. Visual interface components that might normally be displayed at the bottom of the screen, for example, will often be accessed through a series of menus. The Nintendo DS—with its dual-screen display—allows for twice the amount of room. Some designers utilize one screen for the game's interface. Others use two screens for dual perspectives (such as simultaneous first- and third-person) and game views (such as simultaneous overall and close-up displays—macro and micro).

Visual Interface Components

There are several components used in the visual interface of a game, regardless of whether the interface is active or passive. These components consist of either *information* that players access or *actions* that the players must take in order to complete tasks during the game.

Here are just a few examples of some widely-used visual interface components:

Strategy First, Inc.

Interface (bottom of screen) from *Kohan: Immortal Sovereigns* includes a combination of information and action components: map, status awareness indicator, and menu buttons.

Score

The *score* is a numeric indicator that measures the player's success in the game. A high-score indicator keeps track of past scores and gives players a standard by which to measure themselves. This is the simplest of all basic score indicators and can be shown on-screen at all times, especially if score is a primary concern in the game.

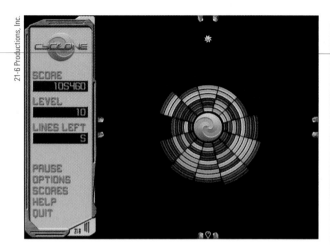

Score displays in *Cyclone* and *Super Collapse*

Some games might display scores only after a player completes a section of a game—such as a mission in a strategy game. At that point, the game might reveal whether the player not only attained a particular numerical score, but a grade. For example, in *Advance Wars*, players discover at the end of each mission whether they received a traditional letter grade (such as an A, B or C) or a "superior" grade (designated by "S")—which is even better than an "A"! This display appears on-screen after the end of a mission – but it does not appear on-screen as a passive display while the game is being played.

Many current games do not rely on ongoing scoring to assess how a player is doing. Instead, players can access their "score" based on where they've been able to go in the game environment, the number of levels they've been able to access, and how many obstacles they've been able to overcome.

Lives and Power

Lives remaining used to be shown with the score indicator. It reflects how many chances a player has remaining—often visualized in a number of mini-icons (usually representing the player's avatar) or a numerical display. Current games often do away with the remaining lives display and allow players to re-spawn (come back to life) infinitely. If a player can save the game at any point, the concept of "remaining

Nintendo of America, Inc.

Konami

Lives remaining display in *Super Mario Sunshine*, and power display (lower left-hand corner) in *Tour de France*.

lives" is no longer relevant. (Issues related to saving the game are discussed later in this chapter.) Often, lives remaining displays show both the number of lives (represented by a number—such as "3") and a graphical representation (such as 3 stick figures representing the player character). Early arcade games often displayed "lives remaining" to the player on-screen at all times. This is essential information needed by players to assess their status in the game. It also provides a feeling of how much time might be left in the game if the player goes along at the same pace (and doesn't necessarily improve on skill level).

A related component, known as the *power* (or health) bar indicator, is used in many current games. This indicator consists of a horizontal bar colored in full. A power bar might appear in a corner of the screen, showing how much power the player has left. This bar is usually color coded as well as spatial—illustrated in the form of a bar with "0" on the left and "100" (as a percentage) on the right. If a player has full power, the bar will be full of color. As power depletes, the color drains from right to left—like a thermometer—down toward "0". Sometimes a "happy" color such as yellow is used toward the right. As the power decreases, the color might darken—becoming red when the player is in danger of losing all power. The player then has only one life (that can be re-spawned), but a limited amount of power. The color drains from the bar until the player dies. Some simulation games use "dials"—a variation on the power bar—or bubbles (as in *Diablo* and *Dungeon Siege*).

The Interface Symphony

All the components of an interface are equally important. It is like a symphony orchestra. If the performance is to be effective, all instruments must be in tune and all notes must be played correctly. If the interface is to be successful, all components must work together.

— *Jan McWilliams*
(Artist/Educator; Director of Interactive Design,
Art Institute of California, Los Angeles)

Map

For players to get a larger view of the game world and find their way around it, a map is often necessary. Many strategy games—such as the *Civilization* and *The Age of Empires* series—display a map as part of the game interface located at the bottom of the screen. A game map allows for "macro" and "micro" views of the game. In a macro view a player is able to oversee all aspects of the game world, while a more micro view of the game involves a close-up of one tiny portion of the map.

Usually, this closer micro view is displayed on-screen in the main game area—while a macro view is displayed as part of the interface. However, some games allow a player to toggle between the macro and micro view during the game. This option may be necessary to see what might be happening in far-off areas of the game world and to help players answer questions, such as, "What if a natural disaster or an enemy's troops are heading in my direction?"

> **M**y favorite onscreen game interface is a map. I'd be lost without one.
>
> — *Mason Batchelder (Game Art & Design student)*

::::: Active & Passive Maps

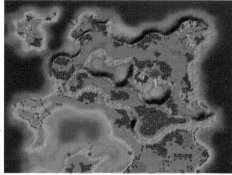

Maps from *Age of Empires II: The Age of Kings* and *Age of Mythology: The Titans.*

Maps can be effective interface elements, whether they appear passively on the outside of the game's "playing field" (common in strategy games), or are accessed actively as their own menu systems (often as part of a tutorial campaign).

Character

A *character creation* interface can sometimes be a highly complex series of screens that allow players to create and customize their own characters. Everything from physical appearance (including clothing, hair/eye/skin color, gender, ethnicity, height, and body type), sound of voice, personality, accessories, race, class, and even history/biography can be selected and combined through this interface. This type of selection is most popular among games that involve a lot of character advancement, such as RPGs. Usually accessed during the initial setup of the game, this interface might also be available at any point during the course of the game – allowing the players to go back to the interface during play and modify characteristics as needed.

Player characters often have a certain set of *skills and attributes* that are either intrinsic to the type of character

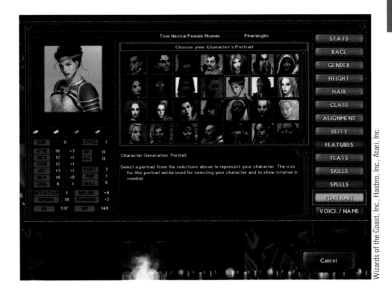

The *Temple of Elemental Evil* RPG utilizes a sophisticated character creation and management interface.

selected or that can be attained during the course of a game. This sort of information is essential for games that involve character advancement—such as role-playing games (RPGs). Skill and attribute information is provided during the character selection or customization process – but it can also be accessed throughout the game. Since the amount of skills and attributes can sometimes be extensive, a full-screen window might need to be accessed through the manual interface in order for players to see the amount. Constantly displaying this sort of information on-screen as the game is played can cause the game to look cluttered. Therefore, some games have an action button in a corner or at the bottom of the screen that triggers a skill and attribute display.

Associated with a player character, *inventory* is also an important game interface component. It helps players keep track of the items that are available to their characters, especially in games that involve collecting and gathering items (such as adventure games and RPGs). Some of these items might be weapons that can only be used in certain circumstances or spells that need to be cast at certain points in the game. The ability to manage this inventory and keep track of what items are available to the player character greatly helps the player make certain decisions during the game. The inventory might be part of a screen that

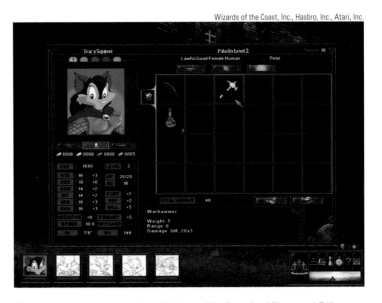

Wizards of the Coast, Inc., Hasbro, Inc., Atari, Inc.

Player character inventory interface from *The Temple of Elemental Evil.*

contains other character information (such as skills and attributes). It could even stand on its own. In either case, a player character's inventory often needs space to be displayed. Therefore, it will often need to be accessed through a menu or a manual interface—just like a skills and attributes display.

Start Screen

Early arcade games often employed *start screens* which would contain the title of the game, credits, instructions, and the ability to choose player mode (usually one or two players). Similar screens are used in online puzzle and other quick, action-oriented games. Other more extensive games might either use a simplified start screen that contains a high-end graphic representation of the game (often an exact replica of the game's box art) with just a "start" button—or a more detailed screen containing a menu of buttons with some of the following functions:

- Play Game
- Multiplayer Mode
- Setup
- Load Saved Game
- Select Character
- Instructions
- Tutorial
- Quit

Nexon Corporation

The *Crazy Bunker* start screen utilizes a simple interface consisting primarily of a start ("go") button, and the ability for players to enter their usernames and passwords.

Depending on how the game is designed, the start screen can provide an introduction to the mood and style of the game in addition to the player interface. It can also allow players to customize controls and get help before starting or resuming play.

Genre-Specific Interface Design

Most current game genres have very specific content structures and expected interface styles. What distinguishes these interface styles? What purpose do they serve? In order to understand why certain interface styles are used with particular genres, it's important to analyze the gameplay goals associated with each genre. Let's look at some popular game genres covered in Chapter 3 and discuss interface elements that are often associated with each.

Action

Since *action* games are fast-paced—requiring eye-hand coordination, reflexive movement, and quick decision-making—players don't have time to interact with a complex interface. Passive heads-up displays (HUDs) are best; players cannot pause the game in order to open a set of menus. A status panel—one of the most straightforward passive interface displays—allows players to check status indicators (lives, energy, time remaining, score) associated with their characters throughout the game.

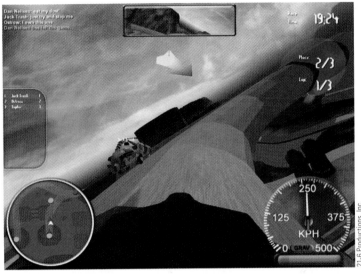

Heads-up displays (HUDs) are common in action games such as *Grav Rally.*

Adventure

More than most other genres, *adventure* games try to hide the fact that the player is using hardware in order to navigate through the environment. Player goals include moving through the world, communicating with other characters, and collecting objects in a way that will not interfere with the sense of immersion. Navigation through adventure games is often accomplished through *point-and-click* or *direct control* interfaces—in which a player clicks somewhere on the screen, causing the player's avatar to move to that location. In a direct control interface, the player steers the avatar around the screen. Inventory is often shown as a pop-up box containing icons representing all items the player is carrying.

In adventure games such as *Syberia,* character movement is controlled through a point-and-click interface. In the above screenshot, the player has placed the cursor (which has the appearance of a gold ring) in the fireplace; if the player were to click at this point, the character would walk toward the fireplace.

Black Isle Studios/Interplay

Character management interfaces are common in RPGs such as *Icewind Dale*.

Microsoft Corporation

Simulation games require realistic interface components, such as the complex cockpit controls for *Microsoft Flight Simulator 2004*.

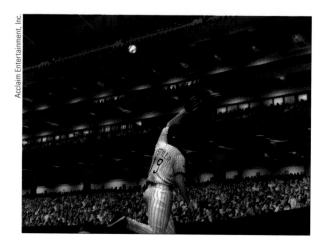

Acclaim Entertainment, Inc.

Interfaces for team sports games such as *All Star Baseball 2005* allow players to control one athlete at a time.

Role-Playing

A *role-playing game (RPG)* interface is often split up into three segments—character management, navigation control, and inventory. The range of actions that a player can take in an RPG is often much greater than in any other form of game. There is a corresponding increase in the complexity of the interface for this reason. To compensate, the manual interface is often more involved.

Simulation

Since all *simulation* games depend on real-world rules, how can an interface be designed so that this reality isn't disrupted? The most straightforward way to establish a seamless interface is to replicate the controls that might actually be used in a simulation. This is done most effectively in vehicle sims—especially flight simulators. Visual interfaces may include an instrument panel consisting of just a few buttons (providing altitude, speed, power, fuel, coordinates) to a more complex panel which could perform upwards of 40 different functions! These panels often have the look and feel of the controls you might actually see in a cockpit.

Sports

In most genres, the interface design changes only in response to explicit actions taken by the player. However, *sports* games are unusual in that the user interface often changes by the second—depending on the conditions in the game. The most difficult aspect of sports game interface design is that you have to map athletic activities (such as jumping) onto a game's input device—which is typically a handheld controller with buttons. In team sports games, the player will often control one athlete at a time—indicated by a circle or star displayed right under the athlete. Symbols might also appear on the field to help the player see exactly where a flying ball should land. Players should be able to see which athlete will be in control at any time. In this way, team sports game interfaces are similar to those of many strategy games—where players might control a set of military troops, each of whom may have different skills.

Microsoft Corporation

Interface design for strategy games such as *Age of Empires* focus on ensuring players can effectively manage resources.

Strategy

Most *strategy* games involve themes of conquest, exploration, and trade. The primary player strategy in these games is resource management, where the player must make decisions involving acquiring, building, expending, and exchanging resources such as food, weapons, buildings, and units (often military troops). Interfaces for these games are extremely specific. In fact, sometimes it's difficult to differentiate between strategy games by looking at isolated screenshots. The game view is often large-scale—displaying a landscape with terrain, structures, vehicles and units.

Data in strategy game interfaces are presented in windows—often containing a map and a series of icons that link to more in-depth information. Since this genre focuses so heavily on managing a great deal of information, it's important to divide the information up so that players don't have to look at everything at once on-screen. One way to do this is to provide context-sensitive information that appears only when needed. Another helpful consideration is to provide both a beginner and advance mode to facilitate different levels of experience.

Components of strategy game interfaces include general information (such as a map and statistics related to the condition of the environment [temperature, elevation, population]), and more specific information (such as inventory, skills, and status indicators related to a particular resource or unit).

Genre Interface Restrictions?

Do you think it's necessary to have specific interface elements for each genre? Choose a genre, analyze its interface components, and consider how you might change these elements to better suit players' needs and goals. What interface components would you include in a hybrid genre – or a new genre of your own?

Usability

The primary purpose of the user interface is functionality—not aesthetics. If an interface is functional, it is considered *usable.* The concept of *usability* is a vast area of study in many areas of interactive design, including web development, DVD authoring, and wireless display design. Since games represent the highest form of interactivity, player-centered design must incorporate a high level of usability. The main idea behind designing for usability is to think like an "engineer" rather than only like an "artist." An aesthetically-appealing interface is definitely desirable. However, an interface that looks great but is not functional will be useless to both the player and the developer. The most important function of the interface is to allow the player to *play the game!* An interface is considered "dysfunctional" when it is:

- **cryptic:** containing unintuitive controls or obscure graphics due to aesthetic over-enthusiasm
- **complex:** providing too many options so that a starting point is unclear
- **simplistic:** limiting player choice by including few components
- **inconsistent:** confusing players with style and logic clashes between the interface and the game itself, or within different areas of the interface
- **inefficient:** forcing players to interact too many times with the interface before they get to their destination
- **cluttered:** taking up too much screen space and obstructing the game content area, or incorporating crowded controls that are physically difficult for some players to use

The User Interface Experience

The effectiveness of an interface depends on the quality of the user *experience*. This is what sets interface design apart from traditional design.

— Jan McWilliams
(Artist/Educator;
Director of Interactive Design,
Art Institute of California, Los Angeles)

Task & Needs Analysis

When designing interface components, it's important to conduct a *task and needs analysis* to determine whether the interface will help fulfill player goals. One aspect of this analysis includes usability testing for frequency. Which of the tasks will need to be completed most frequently by the player? What if you designed an interface so that it took three actions to access a character's status screen—but you discovered that players needed to access that screen every time their characters added objects to their inventories? A simple redesign might allow a player to access that same screen with only one action—but you might have assumed that this screen wasn't going to be accessed that frequently. Testing your interface on prospective players or with an in-house testing team (discussed further in Chapter 10) could help you avoid having to do major interface redesigns.

The key is to allow the player to interact with the game effectively. During the game development process, placeholders are often used in place of visual interfaces so that usability is tested without the distraction of aesthetics. Only later in the development process is the visual look and feel introduced. Consider the example of an aesthetically-pleasing user interface that players can't figure out how to use and contrast it with a "boring" interface that is simple and easy to use. Which game do you think will be played more often? Which game will ultimately be more successful?

There's a term used among designers, engineers, and programmers known as *elegance*. If a design is efficient, consistent, clear, and functional, it's elegant. Designers are really problem-solvers—not "beautifiers." (The difference between an artist and a designer is discussed in more detail in Chapter 10.) By connecting the player to the game itself, active interfaces provide problem-solving functions (such as saving the game, accessing a tutorial, and communicating with other players). Of course, interfaces that are both aesthetically-pleasing *and* usable give the player the best of both worlds!

::::: A Dual Interface?

Nintendo DS—the dual screen handheld platform discussed first in Chapter 1—could display two interfaces at once. In what ways will this system affect game interface design? If you had the ability to design two standalone interfaces that could be accessed simultaneously on this system, what would be their components and purpose? How would you incorporate dual perspective discussed in Chapter 7?

The Importance of Usability Testing

*U*sability testing means putting the game in front of target users early to see if they can get through the game. One of the reasons that games appeal to such a narrow demographic is because they're inaccessible to most people. Usability testing lets designers see how their audience will deal with the interfaces and gameplay before they've spent much money developing it. Designers learn a lot by putting it through usability testing and often end up drastically changing their interfaces, control systems, and play mechanics accordingly.

— *Chris Swain*
(Professor, USC School of Cinema–Television;
Co-author, Game Design Workshop*)*

Accessibility

Accessibility is a branch of usability that focuses specifically on users with disabilities. According to the World Health Organization, an estimated 180 million people worldwide are visually impaired alone. Of these, between 40 and 45 million persons are blind. More than 40 years has passed since the first computer game was developed, yet the same player prerequisites are still assumed—full sight, hearing, and cognitive functions. The game industry excludes many (or most) disabled, potential gamers. Compare this to the web development industry—which has only been in existence since the mid-1990s and has been focusing on accessibility for years. The International Game Developers Association (IGDA) has addressed this problem by forming a "Game Accessibility Initiative." There are five main disability categories addressed by accessibility:

- visual
- audio
- motor
- speech
- cognitive

Firaxis Games / Atari, Inc.

Alpha Centauri's color scheme can be changed to one suitable for players who are color-blind.

Visual

The visually disabled are those who are visually impaired, colorblind, and partially or completely blind. In order to ensure that an interface addresses the visually disabled, it needs to contain code that allows screen readers such as Jaws to read the information displayed on the screen to the player. Games should also provide audio such as voiceover dialogue and sound effects that cue the player to what is happening in the game. Players should also have the option of making the text larger for ease of reading.

It's also necessary for text to be written for *scannability* so that players can read it quickly. Scannable text is concise, direct, free of unnecessary words (such as the articles "a," "an," and "the"), and it only contains words that are essential in getting the point across. Being forced to plow through linear text dialogue and backstory can be tedious for anyone!

This is one of the inherent issues associated with handheld devices. To address this, keep text options within the player's control. Many Game Boy Advance titles allow the player to opt-out of the linear dialogue and story by clicking on the "start" button. (This solution would not work for new players, who may need to scroll through the text information to fully understand the game.) Hard copy instruction manuals should also be available in Braille.

Civilization III—which displays text information from the player's advisors—does not require sound in order to play.

Audio

People with audio disabilities include those who are partially or completely deaf, along with those who have hearing conditions such as *tinnitus*—which results in constant ringing in the ears and is common with people who listen to loud noises for an extended period of time, such as concert-goers and performers. (William Shatner and Pete Townshend are two of the more well-known victims of this ailment.) Audio disabilities can be addressed by *not* relying on audio as a primary gameplay cue. Subtitles and text should be provided for cut-scenes and dialogue. Visual elements for game notices and alerts help all players.

Motor

Age of Empires and *Command & Conquer: Tiberian Sun* allow players with physical disabilities to play the game using specialized equipment.

Sony Computer Entertainment, Inc.

SOCOM: U.S. Navy Seals—a game that focuses on speech as a communication method—allows players the option of communicating by text.

People with some motor disabilities may have difficulty using a mouse, keyboard, controller, foot pedal, or other input device. Menu systems containing small buttons may be difficult to navigate through if a player has difficulty controlling a mouse in a point-and-click interface. A computer interface can allow for tab navigation as an option, avoiding the necessity of mouse clicking.

Speech

People with speech disabilities have difficulty communicating through voice. Since most electronic games are visual, speech disabilities haven't yet become a primary area of accessibility research. However, games such as *SOCOM: U.S. Navy Seals* that require voice communication between players (through headset/microphone input devices) would be impossible for those with speech disabilities to play without non-speech options.

Cognitive

People with cognitive disabilities have difficulty with reading, writing, and envisioning spatial relationships. Complicated menu systems with several layers should be avoided in order to address this type of disability. Simple sentence structure and vocabulary should also be used in order to avoid the possibility of players misunderstanding the rules of the game. Many online multiplayer games require players to communicate with each other via chat or IM-style windows. This can pose a problem for some players, who don't feel comfortable with text communication due to cognitive disabilities such as *dyslexia*—a common disability that could cause a player to spend extra time creating correctly formulated words and sentences. Games that require time-dependent text responses would be inappropriate and unfair for these players.

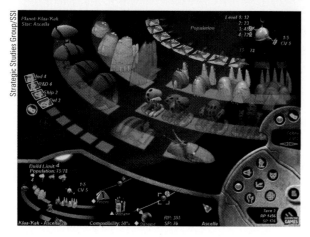

Disciples II: Dark Prophecy and *Reach for the Stars* both utilize an icon-based interface, although players may communicate optionally via text.

Internationalization

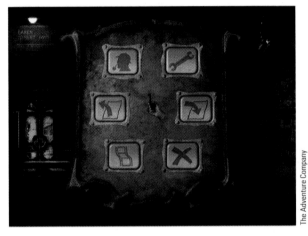

The Adventure Company

The main active menu in the Sherlock Holmes adventure game, *The Mystery of the Mummy*, displays icons that are universally recognizable. When the player's cursor is placed over an action button in the menu, the cursor changes from a pipe into a hand (and the button displays the color green).

Games that are *internationalized* attempt to be usable for players worldwide, without having to develop language-based versions. (In Chapter 11, you will learn more about *localization*—in which versions of a game are developed to address specific languages and cultures.) Internationalization involves techniques such as making menu buttons icon-based rather than text-based. The visual icon can be interpreted and understood much faster than the equivalent text. Buttons should specifically display universal symbols (including those that have become interface standards, such as the question mark to represent "help") to avoid misunderstandings that might result from the use of culture-specific icons, symbols, puns, and phrases. When time zones, measurements, and currency must be specified, they should not be biased toward a particular region (e.g., Pacific Time) or country (e.g., U.S. non-metric system).

Save-Game Options

The various *save-game options* available to a game developer bring up a balance issue between *immersiveness* and *player control.* (Both of these concepts were introduced in Chapter 4.) An active in-game interface often includes a "save" menu item, which can effectively take the player out of the game and compromise the game's *immersiveness.* In contrast, a game could be automatically saved at different *checkpoints* (or milestones) during the game. Although this "save-game" option is seamless and does not take the player out of the game, it compromises *player control.* Game developers have debated which of these concepts might be more important to the player or to the game itself—and the answer usually depends on the game's genre and platform. Let's take a closer look at some save-game options and apply them to different types of games.

Quick-Save

In action games where the player's avatar is in constant danger (such as an FPS), the player can often *quick-save* by pressing one button on a manual interface to save instantly at any time during the game—without ever leaving the game world. In this case, no visual interface exists except for the possibility of a confirmation (the word "saved") being displayed on-screen for a moment—but this does not break the player's concentration and immersion. The disadvantage of this method is that it contains only one save slot. Sometimes, there are several additional slots available—but the player must remember to designate these after pressing the quick-save button. This also takes up extra time, which might be detrimental to gameplay during a fast-moving game. This save option allows for more immersiveness and speed at the expense of flexibility and player control.

Auto-Save

The *auto-save* (also known as *check-point save*) option offers the most immersion and the least amount of player control. The game auto-saves as it progresses, allowing the player to leave and return at any time without explicitly having to save the game. Auto-saves can be continuous, but they more often take place at certain *checkpoints* in the game. These checkpoints are not necessarily revealed to the player—which can prevent the player from undoing earlier mistakes. However, the player is able to interrupt and resume the game at any point. Action games featuring rewind—such as *Prince of Persia* and *Blinx*—allow the player to undo one action.

The Adventure Company

Syberia allows a player to save games to slots and stores a thumbnail image of each save.

Save to Slot/File

Some games allow the player to interrupt play and save the game to a series of named "slots" (console or handheld) or file (computer) maintained by the game. In this case, a "save" item is usually included on an in-game active interface so that the player can conveniently access this option at any time during the game. The player can save either a limited or infinite (only limited by the player's hard drive space) number of games at various points during play, and provide them with distinct names. This method of saving the game is considered most harmful to a game's immersiveness. The interface for managing files or save slots often looks like a file-management system. This can be made more visually interesting, but it will still take the player out of the game unless it is somehow integrated into the experience itself.

The "Save-Game" Debate

There is a debate among developers concerning whether or not to allow players the freedom to save the game at chosen intervals. The debate centers around how gameplay might be affected by saving the game. Developers of some puzzle games are often against the idea because they feel that the player should solve the game by skill rather than trial-and-error. Saving and reloading can also defeat the purpose of an uninterrupted action sequence. When players save and reload at any point, some argue that nothing is really at stake in the game. What if a player's avatar dies or loses resources? Any disaster can be reversed simply by reloading the game. This definitely takes away much of the challenge!

On the other hand, some argue that making a game harder simply by preventing the player from saving the game is not an ideal way of creating a challenge. It most certainly does not show respect for the player. For a more challenging game, create more difficult gameplay challenges! Forcing a player to replay a level or entire game due to a mistake made near the end wastes a player's time and condemns the player to frustration and boredom. This needs to be avoided—not created.

One compromise solution is to allow the player to save at any time but to somehow reward the player for not saving. *Alpha Centauri* has included an "Iron Man" mode. A game played in Iron Man would close automatically when saved, thereby making the save-load process an ineffective way of undoing a serious mistake. As compensation, the player's final score is doubled when playing in this mode. Some games—such as *Halo*—reward players for completing the game without saving at all.

Guidelines for a Great Interface

In order to create a great game interface, keep the following guidelines in mind:

- Be consistent
- Enable shortcuts (as options for hardcore players)
- Provide feedback
- Offer defined tasks
- Permit easy reversal of actions

- Allow for player control
- Keep it simple (and don't strain the player's short-term memory)
- Make it customizable (and allow the player to configure the interface somewhat)
- Include a context-sensitive pointer (that changes form when pointing to an object of interest)
- Implement different modes (including beginner and expert)
- Use established conventions (avoid trying to invent your own)

In the next chapter, you will learn about how audio can enhance the atmosphere of the game—and how it can work with the game interface to help the player connect to the game.

:::CHAPTER REVIEW:::

1. Using one of your favorite games as an example, discuss the ways in which the game's interfaces allow you to feel you have some control during gameplay.

2. How do the components of a game interface work together to make a game usable and functional for the player?

3. There are several unique manual interfaces—such as foot pads, maracas, a microphone, and a fishing pole—that are designed to enhance the game-playing experience. Disregarding the obvious (such as guns for first-person shooters), recommend a unique manual interface that could be used as an alternative manual device for one of your favorite games. If you were asked to create an original manual interface for your own game, what would it be—and how would it make the player's experience of the game more enjoyable?

4. The area of accessibility is gradually being addressed by the game industry. Choose one of the five disabilities discussed in this chapter and come up with a unique way of addressing the disability in a game interface.

5. Knowing that the save-game debate hasn't been resolved, what type of save-game option would you incorporate into your game—and why? Can you think of a new way of saving the game that hasn't been thought of before?

6. Choose a game and analyze its usability features. Suggest at least three improvements to the interface, and create a rough sketch redesigning the interface based on your analysis.

7. Begin a task-and-needs analysis of a game by asking the following questions: What tasks does the visual interface allow the player to accomplish? Do these tasks correspond to gameplay goals? Detail a task-and-needs analysis for your original game idea. Provide a list of five necessary tasks that players will have to complete in order to advance in the game. Provide a list of the top five items or actions that players will need in order to accomplish these tasks during the game. How will your interface address these needs and tasks?

8. Construct a draft interface template for your original game. Define the layout, content, and navigation components of your template.

9. Choose a genre and discuss specific interface design features that correspond to that genre. Add another interface component that has not been discussed in this chapter to address a genre-specific need that may not be immediately obvious.

10. Define the existing visual interface style for one of your favorite games. What if you were asked to redesign the interface so that it incorporated one of the other styles discussed in this chapter? What changes would you make—and why? Would other elements of the game have to change (such as story, character, gameplay, and world)?

CHAPTER

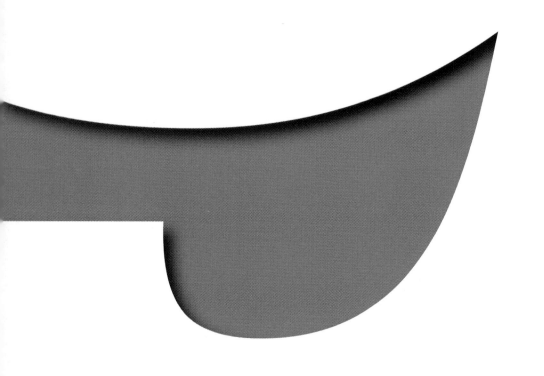

Audio:
creating the atmosphere

key chapter questions

■ Why is audio an important aspect of game development?

■ How are voiceovers, sound effects, and music used effectively in a game?

■ What is the difference between *looping* and *adaptive* music?

■ How is game composing different from film scoring?

■ What are the different formats and tools used in game audio?

Audio is probably the least appreciated area of game development—and it is often overlooked. This neglect is not unusual; it happens in other industries as well. In a film, final audio is not incorporated until the post-production stage—and it is considered an enhancement rather than a core feature of the project. Game developers often focus heavily on graphics, artificial intelligence, and gameplay, without considering the many functions of audio. Once the importance of game audio is finally realized, it is often too late to make the best use of it. This chapter provides an introduction to game audio (including music, sound, and dialogue)—and how it can be utilized effectively to create a rich game atmosphere.

The Importance of Game Audio

Game audio can range from *sampled* (recorded) sound such as voices and music; interface sounds such as beeps and button clicks; and in-game effects, such as explosions and footsteps. Audio can be extremely important for a game's atmosphere, setting the mood as well as changing it. Audio can also provide gameplay cues, heighten player satisfaction, and enhance the quality of a game. While graphics will draw a player into a scene, game audio has an immersive effect on the player that can seldom be achieved with graphics alone. This may be partially because real-life sounds can be reproduced on a computer much better than real-life visuals. (Although a digital image of a gorilla pounding on its chest can be striking, contrast this with a well-sampled gorilla's threatening roar.) Since the game's screen is limited in size, players can conceivably be taken out of the game's visual world. In contrast, players can be enveloped by the sounds of a game world—which can exist all around them.

Russell Burt on Paying Attention to Audio :::::

Russell Burt has been living in Los Angeles for 15 years and has worked extensively as a keyboardist, recording engineer, and producer. His recording credits include Warrant, Boney James, the Temptations, Bruce Hornsby, and the Doobie Brothers. Russell has also worked as a sound designer and composer for many audio dramas, including the *Star Wars* audio book series. He has programmed and produced several interactive CD entertainment titles, as well as corporate training projects. Russell now teaches full-time at the Art Institute of California–Los Angeles in the Interactive Design department.

Russell Burt (Sound Designer/ Engineer; Interactive Design Faculty, Art Institute of California–Los Angeles)

The role of audio cannot be overstated in games! As an audio engineer, keyboardist, and sound designer, I am continually amazed at how poorly audio in general is appreciated. A common adage states that people don't pay attention to sound in entertainment unless the sound is bad. Specifically with games, audio needs to be handled subtly, for it creates a mood whether or not the gamer is actively listening. Audio can be used effectively for dialogue, sound effects, and music—but if it's used ineffectively, it can ruin an otherwise great project.

The Best Audio Tools

Since there is really no central audio tool kit for development over all platforms right now, I would have to say that the best game audio development tools are: imagination, creativity, persistence, patience, enthusiasm—and lots of cool synth and sampler plug-ins! (Patience will help with getting them *all* to work with your current operating system!)

—Bill Brown
(Composer & Director of Music, Soundelux DMG)

In Chapter 8, you learned about the importance of a game's interface. Audio can also effectively reinforce a player's physical sensations, so it is an essential part of that interface. Even in menu buttons, sound can convey a solid tactile feeling of switches being flipped or buttons being pushed. Accessibility must also be considered as a usability principle with audio interfaces. Since some players are hearing-impaired, make sure a visual cue is always given as a complement to an audio cue—or at least have visual cues be a potential option that the player can set. Anytime there is spoken dialogue, subtitles should also be included. Allow players the option of adjusting the game audio volume without affecting the sounds on their machines. Finally, be sure to separate volume controls for dialogue, sound effects, and music.

Game Audio Formats

In the 1980s, game audio was limited by game hardware to simple beeps. Early computer-based audio revolved around *frequency modulation (FM) synthesis,* which uses algorithms to re-create and combine sound waves of different shapes, frequencies, and volumes. Often, these sounds were used to approximate real-world sounds and musical instruments—and the results were less than spectacular.

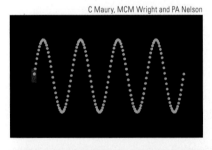
C Maury, MCM Wright and PA Nelson

FM synthesis (used by synthesizers such as the DX7) involves generating sounds from mathematical data associated with sound waves.

Yamaha Corporation of America

The MOD (module) music format, popularized by the Amiga, used real samples instead of mathematical approximations. MOD supported four tracks, each of which could be playing one sample at any pitch. Since computers had enough memory to store instrument samples—and enough pro-

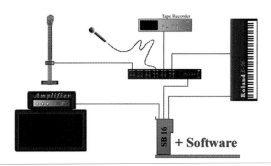

A MIDI setup incorporates several different devices that work together to create sound.

cessing power to manipulate the pitch of those instruments in real-time—MOD was a vast improvement over FM synthesis. This technique was an earlier version of what is now known as *wave table synthesis,* in which the creation of audio relies on a table of sampled sound waves.

Tracked audio followed, with software such as StarTrekker, ProTracker, and ScreamTracker (STM). Parallel to the development of FM synth and tracked audio, the *MIDI (musical instrument digital interface)* revolution was also taking shape.

Unlike tracked audio (which is a closed, CPU-based system that stores instruments, applies effects, and plays the finished process through one device), MIDI incorporates several different devices that work together to create sound. A MIDI setup might include a drum machine, keyboard, instrument banks, computer, and effects processors—and MIDI allows them all to communicate with each other. MIDI is a sort of networking protocol that specifies how musical notes are stored and transmitted across wires to different devices. Following the advent of MIDI, many performers began using synthesizers (electronic keyboards) to control multiple instruments during live shows. MIDI has been responsible for the development of hardware and computer-based sequencers, which can be used to record, edit, and play back performances.

The Fairlight CMI (expensive hardware-based pioneer), Emu E4 (modular unit), and Gigastudio (software) represent three different eras in sampling tools.

Instead of generating sounds from mathematical wave data, *samplers* digitized sound from an external audio source (such as an analog musical instrument) at particular pitches and played these sounds back digitally.

In the 1990s, MIDI and tracked audio were the most popular technology approaches to game audio. MIDI files are typically very small because the instruments playing the music weren't stored within the files. However, this means that good playback of a MIDI song depends on the quality of the hardware/instruments; game audio would often sound great on a composer's professional setup, but would leave much to be

chapter 9   Audio: creating the atmosphere

desired on a player's system. Tracked audio was great because the instruments were contained in the audio, which sounded the same regardless of the hardware used to play it—but the audio took up way too much space and CPU power on the player's system.

Tracked audio and MIDI eventually merged in 1997 in the form of *DLS1 (Downloadable Sounds Level 1),* which also allowed each instrument to have

Microsoft's DirectMusic Producer—which supports DLS2—is a popular tool used by game audio professionals because it allows for game-specific dynamic audio creation.

multiple samples based on frequency. In 1999, *DLS2,* an even better improvement, was introduced, and is supported by Microsoft's DirectMusic.

For commercial games distributed on CDs, *Redbook Audio (CD)* is the best music storage format. A game composer needs to know the game's target hardware platform and what type of music it will support. Computers and all next-generation consoles allow you to use full Redbook Audio (regular CD audio), but handhelds and Internet-delivered games often require MIDI music—which doesn't sound as good but uses very small files.

Redbook Audio is used for commercial games distributed on CDs.

ProTools is considered to be industry standard for audio recording, editing and mixing.

Digidesign (a division of Avid Technology, Inc.)

Practically falling into the game industry 7 years ago, Aaron Marks has amassed music and sound design credits on touch-screen arcade games, class II video bingo/slot machines, computer games, console games—and over 70 online casino games.

Aaron has also written for *Game Developer Magazine,* Gamasutra.com, and Music4Games.net. He is the author of *The Complete Guide to Game Audio,* an expansive book on all aspects of audio for video games. He is also a member of the advisory board for the Game Audio Network Guild (GANG)—and he continues his pursuit of the ultimate soundscape, creating music and sound for various projects.

Aaron Marks
(Composer & Sound Designer; President, On Your Mark Music Productions)

It is essential that you have a good audio editing program; you can't do the job without it! My main editor is Sound Forge, but I also use Wavelab and Goldwave for their unique capabilities. Whether you are doing sound design or composing, taking a final look at the sound will ensure that the file is "healthy" and doesn't have unwanted silence or clipping. Also, a good multi-track audio program such as Vegas Video is a nice addition. Having the flexibility to layer various sounds and adjust their parameters separately really adds to the overall sound, plus it makes it easy to go back and edit later. The one tool I can't live without is Sound Forge's Batch Converter. All of the sound effects and music are created as at least 44.1-kHz, 16-bit, stereo .wav files. Since I initially create up to several hundred sound effects and music cues per game, I could easily end up spending an entire day just doing sound conversions if I didn't have this awesome tool!

Lennie Moore has developed a career in Los Angeles over the last decade as an accomplished composer, orchestrator, and arranger of music for film, television, and games, with a wide range of writing music in many styles—from jazz to pop to symphonic orchestra. He has composed music on 10 films and over 100 commercials, orchestrated for other composers on dozens of feature films and television movies, and completed a breathtaking 60-minute symphonic score for orchestra and choir for the hit game *Outcast.*

Lennie Moore (Composer)

Recently, Lennie composed music for *The Lord of the Rings: War of the Ring* (Vivendi Universal Games) and *Plague of Darkness* (Namco). He has worked with many orchestras around the world as a composer/conductor, including the Moscow and Munich symphony orchestras, the San Francisco Opera, as well as orchestras in Los Angeles, Toronto, Seattle, and Salt Lake City. Lennie Moore began composing at an early age. "I remember being about four five years old, sitting at the piano, with my mother transcribing on music paper for me, as I was plunking out a melody and saying things like 'I want that note!'" He has studied writing with jazz icons Toshiko Akiyoshi, Julian Priester, and Kim Richmond, and he has also been under the tutelage of the outstanding faculty at the Berklee College of Music, where he refined his skills as a composer and arranger and received a Bachelor of Music degree.

Currently I'm using Cubase SX on a PC, three Gigastudio PCs, Sonic Foundry Sound Forge, SawPro (audio editor similar to Pro Tools), Spectrasonics Stylus/Trilogy/Atmosphere, and tons of sample libraries like Project SAM Brass and Sonic Implants Strings. If I am developing music for specific consoles I utilize the Microsoft Xact system for Xbox titles, the Scream system for Playstation2 titles, or Microsoft DirectMusic Producer for Direct Music titles....We keep raising the bar every day. The compositional and sonic quality of music keeps improving as we start to explore surround environments, improve on audio bit resolution, not to mention all the great tools and technology that are now available.

Sound Effects

Game *sound effects* are used to provide feedback and cues to a player. In a vehicle simulation game, audio representing the pitch of an engine can be used to indicate when a player needs to shift gears. Audio can also be used to warn a player that an enemy is approaching through the sound of footsteps, heavy breathing, or a muffled roar behind a locked door.

As you're reading this book, what sounds do you hear around you? In real life, sound is everywhere. Pure silence only exists in artificial environments, such as soundproof chambers. In games, background sounds can be used to help immerse players in the game by providing a realistic atmosphere. Players do not focus on the background ambience in a game, but they would notice if this ambience were to suddenly cease. If you've ever experienced a sudden power outage, you have a small idea of what this feels like.

Event-based sounds serve as feedback to the actions the player takes. These sounds can be realistic, such as a vehicle accelerating—or artificial,

*M*edal of Honor: Allied Assault has the most uncanny sound effects of explosions and bullets whizzing by. I can't count the number of times I actually tried to move my head around those bullets.

—Aaron Nash,
Game Art &
Design student

> The best sound effects I've heard in a game were from *Tony Hawk's Underground.* They were tailored to real life—from the rustle of leaves, to dogs barking, to the sounds of pigeons flapping away.
>
> —*Melissa Adkison,*
> *Game Art & Design student*

such as a special sound that only occurs when a magical spell is cast. Sounds can also provide clues to the player. If a player's avatar is walking down a dark street and is being followed, the player might hear the sound of footsteps coming from behind the avatar—getting progressively louder.

A sound designer creates the bigger sound effects (such as vehicle acceleration, explosions, and the hum of machinery) and the smaller *foley* sounds (such as a key turning in a lock, footsteps, and doors swinging shut). Foley is used in movies and is named after Jack Foley, who helped make the transition from the silent era to talkies. He re-created noises in a sound studio that were not easily captured on the movie set and then synched them to the action on the screen.

> When I heard the crunching and cracking sounds in *Tekken,* it put shivers down my spine.
>
> —*Vincent Ramos,*
> *Interactive Design*
> *student*

Creating an Audio Identity

Once the initial 'feel' for a game is defined, it's up to the sound designer to match that vision and create an audio identity for the game. Even something as simple as a gun shot, for example, has to be unique for each game. I know a sound designer has done a good job when I can hear a sound playing in another room and I can tell what game it's from. Sometimes creating this 'uniqueness' can be a difficult task.

We've all heard games where the sound detracts from the experience—and we've turned the volume off altogether…. Now, it's not to say that sound alone will make or break a game, but experiencing one where audio is a priority can literally be mind-blowing, and an experience a player will want to relive again and again. *Halo* and the *Medal of Honor* series immediately come to mind. These types of games are successful in totally immersing the players into the game world and giving them the ride of their lives! With sound providing one-third of the overall experience, it better be good!

When I'm creating, I often find myself very focused on the task at hand. I was once creating sound effects for a sword fight in my studio, getting all the standard metal hits and scrapes recorded. The next sound on the list was a series of 'sword breaking rock' effects, which was to be used when the swordsman missed his opponent and hit one of the many rock features in the arena. Not even thinking, I brought in a bunch of rocks, bricks, and concrete blocks into the control room, pressed record, and proceeded to start smashing and throwing debris everywhere—really getting into the scene and trying to make it sound realistic. Once I felt I had enough to work with, I stopped and stood back to contemplate the session. That's when I realized dust and rock debris was covering everything! I'd made a complete mess out of the place! I'm still finding bits and pieces of that session in the oddest places.

—*Aaron Marks (Composer & Sound Designer;*
President, On Your Mark Music Productions)

Sound designers often purchase entire sound libraries to help with both large sound effects and foley. Although these libraries can provide some highly effective sounds, I suggest that they only be used as a starting point or to provide ideas. Many game audio professionals—as well as the players themselves—have come to recognize (and sometimes grow tired of) some commonly-used library sounds. The best sound designers will go out in the world with a recorder, capture natural sounds, and tweak them into original sounds in a studio.

> *Silent Hill* scared me so incredibly the first time I played it that I literally had nightmares. When a game uses sound effects correctly, they seem invariable and invisibly structured. They happen just when they should—no sooner, no later, no anticipation possible. *Silent Hill* scared the hell out of me; every time I heard a noise, I turned white!
>
> —*Stephen Toth,*
> *Game Art & Design student*

Using digital or analog recorder, you can capture effects for a variety of sounds—such as gunshots and footsteps—by either recording them in the environment or by using foley techniques. Here are just a few sounds that are fairly easy to capture using foley:

- *Car crash:* Fill a box with scrap metal and chunks of wood. Shake vigorously.
- *Fire:* Open an umbrella quickly for a burst of flames. Crumple up thick cellophane for the crackle.
- *Body collision:* Strike a pumpkin or watermelon with a piece of wood.
- *Gunshots:* Hit a leather seat with a thin wooden stick, such as a ruler (or fold a belt in half and snap it).
- *Bushes:* Rustle some broom straw.
- *Boiling water:* Blow through a straw inserted in water to make bubbles.
- *Aircraft:* Record a hairdryer starting up and turning off. Slow down or speed up the sound in an editing program.

Once you've connected your device to the computer, you can use a program such as CoolEdit to record and save the sample into the computer.

> The *Resident Evil* series uses great sound effects because many different objects and weapons are used to generate them. A zombie dragging itself across the floor could be a fruit of some sort being mashed to make that "sloshing" sound!
>
> —*Mason Batchelder,*
> *Game Art & Design student*

Game Sound Design Challenges

The challenges of game audio are many and varied. First, there are the technical limitations—including the amount of RAM, compression type, amount of streaming, number of channels, and amount of CPU allowed to the audio bits. Once you have this worked out, you have to design your implementation—which accounts for more than 50 percent of a game player's experience with audio. The best assets in the world won't matter if the implementation of that audio is bad. This is the one area where most titles fall short. Ever hear that endlessly repeating sound? Been unable to hear dialog? Get distortion when too many sounds play together? Been unable to distinguish between all the different sounds going on at any one time? This is all implementation. I'm hopeful that the middleware that is currently emerging is going to solve the majority of the implementation problems in the near future.

After all the technical issues are sorted out, there are still the challenges of how to get or create the assets. Depending on the scope of the project, this can be a sizeable task. Managing the files, milestones, and quality are all challenges that are faced by the sound designer.

Assets and implementation have to be connected to the game. The sound design has to be just that—a design. Too often sounds are just slapped in at the last minute—resulting in a lousy audio experience. The design of the sonic space is where the real art is—making sure there is room for voice and low-frequency effects (if any), that sounds attach to the objects they are a part of, and that the whole game is mixed properly.

The non-linear nature of game audio also provides a challenge. With games, you don't know exactly what is going to be played when; once you add the dynamic nature of the playback, the game changes dramatically from other media. Also, you have the added annoyance of not knowing what type of system the end user will be listening to you on. Do I mix for stereo $5 speakers? Or 5.1 surround systems? The quality and frequency response of these two extremes is, well…extreme.

—Scott Snyder
(Audio Director & Sound Designer,
Dancing Mouse Productions)

Voiceovers

Voiceovers are used in games for spoken dialogue and narration. Voiceovers are often supplied by outsourced talent. The artists are recorded reading dialogue and narration scripts in a recording studio. Make sure the artists understand any specifics about the voices, including accents and how character development needs to be revealed during the reading. Voiceover talent should have previous experience in commercial voiceover work—such as film, television, games, or advertising.

Games: New Opportunities for Voice Artists

Now that celebrities seem to dominate the animation world, voiceover artists are turning to the game industry to play all sorts of offbeat and very mature characters. It's opened a whole new field of fun work to a talented group of actors that otherwise might not be heard. Game players benefit because they can go into a funky new world with a fresh crop of characters.

—Janet Wilcox
(Voiceover Artist & Instructor)

Playing Patrick in *Dino Crisis III*

Doing voiceovers for video games is a unique, fun part of the industry. Throwing your voice behind a character with extraordinary powers is pretty awesome. On some gigs, you get to do a little animated movie (establishing the plot of the game) and then go back in and do all of the reactions and sound bites for the in-game action. It is great experience for other animated work. Voicing Patrick in *Dino Crisis III* was almost like having an acting exercise built right into the job itself. I ended up not only doing the written script, but I also got to imagine Patrick in all kinds of different scenarios and react to those as well. How would Patrick react to a slap in the face by a space bear at the end of a hard day? "OOOF!" Pretty cool!

Actor Mike Yurchak voicing "Patrick"—the hero in *Dino Crisis III*—an intergalactic special-ops hero who leads his troops into some hot water when they meet up with "killer dinosaurs."

—Mike Yurchak
(Voice Actor)

> ## "Convincing Death Noises"
>
> I was doing voice talent for the female player character for id Software's *Quake 2*. At the time, I was working for Crack dot Com, and we occupied offices right next to a title company. For a week, I made all manner of horrible screams, gurgling drownings, leaping grunts, and other assorted tasty morsels into FX files. At one point on the first day, a rep from the title company had to come over to our offices and make sure nothing was going wrong. I make convincing death noises, apparently. Bwahahaha!
>
> —*Carly Staehlin*
> *(Lead Designer, NCsoft)*

As discussed in Chapters 4 and 5, game stories (unlike film) are non-linear. This means that dialogue scripts for the game (other than cut-scene scripts) will often be out of context. Voiceover artists will often speak only one or two lines at a time or make victorious or defeated sounds (such as screams or grunts) that will be used again in many parts of the game. An audio director will most likely want to record many versions of one type of sound from the voiceover artists so that the game is more realistic and varied. For example, an orc grunting in the same way each time it is clicked upon will sound more artificial than it would if it emitted several different types of grunts each time. Similarly, a non-player character (NPC) who states that same line of dialogue every time a player character runs into him ("You really shouldn't head in this direction!") also decreases the immersive experience of the game. Several alternate lines of dialogue should be prepared for this purpose and should be recorded by the same voiceover artist for consistency. The best games typically have 20 or more variants of common sounds.

Bob Bergen & Hope Levy on the Joys and Perils of Voice Acting :::::

Bob Bergen
(Voice Actor)

Bob Bergen started working full-time as an actor at the age of 23. His resume consists of hundreds of cartoons, commercials, and games—as well as on-camera stints on such shows as *The Facts of Life, Days of Our Lives,* and *Gimme a Break.* In 1990, Bob's dream came true when he joined a handful of actors who share the job of voicing the Looney Tunes. Over the years, Bob has voiced Porky, Tweety, Marvin the Martian, Henry Hawk, Sylvester Jr., and Speedy Gonzales in a variety of projects. For 10 years, Bob worked as the grandstand host at the annual Hollywood Christmas Parade. After a one-time "trial" performance of his one-man show in Burbank, CA, he was asked by Ken Kragen—who manages Kenny Rogers—to be the opening act for Rogers' 1999 summer tour throughout California and Oregon. Bob returned from the tour and showcased his one-man show at the Ice House in Pasadena and the Whitefire Theater in Sherman Oaks. Producer Ed Gaynes offered to put the show up commercially at the Whitmore–Lindley Theater in North Hollywood, CA. *Bob Bergen: Not Just Another Pretty Voice* opened to great reviews and ran for three months. Bob has been teaching his animation voiceover workshop for over 15 years, and he is currently working on a slew of animation projects, commercials, and games.

In games, voice actors usually work solo. On an animated series, the producers will try to have as many of the cast members at the session as possible. When voicing games, you need to record all the potential options a player might have in the game. This often takes a while and can get a bit tedious…. One of the most challenging things about voice acting for games in particular is the yelling—which is *very* hard on the voice at times! But the good directors will wait until the end of the session to record those. My most memorable experience during a game voiceover session was when I voiced Luke Skywalker for LucasArts. Luke had the line, "Look at the size of that thing!" I kept laughing and it took a long time to get through the line!

Hope Levy (Voice Actor & Singer) is most recognized as the voice of Resident Evil's Rebecca Chambers.

Capcom Co, Ltd.

Hope Levy recently completed voice work on the Japanese animated film *Pompoko*—to be released in America by Disney. She can be heard singing "Welcome to Duloc" in Dreamworks' *Shrek,* and she was the voice of the "Valley Girl" bear in Disney's *Brother Bear.* She created the voices of Chet Zipper and Melanie on the Emmy award–nominated *As Told By Ginger*—and she has voiced characters on *The Fairly Odd Parents, Rugrats, Ozzy & Drix,* and *Invader Zim.* She is currently re-voicing the Japanese anime series *Shin Chan,* playing Cosmo. In games, Hope can be heard in *Polar Express,* Knowledge Adventure's *Jumpstart* series, and as Rebecca Chambers in *Resident Evil.* On the silver screen, Hope will be seen in *My Big Fat Independent Movie,* playing the Greek Wedding Girl (à la Nia Vardolos). Hope also co-stars as Pam, the wanna-be rapper, in Disney's *Uncle P*—starring Master P and Lil Romeo.

In game voice acting, each emotion—such as laughing, crying, screaming—has to be recorded. Each "action" also has to be recorded; we call these "efforts"—and they include punching, getting punched, sighing, getting attacked, performing full combat, dragging bodies, and being dragged. We also perform *numerous* endings for the game so that the player has more to experience and play with. That's cool, because our characters may actually play good guys or bad guys—depending on which ending the player chooses. The energy it takes to voice act in a game is *endless.* It's a surprisingly physical job. We voice actors throw ourselves into the moment … so when we're being chased, we're running in place—huffing and puffing. After a four-hour session of screaming and really getting into the actions and emotions of what the game requires, we feel pretty spent!

Music

Game *music* is a way of telling the players how they should be reacting to the visual images on the screen. Music can heighten the thrill of action, tell the player when danger lurks around the corner, or set a lighter tone for comedic moments.

> The future of game music? Two words: live orchestra!
>
> —*Tommy Tallarico (Composer; Founder, Game Audio Network Guild [GANG])*

A game's *soundtrack* might consist of a *score* and *songs.* The *score* refers to instrumental music often written for the game itself that creates a mood and atmosphere. Composers often put together scores using home recording systems—including a MIDI synthesizer or keyboard that is hooked up to a computer containing recording, sequencing, and mixing software. For games with larger budgets, a composer might prepare *parts* for live instruments and record this music at a recording studio with a live orchestra or ensemble.

Soundtracks are recorded in a home recording studio (Aaron Marks' depicted) or a professional recording studio (Ron Jones conducting).

Orchestral *Outcast*

My expertise is with live musicians, so I'm seeing a lot more AAA titles with orchestral scores being recorded in Los Angeles, which is wonderful, as the AFM musicians who do the big feature films are now showing up on the big games…. My most memorable experience composing music for games would probably be recording *Outcast* in Moscow with an 80-piece symphony orchestra and 24-voice choir.

—Lennie Moore,
Composer

Bill Brown on Positive Challenges in the Composition Process :::::

Bill Brown has composed music for directors and producers including Steven Spielberg, Oliver Stone, Clive Barker, Michael Crichton, Gus Van Sant, Michael Mann, and Tom Clancy. His evocative, powerful orchestral scores continue to gain special recognition and awards in the industry, including three nominations for BAFTA Awards in the music category. Bill is the Director of Music for Soundelux Design Music Group in Hollywood, CA, and he has composed and produced music for theatrical releases such as *Any Given Sunday, Ali,* and *Finding Forrester.* Bill has also scored television films such as *Scorcher* and *Trapped,* and games including Tom Clancy's *Rainbow Six* series, *The Sum of All Fears, Lineage II: The Chaotic Chronicle, Return to Castle Wolfenstein,* and *Command & Conquer: Generals.*

Bill Brown
(Composer &
Director of Music,
Soundelux DMG)

I always look at challenge as a good thing in the context of creativity. If it is obvious, it's not going to interest me as much. If it is complex and layered, there might be a challenge somewhere in the process—and that's good! Where there is challenge, there is growth—and I keep finding that where there is growth, there is huge reward. For me, the process of writing music for games is like mastery of anything, really. I'm just practicing, and every once in a while, I will notice that I have just stepped up to a whole new plateau. And that is a great feeling … and then I continue to practice.

Audio: creating the atmosphere

chapter 9

New Exposure for Musicians?

As the game industry continues to reach a wider audience—and as music sales from traditional distribution channels continue to decline—record labels and independent musicians alike have begun to focus on the game industry as a new medium for music exposure. Unlike the traditional film-going and TV-watching audience, gamers are an "active" audience—manipulating characters, choosing paths, and sometimes changing the scenery in a game environment. Games are truly an immersive experience, and the music gamers hear while playing—whether looping theme music or adaptive sounds that conform to characters' actions—can make a long-lasting impression on the player. When you consider "persistent-state world" games that might involve players for weeks or even months on end, no wonder the fan base for game music is growing tremendously!

Ron Jones on the Composer-Game Developer Relationship :::::

Ron Jones has scored hundreds of animated series—including *The Flintstones, The Smurfs, The New Adventures of Scooby Doo, Superman, Duck Tales*, and *Family Guy* (which garnered an Emmy nomination for Best Original Song). After a

successful four seasons scoring *Star Trek: The Next Generation,* Ron contributed to two best-selling *Star Trek* computer games—providing orchestral scores for Interplay's *Star Trek: Star Fleet Command* and *Star Trek: Star Fleet Academy.* The National Association of Independent Record Distributors & Manufacturers (NAIRD) awarded him with Best Soundtrack Album of the Year for *Star Trek: The Next Generation—Best of Both Worlds, Parts I & II,* on Crescendo Records. Ron Jones Productions maintains a state-of-the-art studio with full, updated computer systems and software located in Burbank, CA.

Ron Jones
(Composer,
Ron Jones
Productions, Inc.)

The most challenging aspect of game composing is filtering through the language differences of game producers and designers in order to discover not only the essence of the game, but to find the right musical approach. Composers are really on a different planet than the game team. You have to hold true to what you know will be right and what will work best—yet still manage to nail what the game developers want. This is a tricky, slippery task. It involves a great amount of patience, and the ability to really listen.

A *song* soundtrack usually consists of pre-existing songs with vocals (not written especially for the game) that are licensed from the respective copyright holders or publishers to be used in the game. Sometimes songs from well-known artists are used in order to increase the popularity of a game. This can be extremely expensive and create a lot of royalty problems down the road. Although song soundtracks have proven to be quite effective in many films, such as *Pulp Fiction* and *Moulin Rouge*, they have not been as effective in games. There are also several alternatives to licensing well-known recordings. You can get a synchronization license, which allows you to hire your own performers to make a new version of a particular song. Or you can purchase the rights to use songs (and instrumental music) from music libraries such as Associated Production Music (APM), which provide an entire catalogue of music organized by mood and scene.

Alex Brandon on Challenges & Successes in Game Audio :::::

Alex Brandon is currently the audio manager at Midway in San Diego. He began by co-designing, marketing, and managing the game *Tyrian,* by Epic Games. He then went on to score *Unreal,* which used a form of interactive MOD files that had never before been done. The files were in fact adapted for extended use in the hit game *Deus Ex,* by Ion Storm Austin. Both titles have won numerous awards and sold over a million copies. Alex has scored and created sound effects for over a dozen titles since *Tyrian,* focusing heavily on technology and interactivity to make the sound and music drive games forward as a truly advanced form of entertainment. Alex is also an IA-SIG (Interactive Audio Special

Alex Brandon
(Audio Manager,
Midway Home
Entertainment)

Interest Group) Steering Committee Member, a voting member of the National Academy of Recording Arts & Sciences (NARAS), and a DirectX Audio Advisory Board Member.

Making music and sound effects is easy. Making good music and good sound effects is hard. Integrating good music and sound effects effectively is the most difficult part. *Deus Ex: Invisible War* and *Thief: Deadly Shadows* both have excellent models. In fact, *Thief*'s gameplay is driven more directly through audio. On the flip side, I really like *Ballers*. It has a very appropriate licensed soundtrack and a variety of hip-hop styles that help ease repetition.

Rob Cairns on the Role of Music Libraries in Game Audio :::::

Rob Cairns
(Key Account Director, Associated Production Music,)

Rob Cairns has been with Associated Production Music (APM) since January of 2002—working in the heart of Hollywood's production industry. Utilizing his long history with sales and marketing, Rob works with a wide range of clients in many different industries that are in need of music for their productions. As a huge music fan, and occasional campfire guitar player, he loves working at APM. Rob is also an avid gamer, and is pleased to be on the Board of Advisors for the Game Audio Network Guild (GANG).

Music libraries help developers and publishers with their audio needs on many different levels—whether the need is for in-game music tracks, promotional demos, or trailers. … Since 1983, APM's "per needledrop" model for licensing music has almost always been the same across different types of productions. This term goes back to when APM was delivering LPs rather than CDs to studios. Most productions are linear in nature, so our clients paid for *continuous use* of music, reflective of the record needle dropping onto the vinyl. When the needle was lifted, this would constitute the end of the music use—and thus the appropriate fee was applied. Every time that same music starts again in the same production, another needledrop fee has occurred.

With game production, music libraries embrace technology and change by allowing for music to be licensed on a "per track" rate if the music is being programmed into the game engine itself. Game audio professionals have unlimited use of that track without having to worry about how many times it was programmed for different scenarios. All of the "per needledrop" rules still apply to game companies if the music is used outside of the game engine—since those worlds are still very much traditional linear productions.

APM *shares* the licensing fees with its composers for every use of their music. There are other libraries known as "buyout" music libraries—where the composer performs a "work for hire" and the library sells the rights to use that music in an unlimited number of productions without tracking or valuing the exposure levels. Therefore, you end up with music that is over-exploited on an endless number of small budget productions—sometimes heard on late-night infomercials and horrifying training videos!

You might want to take a good look at the independent music scene and license music from unsigned artists. You'll often find fresh new music (at a great price) that hasn't been "licensed to death." My company, Indiespace (indiespace.com), has been providing licensing and music supervision services since 1994—supplying music from independent artists for film, television, advertising, and game projects.

The Indie Music Scene

Independent musicians—who once focused on licensing tracks and composing original scores for film—are starting to ally themselves with game developers.

Several online resources for independent music include:

- Artist Launch (www.artistlaunch.com)
- CD Baby (www.cdbaby.com)
- Indiespace (www.indiespace.com)
- MP3.com (www. mp3.com)
- Music4Games.net (www.music4games.net)
- SoundClick (www.soundclick.com)

Looping Music

Some games use *looping music* to provide a continuous soundtrack. If the loops are long enough, the player might not notice that the music is repeating. A composer might also create different themes with identical beginnings and endings that are put together to provide variation. Keep in mind that a player might spend more than 100 hours with your game, and you do not want to drive the player insane with looping music. Another issue with looping music in many current games is context. Let's say you're playing a game that involves exploring a beautiful forest, and the music accompanying your exploration is a beautiful simple theme that matches the setting. What if an evil pagan god jumps out from behind a tree and starts trying to hypnotize your character with his pan pipe? What if your character falls into a hypnotic trance and starts destroying the beautiful scenery by chopping down trees? If the music hasn't changed by that point to complement the change of mood in the game, it will ruin the immersive experience. This problem can be addressed by providing distinct themes that relate to different events that occur in the game. In order to do this, the composer will need to know what paths can be taken by the player character in the game in order to provide enough musical variety to the developer.

Contractual Issues

Film composers are paid by the score, and they retain rights that provide an income stream from their music for years after they have supplied it. Game developers are leaning toward paying by the finished minute, acquiring all the rights, and avoiding any future royalty entanglements. Developers are also concerned with restrictions that prevent them from repackaging the game and managing it through its normal lifecycle. A common compromise is for developers to make a one-time payment to acquire all the rights needed for the life of the game, while the composer retains rights for "non-interactive" use so that he or she can sell the music again in other media.

Game vs Film Scoring

Many film composers are interested in migrating to the game industry. Just like screenwriters who might consider writing game "scripts," film composers face an adjustment to a new, non-linear medium. In film scoring, composers are able to watch a finished film and will often meet with the director of the film for a *spotting* session. Spotting involves watching the film all the way through and deciding where music should be used by calculating each music cue's start and end points, along with any *hit* points—places where the music should be particularly dramatic and "hit" on a particular action, such as a bullet being fired from a gun or the sudden appearance of a magical creature. In contrast, there isn't a way to view a finished game. In order for a composer to see all paths a character might take in the game, the composer would have to play the game several times over—which could take hundreds of hours. Instead, the composer needs to see various characters and settings used in the game, read the story synopsis and character profiles, and be given a list of levels and associated objectives and gameplay elements. Since cut-scenes are more like mini-movies, they can be spotted and scored like films.

Richard Jacques & Rich Ragsdale on the Film & Game Scoring :::::

Richard Jacques is an award-winning composer of blockbuster scores for games, television, and film. He writes, orchestrates, and produces epic anthems and dramatic underscores that blur the borders between Hollywood films and cinematic video game entertainment. His action score for *Headhunter* was the first Western video game soundtrack to utilize the world-famous Abbey Road Studios and record with a full symphony orchestra—the London Session Orchestra—usually associated with the film-scoring world. Richard received the 2002 Game Audio Network Guild Recognition Award for *Headhunter* at the annual Game Developers Conference in San Jose, CA. The game was nominated for GANG 2002 Music of the Year, 2002 Best Live Performance Recording, and 2002 Best Original Instrumental Song ("Jack's Theme"). *Game Industry News* also selected *Headhunter* as finalist for 2002 Soundtrack of the Year. Richard's music for *Headhunter* and the sequel *Headhunter: Redemption* was featured as a world premiere suite in the first-ever symphony concert to celebrate the best music from Western and Japanese games. Richard's works have been exhibited at the Royal Museum of Scotland and at the Barbican in London for *Game On*—the leading international touring exhibition celebrating the art and culture of games.

Courtesy of: Derek Askem

Richard Jacques
(Composer)

Film and television music is linear, and games are non-linear. Therefore, in film or television music, you know exactly what is going to happen at a particular time so you can score the music accordingly. In a game, you don't know what the player is going to do, so you have to make the music react to whatever situation the player is in.

Rich Ragsdale grew up in Nashville, Tennessee. He started playing guitar at age 16, and soon joined local punk and heavy metal bands with "silly" names like Soft Skull Sam and Bombshell. Deciding to get serious about his music, he studied classical guitar and then went to Berklee College of Music, where he majored in both film scoring and composition. He then completed the one-year film-scoring program at USC. After scoring a few independent films, Rich began to write music

Courtesy of: Kevin Ragsdale

Rich Ragsdale
(Composer)

for television and games. He has also scored a number of commercials and has contributed music and songs to several features (both studio and independent). Now he's also a film director—with *Into Something Rich and Strange* winning Best Experimental Short Film, and a horror feature (*El Charro*) in development with Pretty Dangerous Films. Rich has composed music for a number of commercial game projects for Vivendi Universal Games, Fox Interactive, and Music Consultants Group. Game credits include *Aliens vs. Predator, No One Lives Forever,* and *Eight-Legged Freaks* (based on the movie of the same name). His music has been featured on the television shows *Will and Grace* and *King of Queens.*

In film and television, the composer usually comes in during post-production. The picture is more or less locked—so the parameters are often fixed, and your job becomes mainly about finding the correct style and sound for the picture. For game projects, I have generally been brought in closer to the beginning of production—months before I can really see what the game is going to be like. Cut scenes and specific events can have hard and fast parameters as far as timing is concerned, but gameplay is more fluid and does not.

Temp Track Infatuation

A *temp track* is "temporary" music that is traditionally used in a film to provide an idea of what a director might want to hear musically. Usually, the film's editor adds the temp track to an early version of the film and continues to use it while editing. In fact, film editors sometimes edit the film to the music—making it more difficult to part with the temp track. The director often falls in love with the temp track—which often consists of a score to another film, or music from well-known artists that would be prohibitively expensive to license. A composer is often brought in at post-production and must not only write original music quickly so that the dialogue, music, and effects tracks can be mixed—but must also convince the director that this new music will work much better with the film than the temp track. Usually, the composer is right—but the director has already heard the temp track too many times and has difficulty parting with it. Game developers are becoming similar in this way. My advice? Get a music supervisor or composer on the project during pre-production. Don't wait until you're almost ready to release the game. One more thing: If you must use a temp track, try to not to fall in love with it!

Todd M. Fay is the President of Todd M. Fay Media Developments, a provider of production and content development services to the interactive entertainment, television, and music industries. Todd has worked with many cutting edge companies including Creative Labs ATC, Blizzard Entertainment, THQ, Vivendi Universal, Black Ops Entertainment, G4 Media, and Tommy Tallarico Studios. His work has appeared in *Game Developer Magazine,* Gamasutra.com, Music4Games.net, and on G4:Television for Gamers, the 24-hour network dedicated to games and the gaming lifestyle. While at G4 Media, Todd oversaw the development of the shows *Filter* and *Cheat!: Pringle's Gamer's Guide,* as well as the *Icon's Special: Splinter Cell.* While working with Creative Labs, Todd contributed to the development of EAX 3.0, as well as authoring the designer's guide for that technology. Games Todd has worked on include *WarCraft III: Reign of Chaos, Diablo II: Lord of Destruction, Hot Wheels: Velocity X*, and *X-Files: Resist or Serve*. He produced his first book, *DirectX 9 Audio Exposed: Interactive Audio Development,* for Wordware Publishing in 2003. Todd holds a Bachelors of Music from the University of Massachusetts Lowell's award–winning Sound Recording Technology Department.

Todd M. Fay
(President, Todd
M. Fay Media
Developments;
Director of
Development, Game
Audio Network Guild
[GANG])

Unlike other media, game audio has no dedicated tools through which to develop content. Almost every new project requires new technology and new tools which have to be learned and tested. At this point, the aspect of game audio that is most challenging is the overall lack of dedicated resources, either through pre-planning or actual fund droughts. Game audio developers are expected to deliver Hollywood-quality productions on garage budgets. The lack of pre-production for sound and music in games has led to many a nightmare scenario for game audio content developers. While some publishers and developers are beginning to catch on, most don't understand that in order to get the best possible audio for their game, it has to be discussed in the early stages of development. Lastly, there is an overall lack of respect for game audio, from the industry and consumers. And for good reason—so much of what went into games prior to recent years wasn't appealing to the majority of players. Thankfully the quality is starting to turn around, but not necessarily the stigma of game audio being a bunch of "bloops and bleeps."

As founder of the Music4Games.Net service—dedicated to marketing and promoting game composers and the latest game soundtracks—Greg O'Connor-Read has developed a worldwide network that delivers a valuable spotlight on today's highly competitive videogame soundtrack marketplace. Greg has also

Courtesy pf: John Edwards

pioneered publicity campaigns for artists, composers, and producers of music for games via Top Dollar publicity services. Recognized as a leading promoter of game music, Greg moderated the Society of Composers & Lyricists' (SCL) first seminar on "Writing Music For Games," and also lobbied for and secured the Music category in the BAFTA Games Awards. He is a music consultant for *Game On*—the first international touring exhibition celebrating the art and culture of games—and a recipient of the Game Audio Network Guild (GANG) Recognition Award.

Greg O'Connor-Read (Game Music Promoter; Founder, Music4Games, Inc/ Top Dollar Publicity Services)

Similar to film, music in games establishes the emotional context—providing the player with an emotional connection to the visuals on the screen. Music feeds into the gameplay and, if implemented well, the music and visuals will fully immerse the player in the game environment…. Music is an essential component in elevating the game experience…. Unfortunately, game composers do not often get the credit they deserve for their contribution to the overall product. Most game composer deals are "buyouts", with no royalties involved. Finally, game composers working on big budget games have smaller budgets to work with than film composers working on big budget movies.

Adaptive Music

A more immersive way to incorporate music in a game is for a composer to write *adaptive music*—which changes to conform to a player's actions within the game. This requires writing music in very small segments and embedding flags in the code to signal the rapidly changing states in the game. In the example already discussed (pp. 277-278), the music would begin with the original beautiful simple theme that matches the pastoral setting. When the evil creature jumps out from behind the tree and begins to hypnotize the player, the music might change to reflect a mixture of playful, evil, and hypnotic themes. When your character starts to destroy the scenery, the music could rise dramatically—emphasizing the evil theme. Creating this kind of music requires very close coordination between the game designer, programmer, and composer. The composer will not only know what the game is about, but the many shifting moods that need to be interpreted for the player.

David Javelosa on Adaptive Music :::::

David Javelosa is a composer/technologist and game industry specialist based in Santa Monica, California. David is currently an instructor at Santa Monica College's Academy of Entertainment and Technology, teaching interactive media, and composes electronic music for the Internet and live performance. Previously, he worked with Yamaha Corporation of America as an evangelist for their game audio technology. David has created soundtracks for most of the major game consoles and has been involved with digital media since its inception. As David Microwave, he released a solo EP in 1980 with catchy Synthpop and the Zonk (Zolo+Punk) "Record Player." His Los Microwaves group released *Life after Breakfast,* which contains Zolo, Synthpunk, and New Wave—and he collaborated with Charles Hornaday and members of Los Microwaves in the group Baby Buddha, which released *Music for Teenage Sex.* His interests include vintage synthesizers, remixing pop bands and sci-fi soundtracks, yoga, scuba diving, skiing, and raising his protégé.

David Javelosa
(Composer
& Music
Technologist)

With adaptive music, we look at both the vertical and horizontal structures of the score. The vertical structure generally describes instrumentation, arrangement, and "mix" of the music, sometimes referred to as the density or the intensity of the game scene. As the player gets in and out of situations, the ability of this quality to change with the state of the game is immensely effective.

On the horizontal axis, we look over the arrangement of musical segments, or sequencing of the musical development. Having different themes associated with certain scenes or the appearance of characters actually allows the player to have an unconscious hand in the playback of the arrangement. If done too simplistically, the player can become aware of these changes and actually "play" the soundtrack by repeating scene transitions in a non–gameplay fashion. As with most adaptive soundtracks, the more subtle and transparent the transition, the more effective the overall experience. The best soundtracks are the ones that are so well integrated that we tend not to notice them consciously.

::::::Game Music Remixes

Sites such as *Overclocked Remix* (www.ocremix.org) take the online music discovery strategy one step further by allowing fans of game music to remix their favorite tracks for others to sample. Not only does this highlight the popularity of game soundtracks, but this also showcases collaborative features of the Internet. There are reviews of each remix, and tips for making your own. A lot of the music on this site is surprisingly good! (The notion of the player as musician is even being incorporated into some games, such as *Asheron's Call 2* and *Star Wars Galaxies*.)

The *Overclocked Remix* Unofficial Game Music Arrangement Community

Composing Effective Game Scores

Most games I have worked on have gone for a cinematic feel. Using ambient *aleatoric-sounding* (composition depending upon chance, random accident, or highly improvisational execution) orchestral music can work very well in sustaining an atmosphere without calling too much attention to itself. It can be very effective to not have music play constantly as many games do, but to have cues trigger at key moments.

—*Rich Ragsdale*
(Composer)

Audio Variety

One of my most memorable experiences composing game music was for *Milo's Astro Lanes,* a bowling game with a number of level environments. By exploring various entrances from the lobby, the player would get a cross-fade of different music tracks by going from one door to the next. On top of all of this was the specific motion sound for each character, some of which had their own signature soundtrack. The result was a very busy sound design that was completely under the control of the player.

—*David Javelosa*
(Composer & Music Technologist)

Chance Thomas on the Essential Audio Tool Kit :::::

Chance's original music is at the heart of Vivendi-Universal's *Lord of the Rings* game series. Other game credits include *Earth & Beyond, Unreal II,* and *Quest for Glory V.* Chance's music underscored the surprising success of *The ChubbChubbs,* which won an Oscar at the 75th Annual Academy Awards. Chance has also been honored by the Emmy Awards, Telly Awards, Aurora Awards, Addy Awards, Vault Network Awards, and many others. He is a great promoter of game music—frequently linked to the Grammy Awards for his winning game music Grammy campaign in the late 1990s. Chance has served as chair of the Music and Sound peer

Courtesy of: Michael Schoenfeld

committees for the Academy of Interactive Arts and Sciences. He is on the Board of Directors for the Game Audio Network Guild, speaks annually at the Game Developer's Conference, has been a presenter at the Interactive Academy Awards, and is a voting member of the National Academy of Recording Arts & Sciences (NARAS). Chance holds a degree in music from Brigham Young University, and his California-based company HUGEsound.com offers a full range of audio services to quality-conscious developers and publishers worldwide.

Chance Thomas (Composer; President, HUGEsound)

1) **Vivid imagination:** The most brilliant scores always take shape first in the musical workshop of the mind. There's no technology with enough horse-power to outperform the magic that comes of the human spirit.

2) **Quality education:** Learning opens the mind, paves the path to creative flow, and forges habits of intellectual striving. The best inspiration always comes with the best information. Reference books on orchestration, classical literature, music history, music theory, great works of art—all of these enrich the mind and cultivate a fertile seedbed for compelling ideas to rise from.

3) **Reliable equipment:** I've had the same digital mixer for almost 10 years now. Sometimes I'll run sessions around the clock for days on end. That mixer has never been down on me. This is important, not only because I've got Yosemite National Park in my backyard (hours away from the nearest repair facilities), but because I've always got some project going that needs to be done *now.* Downtime is not an option in the pressure-packed world of game and film scoring. Some of my equipment workhorses include 02R digital mixers, Genelec 1031A monitors, PCM 90 effects processors, an old Mac G3, digi HD card and 192 i/o, tons of MOTU gear, Korg Trinity, and several Dell computers.

Audio: creating the atmosphere   **chapter 9**

4) **Amazing sounds:** It's got to tickle your ears, rumble your tummy, caress your soul…. Otherwise, why bother? We're in the business of *sound,* so it's essential to have lots of great *sounds* available. My library includes such pleasers as the Vienna Symphonic Library, Garriton Orchestral Strings, Symphony of Voices, Distorted Reality 1 and 2, Voices of Native America, Bizarre Guitar, and many more.

5) **Obsessive musicians:** Live musicians can make all the difference in a recording—for better or worse, unfortunately. A slightly out-of-tune performance on a Stradivarius will still make your stomach tighten uncomfortably, whereas a passionate and accurate performance on your grandpa's old fiddle can send the spirit soaring. Multiplying the number of players (say, for an orchestra) heightens the situation exponentially. Nothing is more disappointing to a composer than to hear his or her work performed poorly by a large ensemble. But when the musicians truly dial in the performance, get it in tune and in time, and then pour in a little passion—it's a beautiful thing.

Gamers are not only fans of games, but of game soundtracks. In fact, many have been known to listen to game soundtracks from their favorite games while playing other games. In May 2003, game composer and producer Tommy Tallarico put on a live concert at the Hollywood Bowl on the last day of the Electronic Entertainment Expo (E3) in Los Angeles. The concert featured a 90-piece orchestra, 40-person choir, fireworks—and it was shown on cable television. Tallarico is also the founder of the Game Audio Network Guild (GANG) (audiogang.org). Another influential and prolific game composer is George Sanger (a.k.a. "The Fat Man"), who is also a published author (*The Fat Man on Game Audio: Tasty Morsels of Sonic Goodness*) and coordinator of an annual game audio "think tank" conference known as Project Bar-B-Q (projectbarbq.com).

Tommy Tallarico on the Game Audio Network Guild (GANG):::::

Tommy Tallarico's music has been heard all over the world on video games, television, motion pictures, radio, soundtracks—and even on floats in the New Year's Day Rose Bowl parade in Pasadena. Some of Tallarico's top titles include: *Earthworm Jim 1 & 2, Disney's Aladdin, Cool Spot, The Terminator, Madden Football, Prince of Persia*, the *Test Drive* series, *MDK, Tomorrow Never Dies, Tony Hawk Skateboarding, Spider-Man, Pac-Man World, Knockout Kings and the Blitz, Unreal, Unreal 2, Metroid Prime, Scooby Doo, Maximo, Twisted Metal*, and the *Time Crisis* series. Tommy was the first musician to release a game soundtrack worldwide (*Tommy Tallarico's Greatest Hits Vol. 1* – Capitol Records). He has released five soundtrack albums since—including the highly acclaimed *James Bond "Tomorrow Never Dies"* soundtrack. Tommy was also the first to use 3D audio in a game (Q-Sound), and was instrumental in bringing true digital interactive surround 5.1 (6-channel) to the industry.

Tommy Tallarico
(President, Tommy
Tallarico Studios, Inc;
President/Founder,
Game Audio Network
Guild [GANG])

Tommy is the founder and president of GANG (Game Audio Network Guild)—a non-profit organization educating and heightening the awareness of audio for the interactive world (www.audiogang.org). He is also an advisory board member for the *Game Developers Conference* and a nominating committee member for the Academy of Interactive Arts & Sciences. In 1999 Tommy co-designed the award-winning boxing game *Knockout Kings* for the N64 with Electronic Arts, which went on to win the "Best Console Sports Product of 1999" by the Academy of Interactive Arts & Sciences (AIAS). Also in 1999, Tommy was instrumental in getting video game music categorized in the Grammys. Tommy was part of a committee which petitioned NARAS in order to include game soundtracks in the awards show. In his spare time Tommy is the host, writer, and co-producer of the worldwide weekly award-winning video-game television show, *The Electric Playground* (www.elecplay.com)—which currently airs daily on the Discovery network and MTV Canada and was the proud recipient of the 2001 Telly Award for "Best Entertainment Cable Program." Tommy's new television project is a half-hour weekly show entitled *Judgment Day*, which appears on the 24-hour video-game network G4.

I founded the Game Audio Network Guild (GANG) mostly because of the need for *respect*. I was so sick and tired of audio being the last thing everyone focused on in game development. It was ridiculous! I realize that the game industry is currently like the film industry was in the 1950s. We are all still trying to figure this out as we go. However, that is all changing very quickly.

I felt that if something wasn't done soon that other people that were *not* in audio were going to be the ones to decide how things should be with regard to audio—and I didn't want that to happen. I wanted the audio community to dictate to everyone how things should be—from a technical standpoint, a creative standpoint, and even a business standpoint. We can look to the film industry and see the amount of importance they put into all aspects of audio—from voice acting, to music, to sound design. Great attention to detail and care is taken to make it sound incredible because they realize the *importance* of sound. Now the game industry is starting to think the same way— thanks to all of us coming together as one voice to form GANG.

This chapter concludes the content creation section of this book. In the next section, you will learn about the game development process and beyond—including the development of the game production team, cycle, and player community.

:::CHAPTER REVIEW:::

1. What are the many purposes served by audio in games? Why is audio an important (but often overlooked) element in game development? Can you think of a purpose of game audio that was not discussed in this chapter?

2. What is the difference between looping and adaptive music in games? Discuss how two current games use these forms of music. Why can adaptive music sometimes be more effective than looping music?

3. What are some essential tools utilized by audio professionals in the game industry? What do these tools help audio professionals accomplish?

4. How are voiceovers, sound effects, and music used effectively in a game? How would you integrate all three audio forms into your original game? Consider the genre, subject matter, style of play, platform, and mood of your game in your answer.

5. Game and film scoring are very different from each other. Analyze the differences between these processes, and discuss the major distinctions between these two media. Tie these differences into what you've learned about gameplay, story, and character development.

6. How is voice acting in games different from other media? What are the benefits and disadvantages of working as a voice actor in this medium? If you were producing a game dialogue session, how would you change the way the session was structured in order to get the best performances out of your actors?

7. What are some issues facing game composers today? If you were to hire a composer to write music for your game, what would you do to address some of these issues?

8. If you were designing sound for a game, in what instances would you create your own sounds using foley (or by recording sounds from the environment) versus utilizing pre-existing material from a library? Similarly, when would you create (or hire someone to create) original music versus licensing pre-existing material from a library or label?

9. Experiment with foley and come up with new ways to create sound effects that were not listed in this chapter. Capture your foley creations with a recorder. Take the recorder with you wherever you go and capture unique sounds from the environment. Catalog your recordings in a spreadsheet and consider what types of game sounds could be reflected by your recordings. Apply some of what you've recorded to your own original game.

10. In this chapter, you learned a bit about the history of game audio. What do you think will be the next step in game audio development? Consider tools, implementation, and applications in your answer.

Part III: Strategy
team, process, and community

CHAPTER

10

Roles & Responsibilities:

developing the team

key chapter questions

- What are the company roles associated with game development studios, publishers, licensors, and manufacturers?

- What are the team roles and responsibilities associated with producers, artists, designers, programmers, writers, composers, sound designers, and testers?

- What specific techniques and tools are utilized by different team members during game development?

In Part II, you learned about how to develop compelling content for games.
Now, let's look at the process of actually creating a game from start to finish.
This chapter introduces the many roles and responsibilities associated with the
game development process.

Company Roles

There are several roles that companies can play in the game development process. A *developer* (or *development studio*) is the company that creates the game—coming up with a game concept, creating a prototype, and producing the final product.

THQ is an example of a game publisher.

Frequently, a separate company—known as a *publisher*—will fund, market, and distribute a game title. Sometimes a publisher will have an *in-house* development team that creates game titles. Activision, THQ and Atari are examples of publishers. Electronic Arts publishes and develops its own titles in-house. Bethesda Softworks developed and published the Elder Scrolls series—including Morrowind, the popular third installment—and has also published games developed by other companies (such as Call of Cthulu, developed by Headfirst).

Stormfront Studios is an example of a third-party developer.

Raw Creativity, Grunt Work...and Begging

I think the most challenging aspect of game development is just the raw creativity that needs to go into giving life to characters, the world, quests and events. After that, everything is just grunt work that you can muscle through. Oh, and begging for resources. And selling someone on the idea. Then threatening them. Then begging again.

— *Chris Avellone*
(Lead Designer, Obsidian Entertainment)

When a publisher funds or hires an outside developer to create a title, the developer is known as a *third-party developer*. In this case, the developer would present a game prototype to the publisher for approval before beginning the production process. Examples of third-party developers include Konami, Eidos, Infinity Ward, Secret Level, Liquid Entertainment, Stormfront Studios, and Obsidian Entertainment.

Louis Castle (Co-founder, Westwood Studios; Vice President, Electronic Arts–Los Angeles)

Louis Castle on Running a Large Game Development Studio :::::

Louis Castle is co-founder of Westwood Studios and serves as one of the Senior Studio Leaders at Electronic Arts–Los Angeles (EALA). As part of the management team, Louis directs EALA's programming, artwork, audio, and research and development departments, as well as business strategy. EALA creates product for some of the most successful and best-known intellectual properties within Electronic Arts' formidable portfolio, including the original product lines of *Medal of Honor* and *Command & Conquer*, and licensed properties *Lord of the Rings* and *James Bond*. Louis was the general manager of Westwood Studios from 2000–2003 and served in creative, business, and finance roles while expanding Westwood from 2 employees in 1985 to over 250 in 2002 (including the Irvine office). In his creative roles, Louis has contributed to over 100 games created by Westwood over the past 18 years as executive producer, creative director, technical director, programmer, and artist. His business positions include serving as the COO and finance officer for Westwood Studios between 1992 and 2000, a period in which the company negotiated four multinational acquisitions. Louis is passionate about the products and the people who create them. His role as Vice President at EALA allows him to leverage his considerable interactive entertainment experience to add value across the spectrum of EALA's creative and business development.

Running a reasonably large studio (75+ employees) takes you away from most of the day-to-day creative decisions. Your role is more about strategy, timing—and choosing which titles should receive the most resources and funding based on the current progress and competitive environment. You deal with legal issues, employment concerns, communicating to executives or investors—drilling down only occasionally to the details of the operations. Contrary to common belief—if you are the final point of accountability—the larger the company is, the less control you have. You are required to constantly make compromises to maximize your business. I thoroughly enjoyed running Westwood Studios at its peak size of 250 employees, but I missed the day-to-day involvement and focus I got when working with a smaller team.

In Chapter 3, you learned about how console game development differs from computer game development because a *manufacturer* is involved in the process. A manufacturer develops the hardware associated with a game's platform. In order for a game to be developed for a particular console brand, that hardware manufacturer (e.g., Sony, Microsoft, Nintendo) would need to approve of the prototype before the title goes into production. Manufacturers develop titles themselves.

Nintendo is an example of a hardware manufacturer.

A *licensor* is involved if the game's content is adapted from an original source. Licensing fees are notoriously expensive, especially if they are from well-known properties. If you are considering creating a game based on a concept that is pre-existing (and not your original idea), avoid pursuing this until you have the industry clout

NEW LINE CINEMA
A Time Warner Company

New Line Cinema is the licensor for the Electronic Arts game *The Lord of the Rings: The Battle for Middle-Earth.*

Electronic Arts Inc.

and funding to make this kind of deal. Even if you had the money, the deal isn't guaranteed to happen. A competitor may have already secured the rights, you might not have the credibility to convince the copyright holder that you will create something worthwhile from their property, or the copyright holder might simply not be willing to sell the rights to anyone. New Line Cinema is an example of a licensor—which licensed the rights to the film, *The Lord of the Rings,* to Electronic Arts.

If a developer decides to publish its own title for a non-proprietary computer platform, the developer does not have to partner with or get approval from a separate company to begin the production process. This type of developer is known as an independent (or indie) developer. 21-6 Productions (*Orbz* and *GravRally*), Three Rings Design (*Puzzle Pirates*), and eGenesis (*A Tale in the Desert*) are all award-winning indie game developers.

21-6 Productions is an example of an independent developer.

Christopher Bretz on Game Art for Licensed Properties:::::

Christopher Bretz has spent much of the last ten years creating artwork for the video game and interactive entertainment industries. For the past four years Chris has served as the Art Director of San Francisco–based Secret Level—developers

of tools, technology, and game titles for the console and computer game markets. He has worked in all aspects of graphics in the game industry—from concepts, to interface design, to 3D modeling and animation. His work has been seen in game titles published by Nintendo, THQ, Lucasarts, and Atari.

Christopher Bretz (Art Director, Secret Level)

When you work with licenses, you are given the opportunity to bring an established creative world—full of rich detail and history—into a new medium. You are tasked with re-imagining it in a way which remains faithful to the original material. This can be an exciting challenge for a game artist, especially when you are already a huge fan of the property. But changes inevitably have to be made to accommodate an interactive game—and that's the real challenge. Licensors are hoping that the special spark that made the property such a hit in its native medium (e.g., movie, book) will simply translate well into the game space with very little change. Things as simple as scale and color become issues for an interactive character in a way which might not have mattered for the movie or book version. You must also contend with all the preconceptions and biases of the property's creators—who are very protective of their creation, even though they might never have envisioned it as a video game. However, these people are huge assets, since they understand the license like no one else, and can offer insight or solutions to problems from a unique perspective. All parties want as faithful an interpretation as possible, because it is that world we all are sold on, and the one that the audience is following. It is your responsibility as the game artist to respect whatever that special aesthetic was in the original, and ensure that it remains present throughout the metamorphosis into a game.

Indies: The Rise of a New Golden Age?

Indie designers, targeting the gigantic market of casual users with low-end machines, are finding new paths beyond the usual *Solitaire* and *Breakout* clones. A golden age in any creative field typically requires a well-understood source of predictable, reliable, but modest and strictly limited income—along with a few strong visionaries leading a vigorous community that prizes originality. Indie shareware game designers haven't yet ensured the predictability of their modest rewards, but they're closer to that goal than the mainstream game industry. A community has precipitated around the Dexterity Games shareware forums (www.dexterity.com), led by Steve Pavlina. The foundations of the golden age are almost in place. The next five to ten years will show what we can build.

—Allen Varney
(Game Designer & Writer)

Grant Collier on Running a Third-Party Development Studio :::::

Grant Collier has been in the gaming industry for a decade. After spending a year in marketing and advertising, he made the transition to production, at various publishers. After several years and many titles, he moved over to the development side of the business. Shortly thereafter, Grant and company created Infinity Ward.

My duties often involve empowering team members so that they can do their jobs efficiently—from ordering equipment and hiring staff to basic human resources. I eliminate obstacles in project development to provide a positive work environment. A lot of my time is spent collaborating with my partners and publisher on the direction of our products…. Currently, the initial planning for the scope of the game is pretty challenging—although this might change depending on the stage of development. Our design team, our management, and our publisher all have to do a lot of compromising.

Courtesy Kerry Kara

Grant Collier
(President,
Infinity Ward)

Over his 18-year professional engineering career, Justin has held the titles of Senior Software Engineer, Lead Architect, and Development Manager. Justin's hard-core gaming history really started with the Atari 2600. Although he had used other game platforms previously, the 2600 really unlocked his addiction to gaming. Finding a profession that combined his passions for software development and games has been a life-long dream for Justin—a dream that has finally been realized in his latest role as President of 21-6 Productions.

Justin Mette
(President, 21-6
Productions)

I believe that the online distribution market for games is where most independent developers can get started and make a good living. Developing a game in 4 to 6 months with a small remote team means that your costs stay low and your return on investment does not have to be as large as the box or console industry.

You don't have to just build puzzle games anymore to succeed in online game distribution. Many companies have proven that true—with games like *Orbz*, *Marble Blast*, and *Tennis Critters* (all available from GarageGames).

We've also seen an incredibly strong rush of Mac gamers this past year in the online market. For our title *Orbz*, we saw almost a 50/50 split in revenue between Windows and Mac sales during 2003.

It's a great time to be an indie. The Internet allows you to find amazing talent, and work together without an office; technology like Torque makes game development a reality for small inexperienced teams; and a booming online game distribution market all lay out the best opportunity in years for game developers to live their dreams.

If you are interested in starting your own game development company so that you can produce your own titles, you will need to approach a funding source in order to have enough capital to create the game (unless you happen to be independently wealthy)! However, in order to get interest from a prospective funding source, you will have to show them something tangible. If you do decide to go in this direction, make use of the web as an inexpensive and efficient marketing source. (Marketing strategies will be discussed further in Chapter 12.)

More likely, you might be interested in approaching a publisher—who can be both a funding and distribution source for your title. Publishers are usually not interested in reading unsolicited proposals. Unless you know someone in the industry that can get you in a meeting with a publisher, you will need to focus on getting a prototype of your title completed so that you can show something tangible to your prospective publishers. You can reach these people through conferences and organizations—such as GDC (Game Developers Conference), E3 (Electronic Entertainment Expo), and IGDA (International Game Developers Association). (A list of conferences and organizations is available in the Resources section at the end of this book.) Even successful developers often need to develop prototypes to secure a publisher.

Jason Kay on Maximizing Revenue in the Game Industry :::::

Jason Kay is one of the founders of Society Capital Group, a private-capital strategic consulting firm located in Los Angeles, California. Currently, he is a consultant to Home Box Office, Inc. Prior to his work with HBO, Jason worked with a small team of consultants in the sale of Columbia House Company, a direct marketer of entertainment products. Prior to Society Capital Group, Jason worked as Producer and Business Development Executive for Activision in Santa Monica, California. Jason holds a Juris Doctor degree from the University of Southern California Law Center, and a B.A. *magna cum laude* with honors in English from Tulane University.

Jason Kay
(President, Society Capital Group)

People often say that the game business is rapidly becoming like the movie business. While this is true to some extent—the hits are bigger than ever, and the flops more painful—this analogy is imperfect. The feature film business (and to a lesser extent, television) derives revenue through a carefully crafted and maintained "windowing" strategy. Movies are first released at the box office in foreign and domestic markets, then on home video, then on pay-per-view—and eventually on cable and broadcast television. This strategy maximizes revenues across a variety of markets and at multiple price points. There is no analog to this in the game business. Titles are sold at retail at full price, then at discount prices until they eventually are sent to the bargain bin and/or removed from distribution. While Disney can re-release "classic" animated movies to a new generation of young viewers every few years on various home video platforms (including VHS and DVD) at a fairly low cost, the only way to exploit older game properties is to either produce sequels or remakes at increasingly higher costs. The challenge is to find ways to better exploit revenues from game titles in the retail and online distribution marketplaces.

Team Roles

In theory, a game could be created by just an artist and a programmer—but it takes a lot more than programming and art skills to create a working prototype that will form the basis of a successful game. Let's take a look at the various roles and responsibilities associated with those who work together to develop a game. Keep in mind that not all of these roles are always assumed by different people!

Production

A *producer* is someone who "makes things happen." Producers are responsible for making sure the game is released on time and on budget—and that everyone involved is doing what they're supposed to be doing. One of the important and overlooked responsibilities of a producer is the ability to manage people through conflict resolution, to communicate clearly, and to teach consensus-building skills. The lack of these skills can pose a big problem for a project, resulting in a decrease of team morale and even employee attrition. A producer is responsible for balancing time, money, and quality on a project. An *external* producer is the liaison between the game development team and the publisher, while an *internal* producer works for the developer and leads the entire game development team in-house.

John Hight on the Role of Executive Producer:::::

John Hight (Executive Producer, Atari)

After beginning his career as a software engineer for Xerox, John Hight worked with Philips Media during its foray into interactive entertainment, an ill-fated set-top called CD-i. After developing a slew of edutainment programs for Philips, he put together his first game: *CD-i Pinball.* Although CD-i never took off, John was hooked—and he wanted to make more games. John was hired by Trip Hawkins (who went on to start Electronic Arts) to lead the creative team at 3DO—which was outgunned by the Sony PlayStation and failed to achieve its goals. John went back into development with Virgin Interactive and Westwood Studios. One of his external projects showed a lot of promise; the team's president, Mike Booth, sold him the rights to his multiplayer game, *Nox,* and together they started building the solo experience. Within months, they were acquired by Electronic Arts and got the funding to raise the bar. *Nox* is still one of John's fondest projects. He then went on to work with the godfather of RTS games, Brett Sperry, who gave him the task of directing the designers and artists for *Command & Conquer Red Alert 2* and its sequel, *Yuri's Revenge.* While he really enjoyed his creative role at Electronic Arts, he wanted to get back into the producer's job—so he jumped at the opportunity to work as Executive Producer at Atari's Los Angeles studio. In addition to his industry experience, John also has an impressive academic background—having received a B.S. in Computer Science from the University of New Mexico, and an M.B.A. from USC's Marshall School of Business.

As an Executive Producer, I get to decide which games to produce, which developers to work with, and how much money to put into a given property. My job involves scouting for new talent, negotiating deals, creative problem-solving, building teams, and, yes, playing games. I have a team of top-notch producers; each one manages a single game like it's their own business. Every game starts with an idea—whether my own, one of my producers, or one pitched by a developer. I work with my producers and their developers to draft a *high concept*. From concept we go into *pre-production* and a working *prototype*. Our goal at the end of pre-production is to have a solid grasp of the game design and the 'look and feel' of the game. If the game has the potential to be a success, then we green-light it into production. I stay with each game until it ships, and then the process of looking for the next "big thing" starts all over again….

I've done both internal and external production—and I like to switch back and forth. In internal production, you really get into the details of your game. You have a personal relationship with every member of the development team. You get involved in the daily decision-making, and you have a strong awareness of the technology and talent going into your game. In external production you have a broader view, and it's easier to maintain objectivity. You see the works of many studios and see more of the business side. In external production, you have a much better sense of industry trends and consumer tastes.

Executive Producer

An *executive producer* is usually the highest-level producer on a project. Responsibilities include production management, proposal and prototype management, and project support. The executive producer often oversees multiple projects. At some companies, the executive producer might also be the studio head.

Producer

The *producer* is responsible for meeting project goals and establishing policies. This position focuses on priorities, due dates, contractual requirements, payments, budgeting, scheduling, staff support, and reporting to upper management (usually the executive producer). The producer sometimes interfaces with the press and resolves communication problems with partners (e.g., publisher, developer, hardware manufacturer, licensor).

Frank Gilson on the Role of Producer :::::

Frank Gilson
(Producer, Atari)

Before working as Producer at Atari's Santa Monica office, Frank Gilson was Associate Producer at Blizzard for *Warcraft III: Reign of Chaos* and the expansion, *Frozen Throne*. He also worked in Quality Assurance as QA Technical Engineer (*Diablo 2*), QA Lead Analyst (*Starcraft: Brood War*), and QA Analyst (*Starcraft* and *Mac Diablo*). Prior to joining the game industry, Frank was a graduate student at UC Irvine in Mathematical Behavioral Sciences, studying formal models for economics, voter choice, and psychology.

Part of my role as Producer involves business development. We need to look to the future to determine what projects the company should finance, and who should develop them. This involves looking at existing licenses, potential new licenses (e.g., TV, film, fiction), or original Intellectual Property developed internally. Once a project exists, I manage the relationship between my company, a publisher, and the game developer. I will contract for music composition and performance, voice work and audio engineering, and writing, with various groups and individuals. I make sure that the project has a sound schedule for the development of all of its parts, and I correct problems as they occur. I also work to promote the project internally, assuring that our public relations and marketing personnel worldwide have proper visibility of the project.

Associate Producer

The *associate producer* assists a producer on a particular project—providing research, interfacing with the development team, and making sure all areas of the project are running smoothly. Some specific tasks might include managing assets, generating screenshots for the public relations team, and reviewing milestones. The associate producer also works with outsourced producers for motion capture or cinematic video.

Assistant Producer

The *assistant producer* often works under the associate producer, handling any paperwork or other administrative requirements associated with budgeting and scheduling a project. Depending on the company, the assistant producer and associate producer roles might be interchangeable.

Design

Game *design* is often confused with game *art*. Design and art teams are often separated from each other, and some designers do not have any art-related experience whatsoever. Game designers are often more like engineers—taking a problem-solving approach to design functional systems (worlds and interfaces). Some designers also have scripting or even programming experience, which helps them turn the gameplay events they design into reality. *Game designers* focus on gameplay, levels, and interfaces (Chapters 6 through 8). Some game designers are the visionaries behind some very successful games. Sid Meier (*Civilization*), Will Wright (*The Sims*), Warren Spector (*Deus Ex*), Richard Garriott (*Ultima*), and Peter Molyneux (*Black & White*) have formulated game concepts, created compelling storylines, and incorporated gameplay mechanics into successful game worlds.

> ## "A Hive Mind!"
>
> The biggest challenge is probably maintaining a coherent vision. For a game to work, it has to feel like the work of one mind (or at least a hive mind!)—but, in fact, games are (often) created by 30, 40, 100 people or more. Communication is critical and, as in all human endeavors, communication is hard, hard, hard.
>
> — *Warren Spector*
> *(Studio Director, Ion Storm)*

Where is the Writer?

A writer is sometimes outsourced when needed to help develop the story and characters for a particular project. Due to the importance of gameplay over storytelling in game development, traditional writers are not always in high demand. This may change as more game developers attempt to better integrate storytelling with gameplay, and as Hollywood screenwriters and other professional writers start to learn how to apply their skills to this very different medium. Currently, it is not unusual for members of the game design team to write story and dialogue for their respective missions.

Creative Director

The *creative director* ensures that the overall style and game content is consistent with the original vision for the project. The creative director might also help maintain the art style of the game through working closely with the art director (discussed later in this chapter).

Design Director

A *game design director* is another management position that focuses less on hands-on design tasks and more on staff support, documentation, and guiding the design team in creating a game prototype. Depending upon the company and project, this role might be taken on by the lead designer, creative director, or a producer.

Lead Designer

A *lead designer* usually supervises the game design team and is also often involved hands-on in the daily game design process. Some lead design responsibilities include gameplay development, documentation assembly, and level design.

Chris Avellone (Lead
Designer, Obsidian
Entertainment)

Chris Avellone wanted to develop computer RPGs ever since he saw one of his friends playing *Bard's Tale 2* on a Commodore 64. After receiving a B.A. in English at the College of William and Mary, Chris started writing a bunch of short stories and RPG material—some of which got published. His writing got him noticed at Interplay, where he worked for 7 to 8 years before co-founding Obsidian Entertainment, Inc., with other ex-Interplayers. Chris has worked on *Starfleet Academy, Die by the Sword, Conquest of the New World, Red Asphalt, Planescape: Torment, Fallout 2, Icewind Dale 1, Icewind Dale: Heart of Winter, Icewind Dale: Trials of the Luremaster, Icewind Dale 2, Baldur's Gate: Dark Alliance, Lionheart,* and *Champions of Norrath.* At Obsidian Entertainment, he's currently working on *Knights of the Old Republic II: The Sith Lords,* which he's really excited about. He says that his mom still isn't exactly clear on what he does on a day-to-day basis—and neither is he.

As lead designer, the actual duties vary on a day to day basis. Overall, I'm responsible for keeping the vision for the game, the game mechanics, and the "fun" of the game; the overall story (and any specific elements about the game designed to propel the overall story, such as companions, key locations, etc.); and then breaking down the remaining elements into digestible chunks for the other designers in terms of area briefs and area overviews ("This planet is X, the following things need to happen on it," etc.), breaking up the mechanics and play-balancing ("I need you to oversee the feat and class advancement systems as long as they accomplish the following goals," etc.)—and then managing all the parts so programmers, artists, and the producer are getting everything they need to keep moving.

Electronic Arts Inc.

Interface Designer

An *interface designer* determines the layout, content, navigation, and usability features of the game interface (see Chapter 8). The art team might be involved in creating the style of the interface, but this happens after the design stage.

User interface for
The Sims Online.

chapter 10

Level Designer

A *level designer* focuses on building the game environment or world (see Chapter 7). Some level designers only build the physical environment; others incorporate gameplay into the game world (see Chapter 6). Level designers might also be involved in writing the stories (and even dialogue!) associated with missions or campaigns that they design.

Level for
Neverwinter Nights.

Bioware Corp. / Atari, Inc.

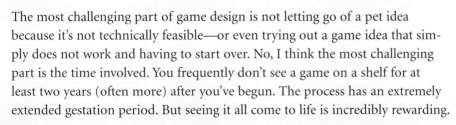

Patricia Pizer on the Greatest Design Challenge :::::

Patricia made her debut in the gaming industry at Infocom in 1988, making games in the days when you didn't even need graphics! She later returned to the fold as a Game Designer for Boffo Games. Over the course of her career, she's worked at CogniToy, THQ/GameFx, and Harmonix Music. Patricia served as Creative Director of *Asheron's Call 2* at Turbine Entertainment, and, most recently, she worked with Ubisoft on *Uru: Online Ages Beyond Myst.* Currently, Patricia does freelance consulting on game design. A founder of the Boston Area Game Developers' Network, she also serves on the Board of Directors of Zform—developers of game software for the visually impaired. Mostly though, she just likes to play games.

Patricia A. Pizer
(Game Designer)

The most challenging part of game design is not letting go of a pet idea because it's not technically feasible—or even trying out a game idea that simply does not work and having to start over. No, I think the most challenging part is the time involved. You frequently don't see a game on a shelf for at least two years (often more) after you've begun. The process has an extremely extended gestation period. But seeing it all come to life is incredibly rewarding.

Art

Game *art* involves creating concept art or assets that will be used in the game. There are four basic art tasks that differentiate game artists: drawing (analog or digital), modeling, texturing, and animation. There are also different applications that artists focus on—including characters, props, vehicles, interiors, exteriors, environment, effects, cinematics, and interface. Artist roles are often distinguished by their task and application focus. A *2D artist* creates and refines two-dimensional art assets used in the game itself—including textures for characters, environments, objects, interfaces, and game packaging (also handled by the marketing department). A *3D-artist* creates and refines three-dimensional art assets—including modeling, texture-mapping, and lighting.

Art Director

The *art director* usually operates the art department, overseeing scheduling, development, budgeting, and hiring. Responsibilities of an art director include directing the style of the game's art—including determining the mood, look, and feel of the game. The art director improves the process, quality, and productivity of art development throughout the company.

Marc Taro Holmes on the Role of Art Director :::::

Courtesy of Laurel Holmes

Marc Taro Holmes
(Art Director, Obsidian
Entertainment)

Before becoming Art Director for Obsidian Entertainment, Marc Taro Holmes was Art Director and Production Designer at Turbine Entertainment Software and Bioware Corp—contributing to various computer RPGs, including *Neverwinter Nights* and *Middle-Earth Online*. He holds a B.F.A. in graphic design from the Alberta College of Art and Design, and he has worked as an illustrator, designing annual reports and a great deal of fantasy artwork. His neglected hobbies include traveling and filling sketchbooks.

The Art Director role, as I have experienced it, is very bipolar. Art Directors have to be equally interested in the creative aspect of production design as they are in planning and monitoring the project schedule. I actually spend a lot of my time drawing. This is usually done in Photoshop (to save time with color tests and revisions), but I'll occasionally dust off the brushes and paint to do some free-form sketching. (This would only occur at the very early brainstorming stages.) Either way, my goal is to create a tangible example to direct the team's efforts—a set of images that define a visual language. It's about setting limits and boundaries, by actual example: *This is what trees look like in this world. These are the materials the clothing is made of. These imaginary people have these body types.* These sorts of questions need to be answered up front, so that, down the road, the team can be making decisions on a day-to-day basis.

Team members need to be able to answer for themselves: *Does this fit into the world we're making? Is this character the right style?* I know that I cannot personally design every single object in the game (even if I might want to—the project can't have a two year pre-production cycle just for my own amusement). It has to be a collaborative effort, not a dictatorship—and, ultimately, that is a good thing.

At the same time, over on the other side of the brain, I do a lot of project scheduling. Excel sheets, meetings, email, design docs—all that fun, fun administration that goes on behind the scenes. One of the problems with a creative endeavor like this is that quality work takes an arbitrary amount of time. You can't really say to an artist, "Make something clever by Friday … or else." This is the kind of business where our projects are defined by features. This game has a great sniper feature, that game has a better stealth feature…. We are always trying to find some way to stand out from the crowd. Combine that with the fact that we are frequently prototyping new technology on the fly, and you really have a volatile situation on the project planning front. This ends up meaning that I am in the Excel file every day, looking to see if we are still on track, what is going to need more time, what can be cut to allow that, and what rare gem of an item is actually ahead of schedule. I have heard it said that "no plan survives first contact with the enemy." This is certainly true in my experience….

If you're lucky, there's a budget to get this work done—but, in my experience, the actual game is taking so much time and energy that this work has to be handled on nights and weekends. There seems to be some unwritten rule that if an artist wants to make the pretty pictures, they have to suffer for that privilege!

Lead Artist

A *lead artist* usually supervises the game art team and is also often involved hands-on in the daily game art production process. Most lead artist positions are based on specialty—such as Lead Concept (or Storyboard) Artist, Lead Modeling Artist, Lead Texture Artist, and Lead Animator.

Concept Artist

A *concept artist* usually creates drawings and sketches of the game environment, props, and characters. Storyboards are used during the concept development process and are often included in concept documentation. (See the "Documentation" section in Chapter 11 for more details.) The concept artist can be key to securing a publishing deal by providing a low-cost way to visualize the game before it is made.

Destination Games / NCsoft Corporation

It all starts with concept art: concept sketch, wire mesh, and model of Thrax soldier in *Tabula Rasa*.

Technical Artist

Some artists bridge the divide between art and programming. They understand the 3D technical requirements and game engine. They help set standards with the tools, work on the art "pipeline," and make sure assets are created and stored in the appropriate formats. They are often experts with particular art packages and scripting.

Modeler

Modeling involves creating 3D assets from 2D drawings—often for game characters, props, environments, and structures. Modelers create all of the final art assets for the game, unless the system being used to create the game is a 2D (or *sprite-based*) system. Modelers create 3D wire meshes from the concept art, and apply textures to the meshes in a process known as *skinning*.

Sometimes models are created from scratch within a software package, or they are created from scanning a real-world 3D clay model into a software program such as 3D Studio Max or Maya. Environmental modelers build 3D spaces and worlds through which characters move, starting with geometric shapes which are combined and re-formed to create the game environment. After completing a 3D mesh for the environment, the modeler provides shading, texturing, and lighting. Types of modelers based on application include Character Modeler, Environmental Modeler, and Structures Modeler.

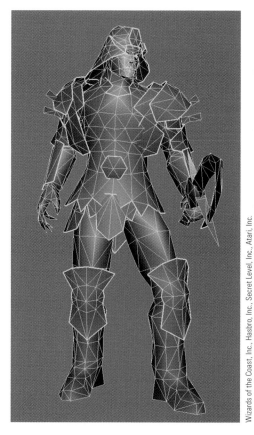

Wizards of the Coast, Inc., Hasbro, Inc., Secret Level, Inc., Atari, Inc.

The many faces of Mishra: Wire mesh, character model, loading screen, and card (modeled after the original *Magic: The Gathering* 'tabletop' card game), used to create Mishra in *Magic: The Gathering—Battlegrounds*.

Wizards of the Coast, Inc., Hasbro, Inc., Secret Level, Inc., Atari, Inc.

Texture Artist

Texturing involves generating 2D image maps that are applied to 3D models. These texture maps include surfaces for characters (skin, clothing), structures (building interiors/exteriors), and objects (vehicles, props). Sometimes texture artists photograph an existing surface, scan it into a software program such as Photoshop, and then touch it up. Another method of texturing involves creating a texture from scratch and building it up by layer.

Animator

Animation involves applying movement to objects and characters in the game world. In addition to in-game motions and performances, some animators also get involved with *cinematics.* In Chapter 5, you learned that a character's movement can reveal personality. Animators need to understand character development. Techniques used in animation include *keyframing* (where an animator makes each pose of a movement and sets sequential keyframes to generate animation files) and *motion capture* (where an animator captures the motions of real people, placing markers on joints of the person in order to track movement and create motion data). Types of animators based on differing applications include Character Animator, Cinematics Artist, and Effects Artist.

Meta Motion

An alternative to keyframing, motion capture ("mocap") devices—such as Meta Motion's "Gypsy 3W"—allow animators to capture actors' motions and live performances.

Programming

Game *programming* can involve anything from creating the *game engine* (the core code for the game) to in-house database, graphics, audio, and world-building *tools* that other team members can use during the game production process to manage assets and create art, sound, and game worlds.

Technical Director

The *technical director* creates the technical design for the project, oversees its implementation throughout all phases of production, and selects the tools, hardware, and code standards.

Lead Programmer

The *lead programmer* usually supervises the programming team (and often reports to the Technical Director). and is also often involved hands-on in the daily programming process.

KyungMin Bang on the Role of Lead Programmer::::

After graduating from Seoul National University with a degree in electrical engineering and computer science—and a focus on networking and graphics—KyungMin Bang started as a game programmer at Nexon in 2000. KyungMin is now leading *Project NG* (a new 3D online golf game) at Nexon.

As Lead Programmer, I focus primarily on system design and time management. There are many technical ways to implement one gameplay feature. It's my responsibility to design the whole system to implement the feature and lead the programming process. I have four programmers on my team, and I need to make a very detailed task list and schedule for them. For instance, if I need to implement a task (from the design team) such as "two characters are playing golf through the online environment," then the tasks to be done would include:

KyungMin Bang
(Project Leader &
Main Programmer,
Nexon)

- 3D max plugin to export character model

- Enhance rendering engine

- Play scripting

- Network sync design

- Network protocol design

I have to make these separate tasks, assign them to the programmers, and check to see how much of each task has been completed on a daily basis.

Engine Programmer

The *engine programmer* creates the core game engine, which usually handles graphics rendering as well as collision detection between game objects. Collision detection involves checking the intersection between game objects and calculating trajectories, impact times, and impact points. The term "game engine" arose in the mid-1990s when id Software began to license its core software for *Doom* and *Quake* games, which allowed the company to have an additional revenue stream. Other developers were able to design their own game content and assets using id's game engine instead of working from scratch.

Tools Programmer

The *tools programmer* designs tools to assist members of art and design teams incorporate their work into code so that it can be included in the game. This programmer might create level-editors to help designers create worlds—or write plug-ins for graphics software like 3D Studio Max and Maya to make it easier for artists to create game assets. The tools programmer also designs performance tracking tools, as well as script engines.

John Ahlquist on Game Engine & Tools :::::

John Ahlquist
(Lead Programmer,
Electronic Arts -
Los Angeles)

John Ahlquist has developed the tools and engine for *Command & Conquer: Generals,* the *Zero Hour* expansion, and *The Lord of the Rings: The Battle for Middle-earth.* John previously worked for Altsys/Macromedia on Aldus Freehand and was one of the creators of Macromedia Fireworks. Prior to Macromedia, John spent seven years working for Texas Instruments, programming Integrated Circuit CAD tools in the Design Automation Department. He is a second-degree black belt in Tae Kwon Do and has been playing video games since *Pong.*

My first responsibility is to analyze what the designers and artists need the game engine and tools to do—and I design and implement efficient solutions. There are two keys to *efficiency:* The first is to develop the code quickly, since we are always longer on features and shorter on time. The second is runtime performance for the engine. The tools are less critical, but engine performance is very important. Tasks include anything from designing and implementing a map layout tool (we call ours Worldbuilder), to creating a motion blur transition from a movie trailer clip. As we get closer to shipping the game, debugging and optimization become my main responsibilities.

Graphics Programmer

The *graphics programmer* (a mix between a programmer and an artist) is also known as the 3D Programmer—and is responsible for programming solutions to specific graphical game issues. This programmer must understand code animation and effects using 3D graphics APIs such as DirectX or OpenGL.

Jay Moore on the Torque Engine :::::

Jay Moore's wildly diverse background includes serving as marketing director for a computer magazine publishing company—retiring the cult classic coding magazine *Programmer's Journal* and launching the now defunct *Windows Tech Journal;* working as sales and marketing director for a K–12 educational software distributor; and founding a small advertising design firm, where he held the title of Director of the Time/Space Continuum. Jay started his game career with *The Even More Incredible Machine!,* taking the game into the classroom. Jay worked to bring all the Sierra educational games into the educational channel—then worked with Dynamix in 1997 to successfully launch category creator *Driver's Education.* Jay joined GarageGames in July of 2002.

Jay Moore
(Evangelist,
GarageGames)

The Torque is a powerful, full-force AAA game engine with an indie license price. Developers get the engine's source code. Being an interior/exterior, multi-platform engine with award-winning netcode makes Torque the standard for independent developers. One of the biggest advantages for Torque is the GarageGames community, which shares resources and knowledge in the pursuit of those building their games.

Game Engines for Indie Development

With the erratic work schedules of indie developers (which is usually in the evenings after a day job or on weekends), there isn't enough time to develop a game engine yourself and still make money with your business. Instead, spend the time designing and developing a fun game. Even with a full-featured game engine like Torque (from GarageGames), our first 3D game *Orbz* took three months to develop version 1.0, and another three months to develop version 2.0 with a five-person team. Our latest title, *GravRally*, which also uses Torque, has a team of eight and has been in development for nine months already, with a few more to go before it's complete. As you can see, even with experience and a great game engine under our belt, it still takes a long time to design and build fun games. The other reason to use an existing game engine is testing liability. Developing computer games comes with the large burden of testing on many different hardware combinations (e.g., CPU, memory, operating system, video card, sound card). Using a proven game engine will greatly reduce your testing liabilities and make it worthwhile to take on computer game development.

— *Justin Mette*
(President, 21-6 Productions, Inc.)

Networking Programmer

The *networking programmer* specifically programs the multiplayer component for online games and must understand database management, client/server architecture, security, and writing code using network protocols such as TCP/IP, Winsock, and UDP. DirectPlay (the DirectX interface to networking) is a popular tool for network programming. Sometimes a network programmer will also need wireless protocol knowledge (BlueTooth, Infra-Red).

Artificial Intelligence (AI) Programmer

The *artificial intelligence (AI) programmer* is responsible for making the game "intelligent" and incorporating gameplay design elements such as balance and flow into the game so that it's challenging and fun to play. AI, also known as machine intelligence, is the practice of developing algorithms that make machines able to make seemingly intelligent decisions on a human scale.

Audio Programmer

The *audio programmer* implements sound and music into the game. Responsibilities include effectively accessing the sound card, loading different sound formats, and programming music.

Physics Programmer

The *physics programmer* researches, develops, and optimizes efficient physics, collision systems, particle systems, and body dynamics.

Interface Programmer

The *interface programmer* designs and creates expandable, customizable, graphical user interface systems.

Quality Assurance (QA) Programmer

The *quality assurance (QA) programmer* develops automated testing tools for the QA team to test product releases.

Associate Programmer

The *associate* (or junior) *programmer* adds small elements to a game project, using a game company's own scripting tools and languages to program events or actions in a game. Sometimes, this scripting responsibility is assigned to members of the game design team who have the required skills. A game designer with some programming experience can then make gameplay events happen in a particular mission or campaign.

Audio

As discussed in more detail in Chapter 9, *audio* for a game project might include music, sound effects, and dialog. Some companies do not have audio departments or teams of their own, and will instead outsource audio services.

Audio Director

The *audio director* is responsible for managing the audio department; interfacing with the audio programmer (or team) to ensure that the audio assets get properly incorporated into the game; hiring personnel such as composers, sound designers, and voiceover artists; and licensing pre-existing songs for use in game soundtracks.

Composer

A *composer* writes the musical score for a game, and is often outsourced. Unlike a film composer—who writes music to fit various scenes in a linear medium—a game composer is unable to preview the entire game before writing the music. As discussed in Chapter 6, there are often many paths players can choose to take within a game. Music must be written to fit each of the possible paths and events that could occur.

Sound Designer

A *sound designer* is responsible for creating sound effects and ambient sound for a game. This position often involves collecting sounds from the environment with an audio recorder, editing them, and incorporating them into the game engine (or providing audio assets to the audio programmer for this purpose). Unfortunately, many sound designers make all-too-frequent use of pre-existing sounds collected in libraries that can be purchased or sometimes downloaded at no charge. Although these sounds can be helpful, they can be overused because they are so easy to obtain.

Voiceover Artist

A *voiceover artist* (also known as a *voice actor*) is often outsourced to provide spoken-word narration and dialogue for the game. There may be several voiceover artists involved in one game project, providing the voice for each character.

Testing & Quality Assurance (QA)

Game *testing* involves playing a game before its release in order to determine whether or not it is *playable*—bug-free, consistent, and entertaining. Similar to starting out in the mailroom in the film industry, beginning your game development career as an in-house tester is an opportunity to network with company decision-makers. Furthermore, these people care what *you* think! If a tester doesn't feel a product is playable, a producer will often take this information very seriously—and have the development team make any changes necessary to pass the playability test. Company management sees testers as a sample of the players that will be buying the game. If the players don't like the product, it will flop. Testers focus on the game's "fun factor," usability, logic, and functionality. Techniques for testing include *black box* or *white box*. In black-box testing, the tester does not know what is wrong with the game and must figure it out during the testing process. In white-box testing, the tester can see the problems with the game almost immediately by running it with a debugger turned on, which reveals code errors.

Quality assurance (QA) is often confused with testing. Unlike testing for playability and compatibility, QA involves establishing standards and procedures for the development of a game. Functions of QA include process monitoring, product evaluation, and auditing—ensuring that games meet the documentation, design, programming, and code standards set by the game developer and publisher. The roles of QA and testing are often combined into the same team, though sometimes one or both roles will be outsourced. Compliance is all-important in console publishing and legal/contractual agreements.

Testing Manager

The *testing manager* is responsible for multiple game projects. Several lead testers report to the testing manager—who sometimes also manages the testing budget and interfaces with upper management to ensure that products being tested are completed in a timely manner.

Lead Tester

The *lead tester* usually supervises the testing team and is also often involved hands-on in the daily testing process for a particular game project. Responsibilities of the lead tester include searching for errors and inconsistencies related to 3D geometry, modeling, texturing, aesthetics, and game logic. The lead tester also manages the data entry process of playability testers; ensures that testers are looking for bugs in the correct areas of the product; determines whether bugs are important enough to be repaired; and summarizes the status of the project when requested in written and verbal form.

The "Fun Factor"

Making games fun is the most challenging aspect of the game-development process. Everything else pales in comparison. Games have to be familiar enough so that they are accessible to the audience, but different enough to be novel and challenging. It's such a balancing act when making a game—to find and iterate through game systems, be strongly self-critical of features that aren't adding to the fun of the game, and still be able to defend those that just need a little bit more work to gel into something great.

— Mark Terrano
(Technical Game Manager,
Xbox Advanced Technology Group)

Compatibility Tester

A *compatibility tester* is an in-house, paid position that focuses on whether a game has cross-platform compatibility—functioning equally well on all target platforms and manual interfaces. If a game has been developed for all console platforms, does it run equally well on all? Do all the controllers allow the game to be played smoothly? Compatibility testers might test joysticks, mouse, controllers, operating system standards, and video/sound cards—and they also need to be familiar with the underlying programming and scripting languages associated with any systems being tested. For computer games, compatibility testers might also ensure that the game runs adequately on machines that comply with the minimum hardware specifications of a game.

Playability Tester

A *playability tester* is usually an in-house, temporary, paid position that lasts perhaps four to six months at a time. Unlike a Beta tester, a playability tester sometimes tests the game before it goes into Beta. Playability testers also make suggestions for improving, adding, or deleting features—and they might also compare the game to prospective competing titles. Since this position is in-house, it does provide many opportunities for networking. Company executives and management visit the testing department, observe the reactions of testers, and listen to testers' opinions. Playability testers need to have good verbal and written communication skills. Tools used in the position include spreadsheets such as Excel.

Beta Tester

When a game is at the Beta stage (discussed in Chapter 11), volunteer *Beta testers* are recruited (usually via the Internet) to test the game in the privacy of their own homes. Beta testing is the easiest way to gain industry experience. Since Beta testing does not occur in-house, Beta testing doesn't involve face-to-face networking opportunities—but it still allows for feedback and communication with some company decision-makers online. A drawback of Beta testing for the developer is that a tester's reactions can't be observed during the process.

Marketing

Separate from roles associated with the development team are those associated with marketing the game to the public. Chapter 12 discusses all these roles (including promotion, sales, advertising, public relations, and community management) in detail.

Now that we've become familiar with the many roles associated with the development team, let's discuss the tools used by these team members.

Tools

The game development team uses a variety of tools during each phase of development in order to plan, budget, schedule, create, and test games.

Level Design

Tools used in level design are usually proprietary, built in-house by tools programmers. Versions of these tools are often released with the game so that players can use them to build their own worlds. Level- and world-building tools are packaged with several games—including *Neverwinter Nights* (Aurora Toolset), *Half-Life* (Valve Hammer Editor), and *Unreal (Unreal Editor),* and *Far Cry* (CryENGINE's Sandbox Editor).

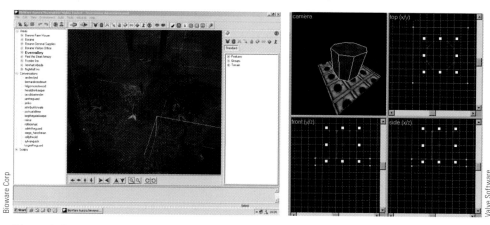

Bioware's Aurora toolset is shipped with *Neverwinter Nights,* and Valve Software's Valve Hammer editor is shipped with *Half-Life.*

Crytek's CryENGINE Sandbox Editor is shipped with *Far Cry*, and Epic Games' Unreal Editor is shipped with *Unreal*.

Game Engine Programming

Programmers use a variety of tools in order to build game engines. Here are just a few examples:

- *Compiler:* This tool takes the code written by the programmer and translates it into machine code that a computer can understand. The GCC compiler is part of the GNU Project, supported by the Free Software Foundation. Other compilers include freeware DJGPP, as well as Microsoft Visual Studio and Metroworks CodeWarrior.

- *Debugger:* This tool is used after a program is compiled to find any *bugs* (defects) in the code and help fix them. The GNU Visual debugger is free and can be easily found online. Microsoft Visual Studio contains a debugger, and GDB is the most common UNIX system debugger.

- *IDE (Integrated Development Environment):* An IDE is a tool that integrates applications into one environment for the programmer, allowing increased productivity by not forcing time-wasting swaps of applications. RHIDE will work with the freeware compiler DJGPP.

- *API (Application Programming Interface):* An API is an interface that makes life easier for the programmer by allowing for a pre-built solution, so that the programmer does not have to use the underlying code. SGI's OpenGL (Open Graphics Library) API provides a flexible and powerful tool allowing high-quality graphics to be rendered in a variety of ways.

- *SDK (Software Development Kit):* An SDK is a set of tools designed to help with development for a particular technology. Microsoft's popular DirectX SDK contains tools that help with the use of DirectX, a powerful API that handles 3D graphics, sound, and input for manual interfaces.

:::::*Shattered Galaxy*: The "Minus" Bug

As a programmer on *Shattered Galaxy,* I once had to apply a big game patch. (This is common in MMOGs—where new content, regions, graphics, interface improvements, and other features need to be added on a regular basis to keep the game evolving.) Right after patching, I encountered a strange game bug, and I had no clue why it happened. I tried almost everything I could to fix it. Since the game was commercialized (people were paying subscription fees to play), I had to find the bug no matter how long it might take. After about almost 12 hours of searching, I finally found that I had made a simple mistake by putting a "minus" sign ("-") before a "1" in the code. Due to a single "minus" sign mistake, over 5,000 concurrent players had big trouble playing the game!

— KyungMin Bang
(Project Leader & Main Programmer, Nexon)

Popular programming languages used by game programmers include C, C++, Visual Basic, and Java. Operating systems include Windows 95/98/2000, XP, NT, Macintosh, Unix, and Linux. In Chapter 3, you learned about the various platforms used in game development, along with associated brands. Most game programmers are familiar with requirements associated with programming games for home console, personal computer, and handheld systems. Brands include Sony (PS2, PSX, PSP), Nintendo (GameCube, Game Boy Color/Advance/SP), Microsoft (Xbox), and Nokia (N-Gage).

There are also other programs—such as Flash MX, Java, GameMaker (www.gamemaker.nl), Torque (www.garagegames.com), and The Games Factory (www.clickteam.com) that you can use to develop your own game engines.

:::::: *Orbz*: Better with a Bug!

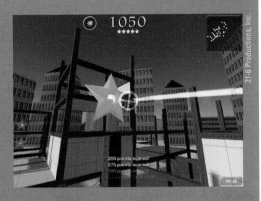

21-6 Productions, Inc.

One of the most memorable moments in developing *Orbz* happened in the early design stages for the game. We were originally developing a quirky golf game. One day, a couple of us were playing a new prototype course together. We were testing out some new scoring code when hitting the targets with the golf ball. I inadvertently introduced a bug in the prototype where the target disappeared after you hit it. During this test session we realized this bug and started playing the game a different way than we had before—to see who could get the most stars before time ran out. We had so much fun with this new way of playing the game that we changed gears on the game design. Instead of building a golf game, we decided to build a game completely based around this simple concept of getting the most stars/points. A couple months later, out came *Orbz*—a unique game that has met with critical acclaim for originality and fun factor (including Best Game of 2003 from *PC Magazine*). We learned a great lesson on *Orbz:* to prototype our ideas early and often. [Author's Note: Prototyping and playtesting will be discussed in more detail in Chapter 11.] What's written on paper doesn't always translate well into gameplay, and it's better to find that out sooner rather than later.

— *Justin Mette*
(President, 21-6 Productions)

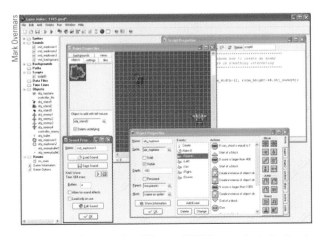

Mark Overmars

GarageGames, Inc.

Gamemaker (freeware) and Torque ($100 license for indie developers) are excellent low-cost game engines.

Flash & the Multi-User Capabilities of Flash Communication Server

Flash has always been a great tool for game development because of its versatility in methodology. One can design almost any type of game with graphics, animation, text, and interactivity, created all in the same program. I use Flash to teach interactive programming concepts, and students are able to generate both simple and complex games during the course. They learn fundamental and advanced programming concepts in Actionscript, while enjoying the challenge of implementing a game idea—and they get to see and share the fruits of their labor at the end of the course.

Flash Communication Server provides more flexibility in gaming with its multi-user functionality. It allows users to communicate and play the same game over a network—even on the Internet. It is fairly easy to implement, as long as the server itself is configured and managed correctly. Having such capabilities expands the possibilities for game design, and challenges game creators to go beyond their previous horizons. Multi-user programming is available for everyone now.

— Russell Burt
(Interactive Design Faculty,
Art Institute of California–Los Angeles)

Greg Costikyan on Java & Mobile Game Development:::::

Greg Costikyan
(Chief Creative Officer,
Unplugged, Inc.;
Consultant,
The Themis Group)

Greg Costikyan has designed more than 30 commercially-published board, role-playing, computer, online, and mobile games—including five Origin Award–winning titles. Among his best known titles are *Creature That Ate Sheboygan* (board game), *Paranoia* (tabletop RPG), *MadMaze* (first online game to attract more than one million players), and *Alien Rush* (mobile game). His games have been selected on more than a dozen occasions for inclusion in the Games 100, *Games Magazine's* annual round-up of the best 100 games in print. He is an inductee into the Adventure Gaming Hall of Fame for a lifetime of accomplishment in the field. In addition to being Chief Creative Officer of Unplugged, Inc.—a mobile game publisher—Greg is a consultant with The Themis Group, which provides community management and consulting services to the massively multiplayer game industry. He also writes one of the most widely-read blogs about games, game development, and the game industry (www.costik.com/weblog).

As an interpreted language, Java inherently runs slower on any platform than native machine code, and games have always been processor-hungry applications. In the mobile world, however, J2ME (Java 2 Micro Edition) and BREW (Qualcomm's Binary Runtime Environment for Wireless) are the dominant languages—largely because there is a substantial installed base of handsets that can run them. As smartphones (used in the generic sense—including Symbian OS and Palm OS devices, in addition to Microsoft's Smartphone OS) become more prevalent, high-end mobile games, at least, will migrate to C++ applications. I expect J2ME and BREW to survive as ways of supporting small, light, mass-audience games installed over-the-air.

Fairlight: A Prelude, Bobby Bearing, & More: 8-Bit Computer to Mobile

Fairlight: A Prelude and *Bobby Bearing* are just two of the 8-bit computer games that EDGE Games is adapting for the mobile platform.

The EDGE Interactive Media, Inc. (d/b/a EDGE Games)

Since 2002, EDGE Games has been actively involved in the mobile game industry—transferring games such as *Fairlight: A Prelude* and *Bobby Bearing* that it developed for 8-bit computers in the 1980s to the mobile phone platform. I am currently working on a cutting-edge 3D engine for mobile devices which is to a large extent device-independent—allowing EDGE to produce games for most mobile phones, smart phones, PDAs, GBA, PSP, and other portable devices. My focus is on creating state-of-the art multiplayer games using Bluetooth and WiFi or GPRS (General Packet Radio Service). I am also focused on creating new artificial intelligence routines based on work we did in the 1980s and 1990s to enhance the game playing experience in both the mobile and video/computer game sectors.

In evolving the 8-bit (and later the 16-bit) game market from the late 1970s to the early 1990s, those of us seeking to always push the envelope of what could be achieved were constantly finding new ways to get devices that had relatively little memory, low processing speeds, and low screen resolution to perform in ways people thought they could not. We thus devised compression algorithms and very tightly written code for displaying 3D space, the physics of rolling and colliding objects, and so on, that would work within a few tens of thousands of bytes—and with screen resolutions as low as 192 pixels wide. With the advent of more capable computers and consoles as the 1990s developed, we left behind much of the need to write such incredibly compact and efficient code because we started to enjoy screen resolutions of 640x480, 800x600 (and now even better)—as well as higher processing speeds and sizable memory.

With the advent of the mobile phone game era in the last two years (as J2ME, in particular, took off), we were once again faced with devices with little memory, limited resolution (both black-and-white and color, and resolutions as low as 96 pixels wide), and slow processors that were more in line with 1980s machines. For this reason, we were able to blow the dust off of some of our best routines and algorithms that we devised in the 1970s and 1980s, which once again became ideal for this new market.... Now we are pushing our 1980s code knowledge to its limits in creating a new 3D engine that, while incredibly compact (so the games will still transmit over the air in under 250k), will rival in many ways what game players have come to expect from games like *Halo, Half-Life,* and so on.

— *Tim Langdell (CEO, EDGE Games)*

Art

Popular 3D software tools used by game artists include Discreet's 3D Studio Max and Alias/Wavefront's Maya. 3D Studio Max and Maya have become standards in the industry, with a large installed customer base, world-building and character modeling utilities, and animation enhancements.

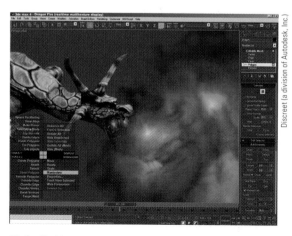

Discreet (a division of Autodesk, Inc.)

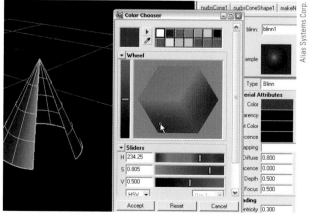

Alias Systems Corp.

3D Studio Max and Maya are the top art tools in the game industry.

3D: Maya and 3D Studio Max Tossup? 2D: "Photoshop Rules All"

For game art, the choice between Maya and 3D Studio Max is a toss-up. At this time, game-quality models are simple triangulated polygon meshes somewhere under 4,000 polys, and closer to 2,000—so using Maya to do in-game work is like cutting cheese with a laser. If you're doing pre-rendered cinematics and want to work more seamlessly between your game assets and some inflated higher resolution version, then Maya might pull ahead…. For 2D, Adobe Photoshop rules all. It's a powerful, flexible tool for concept artwork, texturing, and illustration. There are those who prefer Painter for high-end illustration—but if you want to keep your team on the same platform, Photoshop is the more flexible tool.

— *Marc Taro Holmes*
(Art Director, Obsidian Entertainment)

NewTek Lightwave is another popular game art software program; its modeler and layout modules provide powerful solutions for animating and modeling. Other programs include Bones Pro (skeletal deformation plug-in), Caligari trueSpace, Character Studio, Avid SoftImage, and Mirai. Adobe Photoshop is standard bitmap and vector-based graphics software used by 2D game artists. Other Adobe products used in the industry include Painter, After Effects, Illustrator, and Premiere.

Game Engines as Art Tools

When it finally comes to putting artwork into a game engine, being able to iterate rapidly on the target platform is key—preferably by doing the authoring within the engine itself. For Secret Level, the Unreal engine has been an important tool, which allows our artists to quickly transfer their work and see it "in the game"—giving them a maximum amount of control over their artwork. It is also versatile enough to provide a framework for more than just FPS game types.

— *Christopher Bretz*
(Art Director, Secret Level)

Game Worlds Depend on Game Tools

If your tools make great trees, but suck at architecture, then your game is going to be set in a forest—regardless of what the design doc says. Conversely, if your particle effects editor crashes constantly and doesn't save values, then you will find yourself in a game world that only has ten spells. Make particle effects fun to work with, and you might find yourself in a glowing fantasy world full of mist, fireflies, and paper lanterns.

— *Marc Taro Holmes*
(Art Director, Obsidian Entertainment)

Audio

Popular game audio creation tools include Microsoft's DirectX Audio (and its authoring tool, DirectMusic Producer), Digidesign's ProTools (a standard in almost all music-related industries, including film and studio recording), and Emagic's Logic (a sequencer, which is a device that records and plays back control information for an electronic instrument such as a synthesizer). Analog Devices' SoundMAX Smart Tools allows sound designers to create interactive and non-repetitive audio content, so that game sound effects neither sound the same every time nor occur at regular intervals—like a bird chirping the same exact way every five seconds. For more detail on audio tools, refer to Chapter 9.

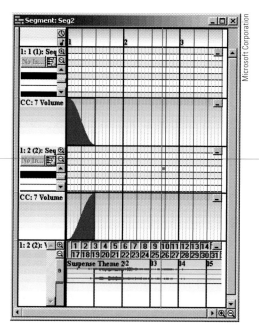

Microsoft Corporation

DirectMusic Producer is one of the most widely-used software programs in game audio.

Now that you have a background on the roles and responsibilities associated with the game development team, let's focus on the process of developing a game from start to finish—and beyond. The next chapter discusses the phases of game development—from concept to release.

:::CHAPTER REVIEW:::

1. How do game development studios, publishers, licensors, and manufacturers work together to bring a game to market?

2. Analyze the different team areas (production, design, art, programming, and testing) and discuss the ways in which a game-production team differs from other production teams in the entertainment industry.

3. What roles in a game-development team are particularly specialized, and what roles are more generalized? Why is this, and how does it affect the game development process?

4. The role of artist and designer are sometimes confused with each other. How do these roles differ? Using one electronic game as a reference, discuss three examples of how art is used in the game, and three examples of how design is used in the game. Does the game utilize art and design successfully?

5. Put together a team for your original game. How many artists, designers, programmers, and producers will you have on your team, and why? What types of specializations will you use? Consider the unique features of your game idea.

6. Experiment with some of the game engines and level editors discussed in this chapter (e.g., Gamemaker, Torque, Aurora, CRYengine, Valve Hammer Editor, and Unreal), and list their features—comparing and contrasting them with each other. Which engine or editor are you most comfortable with—and why?

7. Why do you think 3D Studio Max and Maya are both standards in the creation of game art? Do you prefer one program over the other? Try them both and see which one works better for you. Compare them to other game-art software programs such as Lightwave.

8. What are the benefits and disadvantages of running an independent game studio? How does this structure differ from third-party developers and publishers? If you were running an independent studio and you could initially hire only two team members, what roles would they be?

11

CHAPTER

Production & Management:

developing the process

key chapter questions

- What are the components of each phase in the game development process?

- What are some effective ways to manage game development teams?

- What are the different forms of documentation used in game development?

Now that you have a basic understanding of the roles and responsibilities of game development team members, let's take a look at the game development process itself. This chapter concentrates on all phases of game development—including concept, pre-production, prototype, production, alpha, beta, gold, and post-production. This chapter also includes a discussion of management techniques used by game producers. The final section of this chapter focuses on the functions and features of game documentation.

Development Phases

There are several phases in the development process: concept, pre-production, prototype, production, alpha, beta, gold, and post-production. Each phase involves certain members of the game development team and focuses on specific objectives.

Gordon Walton on Making *Great* Games :::::

Gordon Walton
(Vice President &
Executive Producer,
Sony Online
Entertainment)

Gordon Walton has been authoring games and managing game development since 1977. He currently serves as VP and Executive Producer for an unannounced product at Sony Online Entertainment. Prior to joining Sony Online Entertainment, Gordon was VP and Executive Producer of *The Sims Online* at Electronic Arts/Maxis, and also at Origin Systems managing *Ultima Online*. He also served as Senior VP of Kesmai Studios where he oversaw the development of *Air Warrior* and *Multiplayer Battletech*. Gordon has owned and managed two development companies and has been development manager for Three-Sixty Pacific and Konami of America. He has personally developed over 30 games and has overseen the development of hundreds more.

We need to make our games more *fun* and of much higher quality. Next, we need to work in themes beyond medieval fantasy and sci-fi…. Finally, developers need sufficient *time and resources* to make a great—versus only good—game.

A Three-Day Development Cycle?

After producing hundreds of games, I could probably write a full book of anecdotes about my experiences. I believe that the most memorable experiences have to do with the incredibly talented people that you meet while making games: from engineers to rock stars, graphic artists to composers, everyone seems to discover a new way of expressing themselves….

If I had to outline one single experience, it would be the amazing challenge that we took to produce a game in three days for an important contract when the company was in trouble. After improvising a scenario live in front of the contractor, I had to remember it to tell the technical team and brief the artists. It was in those old days when we only had 8K of memory and 16 colors on the palette to play with. But we made it from start to manufacturing—on tape then—in three days without any sleep. I doubt that this could be done again.

— *Bruno Bonnell*
(Chairman & CEO, Atari)

Concept

The *concept* development phase begins when an idea for a game is envisioned—and it ends when a decision is made to begin planning the project (also known as the *pre-production* phase). During the concept phase, the development team can be quite small—perhaps only consisting of a designer, programmer, artist, and a producer. The goal of concept development is to decide what the game is about and convey the idea to others in written form. The concept document, discussed later in this chapter, is the result of the concept development phase. The goals are to identify a target market, assess company resources, and identify a concept that resonates with developers as well as having a potential market. Often, many short game-design treatments are considered.

The Game Industry: A Victim of Its Own Success?

Developing a game is like trying to assemble an airplane while learning how to fly it. I think that the hardest task is integrating all the disparate pieces—gameplay, sound, 3D engine—in a cohesive format in what seems to be an impossible time-frame. I think that the industry has been a bit of a victim of its own success. The great game designers and programmers out there have consistently blown the socks off of people so many times that when a really solid game comes out that *isn't* a breakthrough in some way, fans are disappointed.

— Jason Kay
(President, Society Capital Group)

Daniel James on the "Conceptual Click" :::::

Daniel James
(Designer & CEO, Three Rings)

Daniel James is founder and CEO of Three Rings, a San Francisco developer and operator of massively multiplayer online games for the mass market casual audience. Three Rings' first game, *Yohoho! Puzzle Pirates,* combines accessible and fun puzzle games with the depth of a social persistent world. Prior to Three Rings, Daniel consulted on game design, toiled for many years on *Middle-earth Online,* and co-founded two profitable UK Internet startups: Avalon and Sense Internet.

For me, the most memorable moment in developing a game is that moment of conceptual "click"—the beginning of the process of development, mirrored by the moments with actual players in the real game, when you feel that "click" reach its fruition. The most challenging part? The last five percent, the polish…getting things just right.

Pre-Production

Once you have received interest in the concept, it's time to develop the proposal and enter the planning (or *pre-production*) phase of development. Additional documentation developed during this phase includes the art bible and production plan. This phase ends with the creation of the game design document (GDD) and technical design document—discussed later in this chapter.

Rade Stojsavljevic on the Challenge of Pre-Production :::::

Rade Stojsavljevic (Senior Producer, Electronic Arts)

Rade Stojsavljevic is a Senior Producer with Electronic Arts. He's worked on a variety of games in different genres such as MMORPG, RTS, adventure, strategy, and military simulations. At Westwood Studios, he worked on *Earth & Beyond Online, Command & Conquer: Tiberian Sun, Firestorm,* and *Blade Runner.* Before joining Westwood and Electronic Arts, Rade worked as a sound designer and video editor for a couple of smaller game developers. He is currently working on an externally-developed title with the EA Partners group.

I used to think that wrapping up a project was the hardest process, but that's not the case any more. After you've shipped a couple of titles, you know what you need to do to get a game out the door. Now I think the hardest part of the development project is pre-production. Generating new ideas for a game is difficult, but the real challenge is figuring out which of those ideas is really good, and which will work together to make a hit. If you don't nail your preproduction goals, you wind up working so much harder in the long run to try and make the game fun and successful.

Prototype

The next goal for most game development teams is to create a tangible *prototype.* The usual definition of a prototype in the game industry is something like this: "A working piece of software that captures on screen the essence of what makes your game special, what sets it apart from the rest, and what will make it successful." However, before moving into the digital realm, I suggest that game designers initially create a *low-fidelity* prototype (often paper-based—using cards, boards, tiles, and/or miniatures) of the game and test it in-house in order to ensure that the gameplay mechanics are tight—and that the game is fun and compelling. Concern about visual style and programming features in a digital prototype can often cause game designers to be distracted from focusing on the game's foundation—the gameplay itself.

Whether or not you decide to begin with an analog prototype, the creation of a digital prototype is essential in the development process—and it could be the single greatest item that influences whether or not the project gets to the next level. Publishers and other funding sources like to be able to look at a screen and understand the game idea right away. If they can't see the vision within a minute or two, they're less likely to fund the rest of the project. Sometimes a development team will be creating new technology during the development process that will be used in the final game. Since the prototype stage is too early for this technology to be available, just try to simulate the feel of the game without it. For example, you could pre-render any material that will be rendered in real-time during the final game.

You might also want to prepare standalone demonstrations proving that the various pieces of planned technology are feasible. The finished prototype shows your vision and establishes that your production path is working—and that you're able to go from idea to reality. Game engines are often used for prototyping, even if entirely new technology will be used for the shipped game.

Early Prototyping

*E*arly prototyping means focusing a team's attention on crude, playable prototypes at the beginning of the design process, before a full production crew is on board. A small group of designers can create a playable version of an idea quickly, using very low production values. The idea is to test and revise the crude prototype over and over using the small team, until you've developed a really interesting play system. Then and only then should the idea be put into production and a full team be brought on board.

— *Chris Swain*
(Professor, USC School of Cinema–Television)

Brenda Laurel on "Make-Believe" Playtesting :::::

Brenda Laurel, PhD
(Chair, Graduate Media
Design Program, Art
Center College of
Design)

Brenda Laurel is a designer, writer, researcher, and performer. She is active as a consultant in interaction design and research. Since 1976, her work has focused on experience design, interactive story, and the intersection of culture and technology. In 1996, Brenda co-founded Purple Moon (acquired by Mattel in 1999) to create interactive for media for girls. The company was based on four years of research in gender and technology at Interval Research Corp. In 1990, Brenda co-founded Telepresence Research—which developed technology and applications for virtual reality and remote presence. Other employers include Atari, Activision, and Apple. Brenda edited *The Art of Human-Computer Interface Design* (Addison-Wesley, 1990), and authored *Computers as Theatre* (Addison-Wesley, 1991 and 1993) and *Utopian Entrepreneur* (MIT Press, 2001). Her latest

book is *Design Research: Methods and Perspectives* (MIT Press, 2004). In addition to public speaking and consulting, Brenda is a Board of Advisors member at several companies and organizations—including Cheskin, the Communication Research Institute of Australia, and the Comparative Media Studies program at MIT. She serves on the Executive Committee of the Digital Storytelling Association and is active in the Association of Computing Machinery (ACM), the International Game Developers Association (IGDA), and the American Institute for Graphic Arts (AIGA).

During the prototype testing for the *Secret Paths* series at Purple Moon, we gave kids paper dolls that represented animals, plants, and other outdoor objects and asked them to make us a play about them. We were expecting *Secret Garden*-type stuff where kids would have magical adventures together. But the girls surprised us; they consistently felt that a place "in nature" would be a place where they would go alone. They wouldn't be taking care of the animals (there goes that nurturing thing); they expected animals and magical creatures to take care of them. What they *wanted* - and what we gave them - was a refuge and a space for personal reflection.

Tracy Fullerton on the Prototyping & Playtesting Process:::::

Tracy Fullerton
(Assistant Professor,
Electronic Arts
Interactive
Entertainment
Program,
USC School of
Cinema-Television)

Tracy Fullerton is a game designer, writer, and educator, teaching at the Electronic Arts Interactive Entertainment Program at the USC School of Cinema–Television. She is also the co-author of *Game Design Workshop: Designing, Prototyping, and Playtesting Games*, from CMP Publishing. She was one of the founders of iTV game developer Spiderdance, and also served as a creative director and producer at the New York design firm R/GA Interactive for a number of years. Her work has received numerous industry honors, including best Family/Board Game from the Academy of Interactive Arts & Sciences, *ID Magazine's* Interactive Design Review, Communication Arts Interactive Design Annual, several New Media Invision awards, iMix Best of Show, the Digital Coast Innovation Award, IBC's Nombre D'Or, and *Time Magazine's* Best of the Web. In December 2001, she was featured in the *Hollywood Reporter's* "Women in Entertainment Power 100" issue. She holds an MFA from the USC School of Cinema–Television, and is a member of the Academy of Television Arts and Sciences, where she serves as a co-chair of the interactive Emmy awards committee. She is also an active member of the Academy of Interactive Arts and Sciences, the International Game Developers Association, and serves as a mentor for the AFI-Intel Enhanced Television workshop.

The most significant elements in prototyping and playtesting are: *when and how often* you do it, *who* you do it with, and *what* you do with the feedback you get. Prototypes are often created these days as demos to sell ideas. While there's value in getting an idea funded, this is one of the worst reasons to do a prototype.

Prototypes are a chance to ask wild, unusual questions, to try ideas that may seem fundamentally unsound, but appeal to you anyway. They provide an opportunity to learn—for game designers to experiment with entirely new mechanics. I encourage prototyping at the earliest possible stage of an idea. And I encourage testing that prototype—no matter how rough or unseemly it feels.

Who should you playtest it with? Playtesting with your core design team is an option of course, but what type of feedback will you get? Informed, but not really objective. As soon as a prototype is functional and stands, albeit precariously, on its feet as a game, I encourage you to recruit objective playtesters from your target group. These are people you don't know. What you will learn from them will be invaluable—and probably hard to hear.

Incorporating feedback is one of the most critical elements to making prototyping and playtesting worthwhile. There is no point to the process if you are not open to change. There is also no point to the process if you don't have player experience goals you are trying to reach—and so are swayed by playtester comments that try to force the game to be a copy of the last game they enjoyed.

The bottom line is: prototype early, playtest often, and have clear goals that you are trying to reach, so that you'll know how best to incorporate the feedback you get.

Production

Once the prototype has been approved, the development team should be ready to enter the longest phase—*production*—in which the game is actually developed. This phase often lasts 6 months to 2 years, and the result is a completed game. You've probably heard about "crunch-time"—involving 100-hour weeks required of most team members during the tail-end of this phase, where many employees might as well sleep on cots at the office for weeks straight. This disaster does not have to happen. In reality, many development teams make the mistake of miscalculating how long it will really take to complete a project. Some projects are given an impossible cycle of under 6 months due to an attempt to make the holiday rush or some other time-sensitive deadline. An even bigger disaster can occur when projects that have a two-year (or more) cycle have the same last-minute scrambling—often resulting in employees quitting, leaving other overworked employees to take up the slack. Initially, two years might sound like a long time—and the initial 1½ years might be spent with team members working a little more "leisurely" than normal. As discussed in Chapter 10, it is the producer's (and other management personnel) job to make sure a project is completed under budget and by the scheduled release date—without causing a mass exodus of dissatisfied employees.

Game Production Challenges: "Are We There Yet?!"

Every facet of the game production process must be handled well or the entire process suffers. If you don't adequately plan during your pre-production phase, you suffer later. If you don't do a good enough job of frontloading your tasks, you'll get bitten later. If you don't manage the team so that they don't peak too early or late, you suffer later. The part I like the least is the middle portion. When you're thinking up cool ideas and planning, you're having fun. When you're at the end and the hours are hideous, at least you have a mostly-finished game and light at the end of the tunnel. The middle part, though, is rough. The game isn't quite there yet, and you have a long way to go—but expectations are high and you constantly have executives breathing down your neck...much like kids on a road trip repeating, "Are we there yet?!"

— *Graeme Bayless*
(Supervising Producer, Electronic Arts–Tiburon)

Localization

If a game will be sold into a market containing a language other than that for which it was originally developed (e.g., an American game being sold into the German market), the development team will need to ensure that the game's content has been *localized* for each respective market. Localization involves language translation (text and voice) and content modification necessary for that market's particular regulations (e.g., on violence, profanity, and sexual content). Keep in mind that some languages, such as German, require more characters per word than others. Gameplay is also often adjusted to suit the tastes of a market (e.g., shooters are easier in Japan, platformers are more difficult for the UK).

Balancing Act: Creativity & Business

The most challenging aspect of the game-production process is balancing creativity with the real business and professional requirements of making a game. Creating an environment where we can be artists and have fun while still getting our work done on time and on budget is quite challenging. However, I believe that achieving this balance is how great games are made.

— *Starr Long*
(Producer, NCsoft)

Alpha

The *alpha* phase is the point at which a game is playable from start to finish. There may be a few gaps and the art assets might not be final, but the engine and user interface are both complete. Instead of focusing on building and creating, the alpha stage is about finishing and polishing the game. If any features need to be dropped in order to make the release date, this is the time to do it. During alpha, the testing department ensures that each game module is tested at least once; creates a bug database and test plan; and records bugs and performance results. Temporary playability testers are brought on during this phase to check for bugs. This is the first time the game is seen by people outside the development team. In order to pass the alpha phase, the following elements should be complete:

- One gameplay path (playable from beginning to end)
- Primary language text
- Basic interface with preliminary documentation
- Compatibility with most specified hardware and software configurations
- Minimum system requirements tested
- Most manual interfaces tested for compatibility
- Placeholder art and audio
- Multiplayer functionality tested (if applicable)
- Draft of game manual

Mark Mencher, in his book *Get in the Game,* does an excellent job of outlining what items are needed (such as the above list) in order to pass one development phase and go to the next.

Game Art Trade-offs

As a game artist, you are frequently making designs and hoping that the technology will work as advertised—or, conversely, you have made a lot of assets, and late in the game some new thing becomes available that suddenly makes them pale by comparison. Now you have to decide: Do you keep to the plan and risk looking dated—or throw out the old work and try and master the new approach in the time remaining? This is always a tough call.

— *Marc Taro Holmes*
(Art Director, Obsidian Entertainment)

Beta

After the game has passed the alpha phase, it enters the *beta* phase. During this phase, the focus is on fixing bugs. All assets are integrated into the game, and the entire production process ceases. The goal during beta is to stabilize the project and eliminate as many bugs as possible before shipping the product. Beta testers are recruited online to test the game for playability. Objectives of this phase include isolating all significant bugs and performance problems; complete testing, bug fixing, and performance tuning; and test on all supported platforms. If the game has been developed for a proprietary hardware platform—such as a console system—the corresponding hardware manufacturer will test the game to ensure that it meets its own quality standards. Games developed for the personal computer platform are tested for compatibility to uncover whether there are any hardware configurations under which the game will not operate.

The last few days or weeks of this phase are sometimes referred to as the *code freeze* period, in which all the work is done and the preparation of master game media begins. The media (usually in disc form) is sent to testing, and the only changes allowed to the game are those that address urgent bugs that show up during this final testing process. The following are elements that must be complete in order to pass the beta phase:

- Code
- Content
- Language version text
- Game path navigation
- User interface
- Hardware and software compatibility
- Manual interface compatibility
- Art and audio
- Game manual

The primary improvements during the beta phase include the development of the game's final code and content, along with the manual and visual interfaces.

Knowing When to Stop

The most challenging part of development, to me, is deciding when to stop. In the end, every game could have a bit more of this or another feature or two. You have to draw the line, finish the title up, and get it into the market. This always results in crunch time for passionate teams, and a good management team ensures that the long hours are being put in to make a good product great, not just to get any product out the door.

— *Louis Castle*
(Co-Founder, Westwood Studios;
Vice President, Electronic Arts–Los Angeles)

Gold

Once the game has passed the beta phase, it is considered *gold*. The game is sent to be manufactured after one of the master game discs has been thoroughly tested and is found to be acceptable. At gold, senior management has reviewed the product and bug database ("bugbase")—and agrees that the product is ready. Manufacturing takes several weeks, as the media is created and packaged. After the game "goes gold," it is released into the marketplace. (Some studios consider *demo creation* to be a phase right after *beta*. In this phase, an isolated experience is created and licensed in limited version to the press. This demo is required by some publishers.)

Rapid Development

The need for *rapid development* is the most challenging aspect of game programming. Time is always short, and the design is always changing because each iteration brings up new gameplay and visual issues, and the designers can always think of more cool stuff than we can possibly code up. We have to identify the subset of possible features that will give us the most bang for the programming buck. Then we get that coded up so the designers can start building the game and identify what is missing—and we repeat this until it is time to polish. There are always more things to polish than time, but polish is what makes a game feel great.

— *John Ahlquist*
(Lead Programmer, Electronic Arts–Los Angeles)

:::::Exceeding Expectations with *Civilization II*

Firaxis Games / Atari, Inc.

Back in 1995 when I was working on *Civilization II*, I lived for a year in Yorkshire (England) during my wife's teaching fellowship—so I was basically just tapping away on a little portable computer in our living room. Management was telling us this game wasn't going to sell very well at all, so it was a very low priority for resources, marketing, etc. But then I came back to the U.S., and one day I happened to be walking around the studio. I saw all sorts of people playing the *Civilization II* beta—including lots of people who had nothing to do with the *Civilization II* team and worked in other departments like marketing and documentation. When I saw how thoroughly we had "infected" the company, it was great—because at that moment I knew we were going to do well in spite of the low sales projection (which we exceeded by a factor of 40)!

— *Brian Reynolds (President, Big Huge Games)*

David Perry on the Amazing $100 Million Piece of Code :::::

David Perry (President
& Founder, Shiny
Entertainment)

A 23-year game industry veteran, David Perry launched his professional career at just 15 years of age by writing video game programming books in his native Northern Ireland. Since then, Perry has developed 32 games—including *The Terminator, Teenage Mutant Ninja Turtles,* and Disney's *Aladdin*—totaling 88 individual retail titles across 23 video game platforms. Perry sits on the Advisory Board of the Game Developers Conference and is a regular speaker at industry events. His latest project was *Enter The Matrix,* the #1 Award Winning Movie Game of 2003—made by working in close collaboration with the writer/directors of *The Matrix* universe.

On *Disney's Aladdin,* I was with a group of great guys trying to meet a really tough deadline. There on my computer was a small file that was worthless to the world. But when I hit the return key, our work was done, we could all relax, the data was heading for a cartridge—and that little piece of code that we had lovingly built was going to be worth over $100 million. It still amazes me to this day.

Cookies at Crunch Time

I was working on an interactive project for a food-service provider, and the lead programmer quit at the worst possible moment: just a few weeks before the deadline. Guess who stepped in? The fact that we were short one programmer meant that I had to work a lot of overtime to get the job done. Fortunately, the project ended well, but those few weeks are a blur in my memory. Thank goodness the producer understood our needs and supplied us with anything we needed. I remember I ate a lot of cookies.

— *Russell Burt*
(Interactive Design Faculty,
Art Institute of California–Los Angeles)

After Crossing the Finish Line...

Like most developers, my fondest memories are usually when the team is gathered around, bleary-eyed from lack of sleep, cheering when our game finally gets released to manufacturing. After a few beers are consumed, we inevitably recount the events, both humorous and dramatic, that led up to that day. My best friends are my colleagues.

— *John Hight*
(Executive Producer, Atari)

:::::A Future *Utopia*

Creating the first computer baseball game and the first computer role-playing game was a lot of fun, but at the time I never realized that anyone would notice or care. We were college students creating games for classmates on mainframe computers,

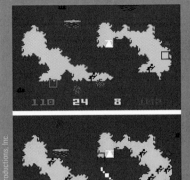

and we had no idea this would ever become an industry. I remember being surprised when my games were shared with other universities across the country and I started getting letters from players. When my first Intellivision game, *Utopia,* was a surprise hit in 1982, I felt like pinching myself—thinking, "How can someone possibly get paid to write games?"

— *Don Daglow*
(President and CEO, Stormfront Studios)

:::::"An Enormous Breakfast at Denny's": Shipping *Age of Empires*

Ensemble Studios was a new company, and it was our first title....Everyone was very passionate and driven to make the game the best it could be. The dozen of us

Microsoft Corporation

worked crunch hours for nearly a year and were completely exhausted in those last few days. The testers at Microsoft were matching us step-for-step, and we'd play multiplayer games until 4am pretty much every night. We set a goal for ourselves of 100 back-to-back multiplayer games without crashing, hangs, or multiplayer problems—and we'd call it good to ship. We were sleep-deprived, going without stopping the last 48 hours—but fueled by being so close to finishing, that we felt like mountain climbers nearing the peak. When the test team called it gold, we all cheered—then got an enormous breakfast at Denny's. We toasted with orange juice, laughed, and slept for a solid week. It was terrible and wonderful at the same time. I'll never forget it.

— *Mark Terrano*
(Technical Game Manager, Xbox Advanced Technology Group)

Post-Production

During the *post-production* (or *post-release*) phase, several subsequent *versions* of the game might also be released that replace and improve upon the original game—increasing its longevity. These new versions are free of charge and are created by applying patches to the original game in order to upgrade it with additional content that enhances the original game. A *patch* can also be applied to fix software bugs—which are not necessarily major software glitches, but issues as innocuous as making the game run properly on an unusual hardware combination. *Upgrades*—additional content created to enhance the original game—are also released during this phase. These are usually created to extend the life of the original game. Expansions are games that are based on the theme of the original game (and sometimes its story and characters). *Expansions* are self-contained games requiring their own software (and sometimes the original game software as well) to run. These adaptations usually cost less than the original game, but are free in rare cases.

Celia Pearce on Virtual Collaboration :::::

Celia Pearce (Arts Research Manager & Associate Director, Game Culture & Technology Lab, TCal-(IT)2, University of California, Irvine)

For over 20 years, Celia Pearce has been a game designer, artist, researcher, teacher, and author. Her publications include *The Interactive Book: A Guide to the Interactive Revolution*—as well as numerous other articles on interactive media, game design, and culture. She is a member of the Interactive Game Developer's Association (IGDA), a founding board member of the Digital Games Research Association (DiGRA), and a regular contributor to *Game Studies Journal.*

I've enjoyed all the games I've worked on, but I think I most enjoyed the process of developing *Virtual Adventures* with Iwerks and Evans & Sutherland. This was done with a distributed team and nobody really had email yet—so the whole project was done by faxing design docs and FedExing videos back and forth. What was fun about it was that it was so interdisciplinary; we were repurposing a high-end flight simulator and turning it into a virtual reality entertainment system. At the time (1993), it was the birth of what we called the "military entertainment complex." In the post–Cold War milieu, a lot of technologies that had been developed by or for the military (the Internet being a prime example) were becoming available to civilians—and people in entertainment had the financial wherewithal and creativity to try and transform them into mass media.

Up until the advent of massively multiplayer online games (MMOGs), my focus had always been multiplayer games for theme parks and attractions. *Virtual Adventures* was particularly interesting because we were trying to appeal to an international and family audience—multiple ages, both genders.…We wanted something that really emphasized collaboration and appealed to the very broad base of a theme park audience. I tried to craft the social interaction in such a way that it afforded a really wide range of play styles so that…everyone could find something that appealed to them. I was especially concerned with making something moms would like, and especially something they'd want to do with their kids. Judging from the tests we ran and the success of the two units that were installed, it was very successful in this regard. At one of the public sites, I once saw a mother dragging her 11-year-old son in for another go-round. That was very gratifying. I also talked to the staff, who said they loved the game so much, they'd sneak in there and play when guest traffic was slow. That was fun because we were inventing something for the first time—a really high-end virtual-reality ride—at the time when titles like *Doom* and *Myst* were just hitting the consumer game market.

Ed Del Castillo on Being a Valuable Team Member :::::

Ed Del Castillo co-founded Liquid Entertainment with Mike Grayson in 1999 and has worked as Creative Director on *Battle Realms* and *The Lord of the Rings: War of the Ring.* At Origin Systems, Ed worked on *Sid Meier's Gettysburg, Alpha Centauri,* and *Ultima: Ascension.* He was Producer on *Command & Conquer, Command & Conquer: Red Alert,* and all the ports and expansions of those titles. Ed's first job in the industry was at Mindcraft Software—where he started in customer support and worked his way into design, which resulted in credits on RTSs and RPGs. Ed received a B.A. in Economics with a double minor in Psychology and Visual Arts at the University of California, San Diego (UCSD).

Edward A. Del Castillo (President, Liquid Entertainment)

When I was starting out, I was given a job answering phones and shipping orders from a folding table. The job had down times, when I read magazines and waited for a call or order. Instead of wasting the time, I offered to write the game manual for *Siege* promising that if they didn't like it they could just throw it away. It was a no-risk proposition for them. They liked my work, so I asked to help with the game, under the same rules as the manual. I ended up building all the levels in the game, and I did a large chunk of the design. After that my boss came to me and said, "I don't know why we're paying you to answer phones!" I was promoted, and that's how I became a designer.

I think the story is important because it's a living example of three principles:

- Hard work and dedication always pay off.

- Never gauge your success by how well you are fulfilling your job description. If you're fulfilling your job description, that's what's expected. You're just passing the class—not getting an "A." Trust me, your boss sees it that way too.

- If you want a job, raise, or a promotion, you have to do the job first!

Management

As mentioned in Chapter 10, the producer needs to balance time, money, and value during the course of a project. If the game has a short production cycle, the producer must make sure that the quality of the product does not decrease due to the lack of time available. This can be done by adjusting the budget or by extending the release date. The producer also needs to come up with a structured development plan for the project.

Iterative Development

Keep in mind that game development is more like software development than other forms of entertainment. Just like games are not films in content, the process by which they are developed is also not anything like film production. The *iterative* development process—used in software and web development (and discussed in detail in Van Duyne, et al., *The Design of Sites*)—also seems to work well for game development. This model incorporates a circular three-stage process: design, prototype, evaluate.

Three-Stage Iterative Development Process

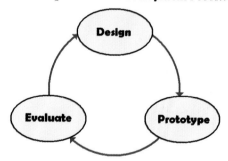

The three-stage iterative development process.

After the *design* phase (which involves planning and pre-production), a *prototype* is developed. After the prototype has been played and tested during the *evaluation* phase, the team decides what works and what doesn't—then goes back to the design phase and modifies the prototype (making it available again for testing). This process is repeated over and over again as needed until the game is no longer a prototype—but a completed game. The key to this model is to continuously refine the design of the game, based on what has been created so far. Don't build assets that you might not need later. Each prototype should have its own cycle of full development—including associated requirements, deliverables, and schedule. This iterative approach is the opposite of *gold-plating*—in which members of the team add "bells and whistles" to a product, costing time and money. When possible, involve prospective players in the evaluation phase so that you can get a player's perspective on usability, gameplay, and the game's "fun factor." This allows the player to take part in the development process (supporting the player-developer connection discussed in earlier chapters)—and it is commonly utilized in games that can be easily beta-tested online.

Common Mistakes

In his book, *Rapid Development,* author Steve McConnell identifies several classic mistakes that managers make on software projects, and discusses the problems that these mistakes cause. Game producers should keep some of these mistakes in mind:

- **Lack of motivation:** Know the team members on your project, and give them reasons to do a good job.
- **Lack of skill:** Make sure team members are highly skilled, instead of hiring people who can get onto the project the fastest.
- **Difficult employees:** If an employee doesn't work well with the rest of the team, it can destroy morale and project efficiency. Removing a problem member from a team will allow for more productivity, even if other team members have to do a little more work to compensate. (They'll be happier!)
- **Restricted environment:** Most game development offices suffer from noisy and crowded bullpens, or even employees crammed into small rooms together without any privacy. It has been debated whether it's more productive for team members to work in their own offices (or uncrowded spaces) or to establish a culture that encourages frequent communication among team members.
- **Insufficient tracking:** Make sure you track the progress of all team members to determine whether you are on schedule.
- **Incomplete task list:** Some time-consuming tasks are overlooked and omitted from the project plan. Examples include interviews, meetings, reviews, and missed days due to conferences or other special events.
- **Misunderstandings:** Make sure that each task is clearly explained. What does it mean to create a demo for a trade show? What does this entail?
- **Unplanned tasks:** Management may ask for unexpected (and sometimes last-minute) tasks that have not been accounted for in the project plan. Assume that this will happen and budget time for this in the project plan.
- **Waiting to fix bugs:** Some developers feel that there's no point in fixing bugs until close to the end of the development process. However, fixing bugs often uncovers other hidden bugs—and it can also create more bugs!

Know Your Limitations

Most game developers are also gamers—and we're always saying things like, "I can make that better," when we play our favorite games. In our early years, we thought we could build these full-blown AAA [high quality] box/console titles, but we were wrong. We needed much more experience with technology, running remote teams, and harmonizing all the creative talent required to make a great game. Understanding the limits of your team is imperative to the success of the project. Don't design features into your game that nobody on your team has developed before or that your technology (e.g., game engine) does not support. You are just asking for trouble, and the project can easily spin out of control as you get deeper into it.

— *Justin Mette*
(President, 21-6 Productions)

Meeting Deadlines

The most challenging aspect of game development is getting the game done on time. It's easy to spend five years experimenting with what you do and don't like—but it's a whole different game when you have a date to meet. Time is something we still find challenging, and I think always will. That said, if it was easy, *everyone* would be making games!

— *David Perry*
(President & Founder, Shiny Entertainment)

Recovery from Mistakes

Game producers also need to avoid falling into the trap of attempting to recover from common management mistakes by doing the following:

- **Planning to catch up later:** This often happens at the beginning, after there's been an unexpected delay that does not conform to the schedule. Don't plan to catch up later, but address problems immediately.
- **Requiring mandatory overtime:** While asking for small amounts of overtime can sometimes be effective for a short time just prior to a major milestone, extended periods of mandatory overtime can result in a significant drop in productivity. As team members tire out, they make more mistakes—which results in more testing and reworking. The most important issue is motivation— thought of as the most significant predictor of productivity—which begins to plummet as a result of forced overtime. Instead of requiring overtime, ask employees to concentrate on making the best use of their standard workweek.

- **Adding people to the project:** This can work at the beginning of an understaffed project. However, if the project has fallen behind after you are well into it, adding people will almost never help you catch up. New people have to come up to speed on the project, and other people might have to take time out to train them. Meetings can take longer, and more misunderstandings might occur.

- **Holding more meetings:** Disrupting a team's workflow by holding status update meetings can greatly reduce productivity. Every time you interrupt people who are immersed in intellectual work, all of the problems they are trying to solve are dropped—and the problem-solving process has to begin all over again later. A workday full of meetings, reports, and other interruptions almost guarantees a drop in productivity.

Managing the Last 20%

The last 20% of the game-production process is the most challenging. It's during these critical weeks where you need the discipline to focus on the things that really matter. As an Executive Producer, you have to keep both your enthusiasm and diplomacy at peak. The team needs you to settle disputes and maintain clarity of purpose.

— John Hight
(Executive Producer, Atari)

Effective Management

Here are just a few guidelines for effective management:

- Ask for input instead of issuing orders.
- Involve the team in the planning stage, and be flexible with the scheduled deadlines when necessary.
- Encourage employees to discuss problems with you so that they do not grow into unmanageable ones.
- Don't panic when problems arise, and don't personalize problems.
- Before making decisions, get the facts and see if the team can reach consensus.
- Make sure employees have several uninterrupted hours of work each day.
- Be forthcoming with your team, and do not hide information from them (even if you feel that they might not be able to handle it).
- Don't just work regular hours when you've asked your team to work overtime.
- Don't make promises to employees in order to get them to make personal sacrifices for the project.
- Provide significant rewards to employees after the project is completed.

Graeme Bayless on Effective Game Project Management:::::

Graeme Bayless
(Supervising Producer,
Electronic Arts–
Tiburon)

Though his career has taken him through many paths (programmer in the U.S. Air Force, computer sales manager, electronics technician), Graeme Bayless has always been fascinated with games. Graeme made his first design contribution to the industry at age 14, and he has been active in the game industry in one capacity or another ever since. In 1987, he finally landed in the computer game industry—and he never looked back. In his spare time, he plays games of every form, reads, watches movies, and wrestles with his two Bull Mastiff puppies. Here are Graeme's tips for effective game project management:

Be honest…especially with yourself: This may seem ridiculously obvious, but it really isn't. Your integrity is critical to your success in life—both business and personal. If you don't have that, you don't have anything. Beyond this, however, is a more subtle aspect: the amazing ability for all humans to delude themselves. Let's say you are the Producer on a big project that is into the mid-production cycle. Upper management comes to you and requests a significant change that you don't have adequate time budgeted for. Assuming that no additional resources are given and no additional time is allocated, this means that you'd probably have to cut something to fit in this change—right? Well, all too often, producers will simply accept the change and expect to "find the time somewhere"—basically convincing themselves it isn't as difficult or large a change as they know it is. Result? A death march and a burned-out team. Simply put, never try to delude yourself or others into believing things aren't as they are. If you're honest at all times, you will save yourself a lot of heartache.

Learn to step back: Producers nearly always come from "the ranks"—former programmers, artists, designers, writers, or testers. However, the job of Producer is not one of these anymore. Unless you're pulling double duty (and if you are, please stop—and re-read rule #1, above), you should not be trying to be a producer and still keep your old job. If you're an ex-designer, please leave the design job to the designer. Comment and carry the vision—but let them do their job. You are a facilitator now—not a "doer."

If you do nothing else…communicate: You've taken a huge step towards success if you keep everyone informed and talking—even if you do nothing else on the team. Every day that is wasted because someone didn't understand that the orders had changed is a day you threw away because you failed to keep the team communicating. Do that too many times and you'll hurt your game…badly. There are a million methods for keeping the communication pathways open. Find the best one for you, and use it constantly!

Starr Long on Online Game Development Management Mantras:::::

Starr Long has been in the business of making computer games for over ten years. Alongside Richard Garriott, he was the original Project Director for the commercially successful *Ultima Online*. Starr worked his way up through the ranks of Origin Systems, starting in Quality Assurance on *Wing Commander, Ultima,* and many other titles. Starr was the Producer for *Ultima Online 2*—and he is currently working with Richard Garriott on *Tabula Rasa* for the Korean online game giant NCsoft, creators of *Lineage* (the world's largest online game). Here are Starr's "mantras" for online game development management:

Starr Long
(Producer, NCsoft)

Mantra 1: "No amount of ego is worth any amount of talent." Developers with professional attitudes are a must. Nothing slows down teams more than intra-team friction—most often created by ego clashes. Ego prevents valuable feedback loops and causes people to get locked into ideas—making them unwilling to be flexible.

Mantra 2: "If you are not having fun making the game, the players won't have fun playing it." Provide a relaxed, professional atmosphere for your team. Engage in team-building and bonding events. Always keep your team at a reasonable size; more than 25 on a team is very risky. Large teams have trouble communicating and staying in synch. With larger teams, managers (including Leads and Producers) spend too much time managing people instead of managing the project.

Mantra 3: "Be a leader, not just a manager." Admit and learn from your mistakes. Use inspiration, not degradation. Positive reinforcement is much more powerful and motivating than negative reinforcement. Ensure that the entire team is always aware of the current status of the project by maintaining a consistently high level of communication; always "show and tell" at team gatherings, and provide regular reports to your team (e.g., daily, weekly, monthly).

Mantra 4: "Fiction explains gameplay—so gameplay should not have to explain fiction." Game design should be about how the game plays, first and foremost. Even genre doesn't need to be defined until the mechanics are sketched out.

Mantra 5: "No plan survives contact with the enemy." Only do enough pre-production on the game design to build an overall schedule. Only do detailed designs in conjunction with the programming team as they are implementing a given system.

Mantra 6: "It's a game and a service." Online games have some unique needs. Know that an online game is both a service and a game—not just one of these. Remember that an online game is a game—not a world, and not a simulation.

Mantra 7: "Stable, fast, fun—in that order." If the game is not stable and does not have a reliably fast frame rate, it won't matter how fun it is.

Managing game projects takes a great deal of inspiration, energy, passion, patience—and the ability to delegate. If you're interested in managing a game development team, consider gaining education in the areas of leadership, project management, business management—and even general "people" skills!

Richard Garriott on Memorable Moments in Game Development :::::

A true veteran of the computer game industry, Richard Garriott is best known for creating and publishing the best-selling *Ultima* series—including the first commercially successful online game, *Ultima Online*. In a career that spans more than two decades, Richard has received numerous awards including *Computer Gaming World*'s "15 Most Influential Industry Players," *Next Generation*'s "America's Elite," PC Gamer's "Game Gods," and *PC Games*' "Designer of the Year." He and his brother, Robert, were also awarded the "Entrepreneur of the Year" award by *Inc. Magazine*. In an industry that now rivals the movie industry in popularity, Richard Garriott is one of the few well-known "stars." Richard's first game was published when he was still a teenager. Under the pseudonym "Lord British," Richard created *Ultima I* (and subsequently the entire *Ultima* series). By the time *Ultima II* was released in 1982, he was sought after by publishers for his expertise and creative vision. In 1983, Richard and his brother, Robert, established Origin Systems, Inc. The company, based in Austin, Texas, is recognized as one of the innovation leaders in the ever-changing world of entertainment software. In 1992, Origin was acquired by Electronic Arts, a global leader in the entertainment software industry. At Origin, Richard continued to add to the *Ultima* series, making it one of the most successful and longest running series in entertainment software history. In 1997, Richard and his team created a new genre with the technologically groundbreaking title, *Ultima Online*. The game's continued

Richard "Lord British" Garriott (Creative Director, NCsoft)

success is measured by the hundreds of thousands of people who enjoy playing the game from all over the world, and by the explosion of online games that have followed since its release. Richard retired from Origin in April of 2000 and formed Destination Games with his brother Robert. In 2001, Destination Games became part of NCsoft, where Richard continues to develop innovative new products. His most recent project, *Tabula Rasa*, was released in May 2004.

After 25 years, there are many memorable moments! Some of my favorite experiences are:

- being killed (unexpectedly and in game, of course) at the end of the *Ultima Online* beta

- the large-scale protest "drunken, naked sit-in" in *Ultima Online*

- late-night jam sessions back at Origin

- the "Killing Children" scene that's been in every *Ultima* since *Ultima IV*. When I made *Ultima IV*, I created the game to test players' virtues. One of the things I did was to put in a room full of evil children who would attack you if you walked your character into the room. I knew players would debate on how to get out of the room alive without having to harm the children and possibly lose points for their moraility. In the end, the players could not be harmed. However, my own family thought this was terrible. They felt like I would be portrayed as some sort of evil advocate for child abuse. But it turned out to be a non-issue. No one complained. And so in every *Ultima* following *Ultima IV*, we always created a room full of "Killing Children" as a memory to this special situation.

- catching one of our developers putting in their own back door (secret room) in an early *Ultima* and then our team quickly modifying the room just before release to keep this cheat out of the hands of players. One of our developers created a back door where he could keep all the equipment he needed to win the game. If this had leaked out, it would have provided a cheat for players to finish the game without really completing it. So what we did was to modify the room so that—when players went through the back door—instead of finding a load of free equipment, Lord British made an appearance and exclaimed, "How dare you cheat in this game!" and summarily killed the player. An *Ultima* saved at the 11th hour.

- playing lots of practical jokes on employees and "modifying" their offices a bit while they were out of town. Ah, those were the days!

Game Documentation

Game documentation is created during the concept, pre-production and production phases in order to convey components of the project to team members and prospective partners (such as a publisher, manufacturer, or licensor). The documentation serves two purposes: to ensure that team members understand their roles in the development process; and to convince companies to develop, fund production, or otherwise help make the game a reality. Keep in mind that the following documentation descriptions and elements are guidelines only. No strict documentation standards exist yet in this industry—although the following represents all the essential components needed for a strong foundation.

The Game Documentation Debate

There is much debate in the industry on the effectiveness of creating extensive game documentation during the planning process. In reality, many elements of a game change drastically during the pre-production and production phases—whether due to problems related to implementation, scheduling, budgeting, market trends...or even a senior executive's change of mind. Lengthy game design document "tomes" should be avoided if at all possible. During the pre-production phase of *Ultima Online II,* Producer Starr Long and his team spent almost three months building "a massive 150-page design document. We ended up completely changing at least 75% of the design, making a lot of that work useless." It's still good practice to put a game project into a structured framework early on so that the development team understands the project's initial vision—even if that eventually changes. Just avoid the unnecessary "documentation dissertation syndrome"!

Don Daglow on the Relationship between Technology & Creativity :::::

Don Daglow
(President and CEO,
Stormfront Studios)

Don L. Daglow has served as president and CEO of Stormfront Studios since founding the company in 1988. Stormfront's most recent titles are *The Lord of the Rings: The Two Towers* (PS2, Xbox) for *Electronic Arts* and New Line Cinema, based on the film by Peter Jackson—and *Forgotten Realms: Demon Stone* (PS2) for Atari. Don's work has earned recognition in publications ranging from *Computer Gaming World* to *Inc., Upside, The Red Herring,* and the *San Francisco Business Times. Electronic Games* called him "one of the best-known and respected producers in the history of the field." Prior to founding Stormfront, Don served as director of Intellivision game development for Mattel, as a producer at Electronic Arts, and as head of the Entertainment and Education division at Broderbund. He designed and programmed the first-ever computer baseball game in 1971 (now recorded in the Baseball Hall of Fame in Cooperstown), the first mainframe computer role-playing game (1976), the first sim game (Intellivision's *Utopia,* 1982) and the first original play-by-email game (*Quantum Space,* for AOL, 1989). Don co-designed Computer Game Hall of Fame title *Earl Weaver Baseball* (1987), and the first massively multiplayer online graphic adventure, *Neverwinter Nights,* for AOL (1991–97). In 2003, Don was elected to the Board of Directors of the Academy of Interactive Arts and Sciences. He holds a B.A. in Creative Writing from Pomona College, and an M.Ed. from Claremont Graduate University.

The huge increase in the power of hardware has reversed the relationship between creativity and technology over the last 25 years. In the early days of gaming, we had big dreams for wonderful eye-popping games. But the limits of screen resolution, memory, cartridge size (remember those?), and processor speed meant that plenty of compromises separated concept and reality. Programmers spent more time making games fit into primitive machines than they spent on the creative process. Today we still have big dreams for exciting games. The only limitations now are our ability to create them, and the need to find a publisher willing to fund a game that may cost $5 - $20 million to produce.

Brian Reynolds on Starting From Scratch :::::

A 13-year industry veteran, Brian Reynolds is recognized as one of the industry's most talented and productive game designers. Honored by *PC Gamer* magazine as one of 25 "Game Gods," Reynolds has masterminded the design of an unbroken stream of hit strategy games—including the million-selling *Civilization II, Alpha Centauri,* and now *Rise of Nations*— the real-time strategy game from Big Huge Games and Microsoft. Highly regarded for his mastery of the art of programming, Reynolds' dual specialty gives him the substantial advantage of being able to bring his own visions to life—and he has built a reputation for finely-tuned strategy games. As President of Big Huge Games, Brian concentrates on the creative side of the company—devoting most of his time to hands-on development of new game concepts and prototypes.

Brian Reynolds
(President,
Big Huge Games)

I think starting a brand new game from scratch is the most daunting part of the process. On the one hand, you have infinite possible choices; on the other hand, most of them are dead ends. Trying to come up with something that's going to be new and innovative—but still functional, and recognizable as a game people will want to buy and play—can be very challenging. You have to break the problem down into smaller steps and then solve it one bit at a time.

Concept

The *concept* document (also known as a *pitch* document) is the result of the concept development stage. The main goal of this document is to convey the goal and purpose of the proposed game. The document helps management (or a prospective investor or publisher) assess whether or not the game idea is viable, timely, and feasible. The purpose of this document is to sell the idea to funding sources, publishers, or other decision-makers in the company. This document should be no more than five pages in length, and it should take no more than a week to create. The producer or creative director is usually responsible for putting together this document. Following is a description of several components that should be included.

Premise

Also known as the *high concept,* the *premise* is the basic idea of your game, introduced in Chapter 4. The premise consists of one to two sentences addressing the player directly, describing the mood and unique "hook" of the game. Think of the premise as something that will be used on posters and on the front of the game's packaging, near the title.

Player Motivation

You learned in Chapter 6 that there are victory and loss conditions in most games. A *player motivation* statement should briefly discuss the game's victory condition. How does the player win? What will drive the player to actually play the game to the end? For example, the player could be driven by a desire to compete, solve puzzles, or explore.

Unique Selling Proposition (USP)

What makes your game unique? Why will your audience choose to play your game over your competitors' titles? Your *unique selling proposition (USP)* is that one thing that makes your title stand out from the others. Why should your game be developed? Why is it special? Briefly state your USP and support it in no more than one paragraph. You might also want to list the features that will make your game particularly exceptional—anything from an unusual graphic style to advanced engine technology. Think of the USP as content that would be included on the back of the packaging for the game.

Target Market

The *target audience* is the portion of the game-playing audience that will be most likely to play your game. In Chapter 2, you learned about player demographics, psychographics, and geographics. Apply this information to the type of player who will enjoy your game the most. Make sure you include a specific age range. The target audience will also tie into the game's genre. This section should be no more than one paragraph in length.

What age group will you target?

You Want Them to Sneeze!

Don't assume that everyone will play your game—because they won't! The key here is to hone in on smaller groups of people that will not only want to play your game, but who will get their friends to play it as well. Marketing guru Seth Godin calls these people "sneezers," who spread an "ideavirus" to others. (Marketing strategies are discussed further in Chapter 12.)

Genre

In Chapter 3 you learned about all the primary *genres* that have been used to classify games. These genres are not based on setting or mood—as in those associated with traditional media, such as film—but on gameplay or style of game. What genre will you choose for your game? If you're considering combining genres (creating a *hybrid*) or inventing a new one, keep in mind that the industry might consider this a risky undertaking. If you are approach-

eGenesis

Genetic Engineering: To increase the efficiency of your guild, you can breed specialized crops... or use mutagens to create truly unique varieties.

Will your game be an MMORPG like the award-winning *A Tale in the Desert*?

ing outside funding or partnerships, remember that publishers and financial backers may need to be convinced that your innovative hybrid or brand new genre will be a success. Without the ability to analyze the sales performance of games in the same genre, your prospective partners might be hesitant to put money and credibility behind something that isn't a "sure thing." If the genre you've chosen is already established, take a few words to name and define the genre with respect to your game. If you are using an original genre or hybrid, discuss it in a paragraph.

What is your game's expected ESRB rating?

Target Rating

In Chapter 3 you learned about the various ratings provided by the Entertainment Software Rating Board (ESRB). Indicate what the expected ESRB rating for your game will be, and why.

Target Platform & Hardware Requirements

In Chapter 3 you learned about several platforms used in game development—including arcade, console, handheld (e.g., mobile, wireless and PDA), and personal computer (PC). Most platforms require a relationship with the hardware manufacturer associated with that platform. As discussed in Chapter 3, the computer platform does not require this, due to the fact that it is not a proprietary platform. The mobile platform requires a relationship with a service provider who acts like a publisher. Major manufacturers of console platforms currently include Sony, Microsoft, and Nintendo. Handheld manufacturers include Nintendo, Sony, and Nokia.

Nintendo of America, Inc.

Will your target platform be a handheld device such as the Game Boy Advance SP?

Mobile Development: The Problem of Diversity

The greatest problem with mobile development at the moment is platform *diversity*. Graphics often need to be reformatted for each new screen size; different manufacturers' phones support different versions of Java; and integrating with each carrier offers its own challenges. Some developers support as many as 80 different versions of a single game.

— *Greg Costikyan*
(Chief Creative Officer, Unplugged)

Choose a target platform for your game, and indicate whether you plan to port the game to another platform as well. If you're developing primarily for the Windows PC, indicate whether you plan to create a Macintosh version. Your choice of primary platform will have a lot to do with your target audience and genre. Discuss your primary target platform and support your choice in one paragraph. If you also plan to develop for other platforms, discuss your reasons for these choices as well. Make sure you also include the minimum and recommended technical requirements for the primary platform you choose.

License (if applicable)

If your game will be adapted from a licensed property, indicate this. Have you made an exclusive deal with the licensor? Include any additional information about the property's popularity and appeal to particular markets. Almost all sports games are also licensed properties for team logos, names, and likenesses.

Competitive Analysis

Select three to five successful titles currently available on the market and discuss how your title will be able to compete with each of them. Make sure you relate this competitive edge to your game's USP. Provide one paragraph per game—and include the title (as a sub-header), genre, and a description of the game's premise. Most importantly, discuss why your game will effectively compete with each game. How will it distinguish itself from the others—and how will it be better?

Goals

What are your expectations for this game as an experience? What mood are you attempting to achieve? Make sure you go beyond the idea of "fun." Are you trying to provide excitement, tension, suspense, challenge, humor, nostalgia, sadness, fear, or a "warm

Atari, Inc.

Will you have the enormous budget to license a film property such as Atari (publisher) and Shiny Entertainment (developer) did with Warner Bros.' *The Matrix*?

Activision, Inc.

Is one of your competitors a top-selling game such as Infinity Ward's *Call of Duty*?

fuzzy" feeling? Do you want players to create their own stories and characters? Discuss how the game will achieve these goals.

Game Proposal

The game *proposal* is a follow-up to the concept document—describing all the components of the earlier document in more detail. The purpose of the proposal is to present the details of the game to a company or prospective partner that is already interested in the idea (perhaps after reading the concept document). This document is much longer than the concept document—usually 10 to 20 pages in length—and it can also be used to explain the game in detail to prospective team members before they begin to plan the game's development. The producer and directors of the art, programming, and design teams are involved in putting this document together. (Sometimes a story-based *treatment* is created at this stage—focusing specifically on the premise and story elements discussed below, such as the backstory, story synopsis, and character descriptions.) All of the sections included in the concept document should be in the proposal. In addition, include the following sections:

Hook

A *hook* is an element that will attract players to the game and keep them there. Why would anyone buy this game? Choose the three to five best features that answer this question. Hooks can be based on visuals, audio, gameplay, storyline, mood—anything that you feel will grab and hold on to a player's attention.

Gameplay

In Chapter 6 you learned about some basic elements of *gameplay*. This section should list 10 to 20 elements that describe the experience of playing the game. What types of challenges are in the game? What paths can a player choose from? Discuss any activities the player can engage in—such as exploration, combat, collecting, puzzle-solving, construction, management, or cooperation with other players.

Online Features (if applicable)

If your game will include an *online* multiplayer component, discuss any pertinent features in this section. You might include elements related to cooperative teamwork, player matching services, and player vs. player modes here.

Technology (if applicable)

The *technology* section is optional and should only be included if you plan to incorporate any special software or hardware technologies into the game. If you plan to license a game engine from a third party, discuss its features here. Will you incorporate innovative features such as character morphing and voice-recognition?

Art & Audio Features

Discuss any unique art and audio features of the game in this section—especially if they may be selling points for the game. Will you license any pre-existing music for the game? Do you plan to hire a well-known game composer to write the score? Will you use motion-capture techniques of relevant real-world people in the character animation process? You might want to discuss related popular media examples.

Production Details

Include a section discussing production details—including your development team, budget, and schedule. What is your current production status? Have you already developed a prototype, or are you at the concept development stage? Spend a few sentences introducing your development team as a whole, and then use subheads for each team member and his or her expected title on the project. Write brief paragraphs (one to three sentences in length) describing each team member's background, credits, and skills related to the role. Provide a rough estimate of how much you expect to spend overall. As a guide, $500,000 means you see this as a small project—and $5 million means you expect the game to be a huge hit. (If you are developing the game independently, your budget would be considerably smaller.) You can also offer a proposed ship date for the product and some key milestones. Keep in mind that the budget and schedule elements you include in the proposal are not final. Instead, they serve as guides to the publisher regarding the project's level of ambition. A rough budget breakdown for each phase is also typical.

Backstory

In Chapter 4 you learned about the backstory—which is a brief overview of everything that has taken place prior to the beginning of the game. Summarize your game's backstory briefly in a short paragraph. (The backstory would also be include in the treatment, if applicable.)

Story Synopsis

Chapter 4 discussed the components of a compelling storyline. Describe your story synopsis in one paragraph. Do not include details on various plot points; just stick to the main story idea. Focus on aspects of the story that might be unique or emotionally compelling. Also incorporate a discussion of how gameplay (discussed in Chapter 6) will reflect the story. What will the player do in the game? What type of environment or scenarios will the player encounter. (The story synopsis would also be include in the treatment, if applicable.)

Character Descriptions

In Chapter 5 you learned about putting together a brief description of each character. Incorporate these short, one-paragraph character summaries into your proposal (and in your treatment, if applicable). Include each primary character's name (as a header), physical description, personality characteristics, background/history, and relevance to the game's story.

Copyright Protection

If you plan to give copies of your concept or proposal documents to potential publishers, developers, or investors, take some steps to protect your intellectual property. If you want to indicate that you have not given permission for copies to be disseminated, include the statement, "Confidential—Do Not Distribute," on the title page and header or footer of all subsequent pages. Only hand out copies to a select group of people. Include a number on each copy, and record the name of the person and company associated with that particular number. You can also provide each person that sees a copy with a Non-Disclosure Agreement (NDA)—a short one-page contract that indicates that the recipient promises to keep your document and ideas within it confidential in exchange for being allowed to see it. Although this is a common business practice, keep in mind that some publishers (or other funding sources) will be put off by this and may refuse to sign it. In fact, most publishers have their own NDAs and often insist on using their format. However, some investors are used to receiving NDAs and won't think twice about signing them. Always clearly define the documents as yours by including your name on the title page, and a copyright notice in the header or footer of every page. The form of a copyright notice is "© [year] [copyright holder]" Mine would look like this: © **2004 Jeannie Novak**

Risk Analysis

This section discusses all the things that could possibly go wrong with the project, and how you should plan to deal with these problems should they arise. Some common risks that threaten projects are:

- Difficulties recruiting personnel
- Late delivery of materials (such as software development kits from console manufacturers)
- Reliance on external sources for key technology components
- Competitive technology developments
- Experimental technology or design decisions that could impact the schedule
- Asset-protection provisions

This section should also include your comments on which parts of the project are relatively safe. If you have any of the traditional risks covered, indicate this. For example, you might have a full team already in place.

Development Budget

A publisher is likely to require a *development budget* (or profit and loss [P&L] analysis) at the proposal stage. This is an estimate of all the costs of bringing the game to market, along with estimates of all anticipated income. Your company will most likely have a P&L statement available to you. If you're an independent developer presenting a proposal to a publisher, you will not have access to that publisher's cost structures. Instead of a P&L, you will need to include your development budget. Here are some items you'll need to list. (A detailed discussion of the following is beyond the scope of this book, but this list should give you a general idea of what's expected.):

- *Direct costs:* These are derived by multiplying person-per-month estimates by the group's salaries, then adding in equipment costs, overhead costs, and any external costs (licensing fees and outsourcing—such as sound, music, writing, and any special graphic effects).
- *Cost of goods sold (COGS):* These are the costs of physical materials that go into the tangible game product—the box, disc, jewel case, manual, etc.
- *Marketing:* The marketing team will need to put together an estimate of how much it will spend to promote the game in print, television, online, point-of-purchase displays, and/or sell sheets.
- *Market development fund (MDF):* These are costs that the publisher pays stores in the retail channel for prime shelf space, end caps, shelf talkers, and circular ads.
- *Income estimates:* Consider the game's unit price and the size of your target market. Assuming only a portion of your target market will purchase your game, what do you expect your income to be from sales of the game? If you are proposing an online multiplayer game that uses a monthly subscription-based financial model, include your expected monthly income from this revenue stream as well.
- *Allowances:* Provide allowances for returns, corporate overhead, and calculations for royalty payments if the game is based on an external license.
- *Return on investment (ROI):* This must show that the company can make more money investing in your game than in some less risky venture, such as putting the money in the bank and drawing interest for two years.

Concept Art

If possible, include concept drawings and sketches of characters and scenes related to the game. The characters should be shown from front, side, and back views. Also, pro-

Concept art of Juzamdjinn from *Magic: The Gathering—Battlegrounds*

Wizards of the Coast, Inc., Hasbro, Inc., Secret Level, Inc., Atari, Inc.

Production & Management: developing the process   chapter 11

vide a few 2D mock-ups of screen shots depicting the game environment and primary characters. Discuss the style of the character and background art you plan to use in the game. Will it be cartoon-like, gothic, realistic, surrealistic, hyperreal?

Game Design Document (GDD)

The *game design document (GDD)* is much longer than the concept or proposal documents. Often running 50 to 200 pages in length, the GDD is not meant to sell your idea. Instead, its sole purpose is to be the reference guide to the game development process. The GDD focuses on the gameplay, storyline, characters, interface, and rules of the game. The GDD should specify the rules of playing the game in enough detail that you could, in theory, play the game without the use of a computer. (Playing a paper version of the game is actually an inexpensive way to get feedback on the design of your game—and paper prototyping should always be considered during the development process.) Due to the length of the GDD, a table of contents should follow the title page. This document will change on almost a daily basis as the project develops. Make sure the document is sitting on a network, and members of the development team are able to make changes to it at any time. In addition to the items in your project proposal, the GDD should include the following elements:

Game Interface

In Chapter 8 you learned about the elements of a functional game interface. In this section, discuss each passive and active interface you plan to include in the game. Include the following elements:

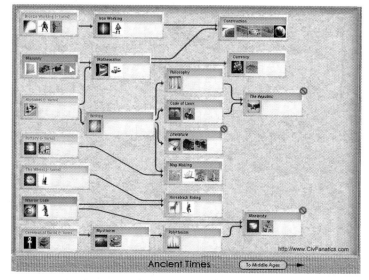

- Elements you plan to include in each interface
- Production time required
- Cost to produce
- Need for each interface and associated elements
- Viability of interface for target audience and genre
- Usability features

Will you utilize a tech tree as part of your interface, similar to the one used in *Civilization III*?

Character Abilities & Items

In Chapter 5 you learned about character abilities and items that might exist in a game. Discuss the acquired, non-acquired, combat, and defense abilities of each player character and non-player character (NPC). What weapons and pickup items might each character control or find during the game? Incorporate concept art and the synopsis that you included in the proposal for each discussion.

Game World

In Chapter 7 you learned about levels associated with the game world. Describe the elements present in each level—including cinematics, art, gameplay, animation, characters, pickup items, and background danger items.

Game Engine

Many misunderstandings arise between programming, design, and art teams over limitations associated with the game engine. It's important for all teams to be on the same page—and for designers and artists to create game worlds and art assets knowing these limitations. In this section, include information from the programming team on what the game engine can and cannot do. Elements in this section might include:

- Number of characters that can be present on-screen at once
- Number of animations per character
- Camera and game view restrictions
- Polygons available per level and character
- Number of colors per texture map
- Support for special controllers (manual interfaces)

Keep in mind that a GDD can vary based on the details of a particular project—and there are many different templates available. (See this book's companion CD for a GDD template and real-world example.)

Nintendo of America, Inc.

Will characters carry items symbolizing their skills or powers (such as Andy's wrench in *Advance Wars 2,* which symbolizes his heightened ability to repair his equipment)?

GarageGames, Inc.

Will you use a cross-platform (PC/Mac) engine such as *Torque* to develop your game?

:::::*Command & Conquer: Generals— Zero Hour*: Developing a Proprietary Game Engine

Electronic Arts Inc.

The key challenge associated with developing a proprietary game engine [as opposed to licensing a pre-existing engine] is that you have to implement every single feature from scratch. As a result, there is usually not enough time left for polish. Sometimes you can squeeze some of that into the expansion pack. I thought we did a pretty good job with *Command & Conquer Generals: Zero Hour* in that respect. Given a decent engine to license, I would go for the license. We created the *Command & Conquer: Generals* RTS Sage engine from scratch—in part because there weren't any RTS engines available for license. However, we did reuse the 3D library and art pipeline from another Electronic Arts title. I'm in favor of using as much existing code as possible. Generally, adapting existing code is much faster than writing it from scratch.

— *John Ahlquist*
(Lead Programmer,
Electronic Arts—Los Angeles)

Art Bible

The purpose of the *art bible* or *art plan* (which is really more of a set of visuals) is to establish the look and feel of the game and provide a reference for other artists to work from. This document is usually assembled by the concept artist and art director—and it ensures that a consistent style is followed throughout the game. Depending on the genre, some of the art in this document can take the form of pencil sketches, but it's also useful to have some digitized images that capture the final look of the game. A visual reference library should also be included that reflects the direction the art should take. Images in this library can come from any print publication or web site—but they should only be used for reference, and not for the final product!

Technical Design Document

The *technical design* document is based on the game design document and is usually written by the game's technical lead or director. This document describes the specifics of the game *engine*—the software in which the game is built—and compares it to other engines on the market. It establishes: how the game will transition from concept to software (known as the *technology production path*); who will be involved in the development of the engine; what tasks each person will perform; how long it will take to complete each task; what core tools will be used to build the game; and what hardware and software must be purchased.

Brian Fargo on Technical Limitations ::::::

Brian Fargo has over 20 years of experience in the software publishing industry, including founding Interplay Entertainment Corp in 1983. While at Interplay, Brian brought Universal/MCA in as a partner, and later took Interplay public in 1998. In addition to Interplay, Brian formed an online entertainment company with partner Softbank in 1996, and sat on the board of Virgin Europe after it was acquired by Interplay in 1998. Brian has served on the board of the Interactive Digital Software Association (IDSA) [now known as the Entertainment Software Association (ESA)] and has given key speeches at the industry's leading shows, such as E3, Global Gaming Forum, and the Game Developers Conference.

Brian Fargo
(CEO, inXile
entertainment)

The most challenging process of development is thinking through all the technical issues upfront. I've always said that games are fun to start and extremely difficult to finish. Those early decisions are critical to determining whether the final product can accomplish the goals that the game set out to do. You can have the greatest game ruined by a technical issue such as frame-rate, texture memory, or art-path issues.

Project Plan

The *project plan*—usually assembled by the producer—outlines the path taken to develop the game. It begins with the raw task lists provided by the technical design document, establishes dependencies, adds overhead hours, and turns all of this into a real-world schedule. The final project plan is broken down into a resource plan, budget, schedule, and milestones that will help in tracking the project.

The *resource plan* is a spreadsheet that lists all the personnel on the project, when they will start, and how much of their salaries will be applied to the project. It takes from the technology design document the timing of the hardware purchases to support those personnel, and it estimates when the external costs (such as outsourced personnel) will be incurred. After applying the overhead costs, you can use these numbers to derive your monthly cash requirements and the overall budget for the game. The project plan is revised and updated throughout the project. Some producers use project management software for this (such as Microsoft Project). Keep in mind that sticking to this schedule and meeting your release date is imperative. If the project is delayed due to poor planning, you might sell less units than expected because all the advertising, cover stories, reviews, and previews are timed by the marketing and public relations teams to appear at certain times based on when the product is expected to be released.

Test Plan

A *test plan* is usually created by the QA department. It involves constructing test cases and creating a testing checklist—itemizing each aspect or area that needs to be focused on during the testing process. The test plan documents the procedures describing how the game will be tested. It is consistently revised throughout the process to cover new and modified areas.

This chapter took you through the intricacies of the game development process—including the phases, management strategies, and documentation. In the next chapter, we'll move from the inner workings of the game development studio to a more public topic: supporting and marketing to the player community before and after a game is released.

:::CHAPTER REVIEW:::

1. Distinguish between the different phases of the game development process, and discuss the purpose and importance of each phase.

2. Leadership is a significant but often under-utilized skill in game development management. Why is this the case, and what strategies do producers and other managers utilize when leading game development teams?

3. Choose three forms of game documentation and discuss the importance of each in the development process. Discuss three components of each form of documentation. Why do you think these components are necessary to include in the documentation?

4. Write a concept document for your original game. Focus on how you will sell the idea of the game. Why will the game do well in the marketplace?

5. Put together a game design document for your original game—focusing on the unique features of your game and all roles and responsibilities involved in developing your game. After reading this document, your team should have a very clear idea of how to develop your game.

6. What is the importance of iterative design? Discuss the three phases of iterative design and what occurs during each phase. How are these phases connected with each other? How is the player market involved in the iterative design process?

7. If you were leading a game development project, what strategies would you come up with to balance time, cost, and quality?

8. Develop an analog ('tabletop' version) or digital prototype for your original game. What elements will you include in the prototype? Give reasons why you won't include certain elements at this time. Have a group of people playtest your game and provide comments on elements related to gameplay mechanics, story/character, mood, functionality, and the "fun factor"!

CHAPTER

Marketing & Maintenance:

developing the community

key chapter questions

- What are the respective functions of the roles associated with marketing—such as advertising, public relations, sales, and promotion?
- What are the functions of customer support in the game industry?
- How are fan communities created and maintained?

Understanding a game's player community is essential in order to develop an effective marketing campaign. Cultivating this community will extend a game's longevity, increase its popularity—and allow for the release of expansions, upgrades, and even new games to a loyal customer base. Online communities are essential for online games—and all channels of online communication (e.g., discussion forums, email, instant messaging, chat, newsletters) should be available to players at all times.

Marketing

Marketing involves targeting the game for a particular player market (discussed in Chapter 2) and persuading that audience to purchase the game. The game publisher usually handles marketing responsibilities (whether the publisher is separate or a part of the game development studio). In Chapter 2, you learned about geographics, demographics, and psychographics—methods used to segment a market into a smaller niche that is most likely to purchase the game. There are several functions that exist under the marketing umbrella—including advertising, public relations, sales, and promotion—all of which utilize these methods while supporting and cultivating player communities. Sometimes these functions are split up into separate departments, but each of them use marketing principles in order to accomplish their goals.

Ivo Gerscovich on Effective Game Marketing Strategies :::::

Ivo Gerscovich
(Director of Marketing–
Youth Entertainment
Group, Vivendi
Universal Games)

Before entering the game industry, Ivo Gerscovich worked for *Professional Sportscar Racing* (a car-racing series featuring Porsche, Ferrari, Lamborghini, and other high-end sports cars). He then helped start Fox Sports Interactive, which launched a variety of sports video games based on sports airing on Fox Television. At Fox Interactive—the film- and TV-based video game side of Fox Television—Ivo did marketing and promotion for titles such as *Buffy: The Vampire Slayer, X-Files, Aliens,* and *Die Hard.* As Director of Marketing–Youth Entertainment Group for Vivendi Universal Games, Ivo markets game titles aimed at youth—including *The Simpsons: Hit & Run, Futurama,* and *Yu-Gi-Oh.*

My main role as Director of Marketing is to work with a talented marketing team to develop a clear vision and solid marketing plan for a product—and then make sure that the team stays focused on executing this strategy. Some of my day-to-day responsibilities include: budget and profit management; market analysis (analyzing competitive landscape and sales trends); marketing plan development and brand management; advertising; sales support; and serving as a liaison between Vivendi and the international marketing group, licensor, and entertainment studios. Here are some of my recommended strategies for effective game marketing:

■ **Use marketing to make your product stand out:** The biggest challenge for any marketer nowadays is getting their new video game noticed by consumers and the ever-important retail channel. For a game to succeed, marketing communication needs to stand "above the noise," which refers to the consumer's perspective of being bombarded with thousands of marketing messages for hundreds of video games. There is so much competition among games for in-store shelf space, consumer mindshare, and consumers' hard-earned money, that everything a marketer does should be designed to make a game stand out in this extremely cluttered marketplace. The rest of the points below filter into this first point...

- **Create excitement around a product:** Build *early* buzz and anticipation for a game by generating pre-launch awareness among both gamers *and* the retail channel that serves them. Video game retailers (stores) listen to their customers—so the more consumers are talking about a product, the more the stores will want to put a game on their shelves. This is an area that Public Relations really can help with as they can work with TV, print, online, and radio to do advanced editorial "sneak peaks" and "previews" to help fuel the hype among gamers long before a game releases.

- **Be different—and be consistent:** Differentiate a title within a crowded market by communicating the unique buzz worthy hooks and gameplay features of the product. Ask yourself, "What makes this game great?" and then consistently hammer this home in all of your marketing communications.

- **Develop killer advertising:** Your advertising does much of your heavy lifting when it comes to delivering your marketing message to the large audience of gamers you want to reach, so it is essential to create compelling advertising that makes consumers stop whatever they are doing and pay attention to your message.

- **Let 'em try your game:** With a great game, getting people to try a game by handing out demo discs before a game is available, or having game kiosks set up at local events for people to play, can really help fuel consumer demand for a game. However, producing demo discs or staffing mall events can be very expensive!

Merchandising & Companion Products

Marketing for big-budget games and franchises—especially those with well-known game characters (such as Lara Croft and Mario)—are often supplemented by companion products such as movies and novels set in the game world, action figures, or licensed properties such as cartoons and *manga* (Japanese comic books).

As discussed in Chapter 2, traditional mass marketing focuses on getting the largest number of people to purchase your product. In contrast, niche marketing focuses on targeting that smaller segment of your market that will become die-hard fans of your product. Marketing analyst Seth Godin, author of *Purple Cow,* calls these early adopters "sneezers," because they will spread your marketing message (or "ideavirus") to friends, family, and colleagues through word of mouth. Instead of trying to get all people who play games to buy your game (this won't happen!), think about what specific type of person wouldn't pass up the opportunity to play your game. You can start by looking at your game's genre. If your game is an RPG, do you really think action gamers will be interested in playing it? Maybe some of them will, but why waste time focusing on action gamers when you've developed a game that has more appeal for RPG gamers? You can hone in further on your market niche by looking at the setting, story, and characters of your game—as well as the environment, levels, and gameplay you've incorporated.

:::::Game Packaging Art

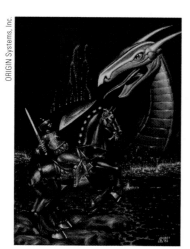  

Game box art from *Ultima* (left), *Command & Conquer: Tiberian Sun* (center), and *Ultima II* (right).

Some game artists specialize in creating art for marketing materials—such as game packaging. These artists are not necessarily on the development team—but might be part of the marketing department. For this reason, game box art may consist of illustrations that do not necessarily reflect art seen within the game itself.

The Art & Marketing Relationship

The worst thing that could happen to you is that you've got a great game, but nobody's heard of it. We don't want that, but we don't want to be distracting the team from the tight deadlines—so it's usually up to the Art Director to fuel the voracious marketing machine with screenshots, illustrations, the occasional bit of concept art that turned out well...whatever you can dig up to put the best face forward for your project.

— *Marc Taro Holmes*
(Art Director, Obsidian Entertainment)

Godin also suggests that marketing should start with the product itself. Examples of what Godin calls "remarkable" products are those with a unique industrial design—such as the Mini Cooper, a car that markets itself just by being driven around by its owner. The marketing process actually starts at the concept stage, when a game's *premise* (or *high concept*) and *unique selling proposition (USP)* are incorporated into the *concept* document (discussed in Chapter 11). What is it that truly makes your game unique? Why would your target market be compelled to play it—and tell others about it? Why might they prefer your game to competing titles? Marketing teams often use the game's premise to help the public form a mental image of the game.

Casual vs. Hardcore Market

As discussed in Chapter 2, there is a tradition in the game industry to divide the game-playing community into two segments: *casual* and *hardcore* gamers. The casual gamer is someone who seldom plays games and might be attracted more by the commercial appeal of the game (e.g., an adaptation of a popular film or book like *The Lord of the Rings*). The hardcore gamer is someone who plays games on a regular basis and who often enjoys competitive features and deep gameplay. Mass marketing would be the approach used for casual gamers, while niche marketing would be more appropriate for hardcore gamers. However—as mentioned in Chapter 2—this casual vs. hardcore market segmentation is not ideal. A better approach would be to divide the market up by genre, platform, geographics, demographics, and pyschographics.

One of the most significant elements of any marketing campaign is the effective use of a web site for the company or game itself. As discussed later in this chapter, online fan communities form the basis of much of a game's word-of-mouth marketing. Godin's notion of spreading an "ideavirus" through "sneezing" is so easily accomplished in the online world. This is due to what Malcolm Gladwell (author of *The Tipping Point*) calls *network effects*.

Sara Borthwick on the Role of Online Marketing Manager

Sara Borthwick has worked as a video game marketer since 2000—first at Atari (formerly Infogrames) and currently at Encore Software. Sara specializes in online marketing and has promoted nearly 100 games, including *Dragon Ball Z: Budokai, Neverwinter Nights, Enter the Matrix, Civilization III, Test Drive, Unreal Tournament 2003, Backyard Sports, Horizons,* and *Sacred.*

Sara Borthwick
(Online Marketing Manager, Encore Software)

At larger game companies, the online marketer would be responsible for crafting the strategy and the marketing communications, while an online producer would create the sites, ads, and other online assets. Since Encore is a smaller publisher, my day-to-day responsibilities involve almost everything that relates to the Internet—and this can be broken down into six basic areas:

1. Online advertising

2. Web sites

3. Online retail

4. Newsletters and loyalty programs

5. Community support/grassroots outreach

6. Research

During a typical week, I do the following:

- Communicate a *marcom* (marketing/communications) strategy to the VP to secure a budget for online advertising, negotiate a campaign with ad sales reps from targeted gaming sites, and kick off creative product with a designer, while optimizing a campaign currently in progress. Tweak copy for search engine optimization purposes, and surf targeted sites to see how the competitors are advertising their products.

- Create product pages, or gather information from producers and brand managers, to update the web site. Work to incorporate beneficial new technology and ensure that the sites are easy to use, relevant, and portray Encore in the desired light. Hire designers to create title-specific sites that provide users with enough information to make a purchase decision.

■ Design promotional campaigns to increase revenue at the corporate online store. Ensure that the site navigation is intuitive and persuasive. Work with the sales team to increase buy-in and sell-through at Encore's online retail partners (including Amazon.com, EBgames.com, BestBuy.com).

■ Grow the customer database with qualified opt-in consumers. Encourage repeat purchases at the online store through promotions, and encourage multiple Encore product purchases through targeted and informative newsletters.

■ Provide a framework for fans of Encore products to interact with each other, the publisher, and the developer. Listen. Address valid concerns as forthrightly as possible. Find and leverage the existing fan base for similar products by establishing relationships with key influencers within the gamer community through grassroots advocacy outreach.

■ Estimate the level of consumer excitement for a game prior to release by gathering and analyzing internal and syndicated log file (web site pages accessed information) data. Gather qualitative opinions from gamers on similar competitive products and on preliminary experiences of our games. Investigate new technologies, consumer attitudes and behaviors, and marketing opportunities.

The game industry is extremely fluid. Games are a mix of art and technology. At any moment, an unexpected problem can pop up that forces production delays and/or the elimination of key elements from the game. This, in turn, can force the ship date to be pushed out by months or years, and the marketing team to re-evaluate and sometimes re-do the entire marketing campaign. The ability to react quickly to changes, while still planning ahead—in addition to extremely strong communication skills—is essential to success in game marketing. Finally, knowledge of games and the player mentality is also necessary to creative, effective marketing communications, and also to gain the respect of the developers—some of whom have rock star mentalities!

You learned in Chapter 3 that online games are "networked" games. This means that players can interact with each other through a network (the Internet) to which their computers are connected. The Internet is not a broadcasting system, but a communication system—more like the telephone than the television. But rather than a two-person phone call, the Internet provides the ability to connect freely with people all over the world simultaneously. This capacity for communication is shown particularly well in email—in which one message can easily be sent simultaneously to thousands of people, who can then forward it to more people, and so on (hence the existence of spam)! Online strategies that take advantage of network effects include newsgroups and forums, chat rooms, blogs, newsletters, reciprocal linking, affiliate programs, and fan sites. These strategies are discussed in the "Community" section, later in this chapter.

Advertising

The *advertising* team focuses on reaching the market through paid ads in media outlets such as television, radio, magazines, newspapers, and web sites. In a niche marketing approach, ads would be purchased in game-related or even genre-related outlets—such as *Computer Gaming World* (a magazine focusing on the computer game platform), *Tech TV* (a cable show focusing on high-technology), or *Just-RPG. com* (a web site focusing on RPG and adventure games).

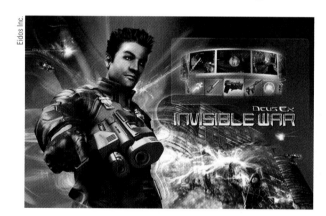

Posters and wallpaper (such as these from *Deus Ex* and *Wario*) are used to advertise games.

Why Is It So Important to Reach the Millennial Market?

Millennials are the largest generation by population. As they mature and define a unique generational style, they will overturn many standard cultural formats popular during the Xer era of the 1980s and 1990s. Those who do not understand the unique aspects of this generation will be caught fighting the "last war," and creating media for a youth culture that no longer exists. In addition, Millennials are more comfortable with games than any earlier generation, and are likely to make them their dominant media as they mature.

—*Pete Markiewicz, PhD*
(Indiespace)

Marketing Multitasking

The most challenging part of the video game marketing process is launching many titles in a short window. Naturally, Quarters 3 and 4 are the biggest launch months because that is when the game industry does the vast majority of its business—and marketing teams must be able to effectively juggle multiple titles, tasks, and work under tight time constraints at any given moment in order to make those crucial dates. There are a tremendous number of things that need to be done on the marketing side to prepare for a game launch. When you have multiple titles releasing around the same time—and you need to familiarize yourself with new properties, conduct market analyses, develop marketing plans, create great packaging, create great advertising, manage budgets, on and on—it can mean many early mornings and late nights. But this is also what makes marketing games very exciting and rewarding!

— Ivo Gerscovich
(Director of Marketing – Youth Entertainment,
Vivendi Universal Games)

Public Relations (PR)

The *public relations (PR)* team focuses on letting the public know about the game—often well before it is released. PR involves targeting the news media and game-related press at magazines, newspapers, radio, television, and web sites. Goals include securing previews, reviews, interviews, features, and cover stories. The PR team often uses assets produced by the art, design, and programming teams—such as demos, videos, concept art, and screen shots—to help assemble analog and digital press kits order to interest the media in the game.

Developer Diaries: A Unique PR Strategy

Developer diaries, such as those found on game and game news web sites (such as gamespy.com), can be seen as a way for developers to communicate their experiences to players—thereby strengthening the developer-player bond. The diaries are also a great PR strategy that lets the public know about a game before it's released. Having the developers become directly involved in the PR process allows the news to be seen as legitimate information—rather than "hype."

Sales

The *sales* team maintains relationships with buyers from online and offline retail stores, wholesalers, discount stores, video rental chains, and hardware manufacturers. This team not only focuses on getting the game into these outlets, but also on positioning the game in stores so that it gets priority shelf space. The team also tries to secure deals with game hardware manufacturers to bundle the game with the hardware platform.

Promotion

Promotion involves putting together events, contests, trials, giveaways, and merchandise in order to get the public excited about a product. Promotional merchandise might include stickers, posters, hats, and T-shirts portraying the cover art of the game. These can be given away to prospective customers at game retail stores or offered along with the product itself. Contests might involve providing cash or merchandise prices to players who win tournaments involving the game. One of the most common forms of promotion for subscription-based online games is to provide a downloadable 10- to 30-day free trial version of the game to prospective customers. Special events might include in-store game signings, preview demonstrations at conferences, online chats with game developers, and educational panels for players interested in learning how games are created.

Customer Support

The customer support team is responsible for fielding questions and concerns related to the game. Issues can range from technical difficulties in loading the game software to complaints about disruptive behavior of other players (specifically in an online multiplayer game). It used to be common practice in massively multiplayer online games (MMOGs) to hand over some of the customer support duties to experienced gamers who might offer to participate voluntarily as *game masters (GMs)*—also known as guides, counselors, or companions. As discussed in Chapter 3, GMs originated in *Dungeons & Dragons*® as those able to change the course of the game. Online GMs are at the forefront of customer service, acting as mediators between game developers and customers. Responsibilities include disciplining players who take part in harassment and cheating; helping new players get situated; answering in-game questions; and accepting feedback from players.

Carly Staehlin on the Importance of Online Player Communities:::::

Carly Staehlin has been a part of the computer game industry for more than seven years. At Origin Systems, she pioneered the first online community services department in the massively multiplayer online game industry—which has served as the model that many other companies have since emulated. Having worked on many titles in the *Ultima* series, she was also the producer of *Ultima Online* during the height of its commercial success. Most recently, she worked with Richard Garriott and Starr Long on the new massively multiplayer online game for NCsoft: *Tabula Rasa*.

Carly Staehlin
(Lead Designer,
NCsoft)

The online community that exists because of an MMOG, *but outside of it,* tends to represent no more than 30% of the player base. That means that 70% of the player base will likely never look at the web site, communicate with game support personnel, submit bugs, or otherwise interact with the developer other than to play the game.

Given these figures, one might imagine that the out-of-game community isn't that important. After all, it's standard practice to only spend your energy on those things that are seen and enjoyed by 70% of the players and to place lower priority on those that impact the remaining 30%. However, I believe that the out-of-game community that grows around a game actually enriches the in-game environment for all players. Out-of-game community 'leaders' tend to be highly active in the in-game environment. Their relative level of happiness and satisfaction with the game can be somewhat measured by the number of in-game activities and groups that they also participate in or create. These leaders provide more content and entertainment within the game environment for all players—even those who do not realize that they are interacting with a 'community leader' of some type. On the other hand, I believe that an MMOG could do fine without any kind of additional out-of-game web support—especially if that game includes the traditional out-of-game features within itself. Once the concepts of community begin to be well understood, they may need to be less distanced from the game itself, and in fact might benefit from a tighter integration.

Any way for a player to get more content, features, attention, or opportunities for fun related to a game will absolutely help that game to be more successful than it would have been otherwise. I don't believe that this is limited to MMOGs either, as evidenced by the FPS and Modder communities.

Eidos Interactive/Core Design, Ltd.

Eidos' official *Tomb Raider* web site provides screenshots, story/character background, and news for existing and prospective players.

Official Web Site

One of the single most important marketing tools is the game's official web site—which can also be a great source of customer support. Whether or not your game is played online, customers will most likely check the web site first for any news, updates, or technical assistance. Customers will also want to provide feedback on their game-playing experience, so make sure that a discussion forum is available on the site for that purpose.

Tutorials

If you have released an online multiplayer game, provide real-time tutorials to new players. Weekly tutorial play sessions were established for the online game, *Shanghai Dynasty*. Not only did these play sessions provide needed customer support for new players, they also allowed developers to receive feedback on the game content, programming, design, and player psychographics—including the thoughts and preferences of the player community.

Newsgroups

Newsgroups existed on the Internet long before the commercialization of the web, so group members who joined during that time do not take kindly to overt marketing techniques. However, these groups contain ideal "sneezer" candidates, because the group members are so highly focused on the group's topic. If a newsgroup has not been formed around your game, create one yourself and moderate it. Join other newsgroups (groups.google.com) that focus on your game's genre or platform, and participate in the group—providing fans with any information they need without trying to sell them the game or

The *Eyes on Final Fantasy* (forums.eyesonff.com) player forum allows players to share their experiences with the game.

Shattered Galaxy: Supporting Player Communities through Interactive Communication Channels

One of the most effective methods of supporting player communities is through *interactive* communication channels. Opening a dialog with the players serves two primary purposes. First, it can be an effective method of learning what the players' opinions and wishes are. Second, it provides the players with a sense of empowerment, increasing their loyalty to the game and the developer.

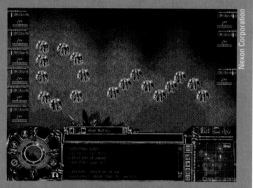

Nexon Corporation

The Dark Mystics player community for *Shattered Galaxy* showed their allegiance by spelling out the letters "DM" with game characters.

Interactive communication channels need not be high maintenance. In *Shattered Galaxy*, we polled players as they logged out of the game to learn their views on game elements or new changes. We also allowed players to vote through the website on which features or issues they most wanted us to address. Through these methods, players had a voice, and we could hear what they were saying with minimal effort on our part.

Bulletin board systems (BBSs) are, in my opinion, a very ineffective method of interacting with player communities. We found less than 5% of the players participated actively on the in-game BBS, while over 30% would take part in the polls. Bulletin boards can be important, but remember that they are dominated by the vocal minority.

Finally, always remember that players will complain. This is good—but don't take it personally. It means that they care about the game and want to make it better. If your players suddenly become silent, then you have a serious problem.

— *Kevin Saunders*
(Senior Game Designer, Obsidian Entertainment)

associated material. Don't create new threads (which might be seen as overt marketing), but participate in discussions begun by fans. Elicit feedback from the group on how to improve upon the game.

Newsletters

Allow players the option of signing up to receive online *newsletters* that are sent out to players on a regular basis. Do not automatically put players on the newsletter list, but allow them to *opt-in* (and *opt-out* if they're no longer interested). The newsletter could contain information on updates, expansions, gameplay tips, other products released by your company, Beta testing invitations, promotions, and anything else related to the game (or your company). Newsletters allow your player community to be reminded about the game and will show them that you care about your customers.

GameSpy Arcade (*gamespyarcade.com*) contains a player-matching service.

Player Matching

If your game is online, consider offering a *player-matching* service for your customers. Existing services such as *GameSpy Arcade* allow players to find prospective opponents and team members based on matching respective multiplayer-enabled games installed on the players' systems. During the matching process, players can determine which other players are online and what games they are playing at the moment. Players can also send out invitations to other players requesting a game session. Interestingly, player-matching services utilize many of the features found in online dating sites!

Online Community: Real or Virtual?

The online world is very real to many players. You learned in Chapter 6 that some will pay tens or thousands of real-life dollars for in-game items and money. (There's an exchange rate between *EverQuest* "platinum" and U.S. dollars.) Players even meet online, fall in love, and then marry in real-life—more often than you might imagine. The social goals of players vary greatly; some players seek cybersex partners, while others connect with family (such as grandmothers playing with their grandkids thousands of miles away).

Stephanie Spong on Participating in Player Communities :::::

Stephanie is a writer and independent consultant based in Los Angeles. She is returning to games, writing, and painting—activities she loved as a child—after a fast-paced business career. Her experience includes running the Los Angeles office of digital design firm Razorfish; working with *Fortune 500* clients on growth strategy, marketing strategy, and innovation while at McKinsey and Monitor Company; implementing systems and customer service progams at Citibank; and working as a financial analyst at Goldman, Sachs. Stephanie holds a BA in Economics and Asian Studies, with minors in Physics and Japanese, from Brigham Young University, and an MBA from the Harvard Graduate School of Business. She has optioned one script, and she currently balances work as a marketing and new product development consultant with her creative pursuits of writing, painting, and game design. She enjoys adventure travel, motorcycling, ballroom dancing—and *Yohoho! Puzzle Pirates.*

Stephanie Spong,
Writer

Curiosity about the genre of persistent-state world MMORPGs has kept me immersed in *Yohoho! Puzzle Pirates* for weeks now, and it has significantly increased my understanding of the attraction of these games. On the personal front, I've now brought several friends and family into the game—so it has become a way to stay in casual touch with my nieces and nephews, brothers, and friends in distant places.

My daily responsibilities in the game include commanding pillage missions, protecting the monarch of our flag, maintaining part of our foraging network, and training and developing young pirates. On the fun side, there are auctions, buying clothes and weapons, fighting monsters, fighting or drinking in tournaments—and designing uniforms for secret crews....I participate in the game community by inventing absurd missions that challenge our skills and teamwork—such as attacking impossible-to-beat opponents or exploring distant parts of the virtual world where newbies don't get to go very often. My captain laughs and gives me the ships and funding to carry out the missions, which keeps the pirates busy and happy. I talked our captain into making an absurdly expensive purchase of an inn at an auction, so we can have a crew place to hang out online. This world is a place to be bold and adventurous without worrying about real death or real disgrace or real bankruptcy. Although, let me tell you, the first time you command a war brig with 25 real people expecting you to bring home the bacon, your adrenaline shoots through the roof! On the social side, I try to include new people and the shy ones, just like I do in real life, so everyone feels included.

I'm motivated to continue playing the game through my curiosity about this complex and surprising world, full of real people with real needs, real goals, and real personalities, and the fun of dealing with them in a virtual world. I want to fully understand the gameplay and social aspects of this genre, from the economic and puzzle skill side as well as the "social puzzle." Surprisingly, this has also been a voyage of self-discovery, as I find myself creating situations within the game that exactly mirror RL (real life) situations.

Prosumerism: Player as Developer

In his book, *The Third Wave*, futurist Alvin Toffler coined the term *prosumer*—which refers to the combination of a producer and consumer. The roles of players (consumers) and developers (producers) are usually separated from each other. But sometimes the line between player and developer can become blurred. Chapters 4, 5, and 7 discussed how players are able to take part in the development of storylines by making certain decisions while playing the game; customize their characters, right down to personality traits; and build physical environments and levels based on a particular game. In these cases, the player becomes a prosumer—a combination of player and developer. Examples of prosumerism that help cultivate a player community also include modding, fan sites, fan art, and "fan fic" (fan fiction).

Beta-Testing: Community & Career Path?

In Chapter 10, you learned about the importance of Beta-testers in the game development process. Many of these testers are recruited from online player communities. In addition to providing a link between the player and developer, Beta-testing can be the first step in a new career. (At least one of the prominent industry professionals profiled in this book started out as a Beta-tester!)

Modding

Allowing the user community to modify, expand, and otherwise customize the content of your game (*modding*) can heighten the value of your game. New missions, models, and settings for a game can also extend its lifespan. Supporting the mod community includes providing players with the ability to customize game variables, scripts, animation, textures, models, audio, and levels.

Wizards of the Coast, Inc., Hastro, Inc., Bioware Corp, Atari, Inc.

Neverwinter Nights mods created by the Midreach affiliation.

Mark Precious on Developing Player Mods :::::

Mark Precious (player name "Fathom") was the Lead DM (Dungeon Master) on the Midreach affiliation of *Neverwinter Nights* from May 2003 to February 2004. (Other players key in Midreach's development include Biocyde, Bonehead, Imago, Tarnaquin, Seancstew, Okiran, T'alia, Starfire, Schwebs, Yagyu Jubei, Hahnsoo, and Dalt Wisney.) Mark is a native of Los Angeles who has played role-playing games for 24 years. He has created a game universe called *The Golden Realm,* which includes the planet Sylgamar (wherein Midreach is located) and several other fully-developed worlds. He's currently working on a novel entitled *The Starflake,* a space fantasy/sword and sorcery epic set in another part of that universe. He says that he also draws "more or less professionally, and paints rather badly."

Mark Precious (Artist & Writer; Former Lead DM, Midreach Affiliation, *Neverwinter Nights* Mod)

Neverwinter Nights (NwN) is revolutionary because it includes not only a toolset similar to previous games' scenario editors, but also a DM (Dungeon Master) client that allows DMs to then run their own campaigns in real-time with their players. This takes role-playing games off the tabletop and puts them fully online. So once it was out, the only question was which pre-existing tabletop world to convert into the *NwN* engine. We chose one called Midreach. In hindsight, though, it seems better to create a new world from scratch for the *NwN* engine, because it doesn't elegantly portray the scale of the world a group of adventurers would "realistically" be operating in.

A key choice for a team developing an online module is whether to make it available as a 24-7 persistent-state world (PSW), or only open it up for play at specific times when the DMs are available. These are two completely different animals. The former allows the game world to take on a life of its own, and the players can form an online community where they can hang out, play, and socialize—but the DMs can kiss control of the world goodbye. The latter is more like the tabletop version of RPGs, but it lacks a lot of the energy of persistent worlds. We took Midreach in the PSW direction because we felt we had enough dedicated DMs to cover most of the hours of play. Wrong. On most teams, a mod developer must do the ordinary DM duties of world creation, upkeep, and prep for the next time they run the story forward. But they also have to maintain thorough communication with the other DMs about what they're doing in the world, help the many players with character development, pop on the server to spend time as a DM between major events, and adjudicate disputes between players and other team members. It can really burn out the lead developer and the person responsible for all server updates.

DM client games are in their infancy; we will see alternative, smoother DM client interfaces, better graphics, and just more toolset options. I've heard that since the vast majority of sales are to single players rather than online players or DMs, there's no incentive for anyone else to push development of the DM client. But I look beyond the current numbers and see a marketing opportunity for someone to really break through and change the direction of computer gaming. I commend Bioware for making their engine open-ended enough to support a thriving array of hacks. Ultimately, the competition to Bioware isn't an economic one, but an artistic one, in attempting to keep their expansions more sophisticated and better-looking than the community's hacks. That ain't easy.

The Modding Origins of Machinima

The *machinima* movement (discussed in detail in Chapter 4) was actually an outgrowth of modding. Player communities making mods from *Quake* and other game engines (such as *Unreal* and *Half-Life*) began to create mini-movies within their mods—inspiring people such as Strange Company founder Hugh Hancock to blend game engines with cinema.

Giving Up Control: Managing Online Player Communities

The most challenging aspect of game online marketing is managing the player community. Game publishers and developers know that most game purchase decisions are heavily influenced by recommendations from friends and general word-of-mouth buzz. Online communities of players provide a window into these interactions, and of course publishers and developers want to influence these communities and the corresponding word-of-mouth buzz to promote their products. However, players are highly resistant to corporate marketing communication. It is one thing for a publisher to say that they will leverage an online community to generate interest in a game, but it is very hard, if not impossible, to make people care about a product. If and when a community of players does latch onto a particular game, the publisher and developer have to be extremely responsive to the players' needs. Players are highly informed, intelligent and fanatical. If the product communications are not consistent, this can cause problems for the success of the product. Finally, when players create a community around a particular game, they are actually shaping the brand. Marketing must be okay with not having complete control over the product image and product communication....I firmly believe that player communities can never be built by design. Instead, the developer and the publisher can stimulate a community through their own enthusiasm for the product and by actively listening and respecting the fan base. A publisher/developer can aid a community by providing tools for players to interact with each other and the game. This can range from simple forums to mod tools to easy map exchanges. Most of all, the publisher/developer can aid the player communities online by becoming part of those communities.

— *Sara Borthwick*
(Online Marketing Manager, Encore Software)

Fan-Produced Content

It is not uncommon in Japan for dedicated fan communities to build on the game world—extending or tweaking the mechanics of popular games. Sometimes these fans even produce *doujinshi*—books and fanzines that contain stories and art based on the characters in their favorite games. These publications are often produced in small quantities and sold to fans at conventions, by mail, or through specialty shops. Fans in Japan have also produced games based on other popular games that have achieved a cult status. The *Queen of Heart* series is one example of fan-produced fighting games that star characters in the popular game *To Heart*.

Watanabe Seisakusho/Himeya Soft

The *Queen of Heart* series (based on the popular Japanese game *To Heart*) is produced by fans.

Reviews: Players as Experts

Online game communities such as Just-RPG.com recruit players from their discussion forums to write reviews for their site: Here's an excerpt from a review of *Dungeon Siege: Legends of Aranna,* submitted by player-reviewer Kevin O'Connor: "To help with the vast inventory management, some new convenient features were added, such as the re-distribute potions function, which, at the press of a button, shifts health potions to fighters and mana to casters—a time saver, indeed, and something other RPG designers should consider implementing." Opportunities to review games can give budding writers and designers some early exposure and credibility.

> Anyone with their eyes and ears open can hear about a new game through a web site or magazine—but I really listen to reviews by people I know and whose taste in games I am familiar with.
>
> — *Robert Ferguson (Game Art & Design student)*

Western game development companies have not thrown enough support in the direction of this sort of fan-produced material, which would provide a great deal of word-of-mouth marketing for a game. There are plenty of spin-off fan art or "fan fic" (fan fiction) works from U.S. game fans based on *Final Fantasy*. The size of this market segment is growing, and this type of fan activity will most likely increase dramatically. The player community gets information and opinions on games from other fans more than traditional channels such as magazines or television ads. Cultivating these fans would help build a terrific marketing strategy. Game studios receive free publicity from fan activity, and these fans are the "sneezers" that will act as a marketing force for the game—endorsing it and encouraging all other members of your target market to play it.

Fan Sites

Encouraging players to construct their own sites centering around your game can greatly increase a game's visibility. This method has been used successfully by independent filmmakers and musicians in order to create a buzz surrounding the release of a product. Sometimes, pseudo-fan sites have been created by the producers (ironically posing as consumers) in order to generate hype. A notorious example of this was when *The Blair Witch Project* filmmakers and colleagues created a series of fan sites that perpetuated the legend surrounding the film—and managed to convince people that the legend really existed. This marketing strategy snowballed into a major campaign (involving plenty of real fan sites) that brought a huge audience into theaters across the nation. Most fan sites contain graphics, audio, video, storylines, character descriptions, and even up-to-the-minute news (usually more current than the official site, which does not get updated nearly as much!) on a game—including rankings, sales figures, reviews, versions, and expansions. Fans might also include a

that happens, content will become a more dominant part of the purchasing decision. In other words, eventually we'll get to the point where players won't perceive the differences in technology any longer and will start buying games because they have good stories or gameplay rather than because they look cool.

David Brin (Author, Scientist & Public Speaker):

Technology-driven realism will push the top game boxes forward as we flow toward full virtual reality. That's a long path, though—full immersion won't come overnight. Each year will feature sports games, shoot-'em games, and zoom games that are slightly more vivid than the previous year's—unfortunately, without a trace of story or originality. The one interesting new development in this area is involvement by the U.S. military. Certain games will appear that spin off from genuine virtual reality software used by soldiers, sailors, airmen, and marines, who are training to use actual equipment in realistic scenarios. Not just combat simulation, but also problem situations that may require judgment calls—for example, decisions: whether to use force, not just how fast you can shoot. Some of these will not only be cool, but vastly more interesting than your typical tactical game play.

Bill Brown (Composer & Founder, Soundelux Music Group):

Games are reaching new levels of emotional expression. More cinematic storytelling is becoming a natural part of the process now. That part of the experience is going to open up a whole new level of creative expression for developers....Audio storytelling will be creative mixing in real-time that goes deeper...more to the subtextual experience...more to the soul of the narrative, and the player.

Rob Cairns (Key Account Director, Associated Production Music):

I have heard the game audio industry referred to as the "wild, wild west." This is really because as far as audio goes, the industry is very young, and there is still a lot of pioneering to do. The advancements in technology have suddenly opened up an incredible opportunity for doing away with primitive bleeps and bloops (however much we loved them), and allowing for the highest quality orchestrations and endless amounts of cutting-edge music. The next natural evolution is for the game industry to settle, and stake their claim into similar territory as Hollywood's very mature film industry. More and more game companies are already relocating to southern California to be closer to these entities and resources. I see game audio heading in a direction similar to film, where you have a mixed recipe of music in a production, and its marketing efforts.

Aaron Marks (Composer; Founder, On Your Mark Music):

Interactive audio is a relatively new concept which is catching on quickly. What better game-playing experience can we have where the music changes as we explore new levels, a door opens where a bad guy is waiting in ambush, or a throng of evil creatures attacks us? Having music change to fit the mood of what we are experiencing is a fantastic element, which adds an incredible amount to the experience. Surround sound is also becoming more of a standard, and this trend will definitely continue. Being enveloped by sound really adds to the believ-ability of what we are seeing on screen. And important clues and foreboding can be conveyed through this type of playback. Knowing that a bad guy is sneaking up from behind makes for a great gaming experience, and that's what our side of the industry is all about.

Chance Thomas (Composer; Founder, HUGEsound):

An exciting trend is picking up steam across the industry, and I couldn't be more pleased. Let's call it Day One Audio, for the sake of simplicity. Day One Audio puts a sound representative (audio lead, composer, sound designer) around the game *design* table…This brings the perspective of a sound professional in at the very conception of a game, where the foundation of interactivity and technologi-cal framework are envisioned and distilled.

Thankfully, this is now happening with many development studios in our indus-try. A second trend that I think you will see take permanent root in games is the standardization of the orchestra as the palette of choice for underscoring dra-matic content. The orchestra is just so rich, so dynamic, so colorful. And increas-ingly, all the top titles will all make use of a live orchestra for their scores, with second-tier titles relying more on digitally sampled production.

Ivo Gerscovich (Director of Marketing–Youth Entertainment, Vivendi Universal Games):

I think the future of game marketing is an exciting one, which will define how other technologies are also marketed. We've seen the leadership role video games have taken in many other technological fields—witness the military's use of game technology for warfare simulation exercises. With all the rapid advancements in game technology—including the rise of subscription-based MMOGs (e.g., *Star Wars Galaxies, Everquest*), wireless games, and the eventual appearance of games on demand—comes the challenge of working closer and closer with Research & Development to figure out what kinds of games a company should focus on bringing to market.

Who Will Develop the Games of the Future?

How will the game industry be structured in the future? Will there still be an interrelationship between publishers, third-party developers, hardware manufacturers, and licensors? Will industry consolidation occur—or will the independent game movement continue to rise? Or could both happen and co-exist in parallel?

As the founder of a company that markets, licenses, and distributes the works of independent arts and entertainment professionals of all types (game developers, musicians, filmmakers, performers, visual artists, and authors)—as well as being an independent musician and composer—I have a stake in the future of the independent games movement. Companies like GarageGames that provide indie developers with the freedom to create, market, and distribute their games without losing ownership or creative control are making a substantial difference in the game community. Events and awards competitions such as the *Independent Games Festival* provide recognition for developers such as 21-6 Productions and Three Rings. And the trend of building startup game companies (often with the intention of remaining privately-held) is on the rise.

Will indie developers prevail?

Gordon Walton (Vice President, Sony Online Entertainment):

More consolidation of publishers is a sure thing. The big will get bigger and the small will get gobbled up.

Jason Kay (President, Society Capital):

I predict that the rising cost of developing games will finally lead to the consolidation amongst publishers that many people have been anticipating for years. With titles easily reaching the $20-million mark for AAA [high-quality] games, one or two failures by a smaller publisher on a $20-million investment will likely force them to merge with another publisher. We are already seeing this somewhat: Square's merger with Enix, and Sammy's slow moves toward Sega.

Chris Swain (Lecturer, University of Southern California):

The game industry is in a position similar to the film industry from the early 1980s. At that time movie studios were producing a lot of formulaic pictures and were not taking much creative risk....Independent film started to blossom, and companies like Miramax took off by producing unconventional films that went on to become hits. The game industry today feels like the film industry from the early 1980s....Players are hungry for something different. Fortunately, a budding independent scene is developing that is starting to make waves. It isn't developing as quickly as the independent film scene did in the 1980s because, among other reasons, producing games is harder than producing movies. However, it is starting to move, with things like the *Independent Games Festival* leading the way. The industry will really start to move when we have some big hits come out of the independent scene.

Jay Moore (Evangelist, GarageGames):

We're going to see more and more areas where player communities can be grown that are profitable to independents, but too small scale to interest larger commercial developers....I predict that independents will lead the way in innovative game play, and the creation of new IP [intellectual property] and building games, that are then discovered and brought to market by a new breed of online publishers.

Justin Mette (President, 21-6 Productions):

I believe that the online distribution market for games is where most independent developers can get started and make a good living. Developing a game in 4 to 6 months with a small remote team means that your costs stay low and your return on investment does not have to be as large as the box or console industry. You don't have to just build puzzle games anymore to succeed in online game distribution....We've also seen an incredibly strong rush of Mac gamers this past year in the online market. For our title *Orbz*, we saw almost a 50/50 split in revenue between Windows and Mac sales during 2003. It's a great time to be an indie; the Internet allows you to find amazing talent and work together without an office; technology like Torque makes game development a reality for small inexperienced teams; and a booming online game-distribution market all lay out the best opportunity in years for game developers to live their dreams.

Greg Costikyan (Chief Creative Officer, Unplugged):

If games are to become what I think they can be—the most important popular art form of the 21st century, as film was of the 20th and the novel of the 19th—

we need to find a way…to innovate, on smaller budgets, in order to find new, successful game styles. Other media do this by supporting a separate, "independent" industry with parallel distribution channels: independent music through small record stores, independent film through art houses and the like. To my mind, finding a way to create a vibrant independent game industry, where innovation and the offbeat are prized, with lower production values than the conventional industry, is the key business issue the field faces today. There are, however, some hopeful signs: The downloadable game market is growing rapidly (~$60m in revenues in the U.S. in 2003), as is the mobile game market (~$80m in the U.S. in 2003). And both in the industry—through venues like the Independent Games Festival—and in academia, there is an increasing interest in games developed outside the conventional industry.

Celia Pearce (Arts Research Manager & Associate Director, Game Culture & Technology Lab, Cal-(IT)², University of California, Irvine)

I'm actually really disappointed with the game industry right now. I think the consolidation of game companies has really hurt innovation. We decided to produce ALT+CTRL, our independent game festival, because we were so appalled by the lack of originality at E3 two years ago. There wasn't a single title on the show floor that wasn't either a sequel to another game, or derived from a film or TV license. The strange thing is that the vast majority of the top 20 games that the ESA (Entertainment Software Association) publishes each year are original titles or derived from existing game-based franchises. By and large, the best-selling games have been original. The *Mario* franchise has made twice the revenue of all the *Star Wars* movies combined. The top-selling games of all time—*Myst, The Sims,* and *Pac-Man*—have all been original titles. I really hope the game industry breaks out of its rut.

The greatest hope I see for the future is the rise of modding culture and game art. There are a lot of people now creating really amazing mods using commercial game engines like Unreal and Torque. The ALT+CTRL submissions had some amazing games that small, independent groups are producing, and really pushing these technologies to make some amazing stuff. A lot of this work—coming out of places like Finland and Australia—is completely off the game industry's radar. Meanwhile, these little stealth teams…have developed very vibrant player communities.

How Will Games Be Developed?

Innovations in the game-development process itself may change the way games are created—through new processes, tools, and team structures. What are some likely advances in game art, design, and programming? As graphics technology continues to get more sophisticated, some game artists have felt the pressure to imitate the latest successful 3D game in color, style, and texture. But, as a close game industry colleague of mine once said: "Where are the Picassos of game art?" Cell shading in *Viewtiful Joe* is a refreshing, eye-catching departure from the grayish, sometimes even cold world of many popular games. Will we see even more focus on replicating the human environment and less on imagining fantastic worlds? Will "synthespians" replace actors as filmmaking and game art share technology? Will non-player characters become more "real" as artificial intelligence becomes more sophisticated? Will story and gameplay both become more complex and compelling?

Will future game development rely less on standard conventions and more on imagination?

Bruno Bonnell (CEO, Atari):

The game industry is growing into a mass market entertainment away from the specialists and experts. It is now competing against the other form of media entertainment like DVDs, music CDs....The big trends are therefore to graphically or musically match the public expectations while simplifying the user interface to make the game as accessible as possible. "The more immersive, the better the game," should be the motto of game designers in the future. Among the major trends will be the growth of online games, which allow people to play together instead of facing the AI of a silicon chip. Another big trend is the development of new interfaces like microphones or digital cameras, which will ease the communication and integration within a specific universe. The paddles are still around, but people want more to interact with virtual worlds.

Tracy Fullerton (Assistant Professor, University of Southern California):

The game industry has come to a point where it needs to reach new markets if it's going to continue to grow. This means designing for different types of players; those outside the traditional gaming audience. The problem with this is that while the industry is extremely skilled at maintaining steady technological innovation and cultivating consumer demand for those innovations, the same isn't true when it comes to developing original ideas in player experience. And, in order to reach new types of players, there are going to have to be breakthroughs in player experience just as surely as there had to be breakthroughs in technology in order for the industry to come this far. The best way I see to approach this problem is to adopt the type of rigorous user testing seen in other forms of software and industrial design, right from the beginning of the design process.... Another important way to create innovation in player experience is to encourage diversity in game design teams.

Warren Spector (Studio Director, Ion Storm):

We will see great strides on the simulation front (encompassing rendering, sound propagation, physics, and object interaction)—so games can look, sound, and feel more like the real world. However, my hope is that all that game engine power can be turned to ends other than increased realism. I think we'll see game artists creating all sorts of non-representational games, too. Honestly, though, there's probably some kid out there somewhere with an idea so revolutionary I can't even imagine what it might be—that's the real future of gaming, something completely and utterly unpredictable and marvelous.

Mark Soderwall (Senior Art Director, Atari):

You will see incredible breakthroughs in dynamic lighting and shading passes that will create incredible moods and tones inside the gaming universe. I see the next level of in-game characters seamlessly interacting (in real-time) with every aspect of their environment through dynamic physics, collision routines, and real-time Inverse Kinematics—a feature that allows a character's hand to actually touch and turn a doorknob instead of just floating in front of it.

Christopher Bretz (Art Director, Secret Level):

The past few years have seen an explosion in graphics processing power. It is allowing games to have ever more complex visuals, approaching that of rendered images previously seen only in movies. The challenge before this was to use what you had available to approximate a real or imagined world with limited polygons and texture space. To use the tools effectively to create a believable simulacrum. Your skills as an artist were all about this filtering. Now these walls are coming down. With talk of the new systems in the millions of polys per second and mountains of memory, the old constraints are less of a concern and the real question for the artist becomes: "How the heck can I build all that—on the same schedule!?" A million-polygon reference character is a wonderful freedom for an artist, but what if you need 50 of them for a game? If environments can have tens of millions of triangles, and hundreds of unique shaders and properties, not to mention realistic lighting setups, how long does that take to make? Many of the new issues for artists beg solutions for these authoring challenges. And what to do with all this power?

As a visual artist, the challenges continue to be compelling characters and inspiring environments, tied to an engrossing narrative. But what is changing is the degree of reality that games can employ to bring you this vision (reality not being "realistic"). "Immersion" is the buzzword from the past few years, and I think it will continue. For the player, jumping into a believable world is the rewarding escapist experience—be it *Unreal* or *Mario* or *Silent Hill*. Coming games, for example, will have characters which can have more than simple scripted/animated responses, but emotional states and automated behaviors. This allows them to express their personalities visually, as the artist envisioned, and not the stilted responses common to past games. True digital actors which can react to, and interact with, their world. All of the things artists previously had to conceal or hint at in their work in the past can now be expressed with these new technologies.

Marc Taro Holmes (Art Director, Obsidian Entertainment):

Real-time 3D technology is getting more and more sophisticated every month. We can pretty much count on our next game looking better than the one before—poly counts go up, new lighting models, in-game physics, material shaders offering added realism—and soon there will be fur on game animals and hair on characters. We're gradually improving toward true photographic realism. The technology has come a huge distance in only five years, and will likely begin to grow even faster. The opportunity to do better and better looking games creates an interesting tension for teams. The minimum bar for artistic skill grows higher every month, as do the requirements for technical training. People can literally be left behind if they are unable to invest in their skill sets. We are finding the need for technical people—artists who write MEL scripts for instance—is growing rapidly…but the requirement for traditional skills (color sense, anatomy, composition) is not going away either. So your team is becoming harder and harder to fill with the right people, and the budget required is growing larger and larger. This has set up a situation similar to Hollywood film, in which big budget games have to live within a mass market creative space. You have to know your potential set of fans is big enough to warrant the investment. This has led to the proliferation of licensed properties—movie games, *Harry Potter, James Bond*…IP [intellectual property]—which has a proven fan base. That is one trend that is going to rule the business for a few years.

However, I feel it is very likely that a related phenomenon mirroring independent film will come to exist. Just as fans of indie film excuse the lack of high-end effects or big-money stars, there are a category of sophisticated consumers that are looking for something different in their games. (Especially as the gaming market widens to include more of the general population, through the emergence of more mainstream platforms like the Web or mobile gaming, for instance.) Fan Mod teams, or small developers who lack a publisher's financial backing, may not be able to make a blockbuster, but they have the benefit of being agile. A ten-person studio can do a game for a niche market, while keeping their costs down. Something that the large studios have no interest in doing—feeding a monster studio means they must seek high-calorie food. Enter *Brittany's Dance Beat.* I'm looking forward to the emergence of an independent game movement that provides a creative infusion—something to keep the big budget mainstream games moving forward and trying new ideas.

Richard Wainess, MS Ed (Senior Lecturer, University of Southern California):

My interests are from the cognitive perspective; that is, how our brains process information and how that knowledge can improve video games—games that educate and games that are played simply for fun. All gameplay is subject to our mental limitations, and virtually no game designer or developer is aware of the nature of these limitations or what has been discovered that can be used as guidelines to improve gameplay from the standpoint of game mechanics, interface, and sound. *Craft* is the application of prior experience to solve real-world problems. *Technology* is the application of science to solve real-world problems. Currently, game design is craft—but it should be a blend of technology and craft. This is the paradigm currently used in video game programming, where computer science works hand-in-hand with creative vision. It will not become the model for design until those who develop games through craft become aware, and confident, that science now exists that can support, and not hinder, their efforts. Then, much of the developer's guesswork will be replaced by the application of sound scientific principles.

David Perry (CEO, Shiny Entertainment):

I expect there to be incredible investment and progress in these topics:

- **Physics**—Everything begins to function. You stick a lamp in a fan and it cuts the top off the lamp; you stick a log in the fan and the blades break.

- **Particles**—Better environmental disturbances—including the air-flow disturbances from your body. Also, better destruction—meaning you can break up a building brick by brick and it collapses correctly.

- **Lighting**—Better self-shadowing, better ambiance, and better cognition of shadows—meaning enemies know what they are and how they work.

- **Tactical AI**—They learn how you play. They actually have memory. They also see your strengths and weaknesses. If you shoot 10 times and miss, they change their opinion of you—if it felt to them like you were aiming.

- **Speech Recognition**—Beyond just a small subset of "chosen" words.

- **Speech Production**—Having them form sentences back to you.

- **Speech Cognition**—Understanding what you said. Is it, "It's fun to recognize speech?" or did I say, "It's fun to wreck a nice beach?"

- **Speech Conversation**—They hear you, get what you mean—and reply.

- **Immersion**—A high level of people achieving a mind state of flow. Time stops for the gamer—like a movie ending and the audience being amazed that two hours have passed.

- **Much Better Storytelling**—You will become more emotionally attached to the game characters. Expect to feel real loss if they die for good.

John Ahlquist (Lead Programmer, Electronic Arts–Los Angeles):

I see the game-programming process using more software engineering practices. The game engines and tools have grown to be large-scale software projects, and seat-of-the-pants methods aren't going to work any more. At the same time, I see it continuing to be a very fluid and dynamic development process…The processes from software engineering that allow quick turnaround, such as rapid prototyping and automated test, are very useful. Complex design processes are not as useful as our design changes on the fly, as the game evolves.

Frank Gilson (Producer, Atari):

Game developers want to own their game engines. They want publishers to pay for the development costs. However, each new game engine is in some sense re-inventing the wheel. This is very time-consuming and expensive. Some few game engines, so far mostly of the first-person-shooter type, have enjoyed ongoing development, maintenance, and extension (such as *Unreal* and *Quake,* etc.). This is more efficient in terms of time and money spent on development. Also, for other aspects of game software technology, various middleware providers have sprung up (e.g., Gamespy for multiplayer matching, Havok for game physics). The future of game development should continue to follow these trends…in fact, much of it may become the licensing of appropriate existing technologies, and putting the pieces together within what really matters—a great creative framework.

Mark Terrano (Technical Game Manager, Xbox Advanced Technology Group):

While the technology that is coming is absolutely stunning, I think we'll finally begin to see some stabilization in tools, middleware, and technology, so game developers can focus more on content. We've been on a steep technical climb for several years, and we'll have to make orders-of-magnitude better tools and production environments to take advantage of more and much higher-resolution audio and video content. Having high quality middleware and vendors that work more closely together (so my physics system is compatible with, and even friendly to, their animation library and someone else's dynamic sound system) is going to be essential for the next step up.

How Will Games Be Played?

Will we continue to play games on a variety of platforms? Will we see further hardware convergence? Companies like Nintendo, Microsoft, Sony, and Nokia continue to manufacture new game platforms that attempt to either converge with home entertainment systems, the online world—and even your mobile phone (Nokia's N-Gage QD)—or focus on perfecting a special-purpose platform for games only (Sony PSP, Nintendo DS). Will online multiplayer gaming increase? Could this cause games to transcend cultural boundaries—forming a global gaming community? As content continues to diversify and MMOG developers explore new financial models and business development opportunities (e.g., partnering with the online distance learning industry), could MMOGs bypass console games as the dominant form of interactive entertainment in the United States? Or will the console platform remain on top—with games becoming home entertainment centers with a cinematic impact?

Will global online games rise in popularity?

Brian Reynolds (CEO, Big Huge Games):

This is still a technology-driven industry. But most of the big paradigm shifts occur not when a new technology is invented or introduced, but rather when it reaches a sufficient level of acceptance to allow developers to take full advantage of it in creating new and innovative kinds of gameplay. Processor speed is no longer the driving technological force it used to be—the exciting opportunities these days are in other technological areas. Some new technologies that are nearing the point of enabling new paradigm shifts include broadband Internet and DVD drives. Developers have already been testing the waters in these areas, but when the technologies achieve sufficient market penetration that "broadband only" or "DVD only" games become marketable, that's the time to look for something really new and innovative.

Don Daglow (CEO, Stormfront Studios):

It may be close to 2010 before it happens, but the video game console is going to become a "routine" component of the living room entertainment system, much as the TV and stereo system are now. Its styling and overall look will change to make it coordinate with the other entertainment devices in the room. As part of the process, the set-top boxes we use to control cable and satellite broadcasts today are likely to be combined into the same box with video game consoles. When this happens, the whole concept of "interactive TV" will be revolutionized overnight.

Brian Fargo (CEO, InXile Entertainment):

The biggest trend in gaming is going to be the socialization of the experience through multiplayer. While this isn't a new concept, we are just now starting to see the proverbial tip of the iceberg. The console business is quickly catching up to the computer in terms of multiplayer impact, and the game designers are just beginning to flex their muscles in this area. There is so much new ground to break here, but people respond to people, and making video games a more human experience will take gaming to another level.

Mark Terrano (Technical Game Manager, Xbox Advanced Technology Group):

With game developers really coming into their own in countries such as South Korea and China, I think we'll see games with different cultural influences and styles of storytelling....MMOGs being developed in South Korea and China will change how we look at social interaction and group stories.

Graeme Bayless (Supervising Producer, Electronic Arts–Tiburon):

As broadband penetrates the market more thoroughly, online components become more and more a key aspect to our games.

Warren Spector (Studio Director, Ion Storm):

Clearly, online play is going to become increasingly important—in the form of multiplayer, and in terms of content delivery and game distribution.

Richard "Lord British" Garriott (Creative Director, NCsoft):

Massively multiplayer online games (MMOGs) are *the* growth segment in my mind—not only from a revenue standpoint, but also a place to look for cool creative innovation. MMOGs are in their infancy, and we are only just beginning to see the variety of play styles and genres the online space will offer in the future.

Daniel James (Founder & CEO, Three Rings):

I believe that massively multiplayer online games will come to dominate the game industry, and grow to be the single greatest entertainment medium of the 21st century.

Carly Stahlin (Lead Designer, NCsoft):

Here are my thoughts on the future of MMOGs:

- **Instantiated Spaces and Persistent Spaces:** The marketing materials for almost every MMOG in development right now includes some mention of providing access to instantiated spaces in addition to persistent spaces. The idea is that the game developers want to blend the best of single-player games with the best of MMOGs by allowing players to have some ability to get away from the crowds of other people and just to play with a few select players, uninterrupted, for a stretch of time. Whether the company comes up with a fancy double-speak name, such as some kind of 'system' or 'technology' to explain the concept to the market, it all boils down to the same thing. MMOGs are trying to provide the experience that players seem to want, which is a massive opportunity for meeting people to adventure with, but with exclusive rights to a location or scenario without having to travel across huge expanses for 8 hours to get to the fun or having to wait for the 50 groups of other adventurers in front of you to have their turn.

- **Online as a Platform Rather than Genre:** Most offerings in the MMOG space are extremely similar to one another. The legacy of MUDs [multi-user dungeons] continues to dominate the designs of MMOG titles. We have begun to see companies play with the concept of what an MMOG looks and plays like. If the nontraditional features and gamestyles prove to be commercially successful, then I think companies will begin to understand that 'online' is more a platform and less a specific genre. Most genres are already trying to find a way to offer an online or multiplayer component, and as more of them become successful at it, the variety of games that will be offered online will begin to look different than those in development today.

- **Regionalization vs. Globalization:** There has been little progress made in understanding the specific criteria that make a game successful in Korea versus North America. One consequence is that companies are considering how to leverage their existing work in other territories without necessarily creating a game that works globally out of the box. Many other industries have recognized that products are hard to globalize. Automobiles are a great example. You can find the exact same car manufactured under different names in different territories expressly because of the expectations of the different markets. Certain markets, even within a territory, have expectation differences. Expecting to sell a GPS feature in a car for a city like San Francisco is logical, but hoping to sell that same feature in a car to a driver in "Small-town" is just plain fallacy—drivers don't *need* a device that tells them directions in very small towns, and almost certainly won't pay for that feature. Electronics hardware firms operate similarly; you can find many examples of repurposed product throughout the global marketplace, including computers, projectors, telephones, and more. Before long, online game developers will recognize that we would be better served by localizing for territories by utilizing developers within those territories.

■ **Player Activity Logging:** There is a growing trend with MMOG game developers to try to trap actual game data about the activities of players in the game, so that more information can be learned about those players, and so that the information about the out-of-game community subjective concerns can be more accurately gauged against objective data.

Titus Levi, PhD (Economist and Media & Arts Consultant):

Online gaming will continue to grow from a niche to a serious market segment. First, some of the most interesting innovations will arise from collaboration through these games. Second, I think this points toward a new kind of interaction and communication between people, particularly groups (or tribes) of persons who bond over the games, as well as other taste and lifestyle connections. Even though broadband rollout continues to drag along, many groups who love these games are already users of both broadband and online gaming, since they group together and their personal (offline) bonds allow them to connect more readily around games and online activities. However, once broadband becomes more widespread, there will need to be some mechanism by which newcomers can integrate themselves into these worlds or form their own. I'm not sure how that will work, but that seems to be a real need.

David Brin, PhD (Author, Scientist & Public Speaker):

The MMOG world is vast, intricate, and immensely capital-intensive. Very few big players can step up to invest in creating these worlds that are driven by a need for huge numbers of subscriber-addicts. Fear of losing their investment makes these companies very conservative and imitative when it comes to story and game design. The problems of social interaction in these games—like dealing with deliberate maliciousness—would be better solved if there were dozens of smaller experimental worlds, trying new things under a rich variety of story-scenarios. That won't happen until somebody realizes that there is a market in offering game *templates*—a "MUD in a box"—that would let much smaller groups create their own online worlds. When this happens, authorship will simplify and the range of products will expand. Many of the problems that plague the online world will be solved by trial and error.

Who Will Play and How Will We Reach Them?

We're entering an exciting new phase in game development, where the stereotypical gamer is no longer an adolescent boy but a whole range of players—where women over 35 top the online game market, a common form of local play involves a mother sitting at a computer with a child on her lap, and people of all cultures compete worldwide in MMOGs. The market for games is growing rapidly.

Will Millennials be the new dominant game market?

Pete Markiewicz, PhD (Indiespace):

Currently, the game industry creates content and markets with a very Xer mindset. While this is a good way to reach the peak gaming audience in their late 20s to early 30s, it is likely to lose appeal during the next few years. One of the largest factors in this is the clear dominance of Millennial women in their generation. Compared to their male peers, Millennial women are taking the lead in education (4-year college freshmen classes were 60% female in 2003), and are taking over leadership positions at an even greater rate. This means that decisions to purchase games will be controlled by women within 10 years. It is also important to understand that members of the Millennial generation have close relationships with their parents. Since most game purchases are actually parent–child co-purchases, any marketing attempting to split parent between parent and child will fail, compared to older generations.

In another trend, Millennials have used interactive media from birth. Whereas Boomers and Xers used non-interactive television to gain information, Millennials trust information exchanged within their peer group. Game marketing will have to address how to "join" the lateral communication of Millennials via the Internet, cell phones, and other media—which, in turn, will require major shifts away from the mass market mindset.

Rade Stojsavljevic (Producer, Electronic Arts):

There's a generation of gamers who grew up with video games and continues to play as they age. This will be a key element that will make gaming a more socially-acceptable activity. Right now you would probably still be labeled a geek or nerd if your friends invited you to dinner or a movie and you turned them down to play the latest *Zelda* game. That's slowly starting to change, and I believe it will impact the types of games that are created.

Patricia Pizer (Game Designer):

At the simplest level, I think we'll see greater diversification in games. Casual games are becoming steadily more widespread. Short but satisfying game experiences will be available on virtually every platform. As games surpass movies and even music sales, I think we'll see more of what equates to niche magazines: games intended to satisfy relatively small groups of players. While many have aimed for giant killer apps, thoroughly appealing to smaller numbers of players in a more meaningful way has tremendous potential.

Brenda Laurel, PhD (Chair, Graduate Media Design Program, Art Center College of Design):

The definition of "play" has a key component: that one's actions do not have serious consequences. The innate problem with gaming as part of a curriculum is that one's play may indeed have the serious consequence of affecting one's grade for a course. Another difficulty with gaming in an educational setting is our desire for transgressive play. (Eric Zimmerman brought this issue to light for me.) We often like to feel that we are coloring outside the lines when we play. Again, this is a problem in an educational context where following the rules has high value. Solution strategies exist for each of these challenges. In the first instance, informal or extra-curricular learning with oblique relationships to coursework may serve to distance a game sufficiently from the "serious" consequences of grading. In the case of transgression, we must remember that literally everything we are taught - from science to civics - is the artifact of some seriously transgressive behavior like Copernicus' outrageous assertions about the solar system or Jefferson's bold strokes in shaping our democracy. The spirit of transgression - of productive change - is the essence of engagement, both in play and in life.

The game industry is continuing to grow. Right now game revenue exceeds box office revenue, and blockbuster games are being marketed like blockbuster movies, complete with 12- to 24-month marketing lead times, significant promotional partnerships and in-game product placement, and multimillion dollar advertising campaigns. The 15 to 25 blockbuster candidates will be promoted based upon their cinematic visuals, engaging storyline, and immersive features. Everything will be done with an eye on mass market consumers. In two to seven years, game consoles will become an entertainment hub, incorporating DVR (digital video recorder—example: TiVo), digital music, and Internet voice communication capabilities, in addition to DVD players. As the consoles evolve, they will become more of a fixture in the average American household. Games are coming out of the basement. With that move, games that appeal to women and older adults will become more popular—although shooters, sports-simulation, and twitch-action games will continue to dominate.

The marketing departments at game publishers have also realized the value of fans. Game developers, particularly First-Person Shooter developers, have known for a long time that embracing the fan community—listening to them and giving them support—reaps long-term rewards in terms of mod to extend the life of a game, brand loyalty to extend the life of the franchise, and a source for creative new ideas to keep the games entertaining. Publishers have been tentatively reaching out to key game influencers through grassroots advocacy for several years, and moderately maintaining the forums. Eventually, the publishers will focus on the key influencer and fan relationships, hiring community managers, and including community features into the game and marketing campaigns.

The Future of Entertainment?

Opinions on where the industry will go are varied—and the mood of most developers ranges from excitement to concern—but everyone agrees that the industry could dramatically change the face of entertainment as we know it. Will games become the dominant form of entertainment in the next 5-10 years? How will you participate in this exciting revolution? I hope this discussion and the topics in this book have shown you the limitless potential of game development, and have sparked an interest in you to contribute to this creative and boundless industry. Read on for some valuable resources that will help you apply what you've learned!

Resources

There's a wealth of information on game development and related topics discussed in this book. Here is just a sample list of books, news sites, organizations, and events you should definitely explore!

Keep the following two online resources on your "favorites" list. You will find yourself accessing them often:

Gamasutra - www.gamasutra.com

Search through developer articles, lists of game development studios and publishers, a directory of schools that have game programs – and employment listings. This invaluable online resource should be your first stop.

Moby Games - www.mobygames.com

Look up game titles, companies and people in this directory. You'll find out what games have been developed or published by which companies, as well as full credits.

News

Blues News - www.bluesnews.com

Computer Games Magazine – www.cgonline.com

Computer Gaming World – www.computergaming.com

Electronic Gaming Monthly – wwwegmmag.com

Game Daily Newsletter - www.gamedaily.com

Game Developer Magazine - www.gdmag.com

Game Music Revolution (GMR) – www.gmronline.com

GameSlice Weekly - www.gameslice.com

GameSpot - www.gamespot.com

GameSpy - www.gamespy.com

Gaming Industry News – www.gamingindustrynews.com

GIGnews.com - www.gignews.com

Internet Gaming Network (IGN) - www.ign.com

Machinima.com - www.machinima.com

Music4Games.net - www.music4games.net

PC Gamer – www.pcgamer.com

Star Tech Journal [technical side of the coin-op industry] - www.startechjournal.com

UGO Networks (Underground Online) - www.ugo.com

Video Game Music - www.vgn.com

Wired Magazine – www.wired.com

Directories & Communities

Apple Developer Connection - developer.apple.com

Betawatcher.com - www.betawatcher.com/

Fat Babies.com [game industry gossip] - www.fatbabies.com

GameDev.net - www.gamedev.net

Game Development Search Engine - www.obtg.net/modules/news/

Game Music.com - www.gamemusic.com/

Game Rankings - www.gamerankings.com

Games Tester - www.gamestester.com/

Online Beta Tester Guild - www.obtg.net/modules/news/

Overclocked Remix - www.overclocked.org

Organizations

Academy of Interactive Arts & Sciences (AIAS) - www.interactive.org

Academy of Machinima Arts & Sciences - www.machinima.org

Association of Computing Machinery (ACM) – www.acm.org

Digital Games Research Association (DiGRA) – www.digra.org

Entertainment Software Association (ESA) - www.theesa.org

Entertainment Software Ratings Board (ESRB) - www.esrb.org

Game Audio Network Guild (GANG) - www.audiogang.org

International Computer Games Association (ICGA) - www.cs.unimaas.nl/icga/

International Game Developers Association (IGDA) - www.igda.org

SIGGRAPH – www.siggraph.org

Events

Consumer Electronics Show (CES)
January - Las Vegas, Nevada
www.cesweb.org

Game Developers Conference (GDC)
March – San Jose, California
www.gdconf.com

D.I.C.E. Summit
March - Las Vegas, Nevada
www.interactive.org/dice

Electronic Entertainment Expo (E3)
May – Los Angeles, California
www.e3expo.com

SIGGRAPH
August – Los Angeles, California
www.siggraph.org

Austin Game Developers Conference
September – Austin, Texas
www.gameconference.com

Indie Games Con (IGC)
October – Eugene, Oregon
www.garagegames.com

ALT+CTRL – Festival of Independent & Alternative Games
Game Culture & Technology Lab
University of California, Irvine
October – Irvine, CA
www.proxy.arts.uci.edu/gamelab/events/alt_ctrl_04.html

Books & Articles

Adams, E. (2003). *Break into the game industry.* McGraw-Hill Osborne Media.

Ahearn, L & Crooks II, CE. (2002). *Awesome game creation: No programming required.* Charles River Media.

Axelrod, R. (1985). *The evolution of cooperation.* Basic Books.

Bates, B. (2002). *Game design: The art & business of creating games.* Premier Press.

Bethke, E. (2003). *Game development and production.* Wordware.

Brin, D. (1998). *The transparent society.* Addison-Wesley.

Broderick, D. (2001). *The spike: How our lives are being transformed by rapidly advancing technologies.* Forge.

Brooks, D. (2001). *Bobos in Paradise.* Simon & Schuster.

Campbell, J. (1972). *The hero with a thousand faces.* Princeton University Press.

Campbell, J. (1991). *The power of myth.* Anchor.

Castells, M. (2001). *The Internet galaxy: Reflections on the Internet, business, and society.* Oxford University Press.

Chiarella, T. (1998). *Writing dialogue.* Story Press.

Crawford, C. (2003). *Chris Crawford on game design.* New Riders.

Csikszentmihalyi. M. (1991). *Flow: The psychology of optimal experience.* Perennial.

DeMaria, R & Wilson, JL. (2003). *High score.* McGraw-Hill.

Evans, A. (2001). *This virtual life: Escapism and simulation in our media world.* Fusion Press.

Fay, T. (2003). *DirectX 9 Audio Exposed: Interactive Audio Development.* Wordware Publishing.

Friedl, M. (2002). *Online game interactivity theory.* Charles River Media.

Fullerton, T, Swain, C. & Weiss, S. (2004). *Game design workshop: Designing, prototyping & playtesting games.* CMP Books.

Gardner, J. (1991). *The art of fiction.* Vintage Books.

Gershenfeld, A., Loparco, M. & Barajas, C. (2003). *Game plan.* Griffin Trade Paperback.

Gladwell, M. (2000). *The tipping point.* New York, NY: Little Brown & Company.

Gleick, J. (1999). *Faster: The acceleration of just about everything.* Vintage Books.

Godin, S. (2003). *Purple cow: Transform your business by being remarkable.* Portfolio.

Hamilton, E. (1940). *Mythology: Timeless tales of gods and heroes.* Mentor.

Heim, M. (1993). *The metaphysics of virtual reality.* Oxford University Press.

Johnson, S. (1997). *Interface culture.* Basic Books.

Jung, CG. (1969). *Man and his symbols.* Dell.

Kent, SL. (2001). *The ultimate history of video games.* Prima.

King, S. (2000). *On writing.* Scribner.

Knoke, W. (1997). *Bold new world.* New York, NY: Kodansha International.

Kurzweil, R. (2000). *The age of spiritual machines: When computers exceed human intelligence.* Penguin.

Laramee, F.D. (Ed.) (2003). *Secrets of the game business.* Charles River Media.

Laramee, FD. (Ed.) (2002). *Game design perspectives.* Charles River Media.

Laurel, B. (1990). *The art of human-computer interface design.* Pearson Education.

Laurel, B. (Ed.) (2003). *Design research: Methods and perspectives.* MIT Press.

Levy, P. (2001). *Cyberculture.* University of Minnesota Press.

Lewis, M. (2001). *Next: The future just happened.* W.W. Norton & Company.

Mackay, C. (1841). *Extraordinary popular delusions & the madness of crowds.* Three Rivers Press.

Makar, J. (2003). *Macromedia Flash MX game design demystified.* Macromedia Press/ Peachpit Press.

Marks, A. (2001). *The Complete Guide to Game Audio.* CMP Books.

McConnell, S. (1996). *Rapid development.* Microsoft Press.

Mencher, M. (2002). *Get in the game: Careers in the game industry.* New Riders.

Michael, David. (2003). *The indie game development survival guide.* Charles River Media.

Moravec, H. (2000). *Robot.* Oxford University Press.

Morris, D & Hartas, L. (2003). *Game art: The graphic art of computer games.* Watson-Guptill Publications

Mulligan, J & Patrovsky, B. (2003). *Developing online games.* New Riders.

Murray, J. (2001). *Hamlet on the holodeck: The future of narrative in cyberspace.* MIT Press.

Negroponte, N. (1996). *Being digital.* Vintage Books.

Nielsen, J. (1999). *Designing web usability: The practice of simplicity.* New Riders.

Novak, J. (1991). "Gender role representation in toy commercials." University of California, Los Angeles.

Novak, J. (2003). "MMOGs as online distance learning applications." University of Southern California.

Oram, A. (Ed.) (2001). *Peer-to-peer.* O'Reilly & Associates.

Rheingold, H. (1991). *Virtual reality.* Touchstone.

Rheingold, H. (2000). *Tools for thought: The history and future of mind-expanding technology.* MIT Press.

Rogers, E.M. (1995). *Diffusion of innovations.* Free Press.

Rollings, A & Morris, D. (2003). *Game architecture & design: A new edition.* New Riders.

Rollings, A. & Adams, E. (2003). *Andrew Rollings & Ernest Adams on Game Design.* New Riders.

Rouse III, R. (2001) *Game design: Theory & practice.* Wordware..

Salen, K. & Zimmerman, E. (2003). *Rules of Play.* MIT Press.

Sanger, GA [a.k.a. "The Fat Man"]. (2003). *The Fat Man on Game Audio.* New Riders. Sellers, J. (2001). *Arcade fever.* Running Press.

Standage, T. (1999). *The Victorian Internet.* New York: Berkley Publishing Group.

Strauss, W. & Howe, N. (1992). *Generations.* Perennial.

Strauss, W. & Howe, N. (1993). *13th gen: Abort, retry, ignore, fail?* Vintage Books.

Strauss, W. & Howe, N. (1998). *The fourth turning.* Broadway Books.

Strauss, W. & Howe, N. (2000). *Millennials rising: The next great generation.* Vintage Books.

Towes, K. (2003). *Macromedia Flash Communication Server MX.* Macromedia Press/ New Riders.

Tufte, ER. (1983). *The visual display of quantitative information.* Graphics Press.

Tufte, ER. (1990). *Envisioning information.* Graphics Press.

Tufte, ER. (1997). *Visual explanations.* Graphics Press.

Turkle, S. (1997). *Life on the screen: Identity in the age of the Internet.* Touchstone.

Van Duyne, D.K. et al. (2003). *The design of sites.* Addison-Wesley.

Vogler, C. (1998). *The writer's journey: Mythic structure for writers. (2nd ed).* Michael Wiese Productions.

Williams, JD. (1954). *The compleat strategist.* McGraw-Hill.

Wysocki, RK, Beck, R, Jr., & Crane, DB. *Effective project management (3rd ed).* John Wiley & Sons.

Index